endgame

# endgame

*Inside the Royal Family and the*
*Monarchy's Fight for Survival*

## OMID SCOBIE

**DEY**ST.
*An Imprint of* WILLIAM MORROW

**DEY**ST.

ENDGAME. Copyright © 2023 by Omid Scobie. All rights reserved. Printed in the United States of America. No part of this book may be used or reproduced in any manner whatsoever without written permission except in the case of brief quotations embodied in critical articles and reviews. For information, address Harper-Collins Publishers, 195 Broadway, New York, NY 10007.

HarperCollins books may be purchased for educational, business, or sales promotional use. For information, please email the Special Markets Department at SPsales@harpercollins.com.

FIRST EDITION

*Designed by Angie Boutin*
*Frontispiece by Omid Scobie*

Library of Congress Cataloging-in-Publication Data has been applied for.

ISBN 978-0-06-325866-2

23 24 25 26 27 LBC 5 4 3 2 1

*To everyone who clicks on, reads, or watches my work—*
*your support means the world. Thank you!*

**endgame** (noun)

ĕndgām

the final stages of a chess game after most of the
pieces have been removed from the board

*also*: the final stages of an extended process
or course of events

# CONTENTS

———·———

PROLOGUE   1

1: *The Queen and Her Piper:*
*Elizabeth II's Final Days*   15

2: *Shaky Ground: The Queen Is Dead,*
*the Monarchy Faces Trouble*   32

3: *"Oh God, I Hate This": King Charles's Premiere*   58

4: *Remembrance of Things Past: The Ongoing*
*Campaign to Make the Royals Great Again*   79

5: *Baggage: The Lingering Trials of King Charles*   93

6: *The Fall of Prince Andrew: Scandal,*
*Shame, and Silencing Jane Doe*   117

7: *Race and the Royals: Institutional*
*Bigotry and Denial*   135

8: *Gloves On: Prince William, Heir to the Throne*   171

9: *Gloves Off: Prince Harry, Man on a Mission*   199

10: *The Men (and Women) in Gray: Royal
Courtiers and the Struggle for Power*   222

11: *Ghost at the Feast: Princess Diana
and Revisionist History*   243

12: *Skilled Survivors: Camilla and Kate, Windsor Women*   267
Part I: Camilla—The Transformation of a Mistress   267
Part II: Kate—Suddenly Front and Center   286

13: *A Dangerous Game: Royals and the Media*   307

14: *The Decay of Years: The Fading
Glory of the Crown*   340

15: *Endgame*   358

ACKNOWLEDGMENTS   371

NOTES   375

# Prologue

When Queen Elizabeth II was in her nineties, there was an element of covering the royals that those around me found a little morbid. Wherever I went, whether it was on a road trip with mates to Wales or a royal visit to Morocco, I always packed a black suit and tie. To friends and family outside the royal bubble, the presence of that ominous suit bag was, to say the least, somewhat gloomy, and a grim reminder that Queen Elizabeth II was nearing the end of her life.

As a journalist who joined the royal beat in 2011, I knew this was a vital piece of the reporting tool kit—an appropriate outfit at the ready so I could spring into action the moment Buckingham Palace shared the news of the Queen's death. While I was at home in London, the suit (a practical polyester blend, because who has time to steam out creases during breaking news?) mostly lived in the trunk of my car.

On September 8, 2022, however, that car and its contents were twenty-odd miles away getting serviced when I was summoned to ABC News' London bureau for what we worried might become the long-feared announcement. I was in the middle of running errands when rumors started to flood through via sources and colleagues, so I didn't have time to race home to grab a backup suit. Feeling the pressure and lack of time, I grabbed a simple black sweater from a nearby Marks & Spencer and took the fastest route, via London Underground, to the Hammersmith studio.

The Queen had been bedbound at Balmoral Castle in Scotland for the forty-eight hours prior, after conducting what later became her final engagements on September 6—seeing out the controversial prime minister Boris Johnson and welcoming in his exceedingly short-lived replacement, Liz Truss. Palace aides announced the day after the monarch's royal duties that she had accepted doctors' advice to rest. The next morning, after a further Palace update warned that her doctors were "concerned for Her Majesty's health and have recommended she remain under medical supervision," an insider messaged me to say, "It's not looking good." For a multitude of reasons, I hoped the warning would turn out to be a false alarm.

Arriving at ABC News' offices that Thursday afternoon, I received a text from someone very close to the family. As I caught my breath in the elevator of the Disney-owned building, "A Spoonful of Sugar" was playing quietly in the background, making a surreal moment even more so. "Please don't say anything yet but I think it's happened," they wrote. I responded with a follow-up, checking that I understood their message correctly. No doubt trying to get confirmation of their own, the source—someone whose word I had come to trust over recent years—didn't reply.

Fifteen minutes later, as I sat in front of the camera and put on my earpiece and mic, my calm in the storm, the network's royal producer Zoe Magee, called across the newsroom: "We've had confirmation." Messages started pouring into my phone within seconds. The statement from the Palace had yet to land, but my heart was already thumping. Though I had been at briefings that described what would happen the moment "London Bridge" (the code name for the monarch's death and the operation that kicked into action straight afterward) went down, nothing could have truly prepared anyone for the news. Not even the two-hundred-page research bible Magee had created in the recent months. The death of Britain's longest-reigning monarch, a woman much loved and revered around the world, had a bigger impact on me in the moment than I expected. The Queen had been a presence in my life for as long as I could remember, a fact shared by most Brits. Whether you cared about the royal family or not, she had evolved into the nation's grandmother—a comforting presence during destabilizing times and easily more popular than the monarchy itself. "New York is going to come to you shortly, Omid!" my producer prompted.

*This is it.*

An astounding amount of royal history happened during the writing of *Endgame*. The world was introduced to King Charles III and Queen Camilla; Prince Andrew was stripped of his titles. Prince Harry released an explosive memoir and a revealing Netflix series, and, of course, Her Majesty Queen Elizabeth II passed away. All these events, along with a litany of startling headlines, greatly impacted this book, including the structure and shape of the narrative and its cast of characters. What should have been a banner year for the royal family, one spent celebrating the Queen and her seventy years of service, was instead a year of more upheaval and strife. The Queen's Platinum Jubilee in the first half of 2022 is but a footnote now because her death followed so quickly in September—a summer of flag-waving celebrations quickly met an autumn of profound change and depth charge revelations. All this proved trying for a staid institution not exactly used to, or adept at managing, such rapid-fire disruptions or change. The royal establishment has now assiduously installed an elderly new king while fending off unyielding accusations and misgivings from an exiled prince.

I started this book in the summer of 2022, so the Queen's passing happened well into the writing process. This meant going back and figuring out how to reframe key chapters while looking through the twin prisms of the late monarch's death and the ascension of her eldest son. Where significant parts of *Endgame* initially theorized about the future of the Firm, I suddenly found myself watching and reporting on that future as it happened in real time. Overnight we were in it: the royal family's new chapter—a moment I couldn't have imagined during my first royal engagement with Prince William and a then Kate Middleton over eleven years earlier. The months following the Queen's death gave me the necessary time to process such a seismic event and an opportunity to peer into the new era before contextualizing it. And that time provided me with a chance to speak with those currently at the center of it as well as the many individuals who had been part of the journey leading up to it. Think of it this way: I started writing the book in the New Elizabethan age and finished in the Carolean era—a dynastic sea change happened in a matter of days. And with it, so did many of my perceptions.

The full reality of Queen Elizabeth II's death hit me ten days later, when I joined a small group of journalists to observe the scene of the former monarch lying in state at Westminster Hall. Members of the public had queued for up to ten miles and over twenty-four hours to pay their respects. For those of us in the press working eighteen-hour shifts, reporting to millions of others around the world, British Parliament's "Operation Marquee" team had arranged prebooked one-hour time slots in Westminster so we could capture this moment in history.

I'd been to the Houses of Parliament before, for other assignments and events, but with all political activity suspended during the ten-day national mourning period, the usually buzzing alley through the length of the Palace of Westminster was eerily silent as we walked toward New Palace Yard. Deep in conversation with one of the staff members guiding us, I wasn't at all prepared for the moment we arrived at the doors of Westminster Hall. Suddenly, there it was: the Queen's coffin resting on a raised ornamental catafalque.

You couldn't hear much else beyond our footsteps and the rustle of coats and bags carried by mourners as we entered the hall's vaulted silence. A solemn usher, obviously weary from his work, calmly directed us up a narrow spiral staircase at the back of the room. We climbed a makeshift riser painted to blend in with the thick magnesian limestone walls of the eleventh-century room—an inconspicuous observation tower for the press.

From this position, about fifteen feet off the ground, my eyes were almost at the same level as the Imperial State Crown resting atop the coffin. As I'm sure it did for so many of the people who quietly walked in and out to pay their respects, the juxtaposition of the crown and the coffin emphasized the finality of it all. Like many journalists covering this story, I had been operating in a suspended state of disconnect up until that moment.

Lying next to the pillowed crown were the orb and scepter. I'd seen them in person before, many times, but being so close to the two symbols in this setting gave me goosebumps. There was the weight of history and tradition, yes, but also the aura of mystery and myth. Ordinary things in and of themselves, really, but an accruement of time, the narratives of power and divine lineage dictated over centuries, and the human desire for meaning and order all alchemized, transmuting those *things* into powerful ideas. It was a strange, commanding magic that I felt that day in Westminster. But the woman, the human form of all that regal authority and mysterious poetry, was lying in a coffin underneath. For so long, she stood for the Crown, and the Crown for her. Without her presence, these ornaments and symbols seemed exposed, naked somehow, as if they had been caught unawares.

King Charles III. Even after all this time, it still doesn't always look quite right on the page. The same can be said of Queen Camilla—those promises of her taking on only the titles Princess Consort, and then Queen Consort, were just white lies the Palace is now keen for people to forget. But here we are. Despite their flaws and many mistakes, it's difficult not to sympathize with the new king and queen. Filling such enormous shoes is almost an impossible task, especially considering that when Her Majesty died, unfortunately so did much of the legend, mystique, and secrecy that enshrouded the monarchy. It's safe to say that very few outside a strict inner circle knew much of anything about Queen Elizabeth II. She inhabited her stately role completely. Her personal life was her own and she fiercely guarded it, knowing full well that to share it was to lose it. She also appreciated and respected the demands of the Crown: service over personal gain, and duty over individual happiness. In public, her resolute composure expressed this in spades, no explanations necessary.

With Charles and Camilla, it's the opposite. The King has lived a full life out in the public as an outspoken environmental activist, an occasional meddler in politics, a successful businessman, a flawed father, and a philandering husband who destroyed the life of Princess Diana—an ignominious legacy he's eager to put behind him now that he is on the throne. He's known to us warts and all. His litany of personal failings and missteps is front-page fodder, and much of the British public will never fully forgive him for his role in Diana's tragic demise. And Queen Camilla, a woman who is finally tolerated by the public but is still not universally *accepted*, remains to many as "the other woman," the third person in Charles and Diana's marriage and someone who caused much pain and chaos within the royal family. Now, no veil of arcane secrecy falls between the new King and Queen and their subjects, providing cover and inscrutable power. Everyone already knows that King Charles might have preferred a life as Queen Camilla's tampon.

Though off to a steady start, the ongoing efforts to boost Charles's popularity will never come easy for the institution of the monarchy, regardless of his new station. As prepared for thronedom as he may have felt, behind palace walls, and in the minds of the public, the question remains: Is he up for the job? Immediately after the Queen passed away and ordinary citizens were still shedding tears, the new King Charles made headlines after cameras caught him throwing a tantrum over a faulty pen. A stubborn eccentric who has spent most of his life waiting and planning for his ascension, even at the cost of his relationships with his own sons, the former Prince of Wales is not only far less popular than his predecessor and his successor, he has also been a thorn in the side of the institution. Despite the fact he's well-liked by world leaders and global power figures, during the life of his mother, he was never fully embraced by power brokers within the system, the Palace operators and partisans with links to the British establishment, including the government. When he was Prince of Wales, some senior Buckingham Palace aides had expressed to me and others that they felt the then next in line didn't quite have the moxie or vision for the family's next chapter. Perhaps they were right. Just weeks before becoming the new monarch, he was knee-deep in controversy involving bags of money, cash-for-honors allegations, and a police investigation into donations accepted by his Prince's Foundation charity.

Or perhaps he was just never allowed to demonstrate his readiness. Many in the Firm's old guard, including the Queen's most senior courtiers—those shadowy men, and now women, "in gray," as Diana famously called them—distrusted and disliked Charles. Personally, I've always admired Charles's efforts in the environmental space, but it's telling that he is also a man who—over fifty-five years into his life as a working royal—failed to truly capture the imagination and interest of those outside the monarchist bubble. His quirks and entitled behavior have, at times, alienated him from the institutional hidden forces that could change that popularity overnight, leaving him to take matters into his own hands, often with disastrous results. His failure to initiate a substantive dialogue with Prince Harry, despite how clearly his son detailed their fracture in interviews and public statements, is yet another sign of his inability to effectively address family matters head-on or navigate constitutional crises.

To add insult to injury, Charles knows his reign will be a transitional one, an intervening sovereignty that must happen before his elder son, William, the Prince of Wales, takes over at a far younger age and attempts to breathe new life into a desiccated monarchical system. Over the years I've watched as, behind the scenes, senior courtiers and other establishment figures groom Prince William for the throne. As a long-serving member of the Queen's most trusted staff put it to me before the monarch's death, Charles may be the next king, but William is "the future."

This brewing power struggle between the favored prince and the unpopular king is Shakespearean—a familial tug-of-war waged both onstage and off that still has the potential to unravel the monarchical tapestry. Scheming and backstabbing began long ago. Jealous of Harry's popularity with the media and William's preferred status in the Firm, King Charles has been known to turn a blind eye while aides leak details about his sons to the press. Camilla, also guilty of the same practices, caused further damage to the family during her long-running campaign to rehabilitate her own image. A tactical masterstroke, a well-timed leak, can pave the way for a beneficial back-scratching relationship with media confidantes in exchange for favorable treatment while also cutting down competition for the spotlight a rung or two. Long before the release of *Spare*, it was well known within the tight circle of royal correspondents that Charles eagerly piggybacked on reports of Prince Harry's teenage drug use by allowing the leak of personal details about his own son to construct a "great dad" narrative that many within the press gladly printed in return.

They say never mix family with business and, though the brothers had in the past put on a good show when needed, William and Harry are the perfect example of why this particular family business often teeters on the brink. Though they were remarkably close as they grew up, Harry's decision to "defect" to America (William's choice of word, according to a source, not mine) widened an already growing rift between the pair. Disappointed in Harry's life decisions and rooted in his ignited, newfound dedication to the Crown, William now considers his brother an outsider, especially since the release of Harry's memoir, which not only gave further details surrounding the Sussexes' decision to step back from their royal roles but also William's part in it. The heir doesn't really "need" the spare any longer anyway, one source admitted to me shortly after the Duke of Sussex left Britain in March 2020.

No longer useful as a helpful distraction or collateral damage, William had been wanting to distance himself from his brother ever since Harry's marriage to Meghan—whom the then Duke of Cambridge took a disliking to from the start. Now firmly established within their own household, William and Kate have become a committed, driven team, focused on their roles in the family and in royal history. Harry's dramas are no longer of any concern to them. Or so they say.

Some might argue that it's unnecessary to bring the Duke and Duchess of Sussex into conversations about the future of the monarchy since they started their separate life in California three years ago. As royal family members now living autonomously and completely disconnected from the institution, they currently play no part in where the Firm goes from here. But their role in the bigger royal story remains as important as ever. The issues raised by the couple, including allegations of bullying, misogyny, racism (or, in Harry's description, "unconscious bias"), and image manipulation, alongside the institutional cruelty they experienced, remain largely ignored and unexamined by the Palace. And any promises made after their departure, including a focus on diversity within the royal households, have proved little more than PR-friendly gloss-overs. Not a great look for an institution whose monarch is sovereign to interracial Britain and the head of the predominantly non-white Commonwealth. Discrediting Harry and Meghan through negative press briefings (no matter how many times Palace sources deny doing so) may have damaged the Sussexes' legitimacy to many, but for the members of the public still horrified by the family's treatment of its first mixed-race royal, it remains a thorny issue.

Beyond the family circle's damaging dramas, the institution of the monarchy is in increasingly desperate straits, too. Supporting a cratered Firm after the Queen's death is a tall order in and of itself. Doubly so when a growing percentage of the population feels that the monarchy is losing relevancy, with many now far more comfortable in voicing their views after Elizabeth II's passing. Recent years have seen an institution scrambling to justify its significance to younger generations who believe it no longer serves a strong enough purpose to justify its growing cost to the state. To stay relevant, the system, in an almost Trumpian twist, leans on patriotism—even jingoism—to shore up its purpose. When in doubt, festoon the palace, unfurl the Union Jacks, and enlist the tabloids.

In the first year of his reign, however, with the memory of the late Queen still fresh in the minds of many, King Charles III has received a healthy amount of support. To many, particularly Britain's royalists, he is still a son who lost his mother. But, as declining popularity polls already show, the good favor of the country can last only so long. And the bigger question remains: How can a former pampered prince who is now an aging king keep the attention of those who already feel the monarchy is less necessary than ever—or, worse, are totally indifferent to it? Charles's mother left a mandate and a clear path forward—a blueprint for how to keep things afloat. But is Charles the kind of king to simply follow the rules? Or will he want to go his own way, as he has repeatedly demonstrated in the past? It's an inescapable fact that the Firm's public ordeals, knee-jerk reactions, and family discord have created a life raft mentality that has long made their "never complain, never explain" mantra impossible to live by. The rot has set in, and it's eating away at the monarchy's undergirding. Without Queen Elizabeth II, who is there to offer a counterpoint? To stop the rot from spreading? Like Dorian's portrait in the attic, the ruinous truth is starting to show.

———

I have followed every important step of the royal story since William and Kate's engagement captured the hearts and excitement of a global audience in 2010, but I never expected to one day find myself in the middle of it. Working as the European bureau chief for Jann Wenner's *Us Weekly* magazine—at the time one of America's most-read publications—my entrance into the royal press ranks was bright-eyed, and I cut my teeth covering the gamut of royal events and news stories: engagements, weddings, births, and many wet Wednesdays in small rural towns for community center openings and plaque unveilings. The job gave me the perfect courtside seat to their world, and it wasn't long before I started to travel around the globe on tours and foreign visits with William, Kate, and Harry— the younger, more exciting stars of the family at the time—while forming bonds with those around them. Whether it was privately sharing strategies in the dawn of the social media age, providing a sounding board during certain media crises, or getting invites to private drinks receptions with the royals, I was a welcome face to Palace aides from the kinder U.S. press. Luckily for me, my work separated me from some of the less savory British media outlets that staff and family members had grown to quietly despise. The arrival of Meghan in 2016 saw my two news beats (entertainment and the royals) collide, and less than a year later I made the decision to focus on the royal family full time. Owing to a unique pool of sources and a refusal to follow the crowd, I quickly became a trusted confidante for many in and around the younger family—a true insider.

But that all changed in late 2020 after the publication of my first book, *Finding Freedom*, about Harry and Meghan's whirlwind journey in, and out of, the House of Windsor. It blew the lid off the Sussex saga, finally revealing the backroom machinations and family betrayals that eventually forced the royal couple out of the Firm. But it also put me on the receiving end of several of the same toxic practices that pushed the couple to their breaking point. "You ended up in a place a journalist rarely finds themselves—in the middle of a family war . . . And you were on the wrong side," a senior aide to the late Queen opined to me as I began writing this book. The fear of damaging revelations scared the family and angered powerful Palace operatives, and it also put a mark on my back. Five months before its release, a close friend of Prince Harry had warned me that the institution—and the media allies that support it—might "play dirty" against those who attempt to expose the truth. They weren't wrong.

I'm still in the mix, but let's just say I'm no longer the journalist who some in the family, or the more royalist-leaning correspondents, are thrilled to see at engagements. Having moved away from playing the Palace game of give-and-take to maintain access, I am now a perceived source of trouble for the institution. Why? Because I know—and share—too much. For four years, some of the most damaging in Windsor history, I witnessed the full scope of the deceptions, malice, and defensive posturing of an unstable family business and an institution in decline. I saw just how far they would go to save their own skin, the deep corrosion at the heart of the royal establishment, and I've witnessed the human damage done because of it.

It's impossible to deny the Queen's achievements during her seventy-year reign—something the world was reminded of during the outpouring of grief and tributes after her death. I was fortunate enough to cover some of the late monarch's greatest moments—

from making the line of succession more equitable to her tireless charity efforts—and I've seen the impact that Her Majesty's unwavering dedication to duty had on a new generation of working royals. Even at the height of his painful battle with the institution, I can't forget how Prince Harry's closest aide told me that the Queen's life of public service continues to inspire and motivate his every step forward in the Sussexes' new American life.

But all that hangs in the balance now. I fear that by continuing to ignore the ongoing constitutional corruption in the Palace's inner sanctum and enabling a cabal of courtiers and the British media to call the shots—as well as quietly supporting those who have brought shame and humiliation to the Crown—the royal institution is risking untold damage to the Queen's legacy. King Charles and Prince William have already displayed signs that they are allowing selfish agendas, a culture of cover-ups and PR trickery, and family discord to take over the House of Windsor. It is an outcome the royal family can avoid, but only if there is change.

In the past I, like others, have held back on revealing some of the darker truths at the heart of the institution of the British monarchy because I didn't want to lose my insider position or my contacts, or experience some of the threats made toward me. But as the once-majestic brocade of the royal family continued to fade and fray behind the scenes and on the front page, I was increasingly convinced that it was time to write this book.

Some of what you will read in *Endgame* may already be known to those in the self-regulated pack of journalists who, just like the White House press pool, shadow the family on their various endeavors. But that doesn't mean you will hear it from them. Though one can usually get away with the occasional rock of the boat, you need to waltz the Palace's dance if you want to maintain access to those off-record briefings and invites to private engagements. Me? Let's just say it's not the path I continued to follow.

The information shared over the pages ahead is sourced from

over a decade of personal reporting files as well as conversations and interviews with the many who have played a part in seminal moments, be they friends or professional acquaintances of the royals and those working for the monarchy, Palace aides and courtiers past and present, insiders from the world of politics and media, and, as you'll see, occasionally royal family members themselves.

Parts of this book will burn my bridges for good. But to tell the full story, there's no holding back. Not anymore. We're in the endgame.

# 1

# The Queen and Her Piper

### Elizabeth II's Final Days

———◦———

*Life seems to go on without effort when I am filled with music.*
—George Eliot, *The Mill on the Floss*

*So the days, the last days, blow about in a memory, hazy autumnal,*
*all alike as leaves: until a day unlike any other I've lived.*
—Truman Capote, *Breakfast at Tiffany's*

On the morning of September 6, 2022, at Balmoral Castle, a fifty-thousand-acre royal estate situated deep in the northeastern corner of the rugged, mystical Scottish Highlands, the piper to the sovereign, Pipe Major Paul Burns, started his day the same as he had done for over a year. Standing below the draped bay windows of Her Majesty's quarters, he fired up his bagpipes at 9:00 a.m. sharp to "wake the Queen." She was, of course, already up at this time (since 7:30 a.m.), but for seventy years of her life it had always been the official start to her day after having a bath and breakfast, and a moment she always looked forward to.

Though his fifteen-minute piping session usually started promptly on the hour, those in charge asked him to commence his tune thirty minutes later on this foggy autumn morning due to the Queen's ailing health and need for rest. As Burns blew air into his instrument's flutelike chanter, a low drone crowned by a haunting melody drifted over the sprawling Balmoral grounds, ascended into the forested hills surrounding the castle, and spread into the cloudy sky. To those within earshot, goosebumps were as guaranteed as his presence. Major Burns's piping prefaced a busy and important day of engagements for the monarch. At the time, of course, no one knew that this piping session would also herald the Queen's final day of royal duties.

At 11:00 a.m. exactly, the Queen met with Boris Johnson to accept his official resignation as prime minister. The conservative Tory party had pushed him out after a series of disgraceful scandals, and this was his official exit. The meeting lasted forty minutes, with Johnson later sharing that the Queen appeared "bright and focused." Professional, too—though the monarch privately disliked Johnson because of his behavior (the only one of fifteen prime ministers forced to formally apologize to the sovereign *twice*), sources said "you wouldn't have known it" during their time together. At noon, she met with the newly elected party leader, Liz Truss, to officially grant her permission to form a new government. The Queen had always conducted this ceremony, known as the "kissing of hands," at Buckingham Palace, but, due to her ongoing health struggles and her officially stamped "episodic mobility issues" from which she continued to suffer, Palace officials decided that Truss should make the trip to the Highland estate instead.

Less than forty-eight hours earlier, concerned courtiers suggested to the monarch that she might be better off letting Prince Charles carry out the task in her place. After all, the heir had already stood in for his mother at the opening of Parliament four months earlier. But this was one duty the Queen—despite the crippling pain she was experiencing in private—would not step aside from. "It's my job," she defiantly told aides.

Her meeting with Truss was short, lasting a little under an hour, and the Queen concluded it by allowing a photograph of the two to be released—the monarch with her walking stick in her hand (a dark wood favorite that once belonged to Prince Philip) and a room-lighting smile. Truss looked somewhat out of her element, which proved to be the case—her time as PM lasted a mere seven weeks. After carrying out light reading and correspondence from her desk, the Queen returned to her bedroom after lunch. Two days later, and after she postponed a virtual Privy Council meeting on the advice of doctors, Major Burns piped the Queen awake for what would be the last time.

A member of the Royal Regiment of Scotland, Pipe Major Paul Burns took over the piping duties from his predecessor, Pipe Major Richard Grisdale, in late 2021. A forty-six-year-old unassuming man with distinguished graying temples, solemn eyes, and a welcoming smile, Burns hailed from Ingleby Barwick, a small North Yorkshire town not far from the heathered valleys and Jurassic scenery of the North York Moors. He served as the Queen's thirteenth piper during her seventy-year reign and was part of a line of pipe majors who stretch back to Queen Victoria's time on the throne. A dutiful, even-keeled man who is proud of his country and honored to serve, Major Burns told his family and friends on several occasions that it was the job of his dreams.

The tradition of the piper to the sovereign began in 1843, after Queen Victoria traveled to the Scottish Highlands to visit John Campbell, the 2nd Marquess of Breadalbane, at Taymouth Castle. The marquess had his own piper, and Queen Victoria fell in love with both the sound of the instrument and the idea of having a piper of her own. She later wrote to her mother, the Duchess of Kent: "We have heard nothing but bagpipes since we have been in the beautiful Highlands, and I am become so fond of it [sic], that I mean to have a Piper, who can, if you like it, pipe every night at Frogmore." After seeking Campbell's sage counsel, Queen Victoria ordered her clerk marshal, a member of her royal household, to swear in Angus Mackay as the first official piper to Her Majesty. Since then, pipers, who are present whenever the monarch is in residence, have served the sovereign in this position, establishing what is an unquestionably affecting royal tradition.

To most of the thirteen pipers taken on by Queen Elizabeth II, their nickname ended up as "Pipes," and all the pipe majors quickly developed a lighthearted, friendly rapport that included jokes and cheerful banter with Her Majesty. Scott Methven, who piped for the Queen from 2015 until 2019, enjoyed a particularly warm relationship with Her Majesty.

Though the friendship was respectful on both sides, the Queen was never afraid to be the first to break the ice with her pipers, knowing that they would probably be nervous in her presence. "Do you know you're the first piper to hold the post that I haven't had to look up to?" she once joked to Methven, who—though broad in stature—stands at just five six. "That was the first thing she said to me," he later shared. "So, I was like, 'Right, is that how it's going to be?! One-liners. Right, here we go!' "

And it wasn't just jokes. The Queen demonstrated her genuine kindness to him when his wife, Morven, was diagnosed with cancer. He was at a loss as to what to do after discovering the tragic news, not wanting to let down the Queen and skip his playing session that evening. But the boss was having none of it. "No," the Queen told him that afternoon. "You're not playing. You're going to go to the hospital now and sit with your wife."

"She treats everyone with the utmost respect," he said, adding that when he took time off to be with his wife during her chemotherapy treatments, the British Army wanted to install a new pipe major who didn't have family matters to attend to. But, once again, the Queen had his back. "I've got one Queen's Piper. And the reason he isn't here is that he's away caring for his wife," she told her staff. "So, you are not replacing him under any circumstances. He is not getting removed from his post because his wife is dying of cancer."

The pipers to the sovereign do more than just pipe in the mornings and at night; they also sometimes play when guests arrive at Buckingham Palace, Balmoral, or any other royal residence where a royal hosts visitors and family members. During the Queen's final summer at Balmoral, Major Burns greeted many of those who came to visit, including family members who had all grown to love the unwieldy instrument and its rustic tone. For the most part, anyway. Prince Harry has amusingly described the instrument as a "drunken octopus" that, depending on your mood, "could sometimes drive you mad."

Balmoral, in any season, is a beautiful place. The Queen often referred to it as her "happy place." Located in Aberdeenshire, Scotland, the huge estate is nestled in the foothills of the craggy Cairngorms, a mountain range that includes some of Britain's highest plateaus and peaks, namely the cratered but towering Mount Lochnagar. It was "Dark Loch na Garr" to Lord Byron, who, in one of his earliest poems, praises the mountain's rugged glory: "Restore me the rocks where the snow-flake reposes / . . . Oh for the crags that are wild and majestic."

With a stunning view of these sublime peaks, Balmoral Castle sits at the heart of the estate and was acquired by the royal family in 1848, when Prince Albert privately purchased it for Queen Victoria. A Scottish baronial castle built from local granite and outfitted with a seven-story tower and pepper pot turrets, Balmoral predominantly functions as a grand country house for the royal family. Inside the fairy-tale home are stone floors, decorative fireplaces, and dozens of rooms—it's cavernous but warm, with dark woods accenting all the granite and stone. It's historically been a quiet Highland retreat for gatherings, shooting parties, and outdoor pursuits such as salmon fishing—the late Prince Philip's favorite pastime—hunting, and hiking. Even during the Queen's later years, she was known to confidently drive her Land Rover Defender over large swathes of the fifty-thousand-acre property—both on and off road. "The roads were bumpy and full of potholes, but she handled them all like a pro," a longtime aide told me. "The further out you go, the easier it is to get lost, but she knew every inch of the estate off by heart."

About a mile from Balmoral's main castle, up on a hill above the cascading, salmon-rich River Dee, is Craigowan Lodge, a modest (at least by royal standards) seven-bedroom guest house where the Queen and Prince Philip would often stay for part of their summers on the estate. It was at Craigowan where the Queen spent the first month of her final summer at Balmoral, before moving into the castle. Her team there was much leaner than her others, but close aides like her long-serving page of the backstairs, Paul Whybrew, and her sergeant at arms, Barry Mitford, were always nearby. After Philip's death, these two men dutifully watched TV with their boss in the evenings and brought in her beloved *Racing Post* newspaper every morning. Also by her side was her personal assistant and advisor, and curator to the Queen, Angela Kelly. A fashion designer and, according to most, a stern woman, Kelly was very protective of the Queen—she even lived with the monarch during her February 2022 bout with Covid, doing everything including reading to her at night and washing her hair. She was one of the Queen's most trusted aides and confidantes, and a source said she was "indispensable" during Her Majesty's final weeks.

By all accounts, it was a peaceful summer for the Queen after her arrival that July. Sources familiar with her itinerary, and those who had visited her there, shared that she enjoyed spending time sitting in the sun when it was pleasant out. Mobility issues kept her from taking her usual walks, but she did use her staghorn walking stick—a cane suitable for outdoors made from locally sourced wood—to take short strolls around Balmoral's grounds and watch her two beloved corgis, Sandy and Muick, scamper around the gardens. As a close aide described, "That summer was walks, picnics, and barbecues—all the things the Queen loved to do at Balmoral." People who spent time with her, including one of the staff members who spoke to me for this book, said she was often "smiling and in good spirits."

Always mindful of the work to be done, the Queen also fulfilled her daily duties without fail—her red box of government papers and briefings was always up-to-date and close by. All play and no work was never the Queen's style. In fact, it was loyal aides who had to make sure she paced herself, knowing that for her to do it all, they would have to find ways to spread out her scheduled duties so they didn't take an irreversible toll on her limited energy. Though she loved attending the annual Braemar Gathering, an historic Highland Games festival near Aberdeen—she missed only two in her life—Palace aides and doctors decided the lively event was not a good idea for the ninety-six-year-old. Courtiers back in London, including the Queen's private secretary Sir Edward Young, Prince Charles's private secretary Sir Clive Alderton, and the master of the household Sir Tony Johnstone-Burt, discussed the sovereign's workload if she didn't return to Windsor at the end of the season— and how other family members, particularly Charles, could help pick up some of that work in her stead. The monarch usually left her Balmoral retreat in late September or early October to return to palace life, but with her health issues, her departure was looking unlikely. Even before she left, a long-serving Buckingham Palace courtier told me a month before her arrival that they were unsure whether Her Majesty would come back at all. "I have a feeling in the pit of my stomach that this will be the last time we see her head up there," they said. "There's a sense that, and I feel scared to even say it, that she may not make it."

Despite her serious health issues and the unwelcome changes to her work schedule, the Queen ensured that Balmoral was a revolving door of close family members sojourning there that summer, including her son Prince Edward and his wife, Sophie, Countess of Wessex, and her grandson Prince William with Kate, then the Duchess of Cambridge, and their children, Prince George, Princess Charlotte, and Prince Louis. And the steadfast Major Burns was there to greet every single one of them who came through the door. The Queen also welcomed friends from every part of her life to Balmoral during her last days. The Reverend Dr. Iain Greenshields was appointed as the moderator of the General Assembly of the Church of Scotland that summer and received a two-day invite on September 3 from the monarch. Unknown to all at the time, his visit would fall on what would become the final weekend of her life.

"You could see her fragility, but as soon as she started talking, as soon as she was engaged with you, a very different kind of person emerged," he said of his time with the monarch. "She was somebody whose memory was exceptional . . . She spoke very warmly of Scotland and the relationship she had with Scotland and particularly the Balmoral estate where she felt very much at peace in her last days as it was going to turn out to be." And despite her physical struggles, the Queen's trademark wit was as sharp as ever. After dining together on the Saturday, the monarch stopped Reverend Dr. Greenshields before he returned to his guest accommodation at the castle's Tower Rooms. "Your Queen is sending you to the tower," she said with a smile, chuckling at her own joke.

The monarch was also in a reflective mood, Greenshields shared, often reminiscing about the joy she had felt while staying in Scotland. "She loved Balmoral estate and [after lunch] she took me over to the window and she was just showing me the different gardens and flower beds that were there and pointing out the estate that brought her so much comfort and peace in her life." The pair also spent time reflecting on Her Majesty's faith and the role it played throughout her seventy-year reign. "[Her faith] was fundamental," he said. "She said she had no regrets, having started that journey of faith, she had no regrets at all."

On the second day of his visit, Reverend Dr. Greenshields presented the monarch with a parting gift—a handmade cross that an inmate in a rehabilitation program at Glenochil prison gifted him on one of his many visits. "I asked what I could possibly give to somebody who had everything, and she smiled at me. I offered her the cross, and she took it very graciously and thanked me for it and wished me the best."

Just four days later, the Queen passed away peacefully at 3:10 p.m. in her bedroom. The official cause of death later given by Her Majesty's official apothecary in Scotland, Dr. Douglas James Allan Glass, was "old age." Her eldest children—Princess Anne, who was in Scotland for royal engagements at the time, and Prince Charles, staying less than ten miles away at his Birkhall residence—each received calls from Dr. Glass to tell them the time had come. Anne spent the night at Balmoral Castle with her mother, and both children got to spend time at her bedside before she passed. "It was what she wanted and what we all prayed for," a close friend of the family shared. "To have her loved ones close by and for that moment to happen in private."

Prince Andrew, Prince William, Prince Edward, and Sophie, still then the Countess of Wessex, arrived at Aberdeen Airport on a private flight just before 4:00 p.m. that day. Prince Harry—already in Britain with Meghan for nonroyal engagements—landed almost three hours later, on a separate flight, a story in itself I will get to later.

Each family member was given time alone with the Queen as she rested in peace. A final moment in private before the world—which was informed of the sovereign's passing at 6:10 p.m.—was invited to join the royal family in grief. That night the group was split in two, with Charles, now King, and Camilla, Queen Consort, leaving for Birkhall with William, now next in line, for a dinner together. A top-of-the-heirarchy gathering of sorts. Meanwhile, Andrew, Edward, Sophie, Anne, and Harry sat down for dinner together at Balmoral. Major Burns—dressed in a Balmoral tartan kilt (the only nonroyal allowed to wear this gray-and-red design)—played the pipes in honor of the Queen before they ate. As he stood outside the residence's dining room, it was the first time Burns had played for guests without the presence of "the boss."

The Queen's passing in Scotland was considered serendipitous by some in the family. The "land of the brave" was not only a country to which she was duty bound, but also a home with ancestral roots (Her Majesty was a direct descendant of Queen Margaret of Scotland). "It was where she was most at peace," said Ailsa Anderson, a former press secretary to Queen Elizabeth II. "There had always been plans in place if she were to pass away there." Indeed, the monarch's death in Scotland called for an extension within the "Operation London Bridge" plans. "Operation Unicorn" took its code name from the lion (England) and the unicorn (Scotland) featured in the coat of arms for the United Kingdom. The protocol included an additional ceremonial procession in the Scottish capital, Edinburgh, and a service at the city's St. Giles' Cathedral.

The processions and rituals that followed her ten-day journey from Balmoral to her final resting place in Windsor saw the Queen's coffin steadfastly accompanied by Princess Anne—a wish the monarch's daughter had made some years before her mother's passing. The Princess Royal—whose strong work ethic and no-nonsense attitude were often likened to that of her mother—became a stoic presence for the nation. The six-hour journey from Balmoral to Edinburgh began with six gamekeepers (known locally as ghillies) carefully carrying the coffin out of the castle's ballroom through to a hearse outside. Major Paul Burns played his bagpipes as the oak coffin passed by him in the dining room. With such an important role to play, he turned to Methven the night before for some sage advice for the days ahead. "He's a cracking piper and a good man . . . I told him he would do a fantastic job," Methven said.

As the hearse drove through Aberdeenshire, and then on to Aberdeen and Dundee, Princess Anne, now joined by her husband, Vice Admiral Sir Timothy Lawrence, remained part of the royal cortege until it arrived in Edinburgh. There, Anne and Sir Tim joined other family members for the procession to St. Giles' Cathedral, where the Queen would lie at rest for twenty-four hours. Reverend Dr. Iain Greenshields, his weekend with the Queen still fresh in his memory, conducted the ceremony that followed, telling the congregation, "Most of us cannot recall a time when she was not our monarch. Committed to the role she assumed in 1952 upon the death of her beloved father, she has been a constant in all of our lives for over seventy years. She was determined to see her work as a form of service to others."

On the final morning of the Scottish portion of the processional, Anne was there again to escort her mother's coffin to Edinburgh Airport. The Queen's final journey from Scotland to England was originally planned and documented in "Operation Unicorn" for the Royal Train, but, due to security concerns, Palace aides and government officials decided that the coffin was safer on a plane. The royal standard of Scotland draped over the Queen's solid oak coffin, and a flowered wreath rested on top, with each flower type representing values and traits that Her Majesty held dear. The dahlias represented kindness, commitment, and perseverance, while the white phlox stood for harmony and understanding. Lovingly picked the day she died by Balmoral staff, the sweet peas—Elizabeth's favorite—meant "thank you for a lovely time" and "goodbye." The Scots who gathered at the airport to bid farewell to their beloved Queen waved and, in some cases, wept as soldiers closed the cargo door of the Royal Air Force C-17 that carried her to London.

"It has been an honor and a privilege to accompany her on her final journeys," Anne said of escorting her mother. "Witnessing the love and respect shown by so many on these journeys has been both humbling and uplifting . . . I am also so grateful for the support and understanding offered to my dear brother Charles as he accepts the added responsibilities of the Monarch."

Five days into the ten-day period of national mourning, King Charles and Camilla, Queen Consort, received the coffin at RAF Northolt, on the western outskirts of London. It was there that the royal family formally handed over her body to the public she served—Her Majesty then lay in state until the day of her funeral. At Westminster Hall, the oldest building on the British parliamentary estate, units from the Sovereign's Bodyguard, the Foot Guards, and the Household Cavalry Mounted Regiment stood watch as members of the public filed past to pay their respects, a tradition that dates back to 1898, and since then, King George V, King George VI, and Queen Mary have all laid in state before their funerals. And so, it would be no different for Queen Elizabeth II, a woman who valued and cherished tradition. Over four hundred thousand people from every corner of the country and overseas lined up for five days for an opportunity to venerate Her Majesty and her legacy or to just be present for this historical moment. #TheQueue trended on social media, and lines—which could even be seen from planes flying to Heathrow—became an important final scene of the Queen's life: a national moment of shared experience.

Dignitaries from all around the world, including President Joe Biden and First Lady Jill Biden, also stopped by to pay their respects. On September 17, all eight of the Queen's grandchildren—Peter Phillips, Zara Tindall, Prince William, Prince Harry, Princess Beatrice, Princess Eugenie, Lady Louise, and Viscount Severn—stood in silent vigil beside the catafalque on which her coffin rested. Each was instructed where to stand and what cues to follow. "You were our matriarch, our guide, our loving hand on our backs leading us through this world," Eugenie and Beatrice wrote in a statement. "You taught us so much and we will cherish those lessons and memories forever."

The morning of the funeral on September 19, 2022, was the culmination of a plan conceived in painstaking detail. A cortege of soldiers and family members escorted the late monarch's coffin, now draped in the royal standard flag, to Westminster Abbey, resting on the same 123-year-old State Gun Carriage that former Palace officials rolled out for the funeral of her father. Behind the carriage and to the beat of marching drums walked the new King; his sons, William and Harry; and immediate family including Princess Anne, Prince Edward, Prince Andrew, and the late Queen's first cousin, the Duke of Gloucester. The processional also included Palace officials—the Queen's master of the household, Tony Johnstone-Burt; the most senior officer of the royal household, Lord Chamberlain Baron Parker of Minsmere; principal private secretary Edward Young; equerry lieutenant colonel Nana Kofi Twumasi-Ankrah; and Keeper of the Privy Purse Sir Michael John Stevens, the man in charge of the monarchy's coffers. With a view of Westminster Abbey from the roof of the neighboring Methodist Central Hall, where ABC News was live on air, the rousing sound of bagpipes dolefully echoing through the streets of Westminster is one I won't soon forget. All air travel was suspended for the solemn occasion, and the silence that immediately followed the procession as Her Majesty was carried into Westminster Abbey by eight soldiers from the Queen's Company 1st Battalion, Grenadier Guards was profound.

The Queen chose the Abbey over the larger St. Paul's Cathedral because of the medieval church's significance in her life. The Abbey was where she married Prince Philip in 1947 at the young age of twenty-one, and where, just six years after their union, she was crowned. Her words on the day of her coronation now served as a reminder of her service. "The ceremonies you have seen today are ancient, and some of their origins are veiled in the mists of the past. But their spirit and their meaning shine through the ages never, perhaps, more brightly than now. I have in sincerity pledged myself to your service, as so many of you are pledged to mine," she said in her first speech as sovereign. "As this day draws to its close, I know that my abiding memory of it will be, not only the solemnity and beauty of the ceremony, but the inspiration of your loyalty and affection."

Her Majesty Queen Elizabeth II's coffin arrived at the Abbey shortly before 11:00 a.m., and it was now her family's turn to say goodbye to her era. As 4.1 billion people tuned in from around the world to watch the first state funeral since Winston Churchill's in 1965 (Prince Philip turned down the opportunity for one, not wanting "the fuss"), it was the first in over seventy years to allow viewers to witness firsthand how the royals pass on their hereditary power. After handing over responsibilities and duties to those more physically able in the final few years of her life, the Queen had already put a spotlight on the new representatives of the royal family. King Charles and Camilla, Queen Consort, stood front and center to illustrate the beginning of the new Carolean era, while Prince William and his son Prince George stood closely behind to reinforce the family's next two generations. For a family that heavily relies on imagery, it was a well-choreographed moment on an emotionally potent day.

Just one part of the most complex security apparatus in British history, the Metropolitan Police watched over all two thousand guests from every corner (and rooftop) as other family members—from the Sussexes to the Wessexes—joined representatives from 168 countries (out of 193 UN member states), eighteen monarchs, fifty-five presidents, and twenty-five prime ministers, including President Joe Biden, President Emmanuel Macron of France, and all of Britain's living prime ministers. (An envoy from North Korea was present, but representatives from Myanmar, Belarus, and Russia all remained firmly on the no-invite list.) All the guests stood as the choir's spine-tingling rendition of the nineteenth-century hymn "The Day Thou Gavest, Lord, Is Ended" filled the Abbey with sorrowful acceptance.

Major Burns waited patiently in the wings of a balcony over-looking the congregation. It was, he admitted to Methven just days earlier, the most important day of his career, and he wanted to get it right. In the days leading up to the funeral, he practiced in private, but, in just over an hour, there would be no room for error dur-ing his rendition of the traditional lament "Sleep, Dearie, Sleep." Dressed in a kilt of Royal Stewart tartan plaid and the piper's tra-ditional Glengarry hat, Burns had received instructions earlier in the morning about where he should stand to allow BBC cameras to capture the moment, a small piece of tape marking the exact spot. He always took pride in his bagpipes, but he went the extra distance for this occasion, deep cleaning and polishing the dark, weathered wood and silver tuning slides, even lint-rolling the pipes' bright blue velvet bag.

But before Major Burns's lament came the religious ceremony led by the Dean of Westminster, David Hoyle. A devout Christian and the proud head of the Church of England, the Queen often spoke about how her faith guided her reign and her personal life. As Archbishop of Canterbury Justin Welby noted during the service, "People of loving service are rare in any walk of life. Leaders of lov-ing service are still rarer."

Every detail, every moment of religious symbolism, was carefully considered by the Queen and her closest aides during the later years of her life. "Her Majesty's state funeral was so God honoring because that's exactly how she lived every moment of her life," a Buckingham Palace courtier said. "The service was a celebration of her life but also a true show of her commitment to God and serving others." A minister who knew her added that she lived her life "immersed [in Scripture]" (she would read daily and worship privately every Sun-day) and wanted people to feel that throughout the service.

For a woman who had purposefully remained so shrouded in mystery during her life, the Queen's state funeral offered new glimpses into her personality, namely through music and readings, as those elements emphasized the things she respected and loved in her personal life, a rich inner existence she kept mostly to herself.

As the national anthem and two-minute silence signaled the end of the service, Major Burns tuned up his bagpipes for his soul-stirring version of "Sleep, Dearie, Sleep." The Gaelic lullaby brought tears to the eyes of many, including King Charles, who, after touring the nation for eleven days as the new monarch, was "understandably exhausted and emotional," a senior aide later explained.

On this unusually dry and sunny day in London, thousands lined the streets to watch as the funeral procession solemnly moved from the Abbey, past her former Buckingham Palace home, and then to the nearby Wellington Arch, where a cortege would head toward Windsor for the committal service that would officially end Elizabeth II's reign. Big Ben's affecting chimes were the only accompaniment to a reigning, powerful silence.

This twenty-two-mile journey to Windsor would also lead to the Queen's final retreat from the public eye. After the high polish of the official proceedings, this homecoming trip returned her from the public to the private sanctuary of her family. For them, the strict protocol of the past eleven days naturally led everyone to demonstrate the famous stiff upper lip and push through the formalities. But there in Windsor, without all the cameras and conventions, they would soon be able to mourn freely as their mother, grandmother, and great-grandmother was returned to the earth.

Since her death, Charles had already become king two times over—the day the Queen died and the day of his September 10 proclamation at St. James's Palace in front of the accession council. At the private committal ceremony that evening, it would happen once again as he symbolically scattered soil on his mother's coffin in the Royal Vault beneath St. George's Chapel.

Before the last hymn at the burial, the Imperial State Crown, scepter, and orb were removed from the Queen's coffin by the crown jeweler. As is tradition, the Lord Chamberlain broke his "wand of office" to mark the end of the sovereign's reign before placing the two pieces on her coffin. Cameras were allowed to capture these final moments for the first time before Elizabeth II was lowered into the vault, but what happened beyond was kept private—all part of maintaining the mystery and intrigue of the royal family, perhaps the Queen's last command. For a family so known for sharing some of their most private moments through back channels with the press, this was the one time they all universally agreed to keep the details to themselves.

Major Burns was also there to pipe for the monarch's final act. The image of the lone piper was one that resonated the most with viewers around the world. As he played "A Salute to the Royal Fendersmith," the haunting timbre of his bagpipes floated over the fields and gardens of Windsor, down to the River Thames, and out to the North Sea. Burns didn't show it at the time, but he was deeply moved by that moment. Right before his final duty for Her Majesty, he learned of the Queen's final act for him—ensuring his job was safe. The new king had assured his mother's dear "Pipes" that he would continue the role under his reign.

Inside St. George's Chapel, as the Queen was finally laid to rest in the King George VI Memorial Chapel, King Charles III wiped away his tears. In a 2011 speech at the Commonwealth Heads of Government Meeting in Australia, the Queen quoted an Aboriginal proverb: "We are all visitors to this time, this place. We are just passing through. Our purpose here is to observe, to learn, to grow, to love, and then we return home." Now, resting by her "strength and stay," Philip; her beloved parents, George VI and Elizabeth; and her sister, Margaret, she, too, returned home.

# 2

# Shaky Ground

The Queen Is Dead, the Monarchy Faces Trouble

———·———

*Above all things our royalty is to be reverenced, and if you*
*begin to poke about it you cannot reverence it . . . Its mystery*
*is its life. We must not let in daylight upon magic.*
—Walter Bagehot, *The English Constitution*

*The Queen is dead, boys. And it's so lonely on a limb.*
—The Smiths

Right after his ascension to the throne, we got a snapshot of King Charles III as a sovereign who might prove more "in touch" and affable than his removed and dignified mother. Just hours after the Queen's death, he ventured outside the gates of Buckingham Palace to shake hands with members of the public during his first walkabout as king. Chatting with those who were close by and smiling at others as they expressed their condolences, the newly minted monarch even allowed one woman to lean forward and kiss him on the cheek. It was a stark contrast to the Queen, whose arm's-length approach might have seen her wave to well-wishers from the rope line but rarely permitted her to indulge in anything more during her seventy-year reign. Charles, on the other hand, genuinely appeared at ease and unafraid to embrace his fellow supporters.

But it's not a stretch to suggest that this moment was orchestrated and planned by Charles and his team years ago. At seventy-four, Charles was the longest-serving heir apparent in the British monarchy's history. He had decades to think about and strategize for his time on the throne—time to outline his vision for the monarchy and calculate ways to delineate his reign from his mother's. And his vision is not a secret; he's continually designed and refined it over the years, even publicly addressed it on many occasions. Knowing full well how difficult it is to get an oversize, slow-moving institution to adapt, Charles has long championed a "slimmed-down" monarchy, one that is more modern, agile, and—more importantly for a public that helps foot the royal bill—cost-effective. More than just trimming the fat, the King, who as the Prince of Wales was known for his compassionate activism and progressive thinking (even if some of it resulted in his reputation as a busybody), has stressed to aides that he wants his version of a "modern" monarchy to be more palatable to younger generations. Where his mother brought a brisk, stately detachment, Charles has spoken about wanting a warmer touch. Perhaps he learned some lessons from the late Princess Diana, queen of people's hearts, both in the tragedy of her life and the genuine value of her work, or maybe his vision was simply born of frustration from a life following the rules and abiding by *the way things have always been*—a rigid code for living and working as a royal that led to countless struggles with his family, the institution, and the public. Or maybe this is just a way of channeling the passion he brought to his service as the Prince of Wales—his dedication to the environment, his desire to unite religions through interfaith initiatives, and his championing of organic farming—into the smaller window he'll serve as King.

But it can be said for sure that the long-suffering prince who now wears the crown has known for years that if the monarchy is going to survive, it will have to present itself to the world as—at the very least—a leaner, more tolerant, and more personable family and organization. And when the King went out to shake hands with his subjects for the first time on September 9, 2022, he was attempting to present just that.

Too bad the image didn't hold. Less than twelve weeks later, on November 29, Queen Camilla hosted a Violence Against Women and Girls reception at Buckingham Palace. It was a high-profile effort for one of Camilla's cherished causes and an issue for which she's advocated over the course of her royal tenure. Held during the United Nations' 16 Days of Activism Against Gender-Based Violence campaign, the event convened three hundred guests, including charity workers, domestic violence survivors, ambassadors, politicians, journalists, royalty (Queen Rania Al Abdullah of Jordan, Crown Princess Mary of Denmark, and Queen Mathilde of Belgium), and even a Spice Girl—Mel B. Declared a success by many who attended, it was a reminder of what Camilla is capable of offering in her new role, and an event that signaled the Firm had the ability to stick its neck out to advance a pertinent, substantial, and brave cause (even if they don't do it often enough).

But the next morning a tweet by an attendee started a fire on social media. Ngozi Fulani, a British citizen born in London of African heritage and Caribbean descent and CEO of Sistah Space—a London-based charity that offers support to women and girls of African and Caribbean heritage affected by domestic and sexual abuse—noted that her experience was vastly different from the positive press surrounding it. "Mixed feelings," she lamented on Twitter, revealing that within ten minutes of arriving, a staff member she referred to as "Lady SH" had touched her dreadlocks without permission and persistently asked where she was *really* from. That aide was Lady Susan Hussey, an eighty-three-year-old lady-in-waiting from Queen Elizabeth II's reign who had recently been moved into a non-salaried position of lady of the household, a role that required her to attend Buckingham Palace engagements and mingle with guests. The daughter of the 12th Earl Waldegrave and a prim-looking baroness, Lady Hussey is also a close friend to many within the royal family, including Prince Harry, and one of Prince William's three godmothers.

In a transcript shared by Fulani, she detailed how Hussey had pestered her about her background and asked at least *seven* times where she was from. After Fulani told her she was British, Hussey pushed back with a follow-up question: "No . . . Where do your *people* come from?" Even after she expressed exasperation and questioned the Queen's former confidante, "'My people'? Lady, what is this?" Hussey continued her offensive inquisition, exclaiming, "Oh, I can see I'm going to have a challenge getting you to say where you're from. When did you first come here?"

This awkward and shocking conversation—witnessed by the leader of the British Women's Equality Party, Mandu Reid—amounted to a privileged white aristocrat berating a Black woman about her origins while refusing to believe she was *only* a British citizen. Within hours it became world news, and, once again, the royal institution was in hot water for racist comments and retrograde thinking. Hussey's casual racism (be it conscious or not) not only scuttled Camilla's successful event, shifting the focus from a noble cause to controversy, it also came at a time when the royal family was still digging out from Harry and Meghan's revelation in their March 2021 Oprah interview that "concerns and conversations" were had in the family about "how dark" the skin of their unborn son, Archie, might be.

Disgraceful and intrusive, the Hussey episode marred an otherwise meaningful royal engagement. "Standing there in a room packed with people while this violation was taking place was so strange, especially as the event was about violence against women," Fulani shared. "That feeling of not knowing what to do will *never* leave me. Almost alone in a roomful of advocates."

There was minimal stalling from Buckingham Palace, who were surprisingly quick to address the issue. "Unacceptable and deeply regrettable comments have been made," a statement read. "We have reached out to Ngozi Fulani on this matter and are inviting her to discuss all elements of her experience in person if she wishes." It went on to say that Hussey had stepped aside from her honorary role with immediate effect.

Despite the statement's claim to the contrary, Fulani didn't receive any official correspondence until almost a week later. The Palace also failed to explain why Lady Susan was put in such a role in the first place. An octogenarian and trusted advisor to the Queen, Hussey might have had respect from the family members, but it was unwise to put her in a public-facing position at an event with such a diverse crowd at a time when they needed to show some proof of modernization. Like so many at Buckingham Palace, she is from another era, and the mealymouthed excuses that rationalize this kind of behavior—well-meaning folks from that generation don't know any better, for example—do not cut it. Large, exasperated swathes of the public are weary of these justifications, and our current cancel culture is hostile to them. The press offices in both royal households should be pumping out good news about the family, not countering allegations from their back foot and expending resources apologizing, fixing, and tap-dancing around scandals.

The fracas was a reminder that despite the promise of a more tolerant and forward-looking monarchy, this institution was still anything but. Repurposing six of the late Queen's ladies-in-waiting, a feature of court life dating back to the Middle Ages, instead of allowing the women (all born in the 1930s and '40s) to gracefully retire set the Firm up for disaster. Ironically, just days earlier, the Palace had made a show of Camilla's "modern" decision to not hire her own ladies-in-waiting, instead bringing on informal "Queen's companions." Though they would not be required to handle correspondence or administration like Queen Elizabeth II's right-hand women, these six would still be around to "support" her at official engagements. In other words, they're ladies-in-waiting with fewer duties—hardly any different to the past. And it was more evidence that, although Charles may have a vision for modernity, the reality is the institution is still entrenched in the past, often knowingly dragging arcane, extraneous traditions along with it.

This also points to a larger issue: modernizing a thousand-year-old monarchy that just lost its longest-serving sovereign in history is immensely challenging, particularly when the family is usually one blunder away from scandal. A royal source said that Charles knows that if he "pulls on the thread" of change too fast and with too much force, he may unwind the knot that holds it all together. It leaves him in the unfortunate position of resorting to virtue signaling and enacting half measures that may come back to haunt him and compromise the monarchy's future. Although King Charles has successfully retreated into the solemn sovereign space, the Lady Susan ordeal indicates that perhaps seventy-four years in a bubble of privilege isn't the most effective training for the top job, and that his decision-making isn't aligned with his own vision of how he wants this new royal chapter to read. The King should be prepared for a reign under a microscope: the press (at least those who aren't in his pocket), the public, and his foes will quickly and mercilessly critique everything he does, and they will be unsparing in their judgment. Because of her long service and her beloved stature in the national pantheon, Queen Elizabeth II was often spared this treatment, but Charles gets no such grace.

Despite the fact that Hussey is his godmother, Prince William was fast to denounce and remove himself from the ugly ordeal. Behind the scenes, William was "furious" and told his team that he needed to distance himself quickly. "There was just this feeling that it could have been easily avoided," said a source in his circle. "[William] asked, 'Why was she there in the first place?!'" Acting the same day the news broke, Kensington Palace spokesman Lee Thompson, who had taken on the job five months earlier, said, "This is a matter for Buckingham Palace, but as the Prince of Wales's spokesperson I appreciate [that] you'll want to ask about it. So let me address this head-on: I was really disappointed to hear about the guest's experience at Buckingham Palace last night." He went on to say, "Racism has no place in our society. The comments were unacceptable, and it is right that the individual has stepped aside."

This was a swift rebuke and a remarkably different PR response to what we've come to expect from the Palace. William's decisive action on the matter demonstrates that he is willing to act independently and, added a source, is proof that he is unwilling to dither and defer to Buckingham Palace when a situation demands an immediate, resolute response. As the heir to the throne, he's savvy enough to know these are moments he can leverage to show the public (and the institution) that he's his own man, and one ready to be king. His father, said sources, didn't share the same approach. "It was a rash . . . knee-jerk response," a Buckingham Palace source remarked. "The feeling was they wanted to disassociate, instead of thinking as a team."

This is quite a different position to the one the Palace adopted when Prince Andrew paid out millions to settle with his sexual abuse accuser, Virginia Giuffre, whose allegations Prince Andrew has always vehemently denied. During this royal cause célèbre, Palace aides told members of the press that Prince William and his father were in "lockstep" over the action to take away Andrew's titles and military honors—a buzzword that then rippled through the media and one the Palace used to suggest that Charles and his son were joining forces to support Queen Elizabeth II at the tail end of her reign. A nice story, but behind the scenes a different one played out. Knowing the Queen's soft spot for Andrew and his father's fear of hurting his brother, sources said it was actually William who encouraged the Queen and Charles to strip the disgraced Duke of York. "William stepped up, but those close to the Queen briefed journalists that it was very much a joined father-son move . . . that's where the term 'lockstep' came in," said a source close to William. Regardless of the details, it worked, but, because it took so long to coordinate necessary action, it also came at great cost: the bad press was relentless.

So much for lockstep now, though. After the Firm's painfully protracted management of the Andrew scandal and the aftermath of Harry and Meghan's departure, Kensington Palace sources say William is keen to ensure his own image is no longer impacted by "poor decisions" made by others—be it his father, his uncle, his brother, or any other family member. The prince, said an insider, knows his father's reign is little more than transitional, if only by virtue of the King's age, and is acting accordingly: "There was rarely a moment where [Charles] stepped on his mother's toes . . . but it's different with William. He's eager to establish himself as his own man . . . He's not giving his father the same space Charles did with the Queen. There's no time for that."

This father-son relationship was beginning to bristle with tension and one-upmanship, so William's solo maneuverings around the Hussey trouble added force to the friction. William's Kensington Palace and King Charles's Buckingham Palace are now hives of competing agendas and different ideas about how to modernize. Behind closed doors, the King and the Prince of Wales are embracing very different approaches.

For William, this isn't just about ego, claimed a source. Rather, it's because the institution itself has always put its weight behind him, giving the prince the confidence required to stand apart from his father. This was evident shortly before the Queen's passing. During June 2022's Platinum Jubilee concert, it was William who had the biggest moment during the televised event in addressing the public and promoting his own efforts on finding solutions to environmental issues. Charles merely followed up with a short speech dedicated to his mother and the introduction of a comedy sketch starring the late monarch and Paddington Bear. As a Palace aide later remarked, "Nothing is ever a coincidence." The tussle for the spotlight has only heightened since Charles became King, including the moment William chose to sit down for a rare interview with the *Sunday Times* scheduled for publication the day after King Charles's first Trooping the Colour parade, essentially wiping any coverage of the special moment off the front page. It's also why joint appearances or engagements have been few and far between during the King's first year on the throne. "Though royal officials don't like to talk about it, particularly after Charles's ascension, behind Palace walls, William represents the monarchy's true next stage." Charles is the bridge to get there.

The prince's unilateral response notwithstanding, the timing of the Hussey controversy couldn't have been worse for William and Kate. The story broke on the morning the Waleses were preparing to leave for the United States to roll out the green carpet for his Earthshot Prize ceremony in Boston—a star-studded event at the MGM Music Hall at Fenway billed by a Kensington Palace aide as Prince William's "Super Bowl moment," whatever that was supposed to mean. Launched by William and Sir David Attenborough in October 2020, the Earthshot Prize awards one million British pounds to five individuals or teams whose work offers "ingenious solutions to repair and regenerate our planet."

After William widely announced Earthshot to the world, sources claimed Charles was quietly annoyed. For much of his adult life, *he* was the one who passionately pushed the environmental cause, often without any acknowledgment. "He had hoped that William would want to involve his father or at least credit him for inspiring him to take on this role, but instead it was as if [Charles's environmentalism] didn't even exist," said a Clarence House source at the time. A glitzy affair for a good cause, the inaugural Earthshot ceremony in London generated a fair share of buzz. The following year's event was shaping up to be no different, featuring celebrity guests such as actress Catherine O'Hara, football legend David Beckham, and actor Rami Malek, alongside musical performances by the likes of Billie Eilish and Annie Lennox.

But by the time they landed in Boston, the furor over Lady Susan was at full volume, drowning out much of the hoopla for the event. The couple flew commercial to make a point, but it was lost on a public already outraged by yet another royal race incident. Both former U.S. secretary of state and current Special Presidential Envoy for Climate John Kerry and the author, diplomat, and member of America's "royal family" Caroline Kennedy, their chief guests, appeared to tap the brakes on joining the engagement—Kerry cited illness and Kennedy "disrupted travel plans" but in reality, it's likely they both wanted to see how the scandal played out. (In the end, Kerry did attend the event, and Prince William later met Kennedy for thirty minutes at the John F. Kennedy Presidential Library and Museum.) On the second night, William and Kate attended a Celtics basketball game at TD Garden Arena, where, to their surprise, many fans booed and subjected the royal couple to chants of "USA! USA!" whenever they appeared on the jumbotron. In all fairness, Boston sports fans will boo just about anyone who shows up on their turf, but the latest scandal, along with all the other baggage William and Kate drag around as royals (including their treatment of Harry and Meghan, for one), only made the jeers louder. In fact, there appeared to be little excitement for the royal visit in general (especially compared to the huge cheers I witnessed when traveling with the couple to New York in 2014). When asked what it was like having the royals courtside, Celtics coach Joe Mazzulla retorted, "Jesus, Mary, and Joseph?" before joking he was familiar with only *one* royal family and didn't "know too much about that [British] one, thank you."

Despite the promotional efforts and high expectations, the

awards ceremony, by most accounts, didn't make the playoffs, let alone the Super Bowl. There was, however, halftime show entertainment courtesy of another royal couple. The first trailer for the Sussexes' intimate Netflix docuseries, *Harry & Meghan*, released that same day (an intentional move by the streamer, I'm told), promising the "full truth" behind the couple's departure. "There's a hierarchy of the family," Harry said in the clip. "There's leaking, but there's also planting of stories." It was all anyone could talk about.

As for the Earthshot ceremony, viewers were less than captivated, to say the least. In the United Kingdom, newspapers claimed the public "switched off" in droves within minutes of the BBC airing it, while the audience watching live in the United States via PBS's streaming platform fell to the hundreds at times. Despite certain celebrity guests flying in to the "green" event at great expense and using thousands of gallons of jet fuel (Beckham flew on a private jet from Qatar), the environmental award winners themselves were strangely forced to stay at home and appear via Zoom. Rather than buying a new outfit, Kate made a statement by renting her off-the-shoulder gown (a genuinely good idea, but one that has never been repeated at a royal event since). The green carpet the couple walked down at the start of the evening was repurposed from the previous year's ceremony, but the Palace refused to comment on the fact it was shipped halfway across the world to make the environmentally conscious statement. As for local media coverage, it focused mostly on the cost of the trip for the city ($170,407) and how it would affect traffic.

For the first time in their lives, William and Kate now have to deal with image challenges of their very own. In the past, the institution and the public viewed them as the safe and relatively fun couple who toed the company line when required but successfully managed a balance between their private lives and their work responsibilities. Kate cut a popular figure in her fairy-tale role, lighting up rooms with her smile and elegant style, while William's awareness and vigor provided a much-needed contrast to older, stodgier family members. They worked within the system and coasted on their star power after their 2011 wedding and for much of their tenures as Duke and Duchess of Cambridge. But perhaps they coasted too long. The higher they rise, the closer they get to the top jobs, the more difficult it has become to separate themselves from all that comes with it. With more pressure on the pair to increase their workloads and deliver more than just agreeable photos for the papers, the Waleses are finally facing more scrutiny from sections of the press and public now unleashed from their respectful relationship with the Queen.

———◆———

It's not like things were going *that* well for the Firm before the Queen's death. After Harry and Meghan shared stories of problematic behaviors and made some damning allegations, and Prince Andrew's slow-motion fall from grace (stemming from his long friendship with sex traffickers Jeffrey Epstein and Ghislaine Maxwell) plunged the family into turmoil, the Palace was in frazzled damage control mode, and Charles—thanks to his plethora of money-related scandals—was doing little right. Even for the usually unscathed William and Kate, their disastrous eight-day Caribbean tour through Commonwealth countries Jamaica, Belize, and the Bahamas in late January 2022 for the Queen's Platinum Jubilee put them firmly in the firing line. What should have been a simple smile-for-the-cameras trip turned into a PR nightmare for Kensington Palace. And instead of solidifying the monarchy's presence in the Commonwealth realms (William's press aides openly billed it as a "charm offensive" when briefing journalists back in London), the tour ended up raising new questions about its future.

The problems began before the couple even arrived, with protestors in Belize voicing opposition to the royals' visit due to a dispute over "contested property" between residents of Indian

Creek village and Flora and Fauna International (FFI), a conservation charity that William supports as patron. "Colonial legacy of THEFT continues with PRINCE & FFI" was just one of the many banners in view. Kensington Palace removed the village from their itinerary, but after flying into Belize (on a costly private jet), William and Kate ran into more demonstrations. One hundred people—including leading human rights advocates, professors, and lawyers—released an open letter with a less than celebratory tone. "During her 70 years on the throne, your grandmother has done nothing to redress and atone for the suffering of our ancestors that took place during her reign and/or during the entire period of British trafficking of Africans, enslavement, indentureship and colonialization," the Advocates Network wrote. "We encourage you to act accordingly and just 'sey yuh sorry!'" continued the letter, which also called for reparations. It was then followed by protestors gathering in Kingston, Jamaica.

But instead of acknowledging the grievances—or taking the opportunity to meet those leading the growing protests—William and the Palace chose to ignore it all. I was one of just a few journalists who initially challenged the silence, pointing out the arrogance of flying into a country that had been colonized by Britain and the royal family yet again refusing to engage in conversation about it. My contention was only met with hostility from Kensington Palace aides on the tour. "I hope you're going to set [Omid] straight," a senior aide said to one of the traveling royal reporters. But there was little reason to—in less than twenty-four hours, the world's media echoed the same points. Photos of William and Kate in Trench Town clutching the hands of young Black boys and girls through a fence that bore an unfortunate likeness to a cage set the tone for the rest of the trip. At best, it was an unfortunate snapshot; at its worst, it was proof that the all-white and undiverse Palace team was just not equipped to carry out such engagements. Their bosses, Prince William and Kate, then the Duchess of Cambridge, were equally oblivious to the poor optics. "If you were there, it wouldn't have been as obvious that this was an entirely inappropriate visual to be sending out into the world. The couple wanted to meet as many people as possible and not ignore anyone," a Kensington Palace staffer explained some months later. Perhaps, I suggested, it would have been avoided entirely if the couple's team included people of color or those with more sensitivity to what would be appropriate and what wouldn't. "*Maybe*," they replied quietly.

The trip was organized months in advance, and all movements were determined by an earlier reconnaissance visit led by members of William's team and the British Foreign Office. Even though the whole scene was drawn up and presented to Palace officials and the couple, no one found the staging of the pair standing in an old Land Rover to re-create imagery of colonial-era trips made by the Queen and Prince Philip a bad idea. The move—which saw the couple in all-white on a raised platform waving at the all-Black crowds below—was greeted with horror and widely mocked. Only after the world reacted to the photos did those around the couple attempt to distance themselves from the decision. "There were questions, including from William, about whether it was appropriate," admitted a Kensington Palace source. "The staging was all at the request of the Jamaican government, not the Palace. They were keen to include the Land Rover, which had been kept for moments like this, but absolutely we should have pushed back." (Curiously, a spokesperson at the office of the prime minister of Jamaica said this version of the story did not ring true.) Still, a Foreign & Commonwealth Office source countered that before the tour, Kensington Palace officials were only "excited" about the itinerary—there had been no complaints or hesitation.

After all this, it hardly came as a surprise that just a day later, Jamaica's prime minister, Andrew Holness, informed William and Kate (who was bizarrely dressed in the orange and white colors of the People's National Party, the party in opposition to the prime minister) that Jamaica was "moving on" and ready to remove the Queen as head of state—to their faces. The pair awkwardly stood and smiled, saying little in response. Later that evening, William was said to be "frustrated and irritated" that he was so unprepared for the moment. So far, everything about the trip looked like a throwback to a bygone era of the British Empire. "Had this have been a personal tour, the itinerary would have been different, but this was a trip for the Platinum Jubilee and we had little say in how it would look," said a Kensington Palace source.

The end of the royal family in the Commonwealth realms (fourteen of which remain at the time of this writing) has been in the cards for some time, as countries move to reclaim their post-colonial independence, but arriving in the Caribbean without anything to say on the matter showed that despite the Palace campaign to position William as a "statesman in the making," he was not as ready for the role as the institution wanted people to believe.

As the tour neared the end, and global criticism stretched from the *Washington Post* to the *Independent* (whose race correspondent Nadine White called it "offensively tone deaf"), Kensington Palace attempted to fix the PR mess. "It needed swift action and, yes, there has been a tendency in the past to sit on these problems or just hope they go away . . . But the feeling at the time was simply 'How can we make this right?'" said a Palace aide. William soon released a statement that claimed "you learn so much" on foreign visits. "I know," he added, "that this tour has brought into even sharper focus questions about the past and the future. In Belize, Jamaica and the Bahamas, that future is for the people to decide upon." His words certainly cooled some of the coverage, but it was too late to save it. Their tour was already marred by ignorant slip-ups, mistakes, and indelible images that those in the Commonwealth still haven't forgotten as many realms continue to power forth with their plans for true independence.

Following his statement, William's private secretary, Jean-

Christophe Gray, sat down with some of the press pack who traveled with the royal couple during the flight back to England. He briefed lines about the lessons learned by William and the "blueprint" for his kingship in the future. Moving forward, he said, the heir and his wife planned to do things "the Cambridge way," which included abandoning the "never complain, never explain" motto favored by his father and grandmother. Aides also shared details about William's own plans to modernize how he works when he succeeds his father as the Prince of Wales. From the outset, it was claimed, he would halve the estimated 137 staff Charles employed to create a more cost-effective and "less formal" team. "It is not a criticism of how it was done in the past," a Kensington Palace aide told *The Sun*, which also reported that William wanted to "rip up" the royal institution's rulebook. "But times are changing."

Though he was not yet next in line, William's remarks came across like a man just years from taking the throne. Charles (who allegedly derived some schadenfreude from his son's recent missteps and public humiliation) was said to be furious over William's effrontery. This kind of declaration was for either the Queen or the direct heir to make, not for the second in line. "It was disrespectful . . . Not only was he dangling the carrot of something his father could not deliver, but he also failed to address how he could actually deliver any of that," an aide huffed. Another source added at the time that William was "out of order" and Charles saw this as a deliberate attempt to upstage him. The Duke of Cambridge screwed up, but he effectively leveraged the moment to tease the public that he could soon be able to bring change. As often envious of his own son's popularity and favored status in the institution as Prince Charles was, this was already a sensitive topic with him, so this breach in royal etiquette, which he has never spoken about directly with William, apparently "left a mark."

And this wasn't the only bruise to Charles's ego. While the trip was still in the planning stages, separate sources said he had advised his son to be "alert and prepared" to the growing calls for reparations. But, as those first days of the visit proved, William ignored his advice, letting bravado obscure his judgment. Distrust and simmering animosity between father and son are nothing new to their working relationship. A source close to William said, "Though [Charles and William] share a number of passions and interests, their style of leadership is quite different." An insider in Charles's camp explained, "Contrary to public belief, [Charles] leads with his head and his heart. [William] is colder in that respect. He just wants to get the job done and has no problem taking prisoners along the way."

Over the years, William has often rejected his father's counsel, keen to avoid the controversial candidness for which Charles has a reputation. The King is a passionate idea man whose instincts, before he took the throne, often drove him into political matters—his climate crusades, his eco-friendly initiatives (such as his quasi-utopian model town project, Poundbury), and his opposition stances on several government policies. He was notorious in the 1990s and 2000s for lobbying with prime ministers and politicians on a plethora of issues. But this outspokenness landed him in hot water. As next in line (or applicable to any senior royal, for that matter), Charles was supposed to always be apolitical, even when he vehemently disagreed with a government position. Those who wear the crown should never express public opinions on political matters or policy, no matter how misguided or noxious they might be—it's why no one ever knew, even posthumously, any of Queen Elizabeth II's political leanings or opinions. For William, who always admired his grandmother's example of political neutrality, "he doesn't want to follow that same path [as his father]," said a source. "There is a lot he wants to do differently."

Since his ascension, however, King Charles has at least proved more reserved than *Prince* Charles. But the question remains, will it last? Considering the ongoing drama in the Firm, it seems unlikely he will be able to rise above it all for long. The new king is still dealing with the fallout from his inability to convene and command his own family. His ineptitude surrounding the Harry and Meghan saga has effectively turned the couple into the disruptors they were feared to become in the first place. "And so much of it could have been prevented," said a mutual family friend. "For so long Harry had made it clear that he and Meghan simply wanted to be heard. That they wanted the opportunity to sit down and talk through the past, from both perspectives, and find a way to move forward. For Harry, it was about seeking accountability and, where appropriate, apologies." Stubborn as ever, it was the one thing Charles refused to give them—even if it meant risking damage to the Crown. A former Clarence House staff member said Charles was encouraged by senior aides and, on at least one occasion, the Queen herself to swallow his pride. "Just tell him what he needs to hear . . . That's what was said," admitted the former employee. Instead, Charles chose to say nothing and turn the other way as the Sussexes shared their story via Netflix in December 2022 and Harry's memoir a month later.

A record-breaking global bestseller on its release day, *Spare* revealed the full unvarnished story of the family's fractures. After watching so many others (including myself) tell their story, Harry quite rightly wanted his turn to put his own voice on the historical record. And that he did, describing decades of simmering resentment between his brother and the true depths of their falling-out. Even more damaging to the Firm were the revelations about how his family, including Camilla, had leaked personal details about his life to save their own skin.

Despite the many opportunities to discuss his grievances ahead of the publication of the book, Charles instead chose to keep his distance for months. Harry and his father swapped a few words over Christmas 2022, but it wasn't until after the January 10, 2023, release of the memoir that they had their first proper conversation.

Encouraged by a close friend, the Duke of Sussex reached out to Charles by phone to try to discuss some of the unresolved issues between them. "It was an awkward conversation, but he knew if he didn't make those first steps, there would never be any progress," said a friend of the prince. "There were no raised voices, no arguments . . . but the King was cold and brief rather than open to any proper dialogue."

With no significant resolution or outcome from the father-son conversation, Charles had once again wasted an opportunity to take the upper hand and let bygones be bygones for the sake of family harmony. "It's complex, but there's increasing frustration from some of the wider circle of family members that Charles won't just fix things for the sake of everyone," said a royal source. And the institution needs it. Just three months after the publication of *Spare*, the royal family's approval rating fell to its lowest level in years: 47 percent, down six points since before the book's launch. In fact, several independent polls have shown that all senior royals (including the Sussexes themselves) have been affected by the fallout.

The responses to claims by Harry and Meghan have followed a pattern of avoidance and dissembling. I've repeatedly witnessed up close how Palace aides do their best to muddy the truths the couple shared with the world (be it with misleading briefings to newspapers or, in some cases, lies to inquiring journalists), but the issues they raised—from institutional cruelty to unconscious racial bias—still loom large over the monarchy. None of this was helped by the fact that the Sussexes remain as much of the royal story today as the day they stepped back from their roles. For most royal correspondents, the couple are still the only surefire way to get prominent headlines and online traffic, whether it was the months of "will they, won't they" stories about the couple attending the coronation or the breathless running commentary about the state of their various business deals in the United States. Instead of completely walking away from the Firm, they've unintentionally taken much of the royal spotlight with them to America. Determined to live their lives apart from the royal apparatus, they have managed to make their own way, enjoying a reasonable amount of support (and experiencing some missteps and failures) all on their own terms.

Both the institution and the family still can't seem to come to grips with that fact. Or move on. I've watched Kensington Palace and Buckingham Palace repeatedly get worried about being upstaged and derailed by the couple, and leak negative information on Harry and Meghan—a tactic that started before they even got married—during moments that could easily be focused on genuine royal news instead. Around significant birthdays, Palace aides are often eager to quietly provide one or two outlets with access to a select group of sources for quotes and background information to use in puff pieces celebrating the life and work of that royal. When Kate turned thirty in 2012, I was pleasantly surprised at how— only eighteen months into my time covering the young royals— Kensington Palace officials happily assisted me with exclusive details as I put together a special issue of *Us Weekly*. For William's fortieth in June 2022, the *Daily Mail*—a paper whose complex relationship with the Firm has shifted over the decades but is currently *very* cozy—provided one of the big birthday reads. With contributions from those closest to William (friends and aides who were given tacit approval), the "intimate portrait" promised the "true story" of a king in the making but, in the end, mostly delivered a list of familial complaints about Harry. Instead of hearing more about William's ambitious environmental plans, we were told in detail by royal sources that he "alternates between grief and anger" over Harry's life decisions and feels his brother "has 100 percent crossed [a] line" by speaking publicly about his struggles within the family. And rather than share how William was preparing for his role as the Prince of Wales and taking over the Duchy of Cornwall, we heard from people close to him about how Harry has been "sucked into an alien world [in California] and there's fuck all [William] can do about it." Still, opined one close friend, "William is absolutely allergic to drama," before proceeding to air his grievances about Meghan. Could have fooled me!

The article had an air of insecurity, and instead of showing a transformational prince at work, it inadvertently cast William as a petulant, grudging brother who is so consumed by Harry's decisions (and his anger over making them all so public) that he, and those around him, are unable to even put it aside to seize his moments. It's one of the many events that highlight William's metamorphosis into what some have described as a hotheaded "company man"—an institutional champion who's privately embraced the draconian tactics of an antiquated and often vicious institution, and an heir increasingly comfortable with the Palace's dirty tricks and the courtiers who dream them up. Famously dubbed the "men in gray," the institution's Palace courtiers and private secretaries form a wall of hard-line establishment types who uphold and preserve the Crown's interests, no matter the cost. With ties to the government and the shadow players who hold the reins of power, these men and sometimes women (though there are still very few in senior roles) are often the operators, strategists, and family confidantes running the show and managing the royal brand behind palace walls. They are both the lifeblood of the institution and, at many times, its most glaring fault line.

Already considered a throwback organization, the institution is increasingly caught up in a self-perpetuating cycle. Most of those who work there are plucked from a tiny minority of British society—white, privileged, and well-heeled. Recent statistics may suggest that Palace staff diversity is on the rise, but when you only look at senior-level aides—and not the junior household staff who check the diversity boxes—the lack of progressive hires has left minimal space for diversity of opinion or thought. They adhere to what they know, and what they know is often outdated and ineffectual. Time and time again, the institutional operatives have demonstrated that they are incapable of managing the scandals that the family routinely throw their way. From the Diana debacle of the 1990s to Andrew's litany of disgraces and the current family feuds, the institutional operators rarely get in front of anything. They often find themselves in a scramble to fix and cover up, and then roll out shoddy PR techniques that stop way short of solving the problem. These over-rehearsed, lacking responses prove there is no learned wisdom—they make the same mistakes over and over again.

Their management of the Harry and Meghan saga is the latest and most glaring example. Back when Meghan married into the House of Windsor, the Sussexes joined William and Kate as representatives of the next generation of royals. Dubbed the "Fab Four" by the press, the two couples commanded global attention and gave the monarchy a new shine and allure. It barely lasted two years. William and Kate have done their best to keep some of that momentum going since Harry and Meghan's departure, and Kate is assuredly the last glamorous figure in the lineup as William assumes a more stolid role, but there is an unmistakable void. And one that is harder to fill than they ever expected.

A short-lived campaign to bring forward Edward and his wife, Sophie, to create a new dynamic foursome failed to inspire an indifferent public and did nothing to make young people interested. As a soft-spoken prince more at home in the West End or on Broadway than on the royal stage, Edward and his wife's quick dispatch to push the family out of the ditch after the Oprah interview did little to help get the show back on the road. Outside of the United Kingdom, few know of the couple, despite both being active working members of the family (they carry out an average of over 130 engagements each per year). In the United Kingdom, few follow them. "Oprah *who*?" the then Countess of Wessex said in a conveniently timed June 2021 interview and at-home-style photo shoot with the *Telegraph*. "You know, if you're not into chat shows, there's no reason why you should know who she is. Certainly not in this country, anyway." The same could have been said about them. Whether it was a "joke" (as a source close to the couple later claimed it was) or not, the comments about the world's most successful Black woman and one of the biggest faces in entertainment made them seem stuffy or tin-eared at best, and casually bigoted at worst. Now the Duke and Duchess of Edinburgh—Charles conferred Prince Philip's title in March 2023 on the condition that their son, Viscount Severn, won't one day inherit it—Edward and Sophie continue with their work, but the media isn't paying much attention. When the couple was dispatched to the Cayman Islands, Turks and Caicos Islands, and the Bahamas in February 2023, the only outlets who covered their movements in the first few days were the *Cayman Compass* and Cayman News Service. As a top Fleet Street editor once told me, "I'd have more luck putting my mum on the front page."

What may seem like a trivial episode by itself, Sophie's Oprah gaffe is yet another page to add to the history of recent royal screwups. Put together, these miscues make up a dossier that could be used to prove that the institution is an anachronistic, intolerant organization steeped in bigotry and privilege. And an expensive one at that. In late June 2023, the Sovereign Grant Report, an annual document that outlines the royal family's expenditures, revealed that spending had risen by 5 percent from the previous year to £107.5 million (the second time in history it had broken the £100 million mark). Despite Charles campaigning on environmental issues, reports for 2022 and 2023 also revealed that he still regularly travels by helicopter between his numerous royal residences at an average cost of £15,000 per flight. William and Kate's ill-fated Caribbean tour cost £226,000 in flights and accommodation alone. For British taxpayers still in the middle of a cost-of-living crisis, the news was once again a tough pill to swallow.

Tone-deaf, racist, and financially reckless are three charges the Firm has had to deal with over the years, but when Queen Elizabeth II was at the helm she managed to keep much of it at bay. She was a unifying force for both the family and the institution—and the monarchy was still valued by the majority, despite its obvious struggles and mistakes. As a sovereign committed to a lifetime of service and duty to something larger than any one person, the late Queen disappeared into the role and allowed the public to project onto her whatever they needed to believe. She symbolized the heavy crown she wore.

By staying true to the old adage "never complain, never explain" and removing herself from her family's unending dramas—sometimes to the point of seeming too distant—Elizabeth II sustained the enigma of the Crown. "She was never born to be Queen but from an early age she got the understanding that when you abandon your duty or put yourself before your duty, bad things happen," said biographer and *Queen of Our Times* author Robert Hardman. "She continued that level of dedication until the very end." Despite the century's upheavals and several anni horribiles, she kept a large part of the public on her side through her voice of perseverance, stability, and defiance against history's pitiless forces. After the September 11, 2001, terrorist attacks, it was the Queen who said, "Grief is the price of love." And during the relentless isolation of the Covid pandemic, she reassuringly reminded us, "We will meet again." She always spoke with a dedication to endurance, no matter the obstacle.

Admittedly this is an almost impossible act to follow and one that may no longer even work in this day, but what we see already is a monarchy struggling to define itself in the reign of King Charles. Two men who had most of their lives to learn from the best are proving they've not learned nearly enough. With clashing approaches and opinions, Charles and William are playing out an increasing struggle between father and son in front of a global audience. The dysfunction goes way beyond parent and child, though. The institution and the family seem unable, even unwilling, to change with the times.

The Ngozi Fulani and Lady Susan Hussey scandal is proof that a monarchy so defined by its own superior, steadfast place in history lacks the agility and improvisational thinking to change with a rapidly transforming world. Seventeen days after the race scandal first made headlines, Fulani was finally invited to Buckingham Palace to sit down with Hussey for a face-to-face conversation. The pair, I'm told, "reluctantly" agreed to allow Palace officials to share a photo of their encounter with the media. According to a Palace statement, the meeting was "filled with warmth and understanding." Lady Susan "offered her sincere apologies for the comments that were made and the distress they caused to Ms. Fulani. Ms. Fulani [has] accepted this apology and appreciates that no malice was intended." For the charity boss, who endured weeks of online trolling, violent threats, and defamatory remarks from radical right-wing media outlets, it all did little to heal her pain. And despite Buckingham Palace's claims that they, too, had apologized for the incident, Fulani revealed on March 8, 2023, that she never received a direct apology from the institution. "If you're sorry, tell *me* you're sorry," she said. "I don't see what is so hard to say, 'I'm sorry.' You sent me the invitation, so you know how to find me. You know how to say sorry." That same day, International Women's Day, the activist announced she would be stepping down from her charity due to safety concerns and continued harassment. Meanwhile, Lady Susan returned to the royal fold, performing official duties on February 21, attending a memorial service of a courtier on behalf of Princess Anne. In June, she was seen laughing and joking with Charles and Camilla in the monarch's box at Royal Ascot—firmly back in the royals' inner circle.

Courtiers, ladies-in-waiting, meaningless PR stunts—they all point to the same problem. Hailing from an incredibly shrinking, old-fashioned world of land barons, polo fields, and posh formality, the royal family is finding it is debilitatingly out-of-touch, even expendable, with an increasing percentage of the public. Those within the institution are aware of the changing public opinion, a growing many of whom are either apathetic to or stand fiercely against the monarchy. The fear is how bad things will get when Queen Elizabeth II is all but a distant memory.

"It's a worry that is discussed on a regular basis," a senior aide who served the late monarch for more than a decade told me after I explained the premise of this book during a private meeting. "How we make that work . . . I'm not sure I have an answer for that yet."

# 3

## "Oh God, I Hate This"
### King Charles's Premiere

———·———

*My days, which are at best but dull and hoary*
*Mere glimmering and decays.*
—Henry Vaughan, "Friends Departed"

*I always admired virtue, but I could never imitate it.*
—King Charles II

Official duties were pressing. On September 13, 2022, just five days after Queen Elizabeth II's death, the new King Charles traveled to Belfast's magnificently Gothic St. Anne's Cathedral for a remembrance service for his mother and to receive a motion of condolence from the Northern Ireland Assembly in nearby Hillsborough Castle. Following a moving memorial that included readings, hymns, a touching Gaelic blessing, and echoing blasts from St. Anne's massive pipe organ, Charles made his way through the gentle slopes and scenic countryside of County Down to the village of Hillsborough. A Georgian mansion built in the eighteenth century, Hillsborough Castle sits at the center of a hundred acres of parkland, where its large walled garden expands out to the edge of a wood and trails meander to a picturesque lake. It is the King's kind of place—a swath of cultivated refinement bordered by unspoiled nature. Inside there is fine art and gilded staterooms, outside an oxygenating forest, wildflowers, and bees.

But even in such a pleasant setting, with an audience present solely to commemorate the late Queen and honor their new sovereign, Charles couldn't contain his frustration and legendary irascibility. While signing the castle's visitor book, he suddenly lost his cool, throwing what can only be called a petulant temper tantrum. His target: a leaky fountain pen.

Caught on video, it was an amusing but revealing scene. Sitting at an antique wooden desk dressed up with a vase of lilies and a gold, royal accoutrement, Charles, already cranky from writing in the wrong date, now faced the calamity of a malfunctioning pen. Noticing the leaking ink, he blurted out, "Oh God, I hate this pen!" After he stood up and brusquely handed it to his Queen, who was equally irked ("Oh look, it's going everywhere!"), the new King grumpily wiped his fingers. He was almost to the point of stamping his feet when he said through gritted teeth, "I can't bear this bloody thing . . . every stinking time!" Shoving his inky handkerchief into his pocket, Charles left the room in a grumble while Camilla calmly sat down and signed the book. She did what most of us would have done in this situation—a simple solution, really: she used another pen.

Now, it's hard to blame him for his crankiness—tradition and duty required a grieving seventy-four-year-old man to tour the United Kingdom and work through an extensive list of "sadmin" just days after his mother's final hours and the traditional obsequies. And who among us hasn't cursed something for not working exactly how we want it to, reverting to peevish, childlike behavior, regardless of our age? The difference, however, is that this particular son who couldn't calmly handle a leaky pen also happens to be King Charles III, the new monarch of Great Britain, the next representative of a bloodline dynasty, and, for many, a symbol of British stability and fortitude. He is the head of state and the Commonwealth, commander-in-chief of the British Armed Forces, and the presiding supreme governor of the Church of England. Some composure is required and expected, especially so when your predecessor was celebrated as the living embodiment of grace under pressure.

A faulty pen is hardly a tragedy. With the world's eyes on him and question marks about his moral character and fitness to serve littering his first days on the throne, it's fair to say the new monarch should have known better. This little "episode" immediately went viral, and the next day nicknames like "Grumpy King" emerged, and news coverage naturally zeroed in on it. "I think in that moment everyone rushed to compare him to his calm mother," said a former Charles aide, "but they forgot that he's also Prince Philip's son, too . . . And that moment was *very* Prince Philip." Added a close source, "The King can be great fun to be around, but he's also a terrible grouch at times. I don't think he knows how to hide it."

This crotchety flare-up might not have piqued and amused the media and public to such an extent had it not been for another sour display of impatience just a few days prior. A mere forty-eight hours after the Queen's death, while signing the historic proclamation of his new position as King in Henry VIII's St. James's Palace, Charles furiously gestured to his private secretary Clive Alderton to remove a tray of pens (*bloody stationery again!*) and inkpot (an old gift from his sons), baring his teeth in a grimace as he nearly pushed the lot off the desk. And, naturally, with little concern for optics, he did this with the world watching and waiting to see the new King in action. Online clips and headlines quickly followed. Despite the occasion's solemnity, there was the new monarch publicly making a fuss over a triviality, bungling his special moment by flashing his temper during the official proceedings for his *own* ascension while signing his very first document as King.

Hadn't the man had decades of training for this exact situation? Are the cosseted prince-cum-king's worst instincts undeterred even by the gravity of history? Is he actually up for the job? These are worthwhile questions, and because of his testy display, they floated to the surface for many even during the deluge of royal pomp that was Charles's first official act as King. The customary royal grandstanding designed to captivate and distort couldn't efface the lasting image of a noticeably prickly Charles. The visual takeaway from his proclamation was an irritable new king passively berating an aide for overcrowding his desk. So, by the time the leaky pen set him off a couple of days later, cantankerous King Charles and his quick temper were ripe for criticism, cued up for memes and punch lines. The Queen hadn't been gone even a week, and already the fragile mystique was cracking.

This was the inauguration of a new sovereign who spent decades waiting for the top job, but it immediately appeared as if Charles was ill-prepared for—and uncomfortable in—his new role as King and that the Palace failed to properly onboard their new CEO. It was a deflating, inauspicious start—insignificant on the surface and at the time, but consequential for the Firm's long-term branding and optics campaign for the monarchy's next iteration. And it was telling. It demonstrated that Charles and the institution still hadn't grasped the power of social media and the internet, a fact that, frankly, seems blindly incompetent at best. Think of it this way: Imagine if Apple had decades to roll out a revolutionary new successor to the iPhone, one they'd spent a great deal of time and money hyping up as an emblem of the next generation of communication, and then clumsily unveiled, with great fanfare, a throwback, temperamental flip phone riddled with software bugs. And doing so while *somehow* unaware that they were under a microscope and at the mercy of trends, unceasing opinion, and the new world order's outrage machine.

Royalist press brushed off the pen blunders as nothing but

harmless gaffes, à la those of President Joe Biden, with one journalist at *The Times* calling them just "a bit of grouchiness," but it was more than that. "Those two moments made me realize we might have our work cut out for us," a Buckingham Palace staffer told me. "People were willing to overlook it because he was a son in mourning, but afterward there were conversations about how those situations can be best avoided in the future." Added another source, "It irritates him when he hears from those on his staff making comments like 'Well, the Queen wouldn't have done it that way' or 'The Queen would have done it like this . . .'" It didn't help that so early in his reign sources close to the King claimed he was already a little frustrated by the burden of daily red box paper shuffling and rubber-stamping—the executive work that Queen Elizabeth II relished and considered an anchoring component of her position. Right out of the gate, Charles was a little overwhelmed by it all, easily irked, and perhaps even a bit wistful for his former job as heir apparent and the freedom it provided. Although he had official duties as Prince of Wales, he was less restricted to express frustration or passion, and in some cases, he was free to crusade for issues like sustainability in the private sector and alternate medicines. As the new role transforms him, the job requiring quiet forbearance instead of vigorous debate (and resistance, in the case of the 2003 invasion of Iraq), the opinionated, activist prince must retreat behind the stately remove of the king's throne. Adopt, adapt, and *abide*, just like his mother did.

This is the expectation of those in the establishment and the institution. But Charles's shaky start proves that it is much easier to mold and coach a newly minted, young Queen than to administer and transfigure the longest-serving intern in the monarchy's history. Just a month after the media had their fun with "Pengate" (eye roll), King Charles's premiere hit another snag in late October, one that presaged a difficult autumn ahead. Before resigning, Prime Minister Liz Truss formally requested that Charles refrain from attending COP27, an annual international climate meeting that the United Nations has organized since 1994 and one he had enthusiastically attended several times in the past. Two years earlier he had delivered the summit's opening address in Paris. The 2022 conference was held in the Egyptian coastal city of Sharm el-Sheikh during the first two weeks of November. Despite his lifelong campaign for a greener earth and his position as an outspoken, stalwart advocate for climate awareness—a cause and a passion that is now almost synonymous with Charles—the new King wasn't allowed to go anywhere near it. And the new prime minister who followed, Rishi Sunak, quickly reminded Charles not to pack any bags for Egypt. He "left [Truss's] request in place," a No. 10 Downing Street spokesperson declared, adding that the climate summit was "not the right occasion" for the King to attend. Buckingham Palace aides told reporters at the time that he "unanimously agreed" with this request, but those close to Charles said that, behind closed doors, the King was frustrated. Because of his reluctance to completely steer clear of the conference, there was a tussle between Charles and the government, resulting in a compromise: government officials gave him the green light to host a November 4 pre-conference reception for many of the attendees at Buckingham Palace. The eco warrior was benched for the big game; the last-minute palace soiree was a chance for the King to hit the field for the warm-up—a way to signal his support from a safe and regal distance.

This flag up the pole from the gated palace was a far cry from Charles's usual (and expected) ardent participation at these gatherings. Standing down on issues near to his heart runs against the grain of his personality and counters his hard-earned legacy as a prince who freely wielded his (leak-free) pen and spoke his mind. As his long-standing biographer, Catherine Mayer, says, "One of the ironies with Charles is, when he was young, he felt that the Palace was blocking him from doing what he wanted to do at every turn, and that everything that he's done, he feels he achieved in spite of the Palace, not because of it." But now, finally in the king's throne, he must assume the Palace position, embrace the established, government-approved point of view, don the requisite mask. The unbending royal system ever at work.

It's only fair to point out that this was also just a bit of bad luck for the new King, a chance turn of events that served as an early reality check. Mayer put it this way: "The very first thing that happens to [Charles as King] is that the whole ordeal around his attendance at COP27 becomes a political hot potato." Possibly stretching the metaphor too thin, it was a hot potato that gave him a proper burn. It was at this point, a source added to me, that Charles begrudgingly accepted that "he can no longer campaign, only highlight." Added another, "The glass-half-full take on that is he still has, and wants to utilize, the power to convene those who *can* campaign."

Later in November, just weeks after the COP reception at the palace, another pointed tête-à-tête with Prime Minister Sunak tested this disgruntled acceptance. During closed-door conversations, Sunak and his team pressured the Palace to rethink Charles's vision for a toned-down, cost-saving coronation, sternly advising them to go big and put on the full show. In keeping with Charles's overhyped conception of a slimmed-down monarchy—a drum that Charles thundered on for years in preparation for his reign—and "keenly aware" of Britain's distressing economic woes, the initial messaging out of the Palace in September 2022 was that Charles wanted a smaller, less grandiose coronation. Like his mother, who was also crowned during a time of great austerity and economic difficulties in 1953 (she even saved up her ration coupons to buy enough material for her wedding dress), Charles supposedly wanted to pay attention to the concerns of the nation. His wish, added the *Telegraph*, was a service that represented "good value." Sources explained that while he certainly wanted the nation to experience the grandeur and tradition of it all, he wanted a celebration that was within reason and in proportion to the intractable realities that plagued the country. "The King and Queen Consort and their advisers are keenly following the debate to ensure they are striking the right balance between this moment of celebration and something that can be done against a very challenging economic backdrop," added a source to the *Daily Mail*.

The country had emerged from the Covid crisis in a bit of a state. After public opinion and "the herd" in the Tory party pushed out Prime Minister Boris Johnson and his successor, Truss, barely had time to unpack her things at Downing Street before the same muttering flock forced her resignation, the government was floundering and in disarray. Twin crises strafed the economy: the Russian war on Ukraine, pandemic aftereffects, and a global supply chain crisis led to a full-on cost-of-living emergency, while a backlog of millions of unbuilt homes, among other issues, precipitated what some argued was a long-gestating housing problem. Workers in various sectors went on strike, including teachers and National Health Service (NHS) employees. And the rippling effects of Brexit continued to rankle a large section of the population. Britain had shunted off the tracks, which further diminished the nation's standing in the world, and internal unrest fueled the country's instability.

Initially, Charles and officials on the Coronation Committee, comprised of privy counsellors, astutely recognized that a scaled-back coronation during these dire times would signal to the public that the monarchical institution wasn't completely out of touch and that the new King was also deeply concerned for the state of the nation. And let's be frank, the King and his team also recognized that a cut-rate coronation was a timely branding and messaging opportunity for the Firm—the new sovereign will do things *his* way; this is the dawn of a new regal era. It was a chance to demonstrate that he would be a more modern, compassionate monarch whose words about slimming down weren't just hot air. Leveraging crisis, in whatever way possible, and maximizing royal benchmarks is all in a day's work for the Palace.

Prime Minister Sunak and the government approached the coronation from the opposite position. While Charles wanted to downsize, Sunak and Whitehall (the government) envisioned a full-fat celebratory weekend—the full monty of carriages, a big concert, and national celebration. The Firm saw the coronation as a chance to exude importance through prudence and sensitivity, but the government wanted to distract and redirect by way of extravagance and ballyhoo. It was a two-for-one deal: a good, old-fashioned royal performance would divert public attention from the crises at home—the pre-coronation media hype would dominate the news cycle for months—and stimulate an image-repair process for Britain on the global stage. A source said it was the Queen's funeral that reminded Sunak and other ministers that a "proper" royal occasion draws an international audience like no other and puts a momentary gloss on reality. The government stance was to harness this moment—the country could use a bit of "Brand Britain" and the public some entertaining diversion. With the Wales children many years away from marriage and jubilees starting only at the twenty-five-year mark, they were also shrewdly aware that Charles's coronation would be the last true royal spectacular for years. This, of course, the Palace agreed with.

Downing Street prevailed, and Charles ceded his vision for a leaner affair. In a later meeting, Sunak's cabinet publicly confirmed that the country would proceed with a full-scale coronation. A cabinet spokesperson said, "Obviously, there will be a great deal of attention on the United Kingdom at that time. It will be a moment for us to show the best of Britain in many different aspects." Immediately following that statement, Palace sources close to Charles backtracked on their earlier words and started to claim that the King rejected the idea of a cut-price coronation weekend. A spokesperson later told reporters in a briefing over Microsoft Teams that the coronation would be a "once in a lifetime" spectacle of glorious pomp and pageantry.

It was a humbling autumn for the new King as he discovered that, in some respects, his promotion occasionally felt like a demotion. He may wear the crown, but the system quickly disabused him of the notion that he could always have his way—the King could no longer act like a prince. The fall season was then capped off by an exceedingly cold and trying end to 2022. Charles's long December was a direct result of the *Harry & Meghan* documentary series, a media juggernaut that commandeered international attention and dominated the news cycle for weeks. Netflix dropped a teaser for the first three episodes on December 1, and, sure enough, hyperbole and screeching immediately followed. The *Daily Mail* reported that "allies" of William and Kate referred to the trailer as a "declaration of war." *The Times* claimed royal sources believed the Duke and Duchess of Sussex "deliberately torpedoed" the Waleses' U.S. visit during that time, while the front page of the *Daily Express* dramatically asked, "Harry, Do You Really Hate Your Family So Much?" Charles was aware that some in other royal quarters were briefing their thoughts and feelings on the series, but within his own court, he requested a wall of silence. "The King was genuinely sad about the entire situation," a family source said three months later. "He was angry but didn't want people to speak ill of his son in front of him, either. It was a brief moment where he paused and realized how bad things had become."

The King's sympathy soon disappeared, however, when it became clear the Harry and Meghan hubbub would overshadow his work, including his participation in a worthwhile cause that received little coverage. Charles personally donated "substantial" funds to the Felix Project, a charity that redirects surplus food from farms, manufacturers, and supermarkets to food banks. A large chunk of their £1 million starting funding came from the monarch, a noble deed, but the Sussexes and Netflix were all the press could talk about.

While the papers and the circus of royal commentators were

still condemning and salivating over the teaser clip, Netflix went ahead with a full-length trailer on December 5 before dropping the first trio of episodes three days later. Once again, the attention was diverted away from Charles, who was traveling to northeast Wales for an engagement his team thought would land him every front page. Set in the beautiful Welsh countryside, Wrexham had recently grabbed the world's attention after actors Ryan Reynolds and Rob McElhenney acquired the local football team, Wrexham AFC—the oldest football club in Wales and the third-oldest professional football club in the world. The motivation for buying the team didn't exactly come from an undying love of the game. After purchasing the Red Dragons for $2.5 million, the two friends created a docuseries about the team, the town, and their first foray into club ownership. *Welcome to Wrexham* was a huge success, and as a result, the largely unknown town of Wrexham and its fifth-tier football team entered the zeitgeist.

Capitalizing on this media focus, Charles and Camilla ventured to Wrexham to celebrate the village achieving city status in a Queen's Platinum Jubilee competition the previous year and to tour the Wrexham AFC stadium with McElhenney and Reynolds. For royal events, this one bordered on the flashy side as photographers captured the King and Queen on the field with the two Hollywood stars. Normally, this would have been fodder for prime, positive royal coverage and grist for the mill of royal watchers, but the spotlight was still on the Duke and Duchess of Sussex. The couple's revelations in the first episodes enthralled millions (Netflix's highest-viewed documentary ever), agitated royalists, lit up social media, and created a frenzy among the papers. The *Mirror*'s front page went with "Stop This Royal Circus," demonstrating the paper has little or no self-awareness, considering it is often a ringmaster for said circus. The *Daily Mail* took aim at the docuseries' description of the Commonwealth as "Empire 2.0" with the pearl-clutching headline "Palace Anger at 'Assault on Queen's Legacy.'" At the Palace, heads were in hands and migraines were brewing. "[The show] took the wind out of everyone's sails," said one aide. "Here you have the King doing his damnedest best and no one is watching." Added a second source, "[He] went from not wanting anyone to talk about his son to openly criticizing 'that fool.'"

It was a rousing mini soap opera within the world's largest soap opera—a level of melodrama only the British royal family can produce. And it eclipsed King Charles at every turn, besting his attempts to highlight his own narrative and promote the monarchy's new Carolean era. And his long December wasn't over yet. In the middle of the month, Netflix released the final half of the series, in which Harry claimed he and his wife were victims of "institutional gaslighting" and revealed new details about how his family leaked stories about the couple to score points with the press and other powerful players. These were true bombshells, but, just as they had done throughout the entire Netflix ordeal, both Buckingham Palace and those working with William and Kate remained silent, offering no official statements, though complaining plenty to preferred journalists in the royal rota in the form of anonymous source quotes. Some of Meghan's claims, including the fact that aides didn't prep her for her job in the Firm, were "a total lie," a royal source told the *Sunday Times*. A "friend" of William's told the paper, "I reminded him to keep his rifle pointed at the target and not to be distracted, even though it's all fucking tedious in every sense of the word."

This silence might have benefited the institution, but it didn't do the King any favors. Up until his first Christmas broadcast from Sandringham, Charles carried on with a few royal events, but he did so in relative obscurity and under a cloud of uncontested accusations and ceaseless media hype about his now excommunicated son. At the December 15 taping of Kate, the Princess of Wales's *Together at Christmas* carol service at Westminster Abbey, Charles and Camilla joined other members of the royal family to present a united front against the damning allegations flying over on Netflix. (Curiously, most of the female family members wore matching burgundy coats, a move the *Daily Mail* called a "dig" at Meghan's documentary claim that she was unable to wear bright colors during her years as a working royal, though a Palace source told me this is "ridiculous.") And the following day should have been a big one for the new King. After attending an anti–hate crime meeting at the Jewish Community Security Trust in northwest London, Charles moved on to a nearby Jewish community center that serves all faiths. He brought along a trunk of rice and canned tuna to donate over the upcoming Chanukah holidays, and, after touring JW3's facility, he joyfully danced with Holocaust survivors, including Anne Frank's ninety-three-year-old stepsister, Eva Schloss. His day out was evidence that he was taking some progressive steps as a monarch and that he hadn't entirely surrendered his passions to the demands of the throne. But in the fallout from Harry and Meghan's latest round of disclosures, few even noticed.

The King's prerecorded Christmas address from the quire at Windsor Castle's St. George's Chapel was perfunctory but heartfelt as he paid tribute to his mother, who was laid to rest in the same location. A few days of holiday rest at Sandringham—where the Wales family, the Wessexes, and Prince Andrew were among guests—were required because the new year was looking ominous. The early January 2023 publication of *Spare* was on the horizon and with it a collateral storm of revelations. Despite the absence of Prince Harry and his family at the royal family festivities, Charles chose not to reach out to his younger son. Instead, it was Harry who made the effort to wish his father well over the holidays. "Charles was cautious," a source close to the monarch shared. "He didn't want to engage in anything other than light chat . . . The message among the family about Harry was he is not to be trusted until they see what is in the book and what he says while promoting it. They all took that seriously." While some were sad to hear about Harry's experiences (Prince Edward was one of the few who felt

Charles should "properly speak" with his son and try to move on), the majority were cross. While gathered at Sandringham, Princess Anne suggested to Charles that it was time he took away the Sussexes' Frogmore Cottage home and Prince Andrew's Royal Lodge residence. "He knew she was right," said a source, who noted that Anne's comments would have been related to the fact that Harry and Meghan, and Andrew for that matter, were no longer working royals, rather than a suggestion for punishments.

Ahead of *Spare*'s release, the Firm endured three days of a rapid-fire prepublication promotional blitz for the memoir. In an interview with journalist and friend Tom Bradby on January 8, the Duke of Sussex detailed his estrangement with his family and told the ITV news anchor he was not sure whether he would attend his father's coronation. The next day's interview with Anderson Cooper for CBS's *60 Minutes* was notable for two things: Harry's candidness and Cooper's on-air disclosure that the Palace demanded to see the full footage of the interview before making any comments (aides also asked the same thing of ABC's *Good Morning America* later that week). Cooper reiterated for the millions watching that this was "something we never do."

The Palace stayed silent. But after its January 10 global release, King Charles made his feelings on the tell-all clear in private, despite not having read a page of the book (just as he refused to watch the Netflix series). The Sussexes' team received correspondence from Buckingham Palace's Keeper of the Privy Purse Sir Michael John Stevens, who informed Harry and Meghan that, as they were no longer working royals or based in Britain, they needed to give up the keys to their royal rental, Frogmore Cottage. Although there were reports to the contrary some months later, I spoke to a source close to the couple on the day they were informed, and there was a clear feeling of shock and disappointment as the news sunk in. Renovations at Frogmore had not only been repaid in full by the couple (£2.4 million in total), but they had also covered a lease on the property well into the future. Given that the couple was now banned from access to royal protection (even if they paid for it themselves), staying on the Windsor estate was the Sussex family's only truly safe option when visiting the United Kingdom, as the grounds are surrounded by armed guards. Several days later Harry spoke about the matter with Charles over the phone. "Don't you want to see your grandchildren?" the duke asked his father. His silence, followed by a half-hearted declaration that they would always have "somewhere" to stay didn't, according to a source, give Harry much hope. Sir Michael followed up with a note that Harry would have until early June to clear out the entire residence and return the keys.

The final blow came when the couple became aware that King Charles had offered the property to his disgraced brother Prince Andrew, who had spent the past twenty years living at the nearby thirty-room Royal Lodge. In 2003, the disgraced prince had signed a seventy-five-year lease on the property, renting it from the Crown Estate for the bargain price of just £250 a week on the condition he covered the costs of the many renovations it needed (believed to have reached a total of £7.5 million over two decades). Now that Andrew was no longer a working royal and didn't have any active financial endeavors bringing in money, there was talk that he could no longer afford to continue running the home, though he defiantly told anyone who asked that he had it under control. For Charles, the issue of Frogmore Cottage wasn't just about punishing his son, though sources say that "undoubtably" played a significant role; it was also part of the effort to streamline the portfolio of properties being used by members of the family. Slimming down the monarchy also means slimming down the privileges and perks enjoyed by family members. Officially, offering the smaller five-bedroom Frogmore Cottage to his younger brother was Charles's way of reducing the number of "nonworking" royals paying discounted rent for grand properties, but the timing and the optics suggested this was also a punitive measure aimed at Harry and his family—one that smelled of bitterness and recrimination.

Nailing an eviction notice on the front door of Frogmore was unsurprisingly hailed as a "strong decision" by the usual chorus of reactionary royalists and royal reporters. But others in the media found Charles's Frogmore move petty, including the respected former BBC royal correspondent Peter Hunt. "Instead of building bridges, the head of state is torching them," he said. "The banishment of his son is cruel, unnecessary, and diminishes Charles." Staying mum about Harry's accusations and remaining publicly unconcerned for his son's well-being while ending his family's lease on a safe U.K. residence was not a decisive action by a resolute King; it was a cheap shot from a wounded father bound by an institutional system that is often intolerant of human emotion.

One all-too-human family complication that the King apparently has a blind spot for is the shameful burden of Prince Andrew and his fall from favor. Stonewalling and expelling his son came easy enough, but it's a different story with his brother. Offering Frogmore is another sign that the King won't completely banish Andrew from the picture. Taking advantage of Charles's brotherly bias, Andrew continued to turn down the keys to Frogmore for months until Sir Michael stopped asking him about it. And despite knowing the uproar that would come from the public, he slithered into an ermine robe for the March 2023 service for the Royal Victorian Order, an event that occurs every four years in the medieval St. George's Chapel at Windsor Castle, and continued the ceremonial role the Queen failed to take away from her son. Charles is aware that his brother wants to slowly step back into some sort of public role, even if it isn't as a working royal (a ship that has long sailed). "He held his hands up and said, 'I can't stop him,' but it felt as if he didn't want to stop him," said a family source of Andrew's outing.

Many questioned the King's judgment, particularly coming on the heels of the Frogmore dustup. Pundits called out Andrew for his brazen audacity and impertinence, including the outspoken former Liberal Democrat politician Norman Baker, who said the Palace allowed Andrew to "play dressing up as a royal for the day when really he should be serving a long period of silence." Considering the depths of Andrew's disgrace, whether or not the King quietly approved or even made the final decision about the duke's appearance at the service is irrelevant. Andrew's mere presence in ceremonial royal garb was dramatically out of step with public opinion. More than that, it exposed Charles as weak-kneed when it comes to his brother (and his family in general).

His judgment came into question once again after he met with Ursula von der Leyen, the president of the European Commission, while she was in London to revise a post-Brexit trade deal between Northern Ireland and the Republic of Ireland. Given the controversial nature of the deal and the mixed feelings toward the monarchy in Northern Ireland (where praise for the royal family vies with disdain), Charles's decision to meet with the EU president on the very day Britain's prime minister signed the new agreement—curiously branded in a press conference as "The Windsor Framework"—was met with skepticism across the political spectrum. To many, this was a monarch sticking his nose into political matters. After outrage intensified, neither government representatives nor Palace officials clarified who decided the meeting between the two was a good idea in the first place. Buckingham Palace told me the King was acting on "government's advice," but Downing Street claimed it was the King's decision.

Circumvented by Netflix, overshadowed by his younger son, humbled by the government and the institutional system, and dragged down by his own poor judgment and that of his wayward brother, Charles often stumbled through his first hundred days as King, encountering one obstacle after another. It seemed he couldn't catch a break. But the monarch did just that at the tail end of an unusually rainy March. The King and Buckingham Palace officials were desperate to carry out the first international trip for the monarch and his consort—an ambassadorial mission to Europe. This was a chance for Charles to promote his new reign and underscore the monarchy's strength, despite the Sussex dramas and the void left behind after Queen Elizabeth II's death. Soft power was on the agenda, too. Part of his mission, on behalf of the U.K. Foreign Office, was also to remind leaders that Britain was still standing tall after Brexit, Covid, and economic and governmental crises stress-tested the country's foundations. Though the tour was originally scheduled to stop in both France and Germany, anti-government protests in Paris and other French cities forced the Palace to postpone that leg until late September. No one's fault, but not the luckiest of starts. So with only Germany left, the pressure was on to knock it out of the park: no gaffes or slipups. The terrible timing and bad-luck traps that Charles knows so well were also set again. The Duke of Sussex was at the High Court in London alongside Sir Elton John and other claimants for an unlawful news-gathering lawsuit against the publisher of the *Daily Mail*, and, because it's Harry, this usually ignored type of hearing chummed the waters for yet another media frenzy.

Taking it in stride and perhaps pulling a page from his mother's handbook, King Charles left for Germany on March 28 showing all signs that he was undeterred, fully prepared, and buoyed by the Queen Consort's presence by his side. After arriving in Berlin with an impressive Luftwaffe escort, Charles and Camilla made their way to the historic Brandenburg Gate, where the German president Frank-Walter Steinmeier welcomed the couple with military honors—an unprecedented move that signaled Germany's strong support for the new King and the monarchy. The following day included another first. Charles shined as the first British monarch to address the Bundestag, the German parliament, with a speech that eloquently enforced the vital importance of both sides maintaining a British-German partnership. Charles further endeared himself to Bundestag lawmakers by speaking German during a portion of his address, one that went beyond the usual royal platitudes and strongly veered into politics with regards to Russia's invasion of Ukraine (and Germany's "courageous" move to give military support). It was a powerful address, and one that Social Democratic Party politician Jens Zimmermann claimed saw Charles send a "clear message" by speaking in the country's native tongue while in the parliamentary chambers. "It was very well-received," he added. "Much more political than you might have expected. It was very connecting."

On the last day of the royal visit, Charles and Camilla visited Hamburg, a city that was leveled by Allied bombs, particularly those dropped by the Royal Air Force, during World War II's "area bombing" campaign. Joined by President Steinmeier once again, Charles laid a wreath of remembrance for all the victims of that war at the magnificently steepled St. Nikolai Church. Before the trip, the *Guardian*—a newspaper unafraid to criticize the royal family when necessary—ran an opinion piece about his symbolic visit to Hamburg with a headline that read, "For Hamburg, Devastated by Allied Bombing, King Charles's Visit Is So Much More Than a Photo-op." He proved that it was, not only in Hamburg but across his entire visit. After a rough start as King at home, Charles proved up for the job abroad. As head of state and a soft-power emissary, he was commanding and unifying—even daringly unconventional—when the situation demanded it.

Returning home to England a little lighter after a trip that was hailed as successful by both German and British media, Charles was bolstered and enlivened by his first mission abroad and relieved that his luck had turned. Foreign trips and mingling with leaders and dignitaries have always been two of Charles's strengths, though it's not known how often he will get to lean on those skills. Sources say that the King and Queen have received advice from doctors that big overseas working trips should be kept "on the shorter side" as a precaution, meaning those grueling countrywide tours of Canada, Australia, and New Zealand lasting ten to fourteen days might just be a thing of the past. For their winter 2023 visit to Kenya, sources say the schedule of engagements was devised with their ages and health in mind. As is the norm during any trip overseas, the monarch is, without fail, accompanied by a doctor.

Although Harry was still in the United Kingdom when he returned from Germany, Charles ignored a request to meet, instead instructing an aide to fob him off with a "too busy" excuse. As for the positive energy generated from his trip, it didn't last long. Charles found himself in the news for the wrong reasons once again just six days later, during a trip to York for his first Maundy Thursday service as King. Commemorating the Last Supper on the day before Good Friday, the ceremony was adopted by the British monarchy back in 1210, when King John became the first sovereign to distribute alms (money, food, clothing) to mark the occasion. After King Charles II handed out new-minted silver coins in 1662, the alms were thereafter called "Maundy Money." Duly obligated, the new King Charles carried on this ancient tradition by handing out two purses—one red, the other white—to 148 senior citizens (seventy-four men and seventy-four women) to recognize their service to the church or community. The white purse contained specially forged silver coins commensurate in value to Charles's age at the time (seventy-four) while the red one held two commemorative coins, signifying the monarch's beneficence.

All in all, it is a rather harmless, if slightly condescending tradition, one that Queen Elizabeth II made her own as only she could do. It was always quite touching to see her perform the service, either as a young, wide-eyed English rose new to the job or a venerated, battle-tested Queen who embodied royal tradition. Charles performed his part of the service with requisite smiles and adequate respect, knowing that his mother especially cherished this event. But while greeting locals after unveiling a statue of his late mother, Charles experienced something that the late Queen never did at a Maundy Thursday service—eggs hurled in protest. Although smaller in number to those gathered in support, a group of anti-monarchy protestors at the engagement were active and loud, with one shouting at Charles, "This country was built on the blood of slaves!" Among them was twenty-three-year-old student Patrick Thelwell, who lobbed five raw eggs that narrowly missed the King and Camilla. As yolks spattered across the ground, some well-wishers tried to drown out the protestors' boos with chants of "God save the King!" The young man was quickly arrested and later sentenced to a hundred hours of community service. The King might have wowed audiences in Germany, but back at home he faced mixed reception, to put it mildly.

Three days after the egg missiles, Charles led members of the royal family into Windsor's St. George's Chapel for the Easter Sunday service. Practically front and center in the group was Prince Andrew. Glum but arrogant, the Duke of York strode tall next to his sister, Princess Anne, and one step behind King Charles. Prince William and Kate, the Princess of Wales, purposefully kept their distance, but Charles appeared unconcerned, still blithely unaware of the message this sends to the public.

The King seemed surprisingly comfortable dragging the baggage of the past into the monarchy's new era. As the Queen told Harry a few years earlier, "Your father always does what he wants to do." Charles has finally got his chance, and only he can squander it.

# 4

# Remembrance of Things Past

### The Ongoing Campaign to Make the Royals Great Again

———◇———

*Though worlds may change and go awry*
*While there is still one voice to cry!*
*There'll always be an England . . .*
*Surely you're proud, shout it aloud*
*Britons, awake!*

—Ross Parker and Hughie Charles, from the popular
World War II song "There'll Always Be an England"

*An element of propaganda, of sales and marketing, always*
*intervened between the inner and the outer person.*

—Julian Barnes, *England, England*

*June 2, 2022*

As far as royal moments go, it was picture perfect. Standing on either side of the Queen was the next chapter of the House of Windsor. Charles, Camilla, William, Kate, Edward, and Sophie, all gathered on Buckingham Palace's iconic East Wing balcony—their children, including future king Prince George—waving and smiling and putting on a model regal display as planes from the

British Royal Air Force, past and present, roared overhead. Trooping the Colour, the official parade for the Queen's birthday, took place right in the middle of Her Majesty's Platinum Jubilee celebrations, a four-day public holiday marking seventy years on the throne. From their privileged vantage point, eighteen members of the family looked straight down the length of the Mall, the 930-meter promenade that runs from the palace's black and gilded wrought iron gates to bustling Trafalgar Square, and skirts leafy St. James Park and Clarence House along the way. It's one of the most beautiful parts of central London—tree-lined, stately, and the only place in the city unbothered by painted lines on the streets (because who would want to spoil such a sight?).

The Mall looked particularly tranquil and grand on that celebratory June day. A stream of Union Jacks danced in the sixty-nine-degree breeze and a summer-blue sky darted in and out of passing patches of white clouds. A sizable crowd gathered there, too, despite the new, upended reality born from the Covid pandemic's global upheaval. Well-wishers, monarchists, and tourists were out in full force—some masked, most not, but all doing their bit to commemorate the Queen or to get a peek at history in the making.

It was hard not to be a little moved by the crowd's presence as they lined the fenced-off pavement in support. The day itself was positive, the family catching a much-needed break from the skies above. I've covered big-ticket royal occasions like that one many times over, and I'm always amazed at how these moments, be it the birth of a new heir or a royal wedding, can magically whip the unpredictably tempered British weather into producing a sun-soaked day that seems lifted out of time. As the Queen waved to her people and the Red Arrows aerobatic team streaked the sky red, white, and blue in perfect formation, I was reminded that *this* was the kind of showpiece moment the royal family had done so well during her reign. And, after a few stormy years, this sunshine was just what the Windsors needed—a cheerful occasion to repackage and reissue the royal brand.

I was covering the event for ABC News, who partnered with the BBC for the official Platinum Jubilee coverage in the United States, and the two networks had exclusive access to every event. Throughout the four-day celebration, I watched as hundreds of workers and volunteers made sure everything was perfect. "When you're asked to perform for the Queen, you drop everything," Ed Sheeran said, smiling backstage on the day of the June 5 concert before he performed his song "Perfect" as a tribute to the monarch and her late husband, Prince Philip. It was a full-circle moment for the singer, who had been inspired by the Queen's Golden Jubilee concert twenty years earlier (and a showstopping performance of "Layla" by Eric Clapton) to start playing guitar and dream of pop stardom. He added, "There's no way I wouldn't be here for this . . . And to be able to pay tribute to the Duke [of Edinburgh] is just the biggest honor." Having overseen and participated in the planning of the commemorative events, one of the Queen's communications secretaries was equally buzzing when I saw them. "It's been a very proud moment for all of us," they said with a smile.

There's an almost school reunion–like atmosphere at big royal occasions such as this. It's often the case that the last time you saw many of the journalists, producers, and TV crews, who flew in from almost every corner of the world, was years prior at the last wedding, birth, or major royal landmark. Even for more critical royal correspondents like me, it's impossible not to get a little swept up in the spectacle of it all. These are huge moments in history to witness firsthand. And it's big business—with the financial struggles most media companies are now facing, mega budgets for special coverage are more infrequent than they used to be. Though that was hardly noticeable over at *Good Morning America*'s plush pop-up studio outside Buckingham Palace. "I mean, this is what you guys do best!" one of the show's anchors, T. J. Holmes, said to me as I was getting mic'd up for my contributions that day. "No one does pomp, circumstance, and all of *this* like the royals."

Image advertising and reputational management are practices about which the royal establishment knows a thing or two—that much is certainly true. The family organization's most famous face, Queen Elizabeth II, was no slouch when it came to crafting visuals to increase the monarchy's core value to the public, and she assuredly left a messaging framework for Charles to build on. She also recognized that it was paramount to manage the family brand out of view and with minimal fuss, something with which her children and grandchildren haven't had much success. The Queen and Prince Philip also famously eschewed going overboard on "strategy," going so far as to half-heartedly embargo the word from the Palace's working lexicon at one point. The Prince once grumbled to a busied Palace aide that "the only two people who talked more about strategy and planning than [the aide] were Hitler and Stalin." But strategically or not, the Queen, with the help of Philip, who provided a fresh take on ideas, repeatedly demonstrated that she—perhaps instinctively—understood the importance of marketing, and that this was something she could effectively administer from her position above the fray. She would no doubt bristle at the phrase, but the Queen appreciated the colossal significance of the monarchy's "value proposition." To survive, the populace must buy into it.

The perception of the Firm unquestionably ebbed and flowed during the Queen's reign. Their image suffered from fate's normal slings and arrows, but it also experienced many crippling self-inflicted wounds, some easily avoidable (Andrew's idiocy and degeneracy come quickly to mind) and others devastating (Princess Diana). Then again, it often projected a healthy glow, conveying well-timed vim and resolve—the Queen's visit to Aberfan in Wales after the mining tragedy that took the lives of 116 children in 1966, and her invention of the "walkabout" during a tour of Australia in 1970, where she decided it would be better to stroll and meet more people rather than cruise past in a car. There were also the weddings of Charles and Diana, William and Kate, and Harry and

Meghan—each of them a grand affair watched by hundreds of millions that elevated the royal family in front of the world.

And through it all, there was the Queen, doing her best to demonstrate the power of tradition and the value of duty. She protected her image and, by extension, the monarchy's, by consistently rising "over and above" all the squabbles and turmoil, even when problematic members of her family (oh, where do I start?) and some buffoons in the establishment (ahem, Boris Johnson) were doing *their* best to drag it all down. As a symbol, she was always there, though what she projected evolved over time. As a young monarch, she was a fresh face after the horrors of World War II; then, as a middle-aged Queen, she was a stiff upper lip in the Cold War; and, finally, in her later years, she was a regal grandmother and a sagacious, maternal comfort in an increasingly haywire world. But, unlike other royal books, I'm not here to tell you that the Queen was perfect. After all, a human being lived underneath that regal facade, but Her Majesty did a masterful job at selling the idea that she lived a life exceedingly close to it. It's one of the things that made her more popular than the monarchy itself. And some, me included, would even argue that her reign often helped mask Britain's relative decline.

For decades, the Queen and her institutional backers expertly maintained and sold this image of unflappable sincerity in a tiara while, behind the scenes, they quietly and steadily reinvented what the monarchy represented and reflected back to the public. As the sun set on the British Empire and the United Kingdom lowered the Union Jacks in the remaining colonies, Great Britain lost its tokens of power and the monarchy much of its luster. The government's focus increasingly returned to its own harbors and the many crises it faced as a declining superpower, until war tempted the country into a different kind of foreign adventure altogether, with wide-ranging results. Margaret Thatcher's Falklands War provided a patriotic jolt, while Tony Blair's risky neoconservative interventions in Afghanistan and Iraq divided the country.

Brexit further split the British citizenry and more forcefully removed the country from the greater world. Excusing itself from the table of global power, the Great Britain of colonial expansion, World War II greatness, and European solidarity decided it was high time to refocus its energies on "Merry England" and other nation-first interests. The totality of all these changes meant a paradigm shift for the country and its royal establishment. Instead of waving to subjects from the backs of Jeeps in far-flung lands or dining out in black tie with European heads of state, senior members of the royal family found themselves more and more on country lane walkabouts greeting their own citizens.

Recognizing these historic shifts and then recalibrating was an essential task for Her Majesty and the Firm. On this front, there were both advances and retreats, but, over time, the Queen and her advisors transformed the monarchy's image from a regal manifestation of empire and preeminent influence to a domestic expression of continuity, civic obligation, and enigmatic "Britishness." The Queen became a national icon. "This was a role imposed on her [by an ancient constitution] that really only required that she simply existed, but she brought so much more to it, she made it her own," said former press secretary to the monarch Ailsa Anderson.

But mostly, she was committed to her title role as a fixed star for the nation and a token of traditional Britain and its "old ways" values. Over the years, however, as countries in the Commonwealth continue to make moves toward independence and Scotland grows more comfortable with republican ideas of its own, this royal emblem of "Britain" and "Britishness" has gradually become more of a totem of "England" and "Englishness." What it really seems to represent is what we might call a "British-Englishness."

To maintain their symbolic position in the British-English firmament, the royal family exhibited what the late author and political theorist Tom Nairn called a "glamour of backwardness" and embraced a "contrived timelessness." Backward because the family has glorified bygone aristocratic ways and means to great effect and sold it as national emblem, and timeless in the way they increasingly joined their dynastic heritage with sentimental nationalism and communal longing for sepia-toned stability. This produced a portrait of a "great nation-family" meant to enchant the public and the press. And in many ways, it worked. Somehow staying both above it all and comfortably entwined with normal British life, the family settled into new roles as tourist attractions and tabloid stars. Their successes and blunders were ceaselessly reported on, and the family narrative emerged as a through line in the national story. As both national treasures (the Queen) and soap stars (the rest of the family), the royals mirrored the state of the nation: a mass-market culture nostalgic for a golden age and in search of itself in the tumult of new global realities.

Nostalgia is a potent energy, and the practice of harnessing that power to advance agendas and undergird isms is nothing new. Governments and social movements have been doing this for centuries—it's now standard operating procedure. The Eton College– and Oxford University–educated Boris Johnson and his elitist chums exploited yearnings for the quaint, rural Britishisms of yesteryear to justify Brexit. And, of course, there's Trumpism. MAGA crowds feverish with grievance and the fear of being left behind gobbled up Donald Trump's platter of "America First" red meat to such a degree that die-hard Trumpists *still* believe that only this particular man of wealth, privilege, and dubious moral character truly stands for real American values; only he can restore the country to its former greatness. The list of those who have manipulated nostalgia for less than honorable purposes is a long one—it seems there's a strong human impulse to practice this dark art. So, when it comes to capitalizing on nostalgia and the feelings that go with it, the royal institution often uses blueprints that history left by the palace gates. And, of course, they've also drawn up a few of their own.

When Elizabeth II was still in the picture, leveraging nostalgia was never a problem. Here was a woman whose life spanned a majority of the twentieth century and twenty-two years of the twenty-first. She witnessed—and worked through—almost a century's worth of history's seesawing—the glories and horrors of the first modern era and the convulsions and breakthroughs in the early hours of the second millennia. In her first radio address in 1940, then Princess Elizabeth, she comforted children around the Commonwealth during the initial spasms of World War II. She was a solemn and strangely comforting presence for many since then— she bucked up the nation when the chips were down and joined us as we celebrated our collective successes and milestones. There's also the ubiquity of her image. For seventy years her visage and the royal iconography associated with her appeared on currencies, stamps, flags, postboxes, and all genres of art. And let us not forget the inescapable photographs: the Queen in her kaleidoscope of bright outfits to stand out from the huge crowds at engagements, Franklin D. Roosevelt–like moments by the fireplace at Windsor Castle, warm and cheerful at Christmas gatherings with her family, in a hat for a day at the races or a tiara for a state occasion, and white-gloved and elegant on the balcony for Trooping the Colour. For a woman we actually knew so little about, she was everywhere, and for a long time.

These photographs and royal representations helped create a type of folklore imbued with that "British-Englishness" redolent of heritage, convention, and fabled civility—the Great Britain of castles, misty green rolling hills, country parishes, afternoon tea, urbane Londoners, and stoic locals standing by the taps in low-ceilinged pubs. This is quite a magic trick when you step back to objectively take it in. Somehow, all at once, an image of the Queen manages to conjure up an assemblage of national myths, stereotypes, and cultural touchstones. She was fortitude in the trenches, Wellies in the English garden, and courtliness in the palace. Her Majesty, her family, and even their creaky system of birthright and superior lineage are bizarrely as essential to the nation's collective understanding of itself—its cherished past, its current decline, its stabilizing hope—as the chords of a Beatles song, the novels of Jane Austen, Big Ben's reverberating chimes, and Stonehenge's prehistoric circle of rock and mystery.

An iconographic transformation like this doesn't happen overnight, and as the royals have demonstrated, it has tremendous staying power, despite what the outside world violently hurls at the royal gates. Its ancien régime has been long associated with military conquest and colonial expansion, as well as the flag-waving and communal pride, whether warranted or not, that frequently accompany these national moments. Leveraging patriotism is tantalizing, low-hanging fruit and comes almost automatically for the Firm, especially when they need to roll out the pageantry to remind the public of their value. It's now pro forma for Union Jacks to come out en masse when there's a coronation, a royal wedding, a funeral, or a milestone like a jubilee.

It must be said that in the past, this patriotic expression for the royal family was often unpolluted by politically charged energies. Because the institution had largely kept the family business out of politics, the public spirit conveyed around royal occasions was generally a celebration of what the monarchy represented to its supporters regardless of their ideological allegiances—the intangibles that comprise national identity. And they waved flags to commemorate their Queen, a singular woman whose elevated, soft power healed and inspired, but always from a dignified distance. This was a preternatural, crowning achievement for the monarchy, given that politics now pervades almost every aspect of our lives.

But, as the saying goes, there's always a chance of having too much of a good thing. Maximizing on patriotic bursts and nostalgic yearnings became established practice for the Firm from the postwar days until the Queen's death to such an extent that the institution and the family started to rely almost exclusively on these national feelings to repair their image and underscore their raison d'être. Prince Harry found purpose in serving his country in the military, an unquestionably honorable thing to do, but it's worth mentioning that his time in uniform also gave his "bad-boy" tabloid image a much-needed "for the Mother Country" makeover. While Harry served, the Palace heavily leaned on the young prince's time on the battlefield in Afghanistan for a boost of its own. It was inevitable that the public would be curious about Harry's military experience, so, in the interest of stopping prying tabloids from putting Harry or his comrades at risk, Palace publicity gurus carefully released details through their own channels and the Press Association. The Firm considered it a PR win to have one of its own on the front lines. "There was a certain amount of pressure put on Harry by the institution to please the press in that situation," a source said. "It wasn't his choice to carry out interviews, but he was told it was the right thing to do." Thanks to those interviews, the world discovered that Harry personally killed several Taliban fighters, a revelation that made the front pages of every newspaper at the time. This moment of patriotic (even jingoistic) fervor saw the prince declared a national hero—and the royal family a pronounced symbol of wartime national pride. It also demonstrated just how entwined royalism and nationalism actually are.

The Firm has seized almost every opportunity to demonstrate the monarchy's value, and they have had quite a good run of moments in recent years. From the Queen's Golden Jubilee in 2002 until the Queen's death in the fall of 2022, the monarchy had many major events to showcase their wares. For all these banner occasions, they spared no expense and played all the hits: street parties, extended holiday weekends, fireworks displays, splashy television specials, and concerts at the palaces.

While the family maintained a unified front (publicly, at least), and with the Queen still on the throne, this reliance on grandstanding kept the monarchy in the papers and front of mind, even if their patriotic swagger and homages to Merry England started to grow increasingly wearisome and transparent. As the Queen aged out of the spotlight and family infighting took its place, their lucky streak came to a discombobulating end. We are entering a potentially uneventful era like the one that endured after Diana's death until the wedding of the Cambridges fourteen years later. Another long winter is coming for the royal family, and it couldn't be at a worse time.

The reality is, King Charles III and his relatively short reign will never reach the national treasure status that his mother achieved, even with Union Jacks fluttering behind him. Aides on his current team say they are "fully aware" of the difference in popularity he holds. "No one is under any illusion that he has the same pulling power," a royal source confided. For Charles, he understands that his primary role is to secure the sail until the next in line can steer the ship into new winds. The institution, royalists, government officials, and media devotees (aka the establishment) are riding out the Charles and Camilla years with the hopes that William and Kate and their three children, particularly Prince George, will have what it takes to make the royals great again.

Just maintaining, however, is proving difficult work, considering the King is facing increasing opposition to his reign and—it must be said—his personality. The protest eggs hurled at Charles in Yorkshire represent more a precursor than an anomaly. More flew in the King's direction a month later while he was in Luton, a small town about an hour north of London. And while none of the eggs found their targets, and both King and Queen were unfazed, it's worth recalling because Queen Elizabeth II was never subject to the egg treatment in her home country. In fact, the only time she faced this kind of protest was during a tour of New Zealand in 1986, in opposition to a treaty the British Crown signed with the country's native Māori in 1840. "New Zealand has long been renowned for its dairy produce," she quipped at the time. "Though I should say that I myself prefer my New Zealand eggs for breakfast."

As proven in recent surveys, there is evidence that a growing percentage of the public is losing patience with the family and respect for the monarchy. Many of the nation's citizens could see themselves in the Queen's representation of the monarchy, with its cohesion of national enchantments and values. With King Charles, well, not so much. With the country facing economic crises at home and reputational bruising abroad, large sections of the public are increasingly less tolerant of royal extravagance and family dramas. Even finding entertainment for his coronation concert at Windsor Castle proved a challenge for the organizers. The list of acts who declined the invitation to perform was long and included Sir Elton John, Harry Styles, the Spice Girls, Adele, Taylor Swift, and Ed Sheeran. Sources close to Kylie Minogue—a regular at royal events in the past and very much an honorary Brit—said she turned down the opportunity because of the growing republican movement in her home country of Australia. Contrast that with the lineup for the Queen's Platinum Jubilee: Queen (with Adam Lambert), Alicia Keys, Sir Rod Stewart, Diana Ross, and, more than happy to clear his schedule for Her Majesty, even Sir Elton.

The coronation refusals may seem frivolous, and no doubt some were down to logistics, but the shrug-offs also suggest something deeper at work. Charles just doesn't have the requisite gravitas, which is understandable, given he's spent a majority of his life in the wake of the grand-class cruise ship of his mother's reputation. In fact, positive opinion of the royal family in the United Kingdom dropped from 68 percent to 54 percent within four months of the Queen's death. In our era of celebrity obsession and pop culture icons, if Elton and Harry Styles can't be bothered, why should we be?

Speaking of Styles, there's also the institution's struggle to connect with or appeal to younger generations, particularly Zillenials, Gen Z, and the ones to follow. During their time as working royals, Harry and Meghan, as individuals and as a couple, put a new coat of paint on the House of Windsor and let some fresh air into the Palace. The couple's generational awareness and interest in progressive social causes fostered a connection between the family and young people of all backgrounds. Three years after the Sussexes' great escape, however, this connection is lost. As older millennials in their early forties, William and Kate should still have some vitality to offer, but many of their overtures—such as their rather stiff guest appearances for BBC Radio 1 and its fifteen-to-twenty-nine-year-old audience—may start to come off as slightly contrived. An attempt to connect with a similar audience through a YouTube channel managed a brief buzzy moment in 2021 (racking up over 600,000 subscribers), but most videos posted these days barely reach 25,000 views.

———•———

If recent cultural disruptions prove anything, it's that progressive millennials and Gen Zers are determined to remain awake to and aware of the world that lies beyond the borders prescribed to them. Pining for a glorious yesteryear and leaning on a love of country that is *partially* defined by long-ago wars and atavistic pride doesn't exactly jibe with the modern worldview. Ready to press reset and usher in a new age of well-informed inclusion, the up-and-coming generations are prepared to jettison the old national emblems in favor of creating a few of their own. When they celebrate their country, they're doing so for a new Britain they see emerging—one of openness, representation, understanding, and cultural fusion. In this light, the traditional royal family seems decidedly off-brand and the institution a dusty relic. British journalist and social commentator Afua Hagan says, "To many young people who hope to see

Britain become a more diverse, equal, and tolerant society, the royal family—or more importantly what they represent—are not part of the picture. They are interested in true modernization rather than trying to force something from the past that is struggling to keep up in a space that has changed dramatically."

As much as the monarchy might like to shoehorn itself into this powerfully reconfigured national identity, it is increasingly unlikely to fully realize this. With the late Queen as the center of attention, it was a less challenging task. Her totemic power meant that a timely public address, staged photo op, or celebration could instantly bring the monarchy back into sharp relief.

Minus the late Queen, those showpiece events are already starting to feel somewhat *énervant* and over-rehearsed. Instead of starting on a new royal chapter, King Charles has simply become the causeway to get to one, and to many, he is exhibiting what Nairn called "a willful failure to quit a darkening stage." And William and Kate, who within the institution are considered the true future of the Firm, have thus far shown they, too, haven't yet figured out how to project new purpose. They may strive to couple some of the old greatness with a fresher perspective, but it's not going to be easy—the support structure below them is crumbling. Still, this won't stop the next King and Queen from carefully choosing their moments to try to re-enchant the public. And to do so they will assuredly continue to play all the dusty hits. They're the only tunes they know.

# 5

# Baggage
## The Lingering Trials of King Charles

———•———

*At the age of eleven or thereabouts women acquire a poise and*
*an ability to handle difficult situations which a man, if he is*
*lucky, manages to achieve somewhere in the later seventies.*
—P. G. Wodehouse, *Uneasy Money*

*There's a lot of baggage that comes along with our*
*family, but it's, like, Louis Vuitton baggage.*
—Kim Kardashian, *Keeping Up with the Kardashians*

There came a time when even Queen Elizabeth II reluctantly admitted she was slowing down. She was undeniably committed to the job until the end, but at ninety-five years old, Her Majesty didn't have the energy or health for every royal event and engagement. If it were solely up to her, she would have kept at it, but much to her chagrin, those around her—including private secretary Edward Young and right-hand woman and dresser Angela Kelly—wouldn't stop reminding her to take it slower. As a matter of practice, understudies Prince Charles, Prince William, and Princess Anne were already enlisted to fill in for her at investitures, events that required standing for long periods of time. After splitting up most of her travel appointments among senior royals starting in 2015 (after completing a final state visit to Germany), with Charles stepping in to lay the wreaths every Remembrance Sunday since 2017, it was pretty rare to see her away from Balmoral, Windsor Castle, or Buckingham Palace for more than a few hours. But it wasn't until spring 2021, toward the end of the pandemic, that the monarch quietly took another step toward relinquishing greater duties by installing Andrew Parker, Baron Parker of Minsmere, as the new Lord Chamberlain, the senior officer of the royal household.

Like the Lord Chamberlain who came before him, Parker oversees the departments and staff that support the royal family and serves as a liaison between the House of Lords and the sovereign. A former British intelligence officer who had headed up the storied MI5 counterintelligence and security agency since 2013, Parker—a bespectacled, salt-and-pepper-haired gent whom one aide likened to a "friendly giant" due to his towering frame when standing next to the petite monarch—was a strategic choice. The Queen, whose health was worsening by the month, was nearing the end of her reign, and a slow transition into King Charles's era was underway. A time of change like this required caution, diplomacy, determination, and sensitivity—essential qualities for a MI5 chief.

These are also qualities that Charles hadn't demonstrated enough of over the years. Indecisive, temperamental, and often in the middle of sticky situations, Charles hadn't exactly proven himself a port in the storm. In an early 2021 conversation with a senior family member, the Queen confessed that Parker would not only become the new Lord Chamberlain of the household but also, unofficially, and in her words, "my new CEO" of the Firm. A source added that "there was a slight lack of faith in her son . . . She needed someone who could be trusted to be her eyes and ears."

The presence of a strong, commanding figure as the Lord Chamberlain is not without historical precedent. After the dingy

1970s, when the embattled monarchy's popularity was at a low point, the Firm brought on David Ogilvy, the 13th Earl of Airlie, as Lord Chamberlain in 1983. A banker and businessman, Ogilvy delivered a bottom-line perspective and business acumen to the monarchy's vision for subtle reinventions. It wasn't exactly "out with the old and in with the new," but more akin to "slow and steady wins the race." Ogilvy and Palace officials transformed the Lord Chamberlain role from a predominantly ceremonial position into an active, participatory job. With the Queen at the helm as CEO, Ogilvy filled in as chairman of the board. He served as Lord Chamberlain until 1997, a guiding force through testing times. He was there for the Queen's notorious annus horribilis in 1992. The Queen was already comfortable with outsiders and change-makers, and this time she was even ready to quietly hand over some of the reins. The previous Lord Chamberlain, Earl William Peel, had been in the position since 2006, and while trusted and respected by the monarch, his close friendship with Charles, at times, saw him caught in the middle of the two. This time, however, the Queen and her team worked directly with Parker behind the scenes to create a strategy for the future and a vision for the monarchy beyond her life. She called on Charles for some of the more public-facing duties that she was ready to step aside from.

It was a long time coming, but on May 10, 2022, the then Prince of Wales—the oldest heir to the throne in nearly three hundred years—finally had his big moment when Palace and government officials invoked the Regency Act of 1937—Section 6, to be specific. It states, "In the event of illness not amounting to such infirmity of mind or body . . . the Sovereign may, in order to prevent delay or difficulty in the dispatch of public business, by Letters Patent delegate, for the period of that illness or absence, to Counsellors of State such of the royal functions as may be specified in the Letters Patent." In this case, that meant Charles would step in to perform the ceremonial duty of reciting the "Gracious Speech" at the opening of the new parliamentary session. It wasn't until the day before that Buckingham Palace announced that the Queen would "reluctantly" miss the event due to "episodic mobility issues"—a well-meaning euphemism for "too old for all that walking" and a convenient way to avoid going into detail about the greater health problems she was privately dealing with. In her seventy-year reign, she missed only two other state openings—those in 1959 and 1963, the years she was pregnant with her spares, Andrew and Edward, respectively. On those occasions, the serving Lord Chancellors read her speech and five Lord Commissioners helped open Parliament, but this time it was Charles's turn. A man who's craved validation and admiration from his family, the royal institution, and the British establishment for decades, the Prince of Wales finally got his solo turn in the spotlight.

Well, sort of. As it turned out, it was more a moment to showcase the monarchy as a powerful, lineal institution, not Charles as an individual or a king in waiting. Charles read the Queen's speech, but not from her seat. Her Sovereign's Throne was removed and replaced with the consort's throne, the ornate chair the late Prince Philip used for occasions (which the Queen first fought to include in 1967). The Queen wasn't physically there, but her presence was felt. Taking pride of place on the dais, Her Majesty's Imperial State Crown rested comfortably on a crimson and gold velvet pillow exactly where her gilt-wood, crystal-inlaid throne would normally command the room's attention.

Also present on the red and gold carpeted rostrum was Prince William, next in line to his father, who looked on from a "chair of state," strategically placed a few inches down from his father and the glittering crown. In the Queen's absence, two counsellors of state* must be present to officiate. The Palace wanted the

---

* Counsellors of state are the five individuals (over the age of twenty-one) next in the line of succession and are authorized to carry out most of King Charles's official duties—such as attending Privy Council meetings and signing documents—if the monarch is absent due to

world to see this as a joint duty. With the two side by side, the vision for the era of transition was in full view. Camilla, soon to become Queen Consort to Charles, was seated nearby on a lower platform. Raffia-hatted, stately in navy, and laden with pearls, she rounded out a portrait of what the family would look like post–Queen Elizabeth II.

Even with a lifetime of training for this ritualistic occasion, Charles looked a little awkward in his down-size throne without his mother by his side. Decked out in his Admiral of the Fleet Royal Navy uniform, complete with medals and gold aiguillettes, the prince appeared deep in thought as he took his seat. He faithfully read a letter penned by the now-disgraced Prime Minister Boris Johnson, which outlined "Her Majesty's Government's" priorities. Charles delivered the pro forma speech without a hitch. He even looked commanding at times, as commanding as one can look while compliantly seated next to the boss's crown on a cushion.

As an anachronistic exercise in mise-en-scène pomp, the state opening was a success. Despite some ginned-up fanfare around the event and media fixation on a "Queen's speech without the Queen," the ceremony proceeded as normal and as expected, which is exactly what the institution and the establishment wanted from Charles. When Charles exited the House of Lords Chambers, a room so full of red—from carpet to benches, cushions to robes—one could mistake it for a set in Kubrick's *Eyes Wide Shut*, the soon-to-be King appeared ready for duty.

The preparation the day before the event tells a different story. To say he was calm, an insider later shared, "would be a lie." Sources in Charles's camp later revealed that chaos reigned during the plan-

---

illness or being abroad. They can't, however, dissolve Parliament, appoint a prime minister, or deal with Commonwealth matters. The current counsellors of state, in this order, are Queen Camilla, Prince William, Prince Harry, Prince Andrew, and Princess Beatrice.

ning stages. Boris Johnson didn't send over the speech until the very last minute, so an irritated Charles wasn't given ample time to practice reading it. ("Johnson has done everything he can to become the most unpopular prime minister the Windsors have ever known," an aide said with a laugh.)

Still, for all the stress, the Firm could count the day as a win. This small victory rolled right into the national holiday hullabaloo and outdoor drinking sessions that accompanied the Queen's Platinum Jubilee. The recently besieged family business took a breath and enjoyed some time in the sun, free of its demons and setbacks. It was short-lived. Just three weeks after the Jubilee, *The Times of London* broke a story about Prince Charles accepting "bags of cash" equaling three million euros from former Qatar prime minister Sheikh Hamad bin Jassim bin Jaber Al Thani between 2011 and 2015. Known as "HBJ" in London's financial circles, the sheikh— a member of Qatar's ruling Al Thani family and chairman of Qatar Islamic Bank—is one of the richest men in the world. To some, he is also "the man who bought up London" thanks to his leadership of the sovereign wealth fund that invested billions into the likes of Harrods, London's Olympic Village, the London Stock Exchange, the iconic Shard building, and Canary Wharf. The optics weren't good, and news replaced the actual image of Charles reading the Queen's speech under the canopy of state with an imagined one where he's reaching out a greedy hand to take plastic sacks (from luxury grocer Fortnum & Mason, of all places) and leather duffels of crisp €50 bills.

The Palace immediately went into their version of damage control. The usual rationalizations and justifications followed as they released a statement to clarify that the money was deposited directly into the accounts for the Prince of Wales's Charitable Fund (PWCF). Clarence House also stressed that it wasn't Charles who physically accepted the bags of money, but an aide who then passed them straight on to the appropriate persons at the nonprofit. Even if this is the case, and there is no suggestion that Charles and the charity behaved improperly in any way, it was perceived to be a wildly irresponsible move for the future King to be casually accepting bundles of cash during a meeting with an official representing a country with an alarming record on human rights. Unconstitutional? Maybe not. Reckless? Most definitely. While Charles can point to documents as evidence that he followed protocol (guidelines state that members of the royal family are allowed to accept a check as a patron of, or on behalf of, a charity with which they are associated), the whole affair raised serious concerns about his judgment and motivations. To banish the story from the news, the Palace offered a half-baked apology, claiming Charles "will not accept bags of cash again," as if he were a child who had just been punished for breaking the rules.

To make matters worse, a month later, on July 30, *The Sunday Times*' Whitehall editor Gabriel Pogrund broke another story about Charles accepting cash. This time the transaction involved members of the forever tarnished Bin Laden family. Charles accepted one million pounds from two half brothers of Osama Bin Laden, Bakir and Shafiq (who had no connection or involvement with terrorism or other illegal activities), after an October 30, 2013, in-person meeting at Clarence House. The private appointment, sources later shared, was only for the purpose of making a donation. "Before the meeting took place, it was made clear that [Bakir and Shafiq] wanted to contribute," one revealed. "Despite the fact aides had told the Prince of Wales it would not be wise, given the family links, he chose to proceed regardless." Again, the Palace set the record straight posthaste, stating there wasn't anything ethically or legally wrong with doing business with Bin Laden family members who were not connected to any terrorist activity. A spokesperson from PWCF went as far as to tell BBC News that "the sins of the father" (in this case, Osama Bin Laden) shouldn't preclude other Bin Ladens from making donations.

The communications foot soldiers at Clarence House quickly put forward Sir Ian Cheshire, PWCF's chairperson, to take the heat off the royal household—highlighting the differences between Prince Charles's obligations and those delegated to the trustees. Cheshire issued a calibrated statement that removed Charles from the equation. At the time he emailed myself and other reporters that the donation was "carefully considered" with "due diligence," and "the decision to accept the donation was taken wholly by the trustees." It doesn't matter that Charles had nothing to do with brokering this donation; the whole sorry episode placed the heir back in the hot seat. To everyone but Charles—and some of those in his orbit of entitlement—it seems obvious that accepting cash from a family tainted by the terrorism of one of its members is not necessarily a smart move. And it begged the questions to even the most ardent of royalists: What the hell was he thinking? Where was his judgment? In only a matter of two months, Charles went from the positive spotlight of opening Parliament to the glaring light of the public's interrogation room.

The imprudence aside, the revelations about his financial affairs couldn't have come at a worse time. Charles's royal household was waist-deep in a cash-for-honors scandal that once again involved the community-focused Prince's Foundation. At the center of this controversy were Dr. Mahfouz Marei Mubarak bin Mahfouz, a wealthy Saudi tycoon whom Prince Charles awarded a CBE (commander of the Most Excellent Order of the British Empire) at an unusually private Buckingham Palace investiture in August 2016, and Michael Fawcett, a former assistant valet to Charles who rose through the ranks to become the prince's senior valet. Curiously, the meeting was never declared on official records.

A leaked letter showed Fawcett offering to support Mahfouz in securing a knighthood and in his application for British citizenship, the infamous "golden visa," in exchange for a sizable donation (reportedly £370,000 to help replace ninety-three windows at the Castle of Mey, the Queen Mother's former retreat on the north coast of Scotland now managed by the foundation). *The Times* broke the story in September 2021, which resulted in a press shitstorm and a bona fide criminal investigation. Under intense scrutiny, Clarence House press secretaries fended off speculation, stating that the "Prince of Wales had no knowledge of the alleged offer of honors on the basis of donation to his charities." The blame fell on Fawcett, who resigned in disgrace shortly after.

This wasn't Fawcett's first rodeo. A ruddy-faced sixty-year-old man who squeezed into expensive suits, Fawcett spent nearly four decades rarely less than a few steps away from Charles. As a long-standing fixture in the prince's court, many believe he knows "where all the bodies are buried" and can point you to the skeletons in the closet. Choose your metaphor, but it is well-known and well-established that Fawcett was Charles's right-hand man, confidante, and fixer. His résumé is a testament to his loyalty and dedication to serving the Firm, and it reads a bit like a "made man" whose years of fealty finally earned him the title of consigliere.

In 1981, at the young age of nineteen, Fawcett joined the ranks as a footman to Queen Elizabeth II. After moving up to serve Her Majesty as first sergeant footman, Fawcett moved over to Clarence House, where staff inside Charles's camp claim he bullied his way into the position of assistant valet to the prince. After that, Fawcett became indispensable to Charles. He held this loyal insider position in some form or another—senior valet, freelance consultant, personal assistant, CEO of the charitable fund—for nearly forty years. His duties ran the full gamut, from laying out Charles's bespoke clothes for the day and managing the prince's social schedule to event planning and heading up fundraising efforts. Despite internal inquiries and controversy around his alleged bullying and racist remarks toward another staff member in the 1990s, which forced a brief departure from his post (until an employment tribunal ruled that the Highgrove Estate was not guilty of racial discrimination),

Fawcett and Charles were basically inseparable. Dickie Arbiter, former royal press secretary to the Queen for twelve years, revealed, "Fawcett has been there for so many years, so close in times of stress, knowing all the ins and outs and all the warts." Several sources have confirmed that at one point, when Charles needed to produce a urine sample after breaking his arm in a polo accident, Fawcett traveled with him to the hospital and held the specimen cup. At some point during their long association, Charles reportedly remarked, "I can manage without just about anyone, except for Michael."

In 2003, however, Prince Charles had to start learning how to do just that, at least on paper. Allegations surfaced that Fawcett, with Charles's blessing, sold unwanted gifts from foreign dignitaries and was allowed to keep a cut of the proceeds. Those in royal inner circles knew about Fawcett's practices—his nickname in the Firm at the time was "Fawcett the Fence"—but kept quiet. An inquiry found Fawcett innocent of any criminal offense, but the incident left a shadow over them. Employing an aide who was barely operating within the law proved too much for Palace officials, so the institution applied the requisite pressure. Against Charles's wishes—it was even reported that he broke down in tears over his adjutant's imminent departure—Fawcett soon resigned as the prince's personal assistant.

Officially, Fawcett was no longer on the Palace payroll, but in a matter of weeks, he set up a new management company, Premier Mode, and Charles hired him as a freelance consultant. The institution might have wiped their hands of Fawcett, but Charles was far from doing the same. The prince not only brought his faithful servant back into the fold as a hired gun, primarily as a "party planner," but in 2018 turned Fawcett the Fence into a chief executive. As head of the Prince's Foundation, he oversaw the entire operation, personally leading many fundraising campaigns that brought in parcels of money (excuse the pun) for the foundation's many initiatives, including renovating the Dumfries House Estate and offering education and training programs in construction and traditional crafts.

Fawcett was indispensable once again, until the leaked letter in 2021 that prompted the investigation into the alleged cash-for-honors deal with Mahfouz, the Saudi billionaire. After this debacle, the heir's loyal aide-de-camp resigned as the Prince's Foundation CEO, and a Clarence House spokesman, as if on cue, trotted out a statement that read: "Michael Fawcett and [his company] Premier Mode will not be providing services to us in the future. We have all agreed to end this arrangement." The criminal probe dragged on at a snail's pace, with authorities confirming they had interviewed two men (one in his fifties, the other in his forties) under caution in September 2022 before proceedings went silent until the following year. Though there were suspicions that the case might conveniently disappear after Charles became king, the Metropolitan Police's Special Enquiry Team went on to speak with a number of witnesses (though nobody from Buckingham Palace), obtained court production orders, and reviewed over two hundred documents. Among those was the 2016 letter from Fawcett, where he admitted that he was "willing and happy" to make an application to change Mahfouz's honorary CBE into a knighthood because of his "generosity." Still, a conclusion was announced in August 2023: no further action would be taken over the alleged "honors for sale" incident. As for Mahfouz, he is now a British aristocrat known as His Excellency Dr. Mahfouz Marei Mubarak bin Mahfouz, CBE, GCMLJ, FRSA, Baron of Abernethy.

After the Metropolitan Police launched the investigation into "honors for sale" offenses in February 2022, Charles faced questions about one of his other projects just five months later. A charity watchdog announced it was looking into the purchase of properties made by a company connected to a Prince's Foundation trustee on land controlled by a subsidiary of the Prince's Foundation. Between 2012 and 2017, the Havisham Group—partly owned by Lord David Brownlow, one of Britain's richest men—spent £1.7 million on eleven houses at Charles's sustainable village of Knockroon. Though

Brownlow was on the board of the Prince's Foundation between 2013 and 2017, it was alleged by *The Sunday Times* that the Foundation had failed to declare information about related-party transactions, despite it being a standard measure required by charity regulators. The Office of the Scottish Charity Regulator confirmed in a statement that "the work of Havisham Group and property transactions relating to [Knockroon] forms part of our overall investigation, work on which is ongoing." Brownlow left his role at the charity in 2018 and was subsequently awarded a Commander of the Victorian Order (CVO), according to a Prince's Foundation spokesperson, "in recognition of his role of chair of the charity the Prince's Foundation for Building Community."

A sequel to his Poundbury, England, green community, but this time in the craggy hills of Scotland's historic Ayrshire county, Knockroon was a disaster from start to finish. Charles acquired the land in 2007 after purchasing Dumfries House, a Palladian country home located in the town of Cumnock, which is managed by the Prince's Foundation. But what he had hoped would become a 770-home "heritage-led regeneration" of the area worth £15 million ended up with a final declared value of only £700,000.

Glasgow-based professor Alan Dunlop, a fellow of Scotland's Royal Incorporation of Architects and Royal Society of Arts, had warned that the project had limited appeal and impossible ambitions. "Ersatz Georgian and mock Scottish vernacular creations . . . and imported pastiche from past centuries" would not fly in the working-class area, he said. "I couldn't see how it could stack up from the start, from a development point of view. No one could understand how you could possibly make it work." Even with the help of the Havisham Group, only thirty-one homes were built over ten years.

To senior aides around the late Queen (and, per rumor, Her Majesty herself), this series of headline-grabbing stories about Charles's financial improprieties were another set of strikes against his name. Ambitious (and, as many would argue, unnecessary) endeavors such as Knockroon, and the predicaments they often led to, are exactly why some of the aides and insiders I spoke to for this book aren't convinced Charles will make a reliable or trustworthy King. "It's the same pattern over and over," bemoaned a senior Buckingham Palace courtier in the summer of 2022. "He starts off with his heart in the right place but makes rash, poorly thought-out decisions to make them [his ideas] happen."

The farmland on which Knockroon was supposed to find its success was part of a larger deal the Prince of Wales made in 2007 when he bought Dumfries House after falling in love with it. Owned by former F1 driver John Crichton-Stuart, the 7th Marquess of Bute, Charles *needed* the countryside home (complete with its original eighteenth-century paintings, artifacts, and Thomas Chippendale furniture) and its two thousand acres of land the moment he laid eyes on it. It was the perfect spot for him to plant a flag and make a statement—a new HQ for HRH Prince Charles, the Duke of Rothesay, the peerage title he uses while in Scotland. The only problem was this grand old manor was valued at an eye-watering £43 million. "I remember trying for years before it actually came up for sale, I tried to find a way to help sort it out or find somebody who might help, a sponsor, a donor or somebody," Charles told BBC's *Hidden Heritage* in 2011. On a mission, the heir managed to raise almost half its value and, while some of his aides implored him not to do it, he took out a £20 million loan through his charitable foundation (he later admitted to his staff that this was a debt that kept him "awake at night"). Originally the bank had offered only half the sum but then doubled it after security for the loan was attached to blueprints for developing Knockroon on the land surrounding the house. News of the extortionate purchase raised the Queen's eyebrows "into orbit," joked one Palace insider. And with good reason. The last Prince of Wales with such a penchant for luxe property (George IV in the eighteenth century) nearly bankrupted the royal family.

Still, sleepless nights or not, Charles was confident he had made the right decision. "His Royal Highness was determined this wonderful asset should not be lost for future generations," a Clarence House spokesman said in an attempt to convince the public of their boss's vanity purchase. Since then, Dumfries House has become the base for Charles's Prince's Foundation and remains one of his passion projects. I remember asking him about it in 2014 and watching his eyes light up as he revealed how much local schoolchildren love to visit the newly renovated farm and stables there. "Some of his charities, such as the Prince's Trust, are clearly doing amazing things," said Gabriel Pogrund, who led the string of scoops on Charles's financial messes. "But [Prince Charles should] ask the question, does he need all that money and to do all these things? Does he need to be raising millions of pounds for Dumfries House? He needs to rethink what he spends his money on. The role of his charitable work should be reassessed."

At a time when Prince Charles should have been making news as an heir to the throne who was ready to assume his future role, he was, instead, in the spotlight for questionable judgment. It was an unfortunate reminder that the King who replaced the untouchable Queen is an error-prone man dragging some heavy baggage as he attempts to fill his mother's shoes.

As much as Charles would like to move past all of this, these issues aren't going away. First, there's the question of Fawcett. He's no longer working for the King, but the two remain in regular contact. Palace sources have expressed concern that he may have his eyes on a return to the King's fold. And there's also the question of who was leaking information about Charles's financial affairs in the first place.

While I was writing this book, a rumor circulated in royal circles that some of these leaks might have come from a party deep inside the establishment who wanted to give Charles a knock before he officially took the throne. Though such rumors are verging on conspiracy theory, the timing makes sense. On June 11, 2022, news outlets revealed that Charles had privately criticized the British government over their plan to deport Rwandan asylum seekers back to their home country. A source (in this case, one of his senior staff) was given permission by Charles to brief *The Times* and the *Daily Mail* that the future King "was more than disappointed at the policy" and "thinks the government's whole approach is appalling."

For a royal, particularly the incoming King, to comment on government policy or function is strictly verboten (even if his empathetic view on the matter was particularly refreshing to hear from a senior royal). Keeping quiet means rising above, and, in a strange twist that only the British monarchy can produce, rising above provides a clear path to maintaining power. Only weeks after opening Parliament in the Queen's stead, Charles opened his mouth on a political matter when he shouldn't have. Sources say he wanted his views on the controversial asylum policy to be heard ahead of the Commonwealth Heads of Government Meeting in Rwanda, where he would represent his mother, later that month.

Charles brings to the throne his deeply held, often vocalized opinions and a lifetime of experience operating outside the rules— written or otherwise—that dictate the life and work of the sovereign. As a successful entrepreneur, philanthropist, and eco warrior, Charles had to play politics, and voicing enthusiastic opinions and generating new ideas that sometimes challenged the status quo were all part of this self-appointed position. The intentions were good, but for someone who should be observing the constitutional rule of not having an opinion on pretty much anything, he should have never entered the conversation in the first place.

His ambitions and dogged persistence have led to some overreach and meddling. During his time as prime minister, Tony Blair complained to the Palace about Charles's interference on several New Labour issues, including the 2001 invasion of Afghanistan led by the United States and the United Kingdom (the prince famously asked to "halt" the invasion to honor Ramadan, claiming, "But

Americans can do anything!"). In 2004, he famously wrote to then environment minister Elliot Morley that protecting Patagonian toothfish must become a "priority" so that endangered albatross could feast on them for survival. In her biography *Prince Charles: The Passions and Paradoxes of an Improbable Life*, Sally Bedell Smith recounts how, at the height of her austere measures in 1985, Prime Minister Margaret Thatcher sternly reminded the prince *she* was in charge after he complained that because of her Tory policies, he would "inherit the throne of a divided Britain" (like Prince William today, Charles was conjuring up his reign long before it was even close to his turn). The Iron Lady's riposte? "I run this country, not you, sir."

Charles's exhaustive history of interfering in political processes and lobbying was laid bare in May 2015 when his "Black Spider memos" (a reference to his spiderlike penmanship) were released to the world following a ten-year freedom of information battle by the *Guardian*. From his calls for homeopathic treatments to be made available via Britain's National Health Service and a 2004 missive calling for Blair to cull badgers to help the country's "lack of self-sufficiency" in producing meat and vegetables, to lobbying for the replacement of Lynx military helicopters (because U.K. troops lacked "necessary resources" in the Iraq War, he claimed), Charles has had an opinion on *everything*.

His busybody campaigning tapered off in his final years as the Prince of Wales, but those who pull the levers will not hesitate to remind Charles, overtly or perhaps in underhanded ways like leaks to the press, that he is far from welcome in the government's legislative process or the establishment's power-brokering. In other words, as King, there's no seat for him at the table in the back room. And when he made those comments about Rwanda, there would have been plenty of figures within the political landscape eager to remind him to keep his apolitical beak out of their business—through whatever means necessary. Charles knows the rules but often still appears divided between what he can and cannot say.

Conspiracies over damaging leaks also extended to his own personal bubble. When some details of private written correspondence between Charles and daughter-in-law Meghan appeared in the *Telegraph* on April 21, 2023, there were worries that the tip-off had come from within. Though fingers of blame are often pointed in the Sussex direction, this was an exchange that *both* parties wanted to keep confidential—letters addressing Meghan's concerns about unconscious racial bias in the royal family in the wake of the Oprah interview. The newspaper's vague reporting, mostly centered on the existence of the written communication, made no mention of the damning details within them, but, said a Palace insider, "there was certainly discussion amongst [the team] that it could be a warning shot from someone . . . something to shake the King up ahead of the coronation." Though they were personal messages, some Palace aides—one of whom later left on less than amicable terms—also caught sight of the letters as they were sent and received.

Charles had initially reached out to his daughter-in-law in spring 2021 to express his sadness over the huge distance between the two parties and his disappointment that the couple chose to go so public with their words. But what had upset him the most was Meghan's disclosure that "several conversations" were had in the family, away from herself and Harry, that featured "concerns" over what color their unborn son Archie's skin might be and "what that would mean or look like [for the Firm]." When speaking with Oprah, both Harry and Meghan chose to refrain from sharing who was involved in this exchange. (A representative for the couple would only go on to clarify that it was not the Queen nor Prince Philip.) "I think that would be very damaging to them," Meghan said. But in the pages of these private letters, two identities were revealed. Laws in the United Kingdom prevent me from reporting who they were.

The King, said sources, wanted his response to make clear to Meghan that he felt there was no ill will or casual prejudice present when the two people had spoken about his future grandson. "He wanted to clear up something he felt strongly about," said a royal insider. For Meghan—who had never used the words *racist* or *racism* in her descriptions of this event or in the letters—her bigger concern was, added the insider, "the way in which these conversations were had . . . Their tone . . . revealed lingering unconscious bias and ignorance within the family that needed to be addressed." The letters, described a second source, were "a respectful back and forth" but "serious." They added, "I don't know if either saw completely eye to eye in the end, but there was at least a feeling that both had been heard." Since then, said a source close to the two families, the pair have had pleasant, if occasional, exchanges. "There are no hard feelings about this specific incident, but there is distance, and everything else remains unaddressed," said the source. For the Sussexes' part, though communication with Charles—who declined an invite to granddaughter Lilibet's March 3, 2023, christening in California due to scheduling conflicts—is infrequent, they "still keep him in the loop on their family life, sending new photos of the children."

———·———

Charles's divided nature sits at the heart of his many family issues. As a child, he was considered a sensitive soul—a quiet boy who preferred books and art to sports and pranks. The age-old story applies here: because of his sensitivity and dreamy nature, Charles was bullied and teased at the strict and demanding Gordonstoun school in Scotland, where he boarded for five years. As a young man, he emerged from his cocoon a bit of a playboy. He took to the finer things in life, happily accepting the boons that his privileged position afforded him. He cut a figure on the social scene, wearing only the finest clothes—Turnbull & Asser shirts, bespoke Savile Row suits, and Anderson & Sheppard tweed. Not an athlete by any stretch, Charles, in an effort to complete his courtly image, stepped out of his comfort zone and took to the polo fields. It is here where Charles met the love of his life, Camilla Shand.

Enter sixteen-year-old Diana Spencer. A darling of the aristocracy who intrigued anyone who caught a glimpse of her, the on-paper version of Diana was perfect for Charles, who was twenty-eight at the time. The institution got one look at her and quickly decided they could easily transform her into what Dame Hilary Mantel later called a "royal body . . . carriers of a blood line." The monarchical machine rejected Camilla and slotted Diana into the system to produce a proper princess for their narrative and approved her as the next delivery mechanism for the royal genes.

This sent Charles into decades of internal conflict between matters of the heart and the demands of duty. His heart wanted Camilla, but the heir's role demanded Diana. The young prince decided to have both. Sometime after saying his "I dos" to Diana at St. Paul's Cathedral in 1981, Charles initiated a decades-long affair with the woman the institution dismissed. The affair became the Firm's worst-kept secret and everyone knew it was wrong. Charles and Diana's tortured marriage was front-page fodder, but for all its luridness, it did result in the required heir and spare. Diana's work was done. Those in power wanted her to step in line, tone down the glamour, and get out of the spotlight. A devoted mother and the "queen of people's hearts," she would go on to do anything but that.

Charles's reputation never fully recovered. Although he has occasionally made forays into the public's good graces, recent polls still reveal that large swathes of the public continue to have a negative opinion of him for how he treated his former wife during their union and her short life. It's why his second marriage to Camilla passed by so quietly. No fanfare, no televised nuptials, just a private

2005 civil ceremony at Windsor Guildhall in the presence of their families. Because of her dedication to her role as the head of the Church of England (which discourages divorce), the Queen felt it was best not to attend the ceremony. Her one bit of advice to her son ahead of the April 9 nuptials was simple: don't rub it in people's faces.

The leaks about his finances and ongoing charity scandals only compound the resentment and disapproval expressed by many about his role as King. As for the institution and the establishment, there are some within it who still see him as a waffler and a dilettante. He remains a question mark to the bureaucrats and éminences grises who privately and publicly run Britain's economic interests and maintain the country's social order.

Even though the heir played a role in Prince Andrew's royal demotion, he is torn here, too. Understandably, he cares for his brother, so much so that a close source said that during the most heightened moments of Andrew's downfall, Charles was tearful over fears for the shamed duke's mental health. Charles has long advocated for a slimmer monarchy with fewer working royals, but he didn't imagine it would become a reality as a result of two things beyond his control: his brother's public humiliation and his son's exit. What could have been a powerful opening gambit for the new King now simply looks like a resigned defensive move to protect what's left on the board.

And what's left on the chessboard, with the exception of the Waleses, isn't much of a side. The older generation have less energy, but the bigger problem is their removed air of entitlement. At the helm of the crew of working royals—Queen Camilla, Princess Anne, the Duke and Duchess of Edinburgh, the Duke of Kent, the Duke and Duchess of Gloucester, and Princess Alexandra—is the King himself, who as the heir was saddled with the unfortunate sobriquets "Prince of Wails" and "Pampered Prince." The latter nickname emerged after staff complained to various journalists about Charles's outrageous service demands and his extravagant lifestyle. The King lives a life of luxury and comfort that is even alien to other members of the royal family—a throwback to monarchs of the past. Those who know him, serve him, and write about him often compare him to Louis XIV, the French monarch who transformed a hunting lodge into one of the most extravagant palaces in the world. Versailles's enduring opulence is testament to the Sun King's commitment to living large. Charles may not own anything to rival Versailles, but Dumfries House (one of six multimillion-pound homes he owns across Britain) is no country cabin.

The details about the cosseted King's habits and way of life suggest a disconnect. Even his late mother, once one of the wealthiest women in the country, repeatedly complained about Charles's extravagantly luxurious lifestyle. We all know he's a man of taste, but some of the particulars leave many gobsmacked. His repair-and-rewear approach to dressing may be the height of eco-friendliness and sustainability, but the multiple changes during the day that four valets prepare for him and help him put on is far from humble. You may have already heard how he likes his soft-boiled eggs *just so* (four minutes—no more, no less, or they'll be sent back to the kitchen in infantile fury), but did you hear about the one-thousand-thread-count bed linen (that *must* be perfectly steamed) he insists on traveling with? There have been reports of temper tantrums at night as well: if the prince's pajamas aren't pressed, sources have claimed, there is hell to pay. Every dandy loves his shoes, and Charles is no different. The King has the same environmentally conscious approach to his footwear as his clothes (never throw them out, always have a cobbler bring them back to life), but his particularness about their shoelaces is a little more unique. When laces get even the smallest bit threadbare, a staff member must quickly switch them out with a fresh, *ironed* pair. There is even a rumor (one that, sur-

prisingly, sources have confirmed) that Charles likes to have someone squeeze exactly one inch of toothpaste onto his toothbrush for
him ahead of his bedtime routine. Paging Michael Fawcett! But
it doesn't end there. The cherry on top of this ridiculous extravagance: the toothpaste must come from a "crested silver dispenser."

In an attempt to lower the chances of further embarrassing coverage, Charles has laid new groundwork for even friendlier media
relationships during his reign. Leading up to his ascension, Charles
and Camilla never stopped ingratiating themselves to media figures and journalists, leaning on aides to leak stories to maintain a
positive image in the press. Hiring a former co–deputy editor of the
*Daily Mail* (and, before that, the *Mail on Sunday*) to lead the Palace's
in-house media team was no coincidence. Tobyn Andreae may have
had zero PR experience before taking the job of head of communications, but with twenty-five years working on tabloids, he quickly
ensured that the likes of the *Daily Mail* and *The Sunday Times* have
had a steady feed of positive stories pumped their way since the
beginning of his tenure in July 2022.

Charles has no problem doing the job himself, either. In February 2020, he invited a handful of trusted royal reporters to Dumfries
House in Scotland for an overnight stay, a grand dinner, and plenty
of schmoozing. With a chance to tour his sprawling estate, Charles
hoped the trip would help keep Britain's most influential newspapers onside during the drama surrounding Harry and Meghan's exit
from working royal life.

As expensive bottles of Laphroaig whisky (from the only single
malt distillery with a Royal Warrant) were poured and laughter
echoed down the historic house's Pewter Corridor, Charles winked
to one of the media guests and said, "This is all off the record, of
course." Knowing full well this is never really the case when dealing
with most royal correspondents (there's a pattern of sticking it in
one's back pocket and then putting it in a story as a "royal source"
after enough time has passed), he went on to pull aside one of the

guests to explain his position on the Sussexes, who had moved to North America just a month earlier: "I made sure they were taken care of [when they left] . . . Their stubbornness doesn't make it easy." While this was hardly a bombshell, anecdotes like these are just the kind of nuggets needed to court favor and find their way into positive articles about him.

With a series of strategically placed "off the cuff" remarks during that period of time, Charles and his aides did their bit to help ensure he emerged from the public family drama unscathed. Shortly after the media get-together (and no, I was not invited—at this point the Palace was already getting jitterish about the release of *Finding Freedom*), details about how much money he was giving his younger son and how he had done all he could for the Sussexes made their way into the papers. Mission accomplished.

Charles may be adept at wielding the media to settle his scores, but it's evidence that he's bringing old habits and coarse practices to the top job—a refined one that the Queen emphatically insisted was to remain untarnished from such scheming. We may have heard snippets about her life from aides and friends over the years, but it was extremely rare to hear her thoughts and feelings via source quotes. (As a friend of the late monarch once told me, "Many of the 'sources' you see in the papers claiming to know her innermost thoughts are clearly made up.") It also demonstrates a recklessness on the King's part: a logrolling relationship with powerful players in the media is a treacherous one. Depending on prevailing trends, capricious opinions, and, of course, ratings and viewership, the very same media he uses to prop himself up can just as easily bring him down if it guarantees clicks and views.

This points to a single important issue when it comes to King Charles. While it was never controversial to support the Queen, it's not the same with Charles. After a long life in the public eye, and one made up of some questionable decisions, Charles was never going to have an easy reign. For much of his adult life, he has been at the center of controversies, both fairly and unfairly. The duplexity of the man intrigues and confounds. His messy trials and tribulations are all too human. The new King, who is supposed to stand above to represent the royal family's solidarity, is in a heartbreaking war with his own son. The reality is that to many who watched as Charles was anointed with holy oil on May 6, 2023, to confirm him as the head of the Church of England, the man in front of the Archbishop of Canterbury was still a philandering husband and an unwise collector of bags of money.

# 6

# The Fall of Prince Andrew

## Scandal, Shame, and Silencing Jane Doe

———·———

*I admit fully my judgment was probably colored by my
tendency to be too honorable, but that's just the way it is.*

—Prince Andrew, 2019, *Newsnight* interview

*I never wonder to see men wicked, but I often
wonder to see them not ashamed.*

—Jonathan Swift, *Miscellanies*

*N*ervous, *frustrated*, and *like shit* were the terms a former aide used to describe the disgraced Duke of York's state of mind as he made the fifteen-minute car ride from his Royal Lodge home to a meeting with his mother on the frigid morning of January 11, 2022. For Andrew—who appeared gaunt and exhausted in his rumpled suit behind the misty windshield of his Range Rover—the rainy journey to Windsor Castle was another chapter in what can only be described as an unfortunate series of events for the royal. After decades of humiliating headlines and disapproval from Queen Elizabeth II, the sixty-one-year-old was finally facing some consequences for his personal failings, particularly his friendship with

Jeffrey Epstein, the wealthy pedophile with powerful cronies whose criminal, contemptible legacy continues to swallow up his victims long after his 2019 suicide in prison.

Andrew's subsequent legal entanglements with Virginia Giuffre, née Roberts, a woman who alleges the duke sexually assaulted her when she was seventeen years old (an allegation that Andrew continues to deny), brought further shame to himself, his family, and the Crown. The court of public opinion had already chastised him, but the punishment from the House of Windsor had, so far, been light—the Firm simply asked him to step away from his royal duties in November 2019, leaving all his royal perks intact. This time, however, Andrew knew the jig was up. Sternly summoned by the monarch without explanation, Andrew was en route to an "official" meeting where the country's head of state would finally strip him of his HRH title, his military honors, and (almost) all his official royal roles.

"He knew it was coming," said a family source. "But given that he also needed to be saved from embarrassment in the courthouse, it was a small price to pay." Five months earlier, Giuffre had filed a civil lawsuit in New York, claiming that she was forced to have sexual encounters with Andrew when she was a minor. Though his lawyer tried to dismiss the case, it now looked like Andrew was going to offer some kind of financial settlement to avoid appearing in court. With few assets of his own, the prince knew he would soon need his mother's deep pockets to help bail him out. Her punishment was something he literally couldn't afford to run away from.

As he pulled up to Windsor Castle, the crunch of the gravel didn't evoke the usual warmth he felt when arriving to meet his mother. At the appropriate entry point to Her Majesty's quarters, an awaiting courtier instructed him to enter the building alone. Andrew had brought his longtime and trusted criminal defense lawyer, Gary Bloxsome, in the hopes that he could help negotiate with his family, but the Queen's aide made it clear that the criminal defense solicitor should wait in the car. Bloxsome's glass-half-full attitude and tendency to focus only on the best-case scenario always put the prince at ease. He was also one of the last remaining close aides on Andrew's team. His private secretary Amanda Thirsk had walked out in 2020 (with a handsome payout), less than ten weeks after Andrew's catastrophic *Newsnight* interview. Now, as he walked toward the Queen's private apartment, he was forced to face his humbling alone.

For many in the family and institution, this day was too long in the making. Though the Queen was the official face of Andrew's reckoning, it was Prince William who set the wheels in motion. William was keenly aware that the horrific allegations, the fallout from the embarrassing interview, and now the prospect of an out-of-court settlement involving money from the family's private wealth were all damaging the monarchy's reputation. "Someone needed to be the firm hand in that situation, and he felt the family [was] being too soft," said a source close to the prince. "The whole thing was casting a long shadow over the entire institution . . . over all of them." Up to this point, the family hadn't done much to mitigate the crisis or make any public moves, even after at least fifty other charities and organizations severed their ties with Andrew, including patronages with the likes of the Children's Foundation, Royal National Institute for the Deaf, Royal Navy, and Royal Marines Children's Fund.

William's snapping point came days before military leaders chimed in on the matter via an open letter to the Queen. Signed by 152 veterans of the Royal Navy, Royal Marines, and Army, the missive called on the Queen as the head of the British Armed Forces to remove Andrew's twelve honorary ranks and titles. They asserted that not only was Andrew's position "untenable," but it also brought shame to the services and "were this any other senior military officer, it is inconceivable that he would still be in post." Considering Andrew is a career naval officer and a Falklands veteran, this was a harsh rebuke from a normally supportive wing of the establishment. The fact that military leadership had joined the already outraged public in questioning the Firm's lack of action was proof that if William had left his intervention any longer, the ordeal would have spiraled to the point of no return.

In a meeting with his private secretary, Jean-Christophe Gray, or "JC" to colleagues—a by-the-numbers, amiable bureaucrat with an impressive résumé who was known to many insiders as a "bean counter" and fiscal hawk—William made preparations for Andrew's ouster, taking the initiative when others suffered from inertia. Even though several working members of the family wanted to see Andrew curtailed, neither Charles nor the Queen appeared ready to take him to task themselves. While Charles openly detested Andrew's indiscretions, he didn't want to be the one to break his younger brother. "You'd find it hard to believe, but [he] has [lay] awake many nights worrying about him," a source close to the then Prince of Wales revealed. Charles's reluctance baffled William, who didn't have much confidence in his father to do the right thing anyway. A source close to the prince said at the time, "William [doesn't] think his father is competent enough, quite frankly. Though they share passions and interests, their style of leadership is *completely* different."

As for the Queen, William admitted to Gray that he understood it ultimately came down to the monarch to drop the gavel on Andrew. But he felt she would remain "soft" on his uncle if he didn't forcefully express his concerns to his grandmother. As the Queen's reportedly favorite son, Andrew has historically received a pass from his mother. In 2011, Andrew was pushed out of his U.K. trade envoy position over concerns about his friendship with Epstein. But the Queen wasn't actively involved—it was Lord Christopher Geidt, her then private secretary, who urged action on the matter. The Queen eventually turned to her stalwart husband, Prince Philip, who outsourced the job to Downing Street, who promptly sacked Andrew with no questions asked. "She always believed in his innocence," a former aide to the Queen said.

Unable or unwilling to admonish her son, the Queen often appeared curiously aloof about the whole affair. Courtiers and royal observers long referred to her spoiling of Andrew as her only notable blind spot. Though her other children may have experienced a stricter side (particularly Anne and Charles), Andrew, said a family friend, "was the one who would make her laugh, keep her company, and, because he was always a little bit lost, she coddled him." As one former member of staff said to me in early 2022, "If anything, her sense of duty means she sometimes turns a blind eye or buries her head when it comes to bigger family issues. The Duke [of Edinburgh] would be the one to take those matters into his own hands." Known as the pillar of the family, Prince Philip was the person they most feared. A gruff but committed, decisive consort who spoke his mind, Philip did not suffer fools, even if the fool was part of the fold. According to a former aide, "*Everyone* would listen to him." His death at ninety-nine on April 9, 2021, prompted the usually Palace-friendly *Times* newspaper to declare, "Without Prince Philip the royal house of cards is falling."

When it came to private family matters, Prince Philip's steady hand was missed by many in the family. While the Queen demonstrated powers of restraint like no other, it was Philip who didn't hold back when it came to toeing the line—especially with their children. "The Queen was the boss, but *he* was the head of the household," said author and family friend Gyles Brandreth. He could also be an exceedingly stubborn man. Those who spent considerable time with him in private described him as a far from easy character. *Thank you* was not a phrase that he often uttered (needless praise was irritating), and anyone expecting an apology from the duke is likely to still be waiting for it. But there was also a sensitive side to the man that the family cherished and counted on. Though very reserved (the modern, emotionally in-touch world was too soft for his taste), his resolute actions of support revealed that he was also thoughtful—in his own particular way, of course. Extracts from letters he wrote to Princess Diana show that he was a caring influence within his family at a time when few were showing any concern for the late princess. He was not a great fan of Camilla at the time and wrote to Diana, "I cannot imagine anyone in their right mind leaving you for Camilla." There were moments, however, when he got it wrong. During discussions about whether William and Harry should walk behind Diana's coffin, it was Philip who nudged the young boys into taking on the mammoth task. "I think you should do it," he reportedly said. "If I walk, will you walk with me?" In 2017, Harry said of the traumatic experience, "I don't think any child should be asked to do that, under any circumstances."

Prince William knew that if his grandfather were still around, Andrew wouldn't have stood a chance. Without Philip there to take charge, it was a different story, so William told Gray he was ready to deal with "the Andrew problem" head-on. He just needed to coax the Queen. In the days leading up to this personal meeting, sources say the "determined" prince was unwavering in his belief that it was time to take out insurance on the Firm's biggest risk. William arranged an appointment with the Queen via Edward Young, her private secretary. Young, too, was keen for the situation to be resolved quickly and efficiently. So, in early January 2022, William met with his grandmother in her residential quarters at Windsor Castle.

Decorated in her own style with items that reflected her passions, the monarch's private living room was less of a stateroom and more of a refuge. Any visitor would struggle to miss the airy room's tall windows or the large, William Morris–style japanned cabinet filled with cherished items, trinkets, and personal photographs. It was the space where William often met his grandmother for tea when she was staying in Windsor, and also a forbidden play spot for him and Harry when they were children. This time, however, it was all business, and the two discussed the Andrew situation for more than an hour, according to sources.

Later that day, the Queen spoke on the phone with Charles, who was in Scotland at the time. The monarch made it clear to her eldest son that it was time to strip his brother of all his titles and duties. A family source described her decision as a "genuinely sad" moment for the monarch and another "gut punch" to the family, particularly coming on the heels of Prince Philip's death. The Queen was distraught over how the media and the public had so quickly turned against Andrew, but, now aware that more drastic action needed to be taken, she was decisive. Charles, on the other hand, didn't want any part of it. On the phone call, he agreed with his mother that now was the time to act, but he left the tough work to her and William. Of course, this wasn't the narrative that aides at Clarence House were cooking up for the press. They soon spun the story that Charles and William acted together from the outset. They were, as many reports cited, in "lockstep" with each other concerning the Andrew predicament. When I spoke to a Charles source regarding this, they said the notion that William took charge of the situation was "off the mark" and part of a personal agenda. "William, or his staff, I should say, will always be quick to play up his efforts," they said. "There is an almost frenzied push for William to be seen as ready for the throne, despite an entire generation coming beforehand."

Two days after Andrew's aforementioned fateful meeting with his mother at Windsor Castle, Buckingham Palace issued a statement, confirming that the Duke of York was to lose his military roles and his ability to use the "His Royal Highness" styling before his title, and be stripped of all remaining royal patronages. They would, said the media release, all be "returned" to the Queen. I had follow-up questions for the Palace communications team: Why didn't the Queen take away his Order of the Garter role? And would the British taxpayers continue to cover his security? "Those will have to be directed to his private office," the press secretary responded. "Private office" meaning "he's not one of us anymore." They wanted nothing more to do with him.

It took them long enough. By this point, Andrew's relationship with Jeffrey Epstein had been in the press for more than a decade. "Andrew has never felt the need to explain himself," said a York family acquaintance. "Entitled, spoiled, and immature. No one in his life has ever called him out on anything, including Fergie [the Duchess of York]." Despite divorcing in 1996, Andrew and his ex-wife have been living together since 2006. Though they have never publicly said much about their unique living arrangement, the pair—who multiple sources confirm are not romantically involved—are closer than ever. Living under the same roof is also about convenience, family, and support, said a source. Plus, both have experienced financial issues, so cohabitating at his cavernous Royal Lodge home (on a seventy-five-year lease for just £250 a week) is a cost-effective arrangement. Andrew, said sources, was Sarah's "rock" after her breast cancer diagnosis and mastectomy in the summer of 2023. Sarah, who now cares for the late Queen's corgis, Muick and Sandy, told *Good Morning Britain* in April 2023, "[Andrew] is a kind, good man, and I think the spotlight needs to come off of him and let him get on with his life to rebuild."

Easier said than done. When Epstein pleaded guilty in June 2008 to procuring a child for prostitution and was sentenced to eighteen months in prison, most of the American financier's horrified friends jumped ship. Andrew, however, stuck around. A former business associate of Epstein's told me that his first arrest was the breaking point for most people who socialized with him: "My wife and I cut things off there and then, almost all of us did . . . Andrew didn't. That was a stupid decision and one, for the life of me, I can't understand. No one can be *that* stupid."

But they were. Despite Andrew's claims that he saw Epstein only once after the horrific conviction (with the "sole purpose" of saying it would be "inappropriate" to be remain friends), court documents reveal that the pair kept in regular touch. In June 2010, while Epstein was still under house arrest—and federal officials had at this point identified thirty-six girls, some as young as fourteen years old, who had been groomed and abused by the businessman—Andrew allegedly visited the criminal's Florida mansion for lunch. Then, six months later, after Epstein's controversial plea deal, Andrew raced to his pal's side, where the pair were photographed deep in conversation in New York's Central Park. On that particular trip, he spent four days at his friend's Upper East Side mansion, the largest in Manhattan. American media called this residence the "house of horrors," where taxidermy animals and sexually explicit artwork adorned the walls (years later police seized drawers filled with CDs containing child porn), but for Andrew this was a home away from home.

On the duke's first night in town, Epstein threw a huge party for his guest of honor, hosting a soiree full of marquee names and celebrities, including director Woody Allen, comedian Chelsea Handler, and news anchors Katie Couric and Charlie Rose. That week, Epstein's former pal and famous literary agent, John Brockman, spotted Andrew receiving foot massages from two young Russian models. In fact, for the entirety of his stay, the entrance to Epstein's Seventy-First Street townhouse was a revolving door of young women. "To Andrew, he never saw Epstein as a bad man . . . The side of him he knew was a kind, intelligent friend and—just like he ignores tabloid rumors about his own family and friends—he did the same when it came to what people said about [Epstein]," a source close to Andrew told me in late 2021.

These were way more than rumors, but Andrew defended his decision to keep Epstein as a friend during his infamous *Newsnight* interview in 2019. The result was a mess, to say the least. The show was full of difficult-to-watch moments as Andrew evaded and parried from the moment he opened his mouth. There were his laughable excuses: he couldn't have been at a nightclub with Virginia Giuffre because he was at a Pizza Express an hour outside of London with his daughters earlier that evening; and that it was impossible for him to have "sweat[ed] all over" Giuffre, due to a post–Falklands War medical condition that prevents him from perspiring. And then there was his complete lack of empathy toward Epstein's victims, evident in his tap-dancing answers to journalist Emily Maitlis's questions. "A ridiculous, misguided, pathetic attempt at fixing his own damaged public image that absolutely blew up in his face," a senior Buckingham Palace courtier vented. "He went in completely unprepared and came out even more of a fool."

Before the public's allergic reaction to the interview finally registered, Andrew bizarrely thought it was a personal win. "This is how far removed he is from reality," a source said. "He thought it did him good." After the interview's taping, Andrew marveled about how well it went to a flabbergasted set crew. The show's producer, Sam McAlister, revealed, "He was in an invidious situation of his own making, but . . . he wanted to vindicate himself, like most interviewees. Everybody thinks they are going to give a good interview."

This lack of awareness and basic common sense is partly why he got sucked into Epstein's world in the first place. Easily influenced and a total pushover when it came to those with impressive credentials or attractive business propositions, Andrew saw not just a mentor in Epstein—whose estate was valued at approximately $600 million—but someone who could help him make wealthy friends and influence others. It was a mutually beneficial relationship: while Andrew used Epstein for his financial connections, Epstein leveraged his connection with the prince to enjoy the trappings and clout that supplements a friendship with a senior royal. Andrew regularly invited Epstein to royal residences and events. Pictures of Epstein and his now imprisoned pimp and sidekick, Ghislaine Maxwell, at one of the Queen's private log cabins during a 1999 Balmoral vacation are proof that he made it as far into the inner sanctum of the royal family as possible. "Within a year [of meeting],

Andrew and Epstein had developed their own strong friendship," said a family source. "He always had a peculiar group of friends, so nothing really stood out in the early days . . . What was strange was that no one told him to distance himself when all the news came out about what Epstein had done."

It was during the early part of this alliance when, on a night out in March 2001, a forty-one-year-old Prince Andrew met the seventeen-year-old Virginia Roberts, just one year after she, too, was swept up into Epstein's world. As a runaway teen and child sex abuse victim, Giuffre was already vulnerable by the time Maxwell offered her a job—at just sixteen—to work for Epstein as a traveling masseuse, providing massages and sexual services for the multi-millionaire and his business associates. For two years, it was a life of private jets, manipulation, and, as Giuffre has later described, a devastating time of being passed around Epstein's associates "like a platter of fruit." In 2007, the FBI identified her as one of Epstein's victims and, after six months of hesitation, she agreed to cooperate with their investigation. Two years later she anonymously filed a lawsuit as "Jane Doe 102" against Epstein, and, in 2010, she shared the details about her encounters with both Andrew and Epstein with the public. She then spoke with the *Mail on Sunday* for a piece that also disclosed a photograph of herself and Prince Andrew and Maxwell at Maxwell's house.

By now, you most likely can recall the image from memory—standing at the top of a stairwell, Andrew has his arm wrapped tightly around a young-looking Giuffre as they both smile for the camera with Maxwell grinning in the background. Without the backstory it looks fairly innocent, but with the gaps filled in, it's stomach churning. Those few who remain in Andrew's corner have long denied the picture's credibility (which has only been seen in the press as a photograph of a photograph). In 2019, Andrew instructed trusted aides to tell friendly journalists at the *Telegraph* and *Evening Standard* that some shadowy figure created the image using digital trickery (the girth of his fingers being the dead giveaway, apparently). Even

Maxwell, who previously admitted the image taken at her London home was genuine, now says (from her prison cell, where she's serving twenty years for child sex trafficking and other offenses) that it is fake. This is all distraction and fabrication, of course—the FBI had already confirmed the authenticity of the four-by-six original, noting that the time stamp on the back of the print proved Giuffre had it developed in a store near her former home in Florida, three days after she returned from her 2001 trip to London.

After the picture made its rounds in the media, Andrew still hoped it would all just go away, knowing Epstein had the means to pressure and stall. A coterie of aggressive lawyers working for Epstein dissuaded some mainstream media outlets from covering the story through various means: a five-figure donation to a *New York Times* reporter's preferred nonprofit at one end of the spectrum, and a severed cat's head in the front yard of *Vanity Fair*'s editor in chief at the other. The royal institution also did its bit to protect Andrew, spending a small (private) fortune on lawyers to work with the prince on his initial defense and making sure certain communication aides were prepped to handle the world's interest. Giuffre, said close sources, was "fearful" about going against one of the Queen's children. "She felt afraid about speaking up," said a source. "It was drilled into her that bad things would happen if you do, that you don't want to get on the wrong side of the institution. And indeed, she was reminded that, like Diana, it could turn on you."

In 2015, Buckingham Palace officials warned media outlets that "any suggestion of impropriety with underage minors is categorically untrue." It's worth noting that the age of consent in Britain, New York, and the U.S. Virgin Islands—the three locations Giuffre alleges Andrew sexually assaulted her—are sixteen, seventeen, and eighteen, respectively. Buckingham Palace still had a shield up for Andrew in 2019, telling journalists, including myself, "It is emphatically denied that the Duke of York had any form of sexual contact or relationship with Virginia [Giuffre]. Any claim to the contrary is false and without foundation." But Giuffre confidently countered, "He denies that it ever happened and he's going to keep denying that it ever happened, but he knows the truth and I know the truth." To this day, Andrew repudiates all allegations.

The journalists who wanted to report further details about Epstein and Prince Andrew also found it difficult to do so. During her time as a *Good Morning America* anchor on ABC, journalist Amy Robach conducted an hour-long exclusive interview with Giuffre that never aired. "The Palace found out that we had her whole allegations about Prince Andrew and threatened us a million different ways," an unguarded Robach admitted during a hot-miked off-air clip that mysteriously surfaced online (supposedly leaked by an "ABC insider" in November 2019 to far-right activist group Project Veritas). "We were so afraid that we wouldn't be able to interview Kate and Will . . . I tried for three years to get it on to no avail." Robach backtracked on her comments a year later while still working for the network, explaining, "I was caught in a private moment of frustration. I was upset that an important interview I had conducted with Virginia Roberts didn't air because we could not obtain sufficient corroborating evidence to meet ABC's editorial standards about her allegations." It would be wrong to assume that this might have been all the work of the Palace (sources at ABC News, where I continue to work as a royal contributor, have said that approaches were also made by lawyers acting for Epstein), but it's impossible to discount this aspect of the story. Even after Giuffre filed a defamation suit against Ghislaine Maxwell months later, putting many of her further allegations officially into the public domain, Robach's interview remained unseen.

A former Buckingham Palace staff member who worked with the Duke of York claimed that many inside and close to the Firm spent "at least four years" actively nudging trusted or easily influenced members of the press away from negative Andrew stories, claiming that "those who could be convinced it wasn't worth dealing with all the legal issues were helped in other ways." This certainly tamed some of the coverage and criticism of Andrew. And soon enough the British media's obsession with the Sussexes pushed Andrew's disgraces further back into the pages of some papers. It's also impossible to ignore that retrograde cultural attitudes around young women and girls being taken advantage of by older white men in power have also played a role in how the story has (and hasn't) been covered.

Still, no amount of media massaging could soften the blow that came from Giuffre's August 2021 decision to launch a civil lawsuit in New York against Prince Andrew, accusing him of "sexual assault and intentional infliction of emotional distress" and seeking unspecified damages. Andrew wanted to fight it. "This is a marathon, not a sprint, and the duke will continue to defend himself against these claims," one of his legal representatives told me at the time. Added a royal source, "He felt there were enough holes in Virginia's story to knock her down. But there was pressure from others [within the institution]" to steer clear of a legal battle and the media circus that would accompany it, especially if it made its way to a courtroom.

It was time to settle, no matter the cost. These pressures primarily came from Sir Edward Young, the late Queen's private secretary; Sir Clive Alderton, Charles's private secretary; and Sir Michael Stevens, the Keeper of the Privy Purse and the monarch's accountant. After considering this position, the Queen came around and agreed to cover the cost. The huge sum of £12 million (approximately) was paid directly to Giuffre's Victims Refuse Silence organization, a nonprofit she started in 2014 to help survivors of sexual abuse and victims of sex trafficking. Even with the rushed sale of his Swiss chalet (also bankrolled by Mummy some years earlier), Andrew didn't have the funds to settle by himself—the Queen's financial support was his only way out.

The case was settled on February 15, 2022, just before Andrew's scheduled seven-hour court-ordered deposition. Giuffre's lawyer, David Boies, explained that it "was never a case where I think he could have afforded to go to trial." He added, "[The] evidence was too strong . . . [The] photograph made it clear that he could not say he hadn't met her. People, when they start to lie, go so far and they make statements that are demonstratively untrue. He could have said, 'Yes I met her, yes I danced with her, but no, there was never any sex.' That's something that may have been hard to disprove. But when he says, 'I've never met her' and you've got that photograph . . . well."

Andrew later pushed staff and friends to inform friendly journalists that he only agreed on a settlement to ease the burden for his mother and the institution, not because he lacked confidence around proving his innocence. On the record, though, the prince stayed silent. As part of the settlement deal, both he and Giuffre agreed to refrain from any public comments regarding the case. This period conveniently encompassed the Queen's Platinum Jubilee (during which Andrew had a fortuitous case of Covid) and, by happenstance, King Charles's coronation. Before her death, the Queen told some of those close to her that she believed Andrew could eventually repair his image through philanthropic endeavors. The rest of the working family—though they predominantly believe in his innocence—would beg to disagree, with some hoping he remains firmly in the background for their sake.

If Andrew has been attempting his mother's style of repair, however, he's off to a strange start. In June 2020, he sent pizzas (not from Pizza Express) and boxes of dates to a charity that helps human trafficking and sexual exploitation victims. Though few want him to, Andrew hopes to one day ramp up his charitable efforts to creep back into the public eye. "William finds this quite extraordinary. The man is a ticking time bomb!" said a Kensington Palace source.

The bomb started ticking years ago. Prior to his Epstein troubles and his official defrocking, Andrew had already proved he was a one-man PR disaster in the making, even as a sideshow to Charles's 1990s humiliations and front-page troubles. Described as an inveterate "tits and bums man" with a penchant for "schoolboy humor" by a close associate, the "Playboy Prince," also previously known in the tabloid press as "Randy Andy," went on a bit of a tear after his divorce from Fergie. Andrew caused a stir because of his associations with a string of glamorous women, including actress Angie Everhart and model Caprice (who, on a 2000 date to Buckingham Palace, Andrew let sit on the Queen's throne). A model ex-girlfriend he dated in the 2010s told me, "I liked him. He's charming, funny, and quick to put his foot in his mouth. Pretty women and money . . . those are the things that he lives for."

That love of money and finer things resulted in a history of poor judgment firmly rooted in debts and financial woes. His fondness for despots, which he fully took advantage of while touring the world as the United Kingdom Trade & Investment special envoy, was also another weakness. At the 2008 World Economic Forum in Egypt, Andrew was heavily criticized for dining with Kazakhstan's autocratic president, Nursultan Nazarbayev, a controversial figure who headed up a family and group of cronies who had just forked over more than a billion dollars for properties in New York, Switzerland, and London. Palace aides initially defended Andrew for "just doing his job," but the chorus of support quieted down when it was reported that Nazarbayev's son-in-law, Kazak billionaire Timur Kulibayev, generously paid $5.6 million over the asking price for Andrew and Fergie's abandoned and collapsing mansion, Sunninghill Park, as a favor.

Then there was the story about convicted gun smuggler Tarek Kaituni, who gifted Andrew's daughter Princess Beatrice a $37,000 necklace for her eighteenth birthday after he and Andrew socialized during a 2008 visit to Tunisia. That same year Andrew dined in Libya with dictator Muammar Gaddafi, a man responsible for the Lockerbie terrorist bombing, among a litany of other crimes and human rights abuses. A year after this trip, the United Kingdom picked up a lucrative oil deal in the region.

Andrew carried on with this brazen behavior and willingness to meet with oppressive regimes long after he was forced to resign as envoy. In 2014, reports surfaced that Andrew was planning a trip to Azerbaijan to meet with billionaire tyrant leader Ilham Aliyev, despite the fact that Aliyev was accused of stealing elections and violently persecuting journalists and political opponents. Sources initially claimed it was a onetime meeting but, as it turned out, the pair had met in secret eleven times prior.

There are believed to be dozens, if not hundreds, more unwise connections to uncover from Andrew's years in the role. Just don't expect to find answers at Britain's Department for Business and Trade. While records of who joined Andrew on his decade of international travel for the government division should be kept on file, Freedom of Information requests hit a brick wall (believe me, I tried). The Foreign Office claim that the documents won't be available until 2065.

Blurring the lines between his personal and professional lives is a repeated pattern for Andrew. His ten years as an envoy saw him live life large, with "travel expenses" and security costing taxpayers an estimated £22 million. With little regard for the public purse, Andrew would settle for nothing less than five-star hotels (the embassies on offer were rarely good enough for him) and first-class or private flights. Up until 2011, he also used his trade missions to plug the work of his friends and associates. According to a trove of emails, internal documents, and regulatory filings, the duke acted as an unofficial "door opener" for financier David Rowland and his secretive bank for the super-rich in Luxembourg, Banque Havilland S.A. Thanks to Andrew's royal connections and envoy role, he was able to pitch the bank's services to potential clients from the ranks of the high-net-worth elite. Rowland even brought Andrew on an official visit to China. In return he had access to a Bombardier Global Express jet and a virtually limitless credit card—Rowland even paid off a £1.5 million loan Andrew owed to his bank.

Now that King Charles *finally* cut off the Duke of York from his £249,000 annual allowance from the Duchy of Lancaster in April 2023, money—particularly how to earn it—is still very much on his mind. Until he figures that out, his big brother continues to provide private financial support. Charles is even footing his seven-figure annual private security bill—a move that surprised Prince Harry after Charles had no problem cutting him off from all financial aid and paid protection when he stepped away from his royal role.

But the close association may end up coming back to bite the King and the monarchy. With the gag order from her settlement with Andrew now expired, it's just a matter of time before the royal family hears from Giuffre again. In early 2023, the thirty-nine-year-old signed a major deal to publish her first memoir. And, though Epstein may be dead, stories from the past—including his friendship with Andrew—continue to trickle out. Still, with Charles's brotherly support, sources say Andrew has been quietly focusing on how to clear his name once and for all, and that discussions with his legal team about contesting his settlement with Giuffre have already taken place. Giuffre's lawyer, David Boies, finds this hard to believe. "He would just be putting himself back into the same dangerous position again, facing the same deposition," he said with a laugh. "But if he wants to go through all of that, his lawyers have my number!"

While King Charles has, so far, shown no inclination of conclusively stopping his support of his wayward brother, Andrew would be foolish to think that William will unquestionably support his uncle in the same way. It's fair to say, the next King is the one in the family who inherited Prince Philip's assertiveness when it comes to protecting the Crown. Until then, though, Andrew remains a wild card and one that can still inflict considerable damage to the monarchy. A source close to the family said, "One would be foolish to assume that Andrew won't bring further shame . . . it's his specialty. For his brother—the *King*, for Christ's sake—to be blindly supporting him, despite the great risk he poses to this entire thing, is crazy."

# 7

# Race and the Royals

### Institutional Bigotry and Denial

———·———

*Perhaps you notice how the denial is so often
the preface to the justification.*
—Christopher Hitchens, *Hitch 22: A Memoir*

*For while we have our eyes on the future, history has its eyes on us.*
—Amanda Gorman, "The Hill We Climb"

You could practically hear the eye-rolling in her voice. "Well . . .
we could already guess what someone like *her* would be like.
I saw it coming from *miles* away." At a March 2021 meeting in her
Kensington Palace apartment, Princess Michael of Kent—wife of
the Queen's first cousin Prince Michael of Kent—couldn't stop herself from indulging in gossip with an aide about Meghan. Princess
Michael has never been much of a fan of Prince Harry's wife, and as
she busily chattered on about the Sussexes' prime-time Oprah Winfrey interview, she let her drawling emphasis on certain words do
all the talking. The seventy-seven-year-old former interior designer
had just spent most of the week with publishing contacts to discuss
a proposal she was working on at the time, so she spoke freely and

with confidence when she said: "[Meghan's] made it *all* about race because that's all everyone does these days."

Her remarks didn't surprise those within earshot, including my source. This is the same royal who, at a 2017 family Christmas lunch, arrived at her first meeting with biracial Meghan Markle wearing a blackamoor brooch pinned to her coat lapel. Blinded by unconscious bias or just callously indifferent, it's hard to say, but she certainly failed to recognize the cultural insensitivity of wearing a brooch featuring a highly exoticized bust of a Black man in servant regalia, much less how others might react to such a thoughtless choice. She later apologized for the indiscretion (though never directly to Meghan), but, according to sources, the princess still shrugs and wrinkles her lip when the subject comes up. "I don't think she particularly cared," a senior royal source told me.

Princess Michael wasn't alone in nonchalantly deciding the resulting outcry over her blackamoor accessory, a style first popularized in the seventeenth century, was "over the top." The same source revealed that "some in the family rushed to comfort her afterward. They didn't feel the [media] onslaught was fair." Meghan, I'm told, did not receive any such overtures. But then, failing to recognize racial or cultural insensitivities is a common theme among certain members of the royal family and a number of those working for and around them. This was but yet another example of ugly, systematic racism bubbling to the top.

During my years covering the royals I have regularly been surprised by the Palace's blasé attitude when it comes to anything to do with race, racism, or the issues that impact those from minority backgrounds. After Minneapolis police officers murdered George Floyd and the resurgence of the American-born Black Lives Matter (BLM) movement spawned international protests against systemic, racially motivated police brutality, unrest hit the streets of London in May 2020. A global civil rights issue was forcing change around the world, but the royal family chose to completely ignore it.

As often as I emailed or phoned the Buckingham Palace communications team (more than weekly during the height of the BLM marches), my requests for on- or off-the-record guidance on whether we may see family members acknowledge this hugely important moment went noticeably unanswered—they responded to other queries I had, just not that one. The Palace famously stays away from anything it considers political, but unlike the political intricacies involved with the movement in the United States, BLM support in Britain simply meant standing up to and against racism. Leaders, activists, and public figures in the United Kingdom all spoke out on the issue (as did other royals in Europe), so the British royals' silence—which followed almost four years of racially charged coverage of their only biracial family member—was hard to ignore.

With Covid still gripping the country, face time with Palace aides was practically nil and almost all engagements were held virtually. I didn't receive any answers about the BLM movement until meeting with a senior aide at a hotel bar in August 2021. "We didn't [reply] because it felt like you were trying to get a headline, quite honestly," they told me. "You would have turned [the family not saying something] into a story." It *was* a story, I argued. To me, it was bizarre that an institution that supposedly works for and strives to reflect modern and diverse Britain—one that now includes a biracial family member who has endured years of racial attacks since joining—couldn't see the importance of speaking out against racism.

The aide added that an op-ed I wrote in my role as royal editor for *Harper's Bazaar* on the Sussexes' allegations surrounding family concerns over the skin color of their son, Archie, was too "pointed" for the family's liking. Titled "Stifling, Toxic, and Racist—Duchess Meghan Never Had a Chance," it underscored the outdated posturing and institutional prejudices that forced Harry and Meghan to make a change. After all the deafening silence on race issues, I wanted it to be pointed. "You called us white supremacists," the aide whispered to me with more than a little exasperation. This wasn't entirely accurate. Here's what I wrote: "If it's not considered appropriate to acknowledge racism or racial ignorance when aimed at a mixed-raced senior royal, then how should the 54 countries of the Commonwealth and its predominantly Black, Brown, and mixed population feel about the realm's figurehead belonging to an institution that claims to celebrate 'diversity' but in practice appears to uphold white supremacy?"

---

But let's pull back for a little history lesson and take a look at the big picture, as ugly and uncomfortable as it is. In the United Kingdom, racism takes a different shape to the United States and other parts of the world. Although sometimes adopting pernicious form in economic policies and political dog-whistling, racism in America, for the most part, is not hidden. It often loudly announces itself in Trumpism, police brutality, the education system, deep-rooted white privilege, and viral "Karen" videos online. In Britain, racism furtively shape-shifts, and it lurks in the shadows as casually accepted discrimination, coded language, and systemic oppression, often revealing itself in conversations about class, crusty colonialist thinking, and well-worn stereotypes. You don't have to dig deep into those aspects of U.K. life that many consider traditional and quintessentially British to unearth some racist roots—post-Brexit, the mawkish Union Jack and St. George's Cross flag-waving often conjures up a yearning for the golden age of empire.

It's often so undercover that many Brits will quickly and confidently tell you, "This is not a racist country," and that Britain is the least racist place in Europe. The latter half is technically true. A 2019 European Union report on race and ethnic disparities found that an average of 21 percent of people of African descent in the United Kingdom had reported or experienced racial harassment in the last five years—in Finland, for comparison, the number is 63 percent. Germany and Italy stood at 41 percent.

But being the "least" racist country doesn't mean there isn't racism. Black women in the United Kingdom are statistically four times more likely to die during childbirth, largely due to wider cultural and structural biases, and young Black men are nineteen times more likely to be stopped and searched by police. The number of non-white people who died from Covid was 50 percent more than their white counterparts, due to factors such as type of work and the toll that living in the crosshairs of racism takes on the body (it has been linked to heart disease, obesity, diabetes, high blood pressure, and kidney or liver disease). It's a similar contrast when applying for jobs. On average, people from minority ethnic backgrounds still have to send 60 percent more applications to get a positive response from an employer compared to a white person of British origin, according to a University of Oxford study.

Many of the issues affecting people of color in the United Kingdom originated in the heart of the British establishment—the institution of the monarchy. It was Queen Elizabeth I who legitimized slavery in 1562 when she allowed naval commander John Hawkins to kidnap Africans in his ship's cargo hold and sell them in the Caribbean. And, during the reign of King Charles II, the Crown financed the African slave trade by founding and maintaining the Royal African Company of England, a trading operation that shipped more enslaved African men, women, and children than any other single institution during the entire period of the transatlantic slave trade. In 1712, Queen Anne landed an exclusive contract for the British nation to provide enslaved people for the Spanish West Indies for thirty years. When the government later sold the contract, Anne received a 20 percent cut of a £7.5 million deal, which equals approximately £355 million in 2023.

By the time British Parliament abolished the slave trade in 1807, more than twelve and a half million enslaved people had been transported from Africa to the Americas and Caribbean. Twenty-six years later, the government paid out a total of £20 million (the equivalent of £17 billion today) to compensate around three thousand British *slave owners* for the loss of "human property." The freed, formerly enslaved didn't receive a penny, nor has the government disbursed any monetary reparations to their descendants.

The murderous and destructive impact of the royal family's role in slavery is rarely covered in British schools to this day, but the remnants of it are all around us, from the man-made canals running through the towns and cities of England and Wales (which transported goods cultivated by enslaved people, including indigo, tobacco, rice, cotton, and sugar) to the striking civic and commercial buildings built with money from the commodities that enslaved people produced. And then there are the dozens of statues confidently associated with the transatlantic slave trade that still stand tall across the country. The sculpture of the political figure and slave owner William Beckford, for example, remains in London's Guildhall, despite the fact he made his name and fortune on the back of the slave trade. To address the BLM protests, City of London officials decided to "retain and explain" the statue. A plaque next to Lord Beckford now "contextualizes" the life of a man who owned fourteen Jamaican sugar plantations and approximately three thousand enslaved Africans.

The history of slavery also explains certain attitudes toward immigrants and foreigners that still persist. When King Charles II financed the African slave trade, the justification of the colonial project was validated by the notion that, other than the West, the rest of the world was corrupt and backward. It was this reasoning—and the widely pushed rhetoric of Black and Brown people as barbarians that accompanied it—that introduced much of the racism and "otherism" that still poisons today's culture. This type of exceptionalism is a seam that runs deep through Britain's politics. Case in point: Brexit and the narrative surrounding refugees, asylum seekers, and migrants (particularly those who are not from the fair-skinned Ukraine). Of course, these policies do not speak for an entire nation.

Compared to other parts of Europe, Britain has managed to grow into a diverse and more tolerant country. But while racial prejudices and learned behaviors are still deeply ingrained into British culture, a lot of it is subconscious.

On my travels with the royals to former British colonies like Singapore and India, I've had the opportunity to talk with Palace aides about the monarchy and race. Almost reflexively, the responses dance around the same theme—that it's unfair to lump the weight of the colonial past on the current crop of family members. They are simply people born into the institution they serve and into a history that was determined long before they entered this world, one senior official told me. Myopic at best, willfully ignoring the issue at worst, this position glosses over the fact that the monarchy they represent—one that emphasizes bloodlines and hereditary power and was built on the backs of others—still profits from untaxed slave-era inheritances. A lot of the £652 million estate inherited by King Charles from the Queen, all untaxed, can be traced back to the slave trade and empire.

And the response to all this? Resolute silence. The family has had plenty of opportune moments to publicly engage in conversations about their past, but instead we have seen a herculean, strategic effort to avoid it. At a 2021 ceremony to mark the transition of Barbados from a constitutional monarchy under Queen Elizabeth II to a self-governing parliamentary republic with a new president, Charles became the first royal to touch on the topic. He declared that the "appalling atrocity of slavery" had "forever stain[ed] our history." But what followed was not an apology for the monarchy's role in the "darkest days of our past," but rote platitudes about how the country's journey had brought Barbadians to "this moment not as your destination, but as a vantage point from which you can survey a new horizon." Charles offered little remorse on the institution's behalf but seized the moment to "reaffirm . . . the close and trusted partnership" between Barbados and Britain. The elephant in the room, of course, was this was Barbados's moment to cast off the label of "Little England," and finally sever ties with the country that turned it into a slave society. And everyone knew it. After the ceremony, protest organizer David Denny, general secretary for the Caribbean Movement for Peace and Integration, told reporters that Charles "shouldn't be here at all" and that the country should ask the royal family to pay reparations.

With much of the public ill at ease with the royal family's ties to the dark history of slavery, the Firm should be doing more than vaguely admitting there is an ugly past. The family's inability to offer a head-on admission that issues to do with race still linger in the corners of the present-day institution is disingenuous, particularly after Harry spoke so candidly about his own unconscious bias in his memoir and in interviews around the book's publication. Vile prejudices are not ancient history for the family. Let's take a minute to recall Prince Philip's comments about "slitty-eyed" Chinese people, the moment he told the traditionally dressed president of Nigeria that he looked "ready for bed," and the time he asked a group of indigenous people if they still "throw spears at each other" (lines that the British media routinely dismissed as "gaffes" or "quips"). The Queen Mother also had a history of making insensitive remarks (she once told a lady-in-waiting that "the Africans just don't know how to govern themselves . . . what a pity we're not still looking after them"), and Prince Charles thought nothing of nicknaming a South Asian friend "Sooty" because he thought his dark skin supposedly looked like soot. And lest we forget, the Duke of Windsor's disturbing friendship with Adolf Hitler and the infamous images of Elizabeth II as a young, no doubt innocent girl giving the Nazi salute—an image the institution is still desperate to bury. The royal family spent much of the twentieth century dealing with, and often trying to cover up, race scandals.

And the twenty-first century has, so far, been much of the same. From Princess Michael of Kent yelling at Black diners in America to "go back to the colonies" (she later defended herself against accusations of racism, declaring, "I'm not a racist—I even pretended to be a half caste") to Prince Andrew's casual slurs (in 2012 he allegedly used the n-word while talking about a senior political aide to Prime Minister David Cameron), and even Prince Harry's own past, which saw the royal caught on video in 2009 calling fellow Sandhurst military cadet Ahmed Raza Khan "rag-head" and "Paki," the House of Windsor may never talk about racism, but their prejudices—conscious or not—have often been on display and speak volumes.

Behind the scenes it's no different, if not worse. In 2001, Elizabeth Burgess, a Black secretary of ten years at Highgrove, told an employment tribunal how Prince Charles's valet Michael Fawcett called her a "fucking n***** typist" in 1996. The tribunal ruled the claim against Burgess as unproven and Charles went on to promote Fawcett to senior valet, but it should have been an opportunity for the Palace to raise their awareness level as a signal that they are listening. It would be careless not to mention the 1968 memo against hiring "coloured immigrants or foreigners" to a number of important roles at Buckingham Palace. Documents in the British National Archives reveal that, at a time when government ministers introduced laws making it illegal to refuse work to an individual on the grounds of their race or ethnicity, the Queen's former chief financial manager informed civil servants that it "was not, in fact, the practice to appoint coloured immigrants or foreigners" to clerical roles in the royal household, although they were permitted to work as domestic servants. It's unknown when the ban was lifted (Buckingham Palace still refuses to engage in conversations about the matter), though records on racial backgrounds of employees from the 1990s do show that the institution hired individuals from ethnic minorities for previously unavailable roles.

"I would be lying if I said it's not a difficult environment to be a person of color," a non-white member of royal household staff told me on the condition of anonymity. "I have not witnessed outright, explicit racism but I have certainly experienced, and seen others experience, microaggressions and prejudice at work. This place still has a long way to go when it comes to *everyone* working here being able to feel completely comfortable." A former member of staff, who worked for more than two members of the royal family during their tenure at the Palace, said, "The ignorance and casual racism is as bad as you think it is. It felt like another era sometimes."

I, too, have experienced and witnessed some of that ignorance and bias. Like the time a seasoned aide who—commenting on my clear English accent—told me, "I never expected you to speak the way you do." Or the staff member who casually called a less developed part of London we were visiting on a royal engagement "the ghetto." Or the senior courtier who hollered, "Oh my God. What a legend!" when they heard that a photographer had commented that Meghan should "be more Black and wear some African garb . . . let her Afro out" at an engagement linked to Nelson Mandela.

A Palace spokesperson previously declined to comment on the views of past employees but admitted to me that there is still "much work to be done." The work to be done is evident in the stubborn avoidance around the issue, even when incidents provide them with perfect opportunities to make amends. Whether it was Lady Susan Hussey's display of racial ignorance toward Sistah Space's charity founder Ngozi Fulani, or the misogynoir-laden bile from *The Sun*'s columnist Jeremy Clarkson, who wrote that Meghan should be "paraded naked through the streets of every town in Britain while the crowds . . . throw lumps of excrement at her," their continued silence is deafening and, perhaps more tellingly, exposes some of the institution's noxious ways and means. Days before the former *Top Gear* host's acerbic rant (which prompted Amazon Prime Video to decline a contract renewal with Clarkson and cost him a presenting gig on ITV's iteration of *Who Wants to Be a Millionaire?*), Camilla, the Queen Consort, was hobnobbing with him at a Christmas party in central London. The pair consider each other dear friends, and, despite public pressure on Camilla to condemn his column and sexually violent language, she remained quiet on the issue. She wouldn't, I was told by a Palace source, "be wading into any culture wars."

Several weeks later, Camilla gave an impassioned defense of free speech and the right of writers to express themselves at a Clarence House event for her Queen's Reading Room book club. Her words followed news that some offensive or outdated terms had been altered or removed in the latest British editions of *Charlie and the Chocolate Factory*, *Matilda*, and other books by Roald Dahl. But it was also considered, particularly by the right-wing press, a rallying cry in the face of the "woke, snowflake culture" she famously detests and has publicly derided.

Other failed opportunities include the number of ignored Black History months—every single one of them up until 2022. You may remember when Prince Edward and Sophie, then the Countess of Wessex, were bizarrely dispatched to pose with alpacas at a city farm in 2021 (the urban farm was marking the start of the annual Black History observance). And who can forget when the same couple was sent to Antigua and Barbuda, Saint Vincent and the Grenadines, and Saint Lucia just one month after William and Kate's flop Caribbean tour? It was the perfect opportunity to patch and correct the mistakes of the March 2022 trip but stopped way short of achieving this. The couple smiled, waved, and danced their way across the islands and in front of campaigners demanding apologies and reparatory justice. A disinterested Edward went on to offend Antigua prime minister Gaston Browne as he guffawed in response to the prime minister's suggestion that the Wessexes should use their "diplomatic influence" to help provide "reparatory justice" for Caribbean countries that were colonized by Britain. "You may not necessarily comment on this issue as you represent an institution that doesn't comment on contentious issues," said Browne. "Our civilization should understand the atrocities that took place during colonialism and slavery, and the fact that we have to bring balance by having open discussions." Edward's response? "I wasn't keeping notes, so I'm not going to give you a complete riposte. But thank you for your welcome today." Later that day the couple's scheduled trip to Grenada was canceled at the last minute following advice from the country's government. The move came just hours after new reports revealed that Britain directly owned hundreds of enslaved Black people in Grenada during the eighteenth century.

Slow progress has, unsurprisingly, not been helped by the majority of the mainstream British newspapers, who—just like the institution of the monarchy—run in the opposite direction when faced with the subject of race. The majority of the country's print media remains lenient and evasive when it comes to conversations about Britain's history of slavery or the accusations of racism in the Palace (racism *anywhere*, for that matter). Spend enough time around certain journalists or outlets and you will find yourself hearing the hard-to-believe argument that the royal family has actually *helped* eradicate the colonial ties of the past. Using an apologist's lens, some commentators have also claimed that over the years the Queen did more to "eradicate" racism while in pursuit of an equal society than any other monarch or politician in British history. There's also the belief that Queen Elizabeth II's years of traveling the length and breadth of the Commonwealth helped modernize the ties between the nations and to move past the fallout from the fall of the British Empire. "She was ahead of the curve," said historian and professor of imperial and military history at King's College London Ashley Jackson. "Unlike many of her ministers and indeed her British subjects, she discerned the need to avoid 'old' ideas of imperial loyalty or Anglo-Saxon superiority and instead to embrace new members. She emphasized the importance of common history, ideas, and values—theoretically shared by the diverse people of the Commonwealth, even if not by their leaders."

And while, yes, the Queen did oversee a decolonization process that played out around the world, she also took her colonial role seriously, sending the following message to "peoples of the British Commonwealth Empire" while still a princess in 1947: "I declare before you all that my whole life, whether it be long or short, shall be devoted to your service and to the service of our great imperial family to which we all belong." That imperial family was, of course, almost exclusively white—its prosperity secured by disposable Black and Brown lives.

When historian and professor David Olusoga claimed on the Sussexes' *Harry & Meghan* Netflix series that the palaces are still filled with "racist imagery," a number of royal commentators rushed to exonerate the monarchy. "Clearly they have never been [to the palaces]," one ranted. But when you look for yourself, the imagery is irrefutably noticeable. Though the royal art collection has more than 7,500 works, it was seventeenth-century Dutch landscape painter Aelbert Cuyp's *The N***o Page* that hung on the wall of William and Kate's formal drawing room at Kensington Palace when President Barack Obama and First Lady Michelle Obama visited in April 2016. The *Mail*'s resident art critic (yes, they have one!) praised the choice, suggesting that the image "featuring a black servant boy . . . would particularly appeal to a History of Art graduate such as Kate." But the critic failed to point out the giant lamp and plant pot that were hastily plonked in front of the 1660 painting to obscure the brass plate featuring the painting's offensive title. I was one of two journalists covering that private engagement, and at the time, Kensington Palace was keen for the art incident to go unreported. Having inside access to the engagements (which, unlike members of the British media–only royal rota, is not guaranteed to any members of U.S. press), I was being careful not to be cut out and regrettably agreed to exclude the incident from my otherwise positive coverage of the meeting.

Take a peek into Camilla's Ray Mill House in Wiltshire, and you can't miss the giant blackamoor statue in the entrance hall—a four-foot muscular Black man holding a lightbulb and lampshade high into the sky. A Palace source says it has been removed "in recent years." It was a similar tale for blackamoor sconces hanging on the walls at Clarence House. When the Google Arts & Culture platform gave the world a look inside Charles's London residence in 2018, eagle-eyed netizens spotted the offending items and officials quickly took them down (both the photos and from the residence).

Removing offending objects are steps in the right direction, but they don't go nearly far enough—many more symbols of slavery, whether in art or jewelery, remain in royal households and in public view. The Royal Collection Trust published a catalog that featured more than forty uncensored uses of racist slurs, including the n-word, in its artifact descriptions. It took complaints over fifteen years before the Trust finally removed *Ancient and Modern Gems and Jewels* from circulation in July 2023. And, despite calls from campaigners for a redesign, one of Britain's highest-honor medals bestowed by King Charles to ambassadors and diplomats for distinguished service still features a depiction of St. Michael, a blue-eyed white angel, standing on the neck of Satan, portrayed as a chained Black man.

More glaringly, looted wealth is visible everywhere. The Koh-i-Noor diamond in the crown last worn by the Queen Mother has only belonged to the monarchical institution since 1849, the year it was stolen from Lahore, India. And the Cullinan Diamond, a showpiece three-thousand-carat artifact of British imperialism incorporated into the Crown Jewels, including the sovereign's scepter, was taken from South Africa in 1905 and "gifted" to King Edward VII by the government of the British Transvaal Colony. Calls for the Koh-i-Noor's return have grown following the death of Queen Elizabeth II. And Camilla's decision to have Queen Mary's crown reset with the Cullinan III, IV, and V diamonds for her May 2023 coronation ceremony reignited questions about the royal family's involvement with the development of diamond resource exploitation in southern Africa. "If the Koh-i-Noor is a symbol of East India Company plunder imperialism in India, the Cullinan is a symbol of a different kind of British racialized settler colonialism in southern Africa—and the royal family and their literal crowns and regalia are one place where these two strains of imperialism come together," said Danielle Kinsey, a professor of history and nineteenth-century Britain at Carleton University in Ontario, Canada.

Revealingly similar to the way in which the Firm avoided the Black Lives Matter movement, Queen Elizabeth II mostly stayed mum on the progress in racial matters during the banner days of the civil rights movement. When Rev. Martin Luther King Jr. requested an audience with the monarch during a visit to London and invited her to his sermon at St. Paul's Cathedral, he received no response. When he was shot dead a little more than three years later in Memphis, though Buckingham Palace made no comment at the time, the Queen did later go on to shape the theme of her 1968 Christmas speech around brotherhood, stating, "Mankind can only find progress in friendship and cooperation." As social psychologist and author Dr. John Petrocelli pointed out, "With a world stage and powerful voice that was inherited by her very position, it could have and should have been the Queen's greatest contribution—she had nothing to lose and most everything to gain by being the real champion she is now ballyhooed to be." British activist, lawyer, and author Dr. Shola Mos-Shogbamimu added, "She was a colonial Queen—monarch of an estate which owned the biggest empire in human history. She was the head of state of the British Empire at the start of her reign. You can't divorce the Queen from the institution that she represented and the institution she represents has one of the strongest known links to the start of, and the pain of, slavery and colonialism."

In other words, it's like saying Pope Francis doesn't represent the Catholic Church.

———•———

*This* was the backdrop on which I based my comments in my aforementioned article that referenced white supremacy, and I stand by that piece today. The Palace aide who admonished me at the time said, "Your statements have huge consequences." It's why, he added, the Buckingham Palace communications team made the decision to exclude me from a media briefing about the funeral of Prince Philip shortly after that article came out (although, after kicking up a stink, the Palace did backtrack and accredit me for Windsor Castle access days later). "If you say things like that, of course you're going to be at the bottom of the list." So much for a free press, I gruffly replied.

I knew this environment, both present and historical, would make it almost impossible for Meghan to flourish in the royal system. And the signs were there even in the earliest coverage of her time in the royal orbit, when news outlets used loaded terms like *narcissistic, social climber, exotic DNA*, and *straight out of Compton* (despite her not growing up anywhere near it) both to describe her, and to establish a narrative. Just eight days after the *Sunday Express* revealed their relationship to the world on October 31, 2016, Prince Harry felt compelled to write a statement, released by his head of communications, Jason Knauf, condemning the "racial undertones" and "wave of abuse" and harassment coming from the media.

"It was something new to all of us," Knauf told me in early 2020. "Harry led the push [against that], but there were others who didn't agree." Though retrospective rumors incorrectly suggested it was his brother, Prince William, who pushed back against Harry's communication efforts, several sources have since confirmed that it was

Charles who felt taking on the papers "so aggressively" was a "terrible" idea. However, this came after the fact. Prior to the statement, Harry's father was kept completely in the dark, because his son had little faith in him to stand on the right side. "[Harry] knew Charles would try and stop him because he's so afraid of the press and damage to his own [media] relationships. Everyone involved had to keep it secret, including William," a senior Palace aide said. Sadly, it was not just his father who was disappointed in Harry's actions. Key members of staff—across all three royal households—thought Harry's "hoo-hah" (the choice phrase of the Queen's then deputy private secretary Edward Young, apparently) was much ado about nothing. Putting his foot down about paparazzi was one thing, but calling out racism in the press? The institution just couldn't see the benefit of publicly addressing the sensitive issue.

As tabloid op-eds and online hate increased, so did the level of denial from Palace aides, who claimed they couldn't really see any racism in press coverage. In the upside-down dimension, some expressed sympathy for those in the press instead. A communication staffer at Kensington Palace comforted royal correspondents whom Twitter users had accused of being racist in their articles or commentary. "I do think the Duke of Sussex and his office will bear some responsibility if a journalist is harmed as a result of that ill-judged statement," tweeted *Daily Express* royal editor Richard Palmer. "But, without naming names, I can say that one of [the Palace aides] is telling royal reporters to ignore the racism nuts." Harry, who monitored Twitter closely back then, noticed the journalist's remark. The Kensington Palace team "would much rather have the media's back than mine," he told a friend.

As the level of online abuse Meghan received increased during her burgeoning relationship with Harry, Kensington Palace struggled with the new reality of their household Instagram account getting swarmed with slurs and hate speech. "You know you can block specific key words from appearing in the comments, right?" I said to one junior aide at the time. The office was aware, they said, but one of its higher-ranking aides felt that at the time it would be "inappropriate" to start censoring comments left for a publicly funded institution. "They just don't think you can start censoring people and it's better to manually take care of anything bad." As a result, thousands of daily comments loaded with the likes of the n-word, as well as monkey, banana, or dagger emojis, steadily appeared, many of them visible for days and weeks before they were deleted. Fans and public supporters of the couple—a movement that had quickly taken on the Sussex Squad moniker—were often the ones trawling through comments and reporting offending items.

"If you'd seen the stuff that was written and you were receiving it . . . the kind of rhetoric that's online, if you don't know what I know, you would feel under threat all of the time," Neil Basu, former head of counterterrorism for London's Metropolitan Police, said. "We had teams investigating it and people have been prosecuted for those threats." Due to the tabloids' ridiculous suggestions that I was essentially an extended member of the couple's team (we'll get to that shortly), threats like the ones aimed at the duchess came my way, too—from disturbing descriptions of violent acts and graphic images, to racial slurs and warnings of physical harm at public engagements. I regularly passed all of these on to the authorities.

In March 2019, Kensington Palace finally ramped up its social media safety efforts, after turning to Twitter and Instagram's owner, Facebook, for help and dedicating a budget for online resources. "We ask that anyone engaging with our social media channels shows courtesy, kindness and respect for all other members of our social media communities," a message posted on the royal.uk website read. "We reserve the right to hide or delete comments made on our channels, as well as block users who do not follow these guidelines."

The efforts were necessary, but pretty late in the game. Meghan was just two months away from giving birth to Archie, the first multiracial child in the family. One British-based YouTube account, a channel dedicated to conspiracy theories about Meghan faking her pregnancy, among other wild tales, had even encouraged followers to try to "pop" the duchess's "moon bump" at a future public appearance. "She's living in fear . . . not just for herself but for the baby. You can't expect anyone to live like that," one of the couple's most senior staff told me at the time. But the fact that Archie faced more security threats than other royal children did not translate to additional safety measures. Hierarchy still took precedence, and as seventh in line to the throne at the time, Archie was not considered a particularly high priority. The Cambridge family had a bigger security team—a point that Harry was very aware of. "No one is thinking about the fact that my wife is biracial, my son is mixed race . . . None of this registers to anyone," Harry told an aide that summer.

In fact, minimal thought ever went into race-related issues when it came to the Sussexes. This is the same institution that suggested that Lady Susan Hussey (yes, *that* Lady Susan Hussey) help biracial Meghan acclimate to Palace life and navigate the royal system. The duchess turned down the offer, probably having already sensed that it might not be the best idea.

When Palace aides later told reporters, including myself, that they "bent over backwards" to make Meghan feel comfortable at Buckingham Palace, this included a follow-up suggestion that perhaps the Queen's Ghanaian-born household cavalry officer Lieutenant Colonel Nana Kofi Twumasi-Ankrah should be the one to help Meghan. Though a charming and intelligent man, it stood out like a sore thumb to Meghan and her friends that, due to a lack of Black or other non-white staff, let alone women, in relevant senior roles, the Palace had to turn to someone who was the Queen's attendant. "I doubt Kate was offered an equerry [for guidance]," a pal said to Meghan.

As for Harry and Meghan's wedding, aides from Charles's Clarence House office put themselves forward to help with the planning for the big day, but Harry, knowing from experience how quickly things leak, especially from his father's camp, put the kibosh on the idea. "Far too big for her boots," one of Charles's staffers—a regular *Daily Mail* source at the time—moaned about Meghan. "Who does she think she is?"

Just who does she think she is? This was a running theme throughout Meghan's time as a working royal. Here was a woman who, in the eyes of many within the institution (consciously or unconsciously), wasn't considered good enough to be part of it—be it because of her class, her family, her ethnicity, or her career history. Or maybe just because she wasn't sufficiently reverential and thankful for the opportunity, a haughty opinion that also stinks of prejudice and privilege.

"Meghan came in and did the work, but she wasn't in awe of her surroundings. It was like taking on a new job, one that came as a prerequisite with her marriage to the person she was in love with," said a close friend of the duchess. "She took it seriously, but the fact she wasn't saying, '*Wow*, this is the greatest thing on earth' made people feel like she wasn't grateful, that she didn't deserve what she had." To some at the Palace, here was a woman of color who was allowed into an entitled, exceedingly white space, so how dare she not show an abundance of gratitude. The fact that later she would choose to step away from it, essentially rejecting the hallowed space she was "lucky" enough to have entered, emerged as the sore point for many.

In the weeks that followed their May 2018 nuptials, the couple embarked on a successful seventy-six-engagement tour of Australia, New Zealand, Fiji, and Tonga. Their popularity grew so big that, according to several Palace staffers I have spoken to over the years, there was intense jealousy over the couple's growing star power among senior courtiers and other family members. "It's a

tricky place to be when you're sixth in line but up there with number one [the Queen] in terms of popularity," one of the couple's
press secretaries told me that summer. "They'll probably want to
bring them down a peg."

And so, the Palace permitted the press to do their bidding. A
month after the couple returned to England, negative stories trick-
led out. "Kicking up a stink" was the *Daily Mail*'s November 30,
2018, headline, which reported on Meghan's alleged "dictatorial"
request to place air fresheners inside St. George's Chapel before her
wedding ceremony (of course, when Kate filled Westminster Abbey
with Jo Malone for her wedding, it was "sweet"). Then the *Telegraph*
reported the now well-worn story about Meghan making Kate cry
at a bridesmaid fitting (which, not even three years later, we heard
was actually the other way around). The same paper also used a report to claim a community kitchen Meghan was working with, run
by a group of mostly Middle Eastern and North African women,
was linked to terrorism—simply based on research carried out by an
"anti-Islam" think tank that "suggested" the mosque it was housed
in may have been attended by three terror criminals a decade prior.
And there was *The Sun*'s reporting that Meghan rejected the wedding tiara the Queen offered because she preferred a different design. "What Meghan wants, Meghan gets!" Harry reportedly ranted
to the monarch's dresser, Angela Kelly. A fatuous and erroneous
story from start to finish, but it had remarkable staying power in the
press (again, never publicly denied by anyone in the Palace). A week
later, the same outlet reported that an "angry" Meghan had "bollocked" a member of Kensington Palace staff. This was around the
same time as a *Telegraph* story about the "garbage patch" Marks &
Spencer tights she berated an assistant for buying instead of a pair
from upmarket brand Wolford. Like most of these tales, this was
not true. In fact, a bemused Kensington Palace staffer even showed
me their text message exchange with Meghan, who had thanked

them for rushing out to High Street Kensington to buy tights from M&S. As the only reporter close to the people working directly with the couple at the time, it was easy for me to see the manipulation for exactly what it was. As I was completely fine with calling it out, my daily reporting often differed from what was in the papers, which quickly put a target on my back, too.

This period was the birth of "Duchess Difficult"—one of the many nicknames given to Meghan by the Palace and tabloids over the years. "Me-gain" (because it's all about "me," a royal insider told society bible *Tatler*), "Narcissistic sociopath," and "Degree wife" (this one supposedly by a senior royal because they felt her marriage would only last the length of a British university degree—three years) are a few others. Inside the Palace was no different to a school playground, except this time the bullies had reporters on speed dial.

For women of color, particularly those of African or Caribbean heritage, the trope of the difficult, angry, emotional woman is a familiar one. The repeated use of "Duchess Difficult" in tabloid reports is typical behavior by large sections of mainstream media, which often use divisive and inciting language—such as *drama queen*, *diva*, *gold digger*, *aggressive*, *bully*—to describe Black women, particularly those who have found success. Just ask the likes of Beyoncé, Michelle Obama, and Serena Williams, who have all been described in the press using similar terms over the years. These labels are why their life experiences, no matter how awful, are often met with little or no sympathy. "Calling someone the b-word, labeling them as difficult, it's often a way to insult and dismiss someone," Meghan explained in her 2022 Spotify podcast, *Archetypes*. "It becomes a way to take their power away, keep them in their place. A lot of times it's tied to the very women who have power and agency."

Palace officials had every opportunity to mitigate some of the attacks and defang some of the dog-whistling in the press, but instead they stayed silent. It was worse behind closed doors. Some aides and staff found the name-calling funny—a few even believed Meghan got what was coming to her. One former aide shared with me that a colleague told them Meghan "kind of deserved it . . . for making our lives hell" during the wedding planning. By "hell," the former Palace employee explained, "they basically meant she had opinions. People didn't like that. They wanted Meghan to just go with everything that was suggested and not create any additional work. It was a combination of her not conforming with how women marrying into the family are expected to behave and certain individuals just being lazy."

The destructive symbiosis between the Palace and the press grew worse with time. Joining the growing list of negative stories about the duchess were new reports about issues with staff. The departure of Melissa Toubati, a Kensington Palace assistant for both of the Sussexes, was the first of many. A report in the *Daily Mail* in October 2018 revealed that the thirty-nine-year-old was leaving her post after just six months. It was accompanied by anonymous quotes (provided by a Kensington Palace aide), which told the paper, "Melissa is a hugely talented person. She played a pivotal role in the success of the Royal Wedding and will be missed by everyone in the Royal Household." When later reports suggested that Meghan had reduced Toubati to "tears" and she'd been driven out of her job, Kensington Palace, including Jason Knauf, refused to comment to anyone on or off the record.

When I wrote in detail about the assistant's departure in *Finding Freedom*, it was intriguing to see how quickly and thoroughly the Palace defended her, from the Palace's positive briefings all the way to a call I received in March 2021 from a senior Buckingham Palace communications aide, after I reported details of the Sussexes' side of the story on air. "Omid, I need you to remember that there is a human being at the other end of these claims," they said. "Melissa has been very upset . . . Please remember that words have very real consequences."

Words do indeed have consequences, but it felt slightly rich coming from the same institution that tacitly permitted cruel nicknames and did little to protect one of their own from a deluge of hateful and damaging reporting. As the racism and threats escalated, I was stunned by their inability to pick up the phone and ask the many journalists, "royal experts," and columnists who were attacking Meghan what had been asked of me.

The pile-on took Meghan to a place she had never been before—contemplating suicide in early 2019. "I just didn't want to be alive anymore," she said. "That was a very clear and real and frightening constant thought." But when she turned to the institution for help, potentially at a facility, she was told it would not be a good look for the Firm and was instead advised to lie low so the papers would give her a break. She responded that she'd left the house only twice in the previous four months.

Her supposedly "private" meeting with Samantha Carruthers, the Palace's head of HR, surfaced as Palace gossip within a matter of weeks. Various staff at Kensington Palace, Clarence House, and Buckingham Palace all tittle-tattled about Meghan's personal crisis, and the chatter even reached some of the reporters in the royal rota. There were few who were sympathetic, and even fewer who did or said anything to help. "The feeling was that she needed to develop a thicker skin," a former Palace staffer recently told me.

The institutional response was regrettably predictable. Instead of lending a hand, they gave her the company line, requiring her to demonstrate some of that clichéd stiff upper lip and suffer in silence, all part of a compulsory effort to protect the company brand. The direction from the Palace was, "Don't say anything," Harry said in the *Harry & Meghan* docuseries. "As far as the family was concerned, everything she was put through, they were put through as well. Like, 'My wife had to go through that, so why should your girlfriend be treated any differently, why should you get special treatment?' And I said, 'The difference here is the race element.'"

The Palace's obvious indifference to Meghan's predicament sent an undeniable message to people of color everywhere. Even a person of color like Meghan—an admittedly white-passing, and privileged biracial woman—is still subject to racial bias and gaslighting in a publicly funded institution that is globally celebrated by leaders and kingmakers. The royal establishment's reluctance to speak out against the racism, or to at least protect a victim of it among their own ranks, indicates how retrograde thinking still poisons the heart of this often-revered family operation.

Contrary to ridiculous reports and endless internet gossip, Meghan and I didn't know each other before she entered stage right into the royal family drama. Other than a brief red-carpet encounter at a fashion event in 2015 (one I doubt she would even remember), she knew as much about me as she did the rest of the royal press pack. Though I had enjoyed covering the royals for more than five years before Meghan's arrival, the majority of my work was largely focused on the family's philanthropic endeavors and picture-worthy milestones. I was an *Us Weekly* editor at the time, and the American appetite for glowing coverage of the House of Windsor's younger members meant that I devoted acres of pages to William and Kate's exciting new lives and Harry's journey as a young royal. Given that I wanted to maintain strong access to their world and work, this approach suited me just fine. Back then, the royal family—alongside the Kardashians—were the outlet's number one franchise for its millions of readers. It's why at one point more than a quarter (all positive) of its fifty-two annual covers was dedicated to the royals. And Kensington Palace loved the arrangement, too, always helping me with reporting and even working closely on a number of stand-alone spin-off publications.

It was the arrival of *Suits* actress Meghan Markle that increased my personal interest in the next chapters of the royal story. Here was a smart, accomplished biracial American woman, every bit the confident, optimistic Californian, joining a thousand-year-old family of hereditary power and a staid institution not exactly known for its openness and tolerance. As a younger, U.K.-born mixed-race journalist who covered the royals day in, day out, I knew this was a significant moment in British and royal history and that Meghan's journey was going to be fascinating and far from easy. A fairy tale this was not.

As I observed many British outlets turn a blind eye or struggle to recognize the thinly veiled racism and bigotry that ran rife through their newspapers and magazines, and as I watched the Palace stand by and say nothing in response, I decided to cover Meghan's journey more objectively, but also from a vantage point closer to her reality on the ground. Hers was an important story to tell. And thanks to connections in the entertainment industry, her former world, I had sources on both sides to provide deeper insight—something the reporters at the papers didn't have at the time. Working only for American media outlets (a decision I made early on in my career), from *Good Morning America* to ABC News to *Harper's Bazaar*, also meant I was lucky enough to be part of more diverse and inclusive teams than one would find in most British newsrooms (only 8 percent of the country's journalism workforce is non-white, and the majority of those aren't in senior positions). These were colleagues who consistently understood and wholeheartedly supported my approach to the job. Back on home shores the response was vastly different. My coverage offering both sides of the story—and an empathetic approach to the journey of a mixed-race woman in the royal institution—was met with criticism and attacks from the press. The likes of the *Mail*, *Telegraph*, and *Express* hastily resorted to name-calling (*mouthpiece* and *cheerleader* being two of their many favorites), and it soon became clear that the presence of a journalist offering a different take enraged them. While other royal reporters quietly got on with their jobs, I found myself dealing with tabloid reporters digging into every possible aspect of my life and, more disturbingly, harassing my family. This type of bullying had two main aims: to diminish my journalistic credentials (and therefore the strength of my reporting) and get back at me for calling out misleading and racially insensitive coverage.

My reporting on Harry and Meghan's story radically and quickly shifted my own social media landscape, too. As a journalist I was no stranger to a heated letter or negative comment here and there, but this was the first time I was the target of regular racially motivated hate. The day the *Daily Mail* started referring to me as "British-Iranian" (despite having never pointed out the ethnicity of other royal correspondents), the personal attacks gassed up, initiating daily tweets that told me I had no right to be speaking about "our" British royals. And as the online vitriol toward Meghan got worse, so did it toward me:

> *"Fuck off back home paki"*
> *"MI6 should keep an eye on this terrorist"*
> *"Needs to be driven through a Paris tunnel"*
> *"Show respect to the monarch who let you stay in this country in the first place"*
> *"Camel jockey who needs to worry about his own country"*

This is just a minuscule slice of the daily tweets, direct messages, and online comments I receive. I won't bore you with the hundreds of variations of messages from furious royalists telling me to kill myself.

As for Meghan, even in the early days, the ugliness was inescapable. In January 2018, the partner of a right-wing populist political party leader was exposed for sending racist text messages about Meghan. In leaked WhatsApp messages, Jo Marney—girlfriend of U.K. Independence Party leader Henry Bolton—claimed Harry's "black American" fiancée will "taint" the royal family with "her seed" and pave the way for a "black king." She continued, "This is Britain. Not Africa." Other extremists shared similar sentiments, many emboldened by the stream of subtle digs in newspaper opinion pieces and on daytime television. Six former Metropolitan Police officers, including one who went on to be employed by the British Home Office, were charged with sending offensive and racist messages, including slurs about Meghan, in a private WhatsApp group they started in August 2018. And a British court also heard how two white-supremacist podcasters said Prince Harry should be "judicially killed for treason" for marrying Meghan, and called their son, Archie, "an abomination that should be put down." The Welshmen, who have since been convicted of terror offenses, claimed their *Black Wolf Radio* podcast comments were simply "freedom of speech." That old chestnut.

By the beginning of 2019, Meghan had become the most trolled person in the world. As she pointed out on an episode of the *Teenager Therapy* podcast, for eight months of this grim period she was pregnant or on maternity leave. "What was able to just be manufactured and churned out, it's almost unsurvivable," Meghan said. "That's so big you can't think of what that feels like, because I don't care if you're fifteen or twenty-five, if people are saying things about you that aren't true, what that does to your mental and emotional health is so damaging."

Again, the Palace did virtually nothing to help, either behind the scenes or in their public communications. During the peak of it in late summer 2018, I received a call that I thought was from the couple's head of communications at the time, Sara Latham. We had been texting back and forth about an upcoming royal engagement. "Hi, Omid!" a female voice chirped. It was different to Latham's northwestern American accent. "It's Meghan." I put my iced coffee down, not quite sure if the call was a prank. "We saw your name keep coming up on the phone . . . and I just wanted to say hi, see how you're doing." Sara had mentioned to her that I was dealing with my own online harassment and threats.

Though I appreciated the conversation, it was also deflating. Here was someone checking in on a journalist she still only really knew through a byline, when so many of the people in her royal orbit—including those on payroll—wouldn't do the same for her. It said so much about the state of the Firm—their ineptitude at protecting one of their own and their failure to comprehend the scope of the damage done because of their silence.

Later that same day, I spoke with a senior member of their team, and they were brutally honest about Meghan's situation. "She will give you the impression that all is fine but it's clearly taking its toll . . . It's really bad, Omid," they admitted, almost tearful themselves. "Without support there's little I can do, either."

The Firm's protective shield—so often used when royals are in crisis, including Prince Andrew's never-ending ordeal—was never offered up for Meghan. And the system wields that shield whenever it's deemed necessary. It's impossible to forget the time Kensington Palace issued an official statement in defense of Kate after a plastic surgeon had suggested to a newspaper that she, then the Duchess of Cambridge, had "baby Botox" injections to reduce wrinkles. And when Charles and Camilla received a barrage of negative comments on Clarence House Instagram posts after the premiere of the fourth season of *The Crown*, aides wasted no time in switching off the ability to comment on posts.

"They didn't see Meghan as important enough to care for—simple as that," said a friend of the duchess. "No matter who asked, no matter what was pointed out, no matter how loudly she told them, or we told them, that she was struggling . . . she was expected to shut up and deal with it quietly." And Harry said, "I thought my family would help but every single ask, request, warning, whatever, got met with total silence or total neglect. I felt totally helpless."

It's revealing that the one family member who has emerged as the most informed and honest about the Firm's racial issues—and his own—is the one who left the institution altogether. Prince Harry's racial awakening has its own story arc, but it's worth remembering that he is the first royal in history to sincerely acknowledge their white privilege, their ancestral role in racial injustices, and, most importantly, their continuing bias and racism, unconscious or not. It was a journey that started the day he met Meghan but one that took on significance and meaning after he left the confines of the palace.

He also called out his own family for not taking on the racist attacks hurled at their own, even linking this institutionalized reticence to Britain's long history of imperialism. "For us, for this union and the specifics around [Meghan's] race, there was an opportunity—many opportunities—for my family to show some public support," he has said.

Support did come from less expected areas. In October 2019, a Labour party political candidate, Holly Lynch, drafted an open letter regarding the racial attacks on Meghan that was later signed by seventy-two female politicians. With no illusions, it resolutely stated: "Stories and headlines have represented an invasion of your privacy and have sought to cast aspersions about your character, without any good reason as far as we can see . . . We are calling out what can only be described as outdated, colonial undertones to some of these stories." After hearing news of the letter, Harry told a friend, "It's more than my family ever did . . . The silence disappointed me."

The Firm has yet to fully learn how to become more initiative-taking when faced with race-related allegations, particularly after Harry and Meghan left Oprah Winfrey speechless over certain family members' "concerns and conversations" about Archie's skin color. The issue may have later been briefly discussed between Meghan and Charles over letter (and this is why the incidents were not repeated in the Sussexes' 2022 Netflix series or in *Spare*), but the Palace's initial response was not a swift one—they would instead wait until the interview's U.K. broadcast aired the following day before planning anything. The family, a Palace aide told me, was keen to hear what the nation thought and see which way the wind was blowing in the court of public opinion. If the Sussexes—whose overall popularity in the country had been on a downward trajectory since they stepped away from their roles—received minimal sympathy from the British public, they would get minimal from the institution, too. After morning television hosts mocked Meghan's stories, newspapers called the couple liars, and a nationwide poll found that more than a third of Britons (36 percent) had more sympathy with the royal family (compared to just 22 percent for the Sussexes), the Palace issued a carefully worded statement to mirror the public's mixed reaction. "The issues raised, particularly that of race, are concerning," Buckingham Palace included in a sixty-one-word riposte issued on behalf of the Queen. "While some recollections may vary, they are taken very seriously and will be addressed by the family privately."

Those three words, *recollections may vary*, artfully submarined the issue by casting it as a he said–she said situation, effectively throwing the hounds off the scent without any mea culpas or promises of investigations. With a large swathe of the public instantly taking the side of the royal family, it felt like mission accomplished for Prince William's then communications secretary Christian Jones and private secretary Jean-Christophe Gray, who helped devise the caveat during multiple drafts of the statement. They worked closely with Charles's chief press aide, Julian Payne, on the perfect response "to plant that seed of doubt in people's minds," said a former staffer, who was also involved in communications efforts at the time. "The last thing they wanted was for people to start pointing fingers at the bosses [William and Kate]." Someone else also keen to protect the family's reputation was Kate. Years later, *The Times'* royal correspondent, Valentine Low, reported that the then Duchess of

Cambridge was the one to suggest that the statement needed something to reflect how the institution "did not accept a lot of what had been said . . . [She] clearly made the point, 'History will judge this statement and unless this phrase or a phrase like it is included, everything that they have said will be taken as true.'" A source later told me, "She was really passionate about defending the family."

Two days later, when confronted by a reporter outside an East London school, Prince William helped reiterate the statement's point, telling TV cameras, "We are very much not a racist family." It was an unplanned response, but William—who admitted to a press secretary earlier in the day that he was "nervous" about stepping out—was keen to avoid any finger-pointing.

More than two years on and, other than Charles, no one in the family has spoken about the Archie conversations with the Sussexes. Meanwhile, the Palace has been on a mission to shift itself away from the perception they represent a racist institution. Less than three weeks after the Oprah interview, "royal sources" (in this case, Buckingham Palace's head of communications speaking anonymously) confirmed plans to appoint a diversity chief, with the "full support" of the family. It was the first time that the royal establishment came close to admitting the important need for the institution's inner workings to be diverse and representative of modern-day society. "We are listening and learning to get this right," I was told at the time.

Unsurprisingly, it turned out to be lip service. Just three months later—after sharing a below-average employment diversity statistic in their 2020–2021 financial report (the first time such information had been publicly shared)—the Palace admitted it would be shelving plans for the diversity role. Though the position has not been completely ruled out for the future, a Palace source revealed that all staff were instead emailed a link to a "diversity survey" with tasks such as ranking (on a scale from "Strongly Disagree" to "Strongly Agree") statements such as "This organisation really values diversity" and "I feel I am respected by my colleagues." A former household employee scoffed, "Lord only knows what was done with the results ... We never heard about it since."

Change is not impossible. In recent years the Dutch royal family has led by example when it comes to addressing their own uncomfortable histories. In 2022, King Willem-Alexander of the Netherlands commissioned independent research into the role of his family in the country's colonial past. The royal personally hired three Dutch historians and a human rights expert to spend exactly three years on the study, including tracing links to the Dutch West India Company, which operated ships that trafficked an estimated six hundred thousand people into slavery over centuries. In tandem, the Dutch government apologized for the country's role in slavery from the seventeenth to nineteenth centuries and devoted €200 million to a fund promoting awareness of the colonial power's role in slavery and €27 million to open a slavery museum. The king followed up with a powerful speech with his own apology on behalf of the family.

In April 2023, King Charles took the British royal family's first baby step toward acknowledging the British monarchy's own role in the slave trade by "supporting" a research project investigating the family's ancestral links with transatlantic slavery. It followed the *Guardian*'s publication of a previously unseen document from 1689 clearly showing that the slave-trading Royal African Company transferred shares in the company to King William III. The collaborative doctoral partnership between the University of Manchester and Historic Royal Palaces (a charity that manages unoccupied royal residences) is allowing historian Camilla de Koning access to specific archives for a PhD thesis on the subject. Though de Koning's collaborative work, which began in October 2022 and will conclude in 2026, would have happened with or without Charles's support, his public show of interest is a start.

As I finished the pages of this book, a spokesperson for King Charles said the institution is still "committed" to improving diversity among household employees, particularly at the senior level. The monarch has, for example, heavily leaned on his former press secretary, Eva Omaghomi, who is now the director of community engagement, to work more closely with minority groups in the United Kingdom and across the Commonwealth. Charles, too, said a source, is planning to do more community-focused work. In August 2022, Charles guest-edited *The Voice*—Britain's only national Black newspaper—and spoke about the importance of "unity through diversity." In a letter properly acknowledging Black History Month in the United Kingdom, he wrote, "My hope is that we can consistently preserve and celebrate the histories of people of African, Caribbean and Asian heritage in Britain, and to expand this beyond Black History Month. Doing so will recognize the rich diversity of cultures and different minority ethnic groups that make this country so special— and in many ways unique." While criticized as "hollow words" by some of its readers, Charles does have a history of supporting minority groups in Britain. In 1976 he launched the Prince's Trust, which has gone on to give thousands of marginalized young people, many from Black communities, financial grants to set up their own enterprises and fulfill their potential. Before they found success, entrepreneurs such as menswear designer Ozwald Boateng, actors including Idris Elba and David Oyelowo, and many Black-owned businesses received support and grants from the charity's various programs.

But it would be hasty to unreservedly believe that real change is on the horizon for the wider royal establishment just yet. In 2023, it was reported that 9.7 percent of employees in Buckingham Palace were from ethnic minority backgrounds (up from 9.6 percent the previous year) and Kensington Palace employed 16.3 percent (up from 13.6 percent). The numbers appear to be ticking up in the right direction, but a closer look at the senior staffers around royal family members reveals a predominantly white lineup (exclusively, in the case of communications team members and private secretaries at William and Kate's household). It depressingly shows that the majority of non-white employees are at junior levels or working in more service industry–type positions (such as the hundreds of housekeeping staff helping maintain royal residences). There are also very few women in senior roles across both royal households. As for the Lord Chamberlain's committee, the five department heads who form the core of it (the Lord Chamberlain, the King's private secretary, the Keeper of the Privy Purse, the Master of the Household, and the office's comptroller) are all older white men.

It's a deep-seated problem, one that has gone unrectified for centuries and one that will take a long time to change. In the twenty-first century, baby steps aren't enough, and incrementalism won't appease recent cultural demands for revolutionary-size change. And it all starts by taking a hard look in the mirror and recognizing all the subtle and insidious ways racism rots away at the center. "Everything they said was going to happen hasn't happened," Harry commented in a January 2023 interview. "I've always been open to wanting to help them understand their part in it . . . For me, the difference is unconscious bias and racism, but if you are called out for unconscious bias you need to make that right, and you have the opportunity and the choice to. But if you choose not to, then that rapidly becomes something much more serious." To put it another way, consciously ignoring or trying to brush away the once unconscious bias is, in and of itself, inherently racist.

The Firm's incapacity—and seeming disinclination at times—to initiate substantive change or even take a truly committed and objective stance on their own history shows a disregard for what the twenty-first century's unstoppable currents demand: cycle breaking and transformation. It demonstrates an unwillingness to truly accept, embrace, and protect what the Duchess of Sussex's inclusion stood for beyond palace walls—how important it was for the millions of Black, Brown, and non-white people throughout Britain and the predominantly non-white Commonwealth to finally see a little of themselves represented in the monarchy because of

Meghan's presence, her background, and her union with Harry. Her role in the royal story symbolized a crack in a glass ceiling that many thought was impossible to touch. But instead of helping her when she needed it most, the Palace discounted her trauma, claiming in a calibrated, well-timed statement that when it comes to Meghan's experiences, well, "recollections may vary." Her story didn't matter.

If Meghan's presence didn't alter anything within the royal family or the institution of the monarchy, then perhaps nothing will. The Firm doesn't like to be told what to do—acclimation and change are not practices and values they have historically embraced. And a deferential press let them get away with it all, and, at times, has made it worse. The family's past will forever discolor their legacy, and their refusal to comprehensively address much of it only deepens the stain. By their very existence, the royal family as a symbol perpetuates the notion of empire and the class system. As a result, it's almost impossible to separate the three. To do so would require a full-scale operation geared toward redressing the Firm in modern colors and populating the institution with diverse opinions and forward-thinking ideas, including a new governing transparency. It's a tall order for a monarchy that stretches back to 1066, and one that desperately relies on tradition, mystery, and memories of the grand old times for its survival. There are just too many blackamoor pieces and tainted historical artifacts that can be neither retained nor explained.

# 8

## Gloves On

### Prince William, Heir to the Throne

———•———

*If you're not careful, duty can sort of weigh you*
*down an awful lot at a very early age and I think*
*you've got to develop into the duty role.*
—Prince William, 2016, BBC News interview

*"I am growing up," she thought . . . "I am losing some*
*illusions . . . perhaps to acquire others," and she descended*
*among the tombs where the bones of her ancestors lay.*
—Virginia Woolf, *Orlando*

A crusader is born. After the Sussexes' allegations and William
and Kate's Caribbean debacle exposed the systemic discrimination within the royal institution, Prince William took the mantle
in the Firm's effort to distance itself from the continued assertions
and presumptions that the royal family is a racist one. Immediately following the bigoted remarks of his godmother, Lady Susan
Hussey, at Queen Camilla's domestic violence event in November
2022, William hastened to rebuke her insensitive comments, even
leapfrogging the Palace's response to do so. Motivated by both justi-

fied anger and atonement for the monarchy's recent blunders, William has now taken the campaign beyond palace walls to admonish and correct in other areas to set himself apart.

On March 18, 2023, he penned a letter to address disturbing claims from a youth football league manager in the north England town of Bradford. The manager had written to the national Football Association (FA) that many of his players—some as young as seven—are routinely subjected to racial abuse and threats of violence from adults on the sidelines, and he asked that the association do something about it. After an internal discussion, board members decided that William, the FA's president-designate of seventeen years (an honorary title more than anything else), should be the one to publicly press the association's executives to take action. The Prince of Wales wrote that he was "deeply concerned" and demanded that those involved "must be held accountable." Not missing an opportunity to use the proverbial megaphone, William declared in his letter that "racism and abuse [have] no place in our society" and "abhorrent behaviour of this nature must stop now and all those responsible be held to account."

It's not the first time William has called out racism on the pitch. On three occasions he has advocated for eliminating racism in football, mainly at the higher levels of Britain's Premier League and on international fields. In 2021, he joined a global chorus that condemned the racial abuse of England players after the team's defeat in the Euro 2020 final, saying he was "sickened" by it and demanded it stop. As president of BAFTA, the British version of the American Academy of Motion Picture Arts and Sciences, he also used their 2020 awards ceremony to decry the lack of diversity in the world of film and television: "We find ourselves talking again about the need to do more to ensure diversity in the sector and in the awards process—that simply cannot be right in this day and age." His reproach, along with those of many other public figures, hit the mark—the 2021 BAFTA nominees were slightly more diverse (although in 2023 it was criticized for falling behind once again, with a winners' list dominated by white cast and crew members). While the royal institution has an embarrassingly poor record overall when it comes to racial issues, these organizations in which William holds honorary roles can't afford to be seen as uninterested or unengaged—meaning the prince can't sit back in silence like other family members.

Plus, said a Kensington Palace source, William is keen to be seen embracing his role as the young, forward-looking heir to the throne. As a close confidante permitted to speak for a 2021 *Sunday Times* profile said, William believes "the public look to him to keep royal work looking modern . . . [He is] carving out his relationship with diverse communities . . . as a way of doing things now that will help a smooth transition when the time comes." It's why in the past year his royal engagements have included a focus on often-overlooked groups, such as visiting the Hayes Muslim Centre in West London to support (and personally donate to) Britain's earthquake relief efforts for Turkey and Syria. In terms of public opinion and optics, it's a win-win for the next king.

While William is certainly solicitous and tolerant in his public role, a more complicated portrait emerges from his private life. What makes his recent civic outcries on racial issues look a tad opportunistic is the fact that he has yet to clear the air with his own brother regarding those cratering accusations of unconscious bias within the family. When the world watched Prince William proclaim "We are very much not a racist family" after the Sussex-Oprah sit-down, no one knew that, behind closed doors, some of the accusations his family was dealing with came from conversations about the Sussexes' unborn son that he and his wife were well aware of. Privately, the issue had been addressed by Meghan and Charles in the letters they exchanged in the aftermath of the interview, but the King also felt the Duchess of Sussex should discuss her feelings with the Waleses, too. Two years on and neither Harry nor Meghan has received any word on the matter from William or Kate, whose reported push for a "recollections may vary"–style clause to be added to Buckingham Palace's public response suggests the princess in particular may not agree with the Sussexes' words. "The silence has caused a lot of confusion and upset," said a source close to the family.

William's handling of the situation reveals a deep divide between his personal life and his approach to the role of heir to the throne. The precarious duality of a high-profile public figure is, of course, nothing new or original to Prince William—a private self often struggles with the public mask, particularly when under duress. With the heir, it's the stark differences between William, Prince of Wales, and Willy, husband, brother, and friend, that place his divided nature in such high relief. Composed on the pitch but unpredictable off, the prince has always had a wall between his observable life and his often very different private one.

In recent years his public persona has taken the hardest hits from persistent online rumors about his private life, which hound him to this day. Although this particular scuttlebutt continues to find its way back as a trending topic on social media, has been tweeted about by multiple public figures, and surfaces as speculation in U.S. tabloids, few British outlets—and zero royal books—have actually delved into the rumors surrounding the Waleses and the Marchioness of Cholmondeley.

Until proven otherwise, rumors are just rumors, but anatomizing the handling of this gossip reveals how hearsay can shape and distort the future king's story. As we know, tittle-tattle has long played a significant role in the history of the royal family. If it weren't for the false tabloid tale that Charles "snuck" a nineteen-year-old Diana onto the Royal Train in 1980, Prince Philip may not have joined the push to get his son—who barely knew the young Spencer at this point—to commit so quickly. The blonde spotted stepping into the carriage was, in fact, the wife of one of Charles's staff who was traveling with the heir, but the mere perception that the innocent, young (and virginal) Spencer was sneaking around to cavort with the Prince of Wales was deemed mortifying by the Palace. The edict came down: either they were a proper couple or nothing at all.

Up until early March 2019, the gossip about Rose Hanbury was restricted to media circles, royal press pens (when aides weren't around, of course), and the society scene. But on March 21, *The Sun*'s executive editor Dan Wootton broke the carefully worded news that the Duchess of Cambridge had "fallen out" with her "glamourous best friend" Rose and instructed William to "phase her out." The article, which referred to the British peeress as Kate's "rural rival," cryptically reported, "It is well known that Kate and Rose have had a terrible falling out. They used to be close but that is not the case anymore." Not included in the final edit for legal reasons, a former employee at the paper told me, was a host of other details. "It was all the newsroom could talk about," says the former staffer.

To royal followers, Rose was a somewhat familiar face. Long connected to aristocracy, her grandmother Lady Rose Lambert was a bridesmaid at her childhood friend Queen Elizabeth II's 1947 wedding to Prince Philip. After a stint as a model and political researcher for Conservative politician Michael Gove, it was announced in June 2009 that she was marrying film director (and former Prince Andrew classmate) David Rocksavage, better known as the 7th Marquess of Cholmondeley. The pair, who are twenty-three years apart in age, enjoyed a whirlwind romance and quickly welcomed twin boys four months after their wedding, and then a daughter in 2016. Home for the family of five is the palatial 107-room Houghton Hall in Norfolk, just ten minutes' drive from the Waleses' Anmer Hall residence (William's thirtieth birthday gift from the Queen). The neighbors soon became close friends.

In 1990, when Rocksavage was just thirty, he inherited the title of Lord Great Chamberlain, making him one of the six "great officers" of state present at the annual openings of Parliament and major royal ceremonies. In July 2017, Rose was photographed in an impressive tiara next to Prince Harry at a Buckingham Palace banquet for Queen Letizia of Spain's state visit. The media's interest in her and the rest of the couple's Norfolk social set—a tight-knit community with generational ties and unimaginable wealth, including pals William and Rosie Van Cutsem; Tom and Polly Cook, the Earl and Countess of Leicester; Laura Fellowes (William's cousin on Diana's side of the family); Lady Laura Marsham and James Meade (an old Eton pal of William's)—quickly saw them nicknamed the "Turnip Toffs." *Turnip* because most of the set own patches of arable farmland across England and also because Norfolk (where they all have homes) is well-known for its turnip crops; *toffs* is British slang for a group of upper-class types.

It was *The Sun*'s story that prompted a blaze of Twitter gossip, but the *Daily Mail* threw a little water on the flames just two days after. The paper's Palace-friendly columnist, Richard Kay, reported that Kate had not fallen out with Rose and was "the real victim of aristocratic dinner party gossip." The "extraordinary" rumors were simply "grist to the mill for the cause of republicanism, bringing a glow to the hearts of anti-monarchists everywhere." He went on to claim the gossip threatened to "disrupt [the couple's] domestic tranquillity." William, Kay added, bears "all the hallmarks of a contented man" thanks to Kate. In other words, nothing to see here. Move on.

At this time, Christian Jones, the former press officer to the chancellor of the exchequer (Britain's equivalent to the U.S. secretary of the treasury), was the head of communications at Kensington Palace, a role he served for both the Cambridges and the Sussexes when they were still sharing an office. I was deep in the middle of *Finding Freedom*, and Jones was helping with some of the information for that book. As the rumors began to spread, he called me, worried about how out of hand the gossip was getting. "Oh my God, I actually had to ask if they were true," he said. Jones had raised the issue in person with the prince and his private secretary, Simon Case, in a closed-door meeting at Kensington Palace. William, he said, was furious when the question came up, and he vehemently said it was not true.

By March 26, hashtags were trending on social media for the fourth day in a row. And things were about to pick up steam when British columnist and *Times* staff writer Giles Coren—coincidentally a close friend of Camilla's son, Tom Parker Bowles—tweeted in reply to someone who had asked about the *Mail*'s recent coverage that the rumors were true. "Everyone knows," he tweeted. He deleted it within two hours, after he had been put under "pressure," sources said. (Coren didn't speak about his loose-lipped comment until three years later, when he wrote in his newspaper column, "Can I please just say that, while it was far from being the worst thing I have ever tweeted, I was JOKING . . . I'd had a boozy lunch talking to fellow hacks about the story and in the cab home went online to blurt.")

Less than a week after Coren's tweet, U.S. tabloid *In Touch* ran a story that took the gossip one step further. The magazine has never been known for its credibility (in its twenty-one-year lifetime, Jennifer Aniston has been "PREGNANT WITH TWINS!" or "BACK ON!" with Brad Pitt about fifty times), but it opened the floodgates for other lowbrow publications and gossip. "It's really bad isn't it," a worried Jones texted me. Palace lawyers at Harbottle & Lewis sent letters out to a handful of newspapers, including *The Times*, stating, "In addition to being false and highly damaging, the publication of false speculation in respect of our client's private life also constitutes a breach of his privacy pursuant to Article 8 of the European Convention to Human Rights."

To many royal watchers, the British media's unusually cautious approach to the story was extremely out of character. It's fair to say that if there were wild rumors about Prince Harry, they would have remained front-page news and fodder for commentary for weeks—even if there was no proof to back them up. (In fact, in July 2023, when the unreliable gossip site Radar Online claimed that the Sussexes' marriage was "on the rocks," many U.K. outlets jumped on the story without even asking the couple's representatives for a comment.) The institution would have handled them differently, too. "It's inevitable," a former Kensington Palace staff member reflected. "There is a greater level of protection around the heir than the spare or any other family member, other than the monarch. It's just the way things go."

For William, there was no "take it on the chin" advice like Meghan received during her media onslaughts. In fact, behind the scenes, William remained in the loop. A senior Palace source said at the time, "We *have* to make this stop." And it did, briefly. As journalists did their best to find details that could possibly back up the rumor, Rose's name stayed out of the press for two months. Even when she attended the June 2019 state dinner at Buckingham Palace for President Donald Trump, headlines merely focused on her outfit. Kate, claimed sources, ignored it all but was "uncomfortable" with the ongoing chatter.

At that moment in time, *The Sun* was less favorable in their royal coverage. On June 13, the paper published a carefully worded update, alleging the cause of Kate's "fallout" with Rose, which they claimed "started because [Rose] had one or two suppers with William in Norfolk when Kate was away. But it was hardly as if they were meeting behind Kate's back—of course she knew they were getting together. And Kate was grateful that a good friend and neighbour like Rose was there to entertain William."

Although the print edition of the paper was out in the wild, the online story didn't remain unaltered for long. Ten minutes after going live, the article was updated with the additional words added to the end of that final quote: ". . . as a platonic friend." Palace lawyers then contacted the tabloid, and within a few hours the two sentences about those alleged dinners were erased. A week later, the entire story was removed. This was the last time the tabloid tried to cover Rose and Kate's fallout. Too difficult, a former editor there told me. Plus, they added, "there was a nice stream of Harry and Meghan stuff coming in, so [the editors] are happy." In fact, it was during this run of Rose stories that the Sussexes—who started their own, separate office at Buckingham Palace in the middle of the gossip run—noticed an uptick in negative or revealing stories about themselves in the *Mail* and *The Sun*. "Funny how [it's] back on us," one of the couple's Palace staff told me at the time. Harry even wondered if someone at the Palace had helped move certain journalists on to other stories—and away from the Rose gossip. He would later find out he was right.

Fast-forward to 2023 and rumors like these still do the rounds, most recently resurfacing as a trending topic after it was announced that Rose's son Lord Oliver Cholmondeley was going to be one of King Charles's pages of honor alongside Prince George at the May 6 coronation. But despite internet lore, there is no "super injunction" on unreported details and there is no proof of unreported information being out there. "It's a reminder that while certain media allies can be controlled, the internet is a whole beast of its own," said a former Palace staffer.

A friend of the Prince of Wales sympathized: "Dealing with nasty, untrue rumors . . . wouldn't you be filled with rage? It's been very difficult for him. And for Kate. But I truly believe these things make you stronger."

The public-facing William appears levelheaded and confident, often to the point of staged—he shows up at the optimal time, asks the right questions, and gives carefully considered answers. A calm and collected character is what the system demands of the heir to the throne, particularly after all the recent turmoil and change, and the Prince of Wales plays it to a tee. As the heir, he's finally fully embraced his roles and responsibilities at Royal Family, Inc. Many people I've spoken to who know him believe William comes by this honestly. It is said that after maturing into his position in the Firm, the prince now aims to follow in the Queen's footsteps. A source within his team at Kensington Palace says that, as an adult in his forties, the former Duke of Cambridge has "fully embraced the path that he's on. Just like the Queen he has learned the importance of duty coming before anything else." The counter to this is that the Firm incrementally institutionalized Prince William—the unyielding pressure from the establishment wore him down into a stoic acceptance of his fate as the next great hope for the monarchy. The truth is probably somewhere in the middle, but, regardless, for public consumption, the system has churned out a disciplined king in waiting.

It's a different story when the stage lights go down, however. While William is a lot like the late Queen in the way he outwardly embodies the institution, when his temper flares behind closed doors, he more closely resembles his famously ill-tempered father. "William is a man that likes to get things done, done quickly, done efficiently . . . In the process of making that happen he can definitely be sharp," said a former aide. Another former Kensington Palace staffer agreed: "He's capable of having constructive conversations, to receive criticism but . . . there's a spikiness when dealing with him, too." Added a third, "You don't want to be the bearer of bad news around him. He's quick to get fed up and blame."

Biographer Robert Jobson wrote in his 2022 portrait of the prince, *William at 40: The Making of a Modern Monarch*, "[William's] fiery temper can blow up at any time—usually when he's frustrated or when it comes to issues regarding his family. Even senior members of his circle will 'check which way the wind is blowing' before becoming too self-assured in his presence or raising problematic issues that might be better addressed at another time. Other insiders confide that William can be an emotional character who is, on occasion, 'difficult to handle.'"

As the next King, a role that requires mental balance and a phlegmatic disposition, William's emotional volatility could be one of his greatest challenges. Much of Queen Elizabeth II's success was her ability to administer a firm grip on her emotions and compartmentalize when necessary. William certainly values this, and he has long championed mental health awareness as one of his anchor issues. Alongside homelessness and environmental causes, he's taken on the cause as a token of how he'll modernize the monarchy as the next sovereign—virtue signaling for his upcoming reign and, once again, delineating his own style and values system from that of his father.

In 2016, William, Kate, and Harry launched Heads Together, a charity that aspires to "change the conversation on mental health." The lightbulb moment occurred during drinks together in 2015. The three landed on it, and Kate wrote the idea on the back of a cigarette packet (although the Palace *loathes* this version of the story, preferring to say it was a paper napkin). Heads Together set out to destigmatize the hush-hush notion around talking about mental health and, largely down to Harry's own candid confessions during its first year, succeeded in this. Although the organization—which falls under the Waleses' Royal Foundation umbrella and is a partner with eight charities—is technically still up and running, it's been more heads apart since Prince Harry's 2020 departure. After all, it's not lost on the public that Heads Together's remaining mental health ambassadors, William and Kate, haven't publicly or privately expressed any empathy for the Duke and Duchess of Sussex.

All this points to a marked change in Prince William. As he gets closer to the top job, in addition to his temper, there's a colder side to him that some friends and also his brother, Harry, have described. For those who have followed him on the royal beat over the years, even his face tells the story—there is less smiling, and his frequently set jaw suggests inner storms could be occluding his sunnier side. My own experiences with William bear this out. Since meeting him in 2011, I've gone from being a friendly face at the many impersonal royal events and a welcome presence on long trips to being a perceived member of the enemy camp. In the early days, on overseas trips, it was William who would often walk over to say hello or make jokes (such as ribbing me for my poor French skills in Canada). "I like the fact that you're present [in the moment], that you're clearly enjoying it and not over it like some of the others," he confessed to me on a 2014 trip to Singapore. And I enjoyed covering his work. Professional, always "on," and willing to make time for everyone, back then William was enjoyable to be around. But while my professional relationship with the Sussex team grew stronger, my Cambridge connection became fractured. There was a noticeable shift after the households divided and Harry and Meghan set up camp at Buckingham Palace in April 2019.

That summer, Christian Jones—who remained at Kensington Palace to oversee all the Cambridges' media efforts—messaged me out of the blue to say it would no longer be appropriate to socialize. Another aide later told me that William had requested this. As we approached 2020, I felt the growing strains on my working relationship with Kensington Palace, who were also much more guarded when it came to their own communication with the Sussex team at Buckingham Palace. I was still invited to the private briefings and announcements but, two months after returning from an October tour with the Sussexes in southern Africa, one of William's aides revealed that William felt "uncomfortable" with my relationship with the Sussex team. The papers would often refer to me, incorrectly, as Harry and Meghan's "pal," another lie largely created to delegitimize the details I was sharing from sources close to the couple that often went against narratives that tabloids were reporting. This didn't help the situation. A Kensington Palace aide said to me privately, "I'm not saying you need to pick a side, but you need to accept that there are sides in this." When William and some of his aides then begged to see certain passages from *Finding Freedom* ahead of its August 2020 release and were told no, I could sense that this was a relationship past breaking point.

Because of the pandemic and the long run of virtual royal engagements, it had been almost eighteen months since I had been in the physical presence of the future King. But in July 2021, standing inches from the front end of his Range Rover, there we were, virtually eye to eye. I had just wrapped filming in Kensington Gardens for *Good Morning America* and, out of all the people, it was William's moving car that I almost walked into outside the gates at Kensington Palace. It was my fault for being so engrossed in my phone, and I think both of us were a little surprised. I mouthed an apology but his unimpressed stare from the driver's seat gave little away as we both paused for a very long second, though his perfunctory apology quickly brought an end to any awkwardness even if it was just a brief smile and a mutely mouthed "Sorry."

Uncomfortable encounters aside, stories about the real William are becoming more common, especially after Harry pulled the curtain back on his own experiences. William's combustible anger reached a boiling point when he physically assaulted his brother in 2019—an allegation from *Spare* the heir refuses to comment on. Harry recounts the moment when William shows up "piping hot" at the snug and storied Nottingham Cottage, a redbrick "grace-and-favor" residence on Kensington Palace grounds where Harry and Meghan lived until they relocated to Frogmore Cottage. According to Harry, William, in full "heir mode," was there to "lay down the law" about Meghan and her "difficult" behavior. Since its release, book reviewers and the media have pored over what happened next, but it's important to note that when Harry describes William grabbing him by the collar and knocking him to the floor, where bits of a smashed dog bowl lacerated and bruised his back, he prefaces it with "it all happened so fast. So very fast." Evidence of a smolder-ing fury turned violent, this lightning-quick assault rattled Harry to such an extent that he immediately called his therapist after order-ing William to get out. What troubled him more than the violence was the look in William's eyes. "He wanted me to hit him back, but I chose not to," Harry later shared. "What was different here was the level of frustration, and I talk [in the book] about the 'red mist' that I had for so many years, and I saw this red mist in him."

As expected, many royal correspondents and Sussex haters (there are a lot of them!) rushed to paint William's attack as nothing more than "brothers being brothers." This may be true with chil-dren, but one doesn't expect this kind of behavior from the future King and head of the Church of England, who was thirty-seven at the time. "Far from seeming cold and unfeeling, William's des-perate collar-grabbing bid to get through to Harry [showed] just how much love he has for his little brother. It made him look *edgy*," wrote the *Telegraph*'s royal editor Camilla Tominey, bizarrely sound-ing like the excuses of domestic abusers everywhere. Imagine if it were the other way around? People would be calling for criminal charges to be pressed against Harry or for his Sussex title to be taken away.

It would take a highly trained psychoanalyst to get to the bot-tom of Prince William's anger, but there are some well-documented triggers. Obviously, his ruptured relationship with his brother tops the list. "I actually love having him around," William once told me about Harry at a private Kensington Palace drinks reception (one of many that took place behind the scenes with the royal press pack). Being forced to walk behind their mother's coffin in 1997 surely solidified a connection between the two—they had to be there for each other in demanding situations like this, especially because their own father wasn't always looking out for them. Wil-liam once said that he and Harry were "uniquely bonded because of what [they] went through" after their mother died. In a 2019

ITV documentary, Harry spoke about this fraternal bond, stating, "Look, we're brothers, we'll always be brothers. And we're certainly on different paths at the moment, but I'll always be there for him, as I know he'll always be there for me." He went on to say, "As brothers, you know, you have good days, you have bad days." Lately, it's been only bad days for the two, and it's a run that started years ago.

Though there had always been rivalry between the pair (not just as siblings but as members of the royal family), true cracks began to appear in 2016, when Prince Harry brought the California sun into the gray skies of his royal life. Meghan Markle's arrival was a jolt to the system, but William soon expressed concerns that Harry was moving too fast with someone who had lived a life so far removed from that of his brother. For William, Meghan was the living embodiment of an "outsider," and he believed Harry was swept up in her glamour and American joie de vivre to the point that he was refusing to acknowledge the rules and risks of managing a relationship within the institutional apparatus. At the expense of the family image, it was felt that Harry was rushing into something that had serious blowback potential.

As Harry continued to feel unsupported by William and the institution, the brotherly relationship went steadily downhill during the months that followed, and the more incendiary moments made headlines thanks to Palace leaks. By 2018, their father reportedly stepped in briefly to referee after Harry accused William of not doing enough to welcome Meghan into the family after their wedding. Charles convinced William and Kate to host the Sussexes for Christmas at Anmer Hall that year (their only holiday invite in the years they lived in the United Kingdom). The Band-Aid didn't hold for long. Over time, William increasingly complained about Meghan to aides and family members. He didn't like how opinionated she was, how she spoke to his staff, and how much of her Markle family dramas were in the press. "William shifted away from acting like a brother and became more like someone only focused [on the Crown]," a source close to the Sussexes said.

Just more than a year later, in January 2020, the Duke and Duchess of Sussex announced they were stepping back from their royal roles to pursue private opportunities in North America, of all places. It was reported in *The Times* that William had "bullied" Harry out of the family. A joint statement denied the story and called out the allegations as false remarks. "For brothers who care so deeply for the issues surrounding mental health, the use of inflammatory language in this way is offensive and potentially harmful," the statement read. Reporters said it was a sign that the brothers could still come together, but the reality was Harry didn't even know about the statement. "I'm so pissed," one of their most senior aides told me the day it was released. "We were completely bulldozed."

For William, the many fractures split wide open when Harry went public with his grievances against the family and the institution—first with Oprah in 2021, then on Netflix in 2022, and then again in his memoir the following year. Harry's sustained offensive was too much for William. In his first post-exit interview, Harry asserted that William (and Charles) are "trapped" in the system—there is no exit for the next in line. While this is objectively true, a source close to William told me that the heir feels "far from [trapped] in *any* system." But we do know that there are persisting reports that William has been—and always will be—envious of Harry's freedom to "break away" from the royal establishment. Couple this slow-burning resentment with William's outright anger at what he perceives as Harry's relentless selfishness in his war against the two institutions he blames for his ills, and it's easy to see why William's fury is bubbling to the top.

The king in waiting believes Harry and Meghan blindsided the family, even the Queen, with their public complaints and their "*oh so* California" self-importance (an opinion he has repeatedly voiced in various ways to friends and aides during the past two years). Convinced Harry's been brainwashed by an "army of therapists," William says he no longer even recognizes his own brother, a source said. Before the family raised the drawbridge and enshrouded the Palace in silence as a response to Harry's incriminating revelations, there were leaks to reporters that William and other family members, including Camilla, covertly sanctioned. The *Independent* claimed that the family feels Harry was "kidnapped by a cult of psychotherapy."

They say deaths and births can bring battling families back together, but neither have helped the Prince of Wales and the Duke of Sussex. In the wake of the Queen's death, the brothers remained in their own separate corners. Over the Christmas holidays that followed, not a single message was exchanged (though gifts were sent by the Sussexes to George, Charlotte, and Louis). And even when Harry came to the United Kingdom in March 2023 for a pretrial hearing in his battle against *Daily Mail* publisher Associated Newspapers, William and Kate kept their distance. "The Waleses are not in Windsor for the [Easter] school holidays," their spokesperson said. Not that Harry had asked to meet.

———•———

William's reactions to Harry's newfound freedom and justice-seeking campaigns to change the British media landscape are certainly more institutional than they are brotherly. At one point in his life, William hated the U.K. newspapers as much as (or maybe even more than) his brother. Which points to another source of William's frustration—the "company man," the monarchy's next sovereign, must fall in line, even when it means eschewing his own brother. Harry and William's estrangement in many ways resembles another sensational fraternal feud in the royal family, but in reverse. Nearly one hundred years ago, Edward VIII contentiously abdicated the throne to his younger brother George VI (Queen Elizabeth's father), because the family and the establishment wouldn't allow him to marry the love of his life, the American divorcée Wallis Simpson. After Edward's abdication, the family was never whole again. The two brothers were effectively ripped apart by institutional duty and personal desire. Different royal players on a different stage, but the storyline is strikingly familiar.

At the center of both morality plays is the monarchic institution. After Harry's trinity of revelations and what a 2023 episode of *South Park* mocked as a "worldwide privacy tour" (both William and Kate supposedly found the show's send-up of the Sussexes "hilarious"), House Montecito's stance on the institution is crystal clear: it's a system of overlords and buttoned-up Machiavellis in cahoots with a tabloid cabal who are all hell-bent on upholding the Crown no matter the human cost. With William, however, it's murkier and more complex. His current positions on Harry, Andrew, and the state of affairs in the outside world certainly suggest that he's in full compliance with the system, that he's accepted his role with few reservations, and that he's prepared to captain the monarchy when called upon.

But let's not forget that a mere six years ago it was a different story. Back then, the prince was not exactly known for his work ethic when it came to royal responsibilities, and the nicknames "Workshy Wills" and "throne idle" followed him, which in March 2017 was to the ski slopes and nightclubs of the Swiss Alps. While on a "boys' trip," the prince skied by day and partied by night in the chic resort town of Verbier. Photographs sold to *The Sun* showed him on the dance floor with an "Aussie beauty" who was most certainly not Kate. William was heavily criticized, of course, but what stirred up the Palace and Fleet Street enough for them to send up the flares was the fact that he was noticeably absent for the Commonwealth Day service, Britain's largest interfaith gathering, held at Westminster Abbey every year, that took place during his trip. It's harder to imagine now, but Prince William was AWOL, and at a time when

Queen Elizabeth II was discernibly slowing down. He had already been skating on thin ice when it came to work, with even the likes of aging Prince Philip carrying out a vast amount more royal engagements than him (128 more, to be precise). A former communications staffer said William was "extremely reluctant" to fully focus on work. "There was a marked difference between William then and William now. There were long periods of time when it was only possible to get one sit-down meeting a month with himself and Kate for forward planning. It didn't feel like his priority."

This isn't to suggest William was work-shy in other areas. Leading up to and after he tied the knot with Kate, William worked at his "day jobs" for several years. In 2010, he signed up as a Royal Air Force search-and-rescue pilot on Anglesey, a large island in northwestern Wales known for its charming rural villages and natural beauty. William and Kate made their home on Anglesey for three years, completely enamored of its sea-swept location surrounded by rolling verdant farmlands, rocky beachheads, and soaring limestone cliffs. White-washed stone on the outside, rustic beams and cozy fireplaces in the inside, and topped with a roof made of locally sourced slate, Bodorgan Hall is an eighteenth-century five-bedroom farmhouse situated on an estate near the Irish Sea. It is here where a baby Prince George spent the first few months of his fairly normal-looking life, where Kate could easily pop out to the nearby Waitrose in the town of Menai Bridge to pick up frozen pizzas on nights she didn't feel like cooking or bags of Haribo candy to stuff in the side pockets of their car. Considering the location of his first home, his meaningful RAF work, and the glow around his new family, it's no surprise William shied away from his royal duties during this time. "It's where they are at their happiest," the couple's former press secretary Ed Perkins told me at the time.

The Firm planned for William to engage in a few years of service before taking on the lion's share of his royal duties, but what they didn't expect was for William to keep extending it. In 2015,

William joined the East Anglian Air Ambulance charity, a helicopter emergency medical team in the eastern county of Norfolk, England. Both Charles and the late Queen supported his decision, but it's now known that a handful of senior courtiers pushed against it. From their view, not only was it time for William to buckle down into his role in the family business, but they also believed this "middle-class job" was beneath the future King. Swooping in with the RAF was one thing, but choppering around with "ordinary people," a source told *The Times*, just wasn't in the royal paradigm. But he forged ahead anyway, and, to his credit, William stuck it out for two years, all the while fending off pressure from Palace busybodies and a nosy press. It was tough work, and he would later discuss how traumatic it was for him at times. I spoke to the prince about his role just a few months after the birth of his and Kate's second child, Princess Charlotte, in May 2015. "Extremely tough," he said of the twenty-four-hour shifts he would sometimes have to carry out, but one of the "most rewarding things I have ever done."

William was motivated by his own individual value system (the Firm's would have to wait), and by his husbandly and paternal instincts to keep his wife, son, and future children out of the media's relentless gaze. He learned the hard way, but it didn't have to be that way for Kate and their kids. After paparazzi continually harassed their children in public and a photographer was even found in the trunk of a car waiting for Prince George to surface at a playground near their home, William worked with his head of communications Jason Knauf on a 1,073-word plea that was then sent out to every editor in the country. The extreme and dangerous lengths certain individuals were resorting to to obtain new pictures of their children *had* to stop.

There were legal threats, too. William and Kensington Palace officials decided that to take away the value of these long lens pictures, they would release their own photos instead. Since then, the couple has released new portraits for each child's birthday, as well as family holidays, Mother's Day, Father's Day, and other milestones, such as first days at new schools. It was a smart move. "He would do anything to keep those children safe," one of his aides shared with me at the time. "And he's not just doing this for himself, but also for others in the family. One day Harry will have kids of his own."

Two years later, William stressed the point when he said, "My mother did put herself right out there and that is why people were so touched by her. But I am determined to protect myself and the children, and that means preserving something for ourselves. I think I have a more developed sense of self-preservation."

For a few years, this impulse for self-preservation served him well. William managed to successfully resist the expectations of others and carve out a private space for family life, all the while reporting for duty when necessary. But, eventually, the institutional demands placed on an heir proved impossible to skirt any longer. In January 2017—following increased pressure from the public, press, and institution, and at a time when an aging Queen Elizabeth II needed more support from other senior family members—he announced the end of his career as a pilot and reported to "Monarchy HQ" for his full-time position in the Firm. "Following on from my time in the military, I have had experiences in this job I will carry with me for the rest of my life, and that will add a valuable perspective to my royal work for decades to come . . . I have loved being part of a team of professional, talented people that save lives every day," he said. And with that, William, Kate, George, and Charlotte left their country enclave in Norfolk to make Apartment 1A at Kensington Palace in London their full-time royal residence.

Since embracing his full-time duties, he's quickly moved up the ladder. In just six years, his job title has already changed once, and it is only a matter of time until he steps into the Firm's top position. William's eleven years as the Duke of Cambridge lasted until the Queen's death in 2022, at which point he automatically became the

Prince of Wales—the Duke of Cornwall in England and the Duke of Rothesay, Earl of Carrick, Baron of Renfrew in Scotland. With this promotion and mouthful of titles, William also inherited the private Duchy of Cornwall estate, a massive land and property portfolio that covers nearly 140,000 acres and was created by King Edward III in 1337. Prince Charles's entrepreneurial efforts (and passion for farming) throughout his fifty years as a prince helped one of Britain's oldest and largest land parcels to grow in worth to somewhere in the neighborhood of £1 billion. Its annual net surplus (£24 million for 2022–2023) is reinvested into the Waleses' charitable endeavors and helps fund the family's public and private lives.

Since William became its proprietor, Kensington Palace hasn't shared much news about his Duchy of Cornwall role, but fully taking over his father's position there was always the plan. Even in 2019, Prince William was already a frequent visitor and a smiling face to the tenants and employees on the rural estate. Having shadowed Charles there on several occasions, the prince became more involved in the business behind the duchy and educating himself on the challenges it may face under his watch. "I'll never know as much as he does, but I'll try my best," he said in October 2019. "I've got the interest and the passion. The countryside is deep in my heart . . . My interest isn't really appearing yet, but it will do in the future." Now that he's the boss (who received a private income of £6 million in 2023), Kensington Palace sources say he plans to do things "his way," cherry-picking from some of the ways his father, grandmother, and grandfather managed estates over the years.

Lee Thompson, his current communications secretary, says William is keen to integrate more of his charitable interests with relevant areas of the duchy, which also covers urban areas. First up is an ambitious plan to build social housing on the estate as part of a longer mission to "end homelessness." It will start small and then scale up if all goes well. The plans tie in nicely with a Royal Foundation initiative he launched in June 2023. Homewards will develop housing and resources for the homeless in six locations across Britain. William says he wants to reach its goal over the next five years and "give people across the U.K. hope that homelessness can be prevented when we collaborate."

The Prince of Wales title and the next-in-line status certainly brings its fair share of perks, but it's also brought more responsibility and pushed William further into the public eye—the same penetrating stare from which he mightily protected his family from just a few years ago. The public-facing Prince of Wales embraces the footlights the institution has switched on for him, but the private William—the son, the husband, the father—remembers his mother's struggles on this very same stage. William's confidence in his role, his slot in the system, and his place in the long line of British kings and queens is visible—he looks every ounce a man of the institution, a king in waiting comfortable calling the shots, doing things his way. But the flip side of this is indifference and harshness and the way he continues to stonewall Harry when all his brother wants from his family is honest conversations and accountability. One is left to wonder if William of Anglesey or William the air ambulance pilot would have left his sibling out in the cold in the same way.

And as the saying goes, it's lonely at the top, or, in William's case, just shy of the top. After Harry's exit, William is considerably more alone in the battle of his two selves. Even though they were always on different paths, Harry and William once shared an office, worked on the same foundations, and wanted to protect their families from the things they both feared. Proximity once allowed them to be each other's sounding boards, particularly in times of crisis, and that "unique bond" William so highly praised tied them together when everything else was pulling them apart. The Queen's death amplified all this. Charles vanished into the sacred Crown's engulfing orbit, leaving William to face the royal family's new chapter and the institution's increasing demands without his brother close by, the one person in the world who can empathize with all that's in store for him. As a friend close to William is quoted as saying, the heir is "definitely feeling the pressure now [that] it's all on him—his future looks different because of his brother's choices; it's not easy." As for how he feels about Harry since the release of *Spare*, a source close to the prince told me, "There's a huge amount of anger there. He feels betrayed and sad about the situation. But he also doesn't agree with the things his brother feels he has done. He feels he has lost Harry and doesn't want to know this version of him." That version, countered a Spencer family source, is simply "Harry being a man who has stepped outside of the institution and sees things in a different light. They will never see eye to eye at this point. They're on completely opposite sides . . . that won't change." Time does heal wounds, but it also hardens grudges, particularly when you've got an entire institution to validate and back your resentment and anger.

Strangely enough, this institutional support has proven problematic and yet another source of frustration for William. For most of his adult life, Palace officials, senior courtiers, and even the Queen herself have paved the way for the future King William. They've envisioned it, planned for it, and, during more private moments, even discussed the fantasy of skipping Charles altogether and installing William as King at the end of the Queen's reign. This support of—and excitement about—William has not gone unnoticed by Charles over the years. In his new kingship, Charles is empowered to prove everybody wrong, and time will tell. Though they grew closer while William learned the ropes for his Duchy of Cornwall position and, added a source, "they have been united in their frustrations with Harry," an emerging narrative between father and son is only just taking shape: two men serving the same institution but with very different visions for how that establishment will run. The Palace may have once pushed the narrative that the two are perfectly aligned, but the reality is William is eager to make his own unique mark. "He respects his father, but he also sees him as a transitional monarch, paving the way for *his* arrival," said a source close to the Prince of Wales. "Their views, their outlooks, are very different, and I can see that becoming an issue over the years ahead."

To avoid repeating this pattern of father-and-son strain and tension with his own children, William has made a concerted effort to be a more involved and protective father. Evidenced by his initial instincts to begin his work life in the private sector to shield his firstborn, George, from the system and the swarming tabloids, this remains an essential condition for William as a father and as a senior member of the Firm. In Anglesey and Norfolk, William drew up plans for a different kind of life for his children, sending a message to the public and the institution that he demands a level of peace and familial security for his children that wasn't afforded to him during his own upbringing. His former private secretary Miguel Head said that after William started his own family, he displayed a "visceral determination to give them a life of consistency and privacy."

In the summer of 2022, the family of five left behind Kensington Palace and moved twenty-four miles outside the capital to Windsor. Adelaide Cottage, a "modest" (only by royal standards) four-bedroom property, is giving the family the opportunity to live a more "normal" life, their team has said. Kensington Palace served them well but the parents to the second, third, and fourth in line to the throne felt it was time to find something less in the middle of everybody else's business. At times, one of the couple's senior aides told me in 2016, Kate commented that it made them feel "a bit like caged animals," due to its heaving central London location and the fact that it was surrounded by tourists in one of the city's busiest parks. Adelaide isn't a permanent home (the couple have their eyes on Prince Andrew's Royal Lodge residence in Windsor

Great Park—if he ever gives it up), but Windsor's quiet, rural environment is exactly what they were looking for. The royal estate, said sources, provides the children with plenty of safe space to run, cycle, and play in privacy, and all three have settled into their nearby Lambrook School (to which Mum and Dad still do the school runs themselves most of the time). During the days, William often uses workspace at Windsor Castle itself, with staff there now more familiar with the sight of the future King making his way back and forth between home and the castle (reportedly by e-scooter). Perhaps on a deeper level this is a way to re-create some of the quiet life they started together in Anglesey.

Sitting down with one of William's former aides, who spoke to me for the purpose of this book, I asked if the release of Harry's memoir—which went into unprecedented detail about the difficulties of being the spare to the heir—has had any impact on how the Waleses plan to raise their own two spares, Princess Charlotte and Prince Louis, the latter of whom was born in April 2018. William, they claimed, has not read it. Hard to believe, I pressed. "He's read passages but not the full thing . . . Harry's experience is very different to [that of William's] own children." One hopes that remains the case.

Of course, William navigates all of this with his wife. Despite the challenges ginned up by persistent rumors, sources said William's marriage to Kate remains solid. "It's a partnership, an alliance, and a lifetime commitment," said a royal source. "They work as a team." And, they added, William remains "incredibly proud" of Kate's growth as a senior working member of the family. "It's all about support, and both feel supported by one another," said a family friend. Indeed, for William's milestone projects over the years, including the Earthshot Prize, Kate has been by his side.

His public role has, however, continued to have slipups along the way, largely down to a premature rush from Kensington Palace to reposition William as a "statesman" within just a year of the prince leaving his pilot job to become a full-time working royal. The much-mocked 2022 Caribbean tour is one of the most notable examples. And there have been the many other false promises along the way. When he visited Israel and the Occupied Palestinian Territories for five days in 2018, Palace aides were quick to brief the press that peace in the Middle East would become the heir's "lifelong mission." In a speech, William told the people of Palestine they "have not been forgotten." Since then, however, there has not been a further word from the prince or his team on the matter, even though violence between the two groups continues to escalate.

In March 2023, William made a surprise visit to Poland to personally thank British and Polish troops for supporting Ukraine and to emphasize Britain's support for Ukrainians in their fight against Russia. Admirable enough, but casually dressed in a black puffer jacket, William conjured up the images of Paul Wolfowitz and Donald Rumsfeld, who wore military-style boots with a jacket and tie when visiting troops during the Iraq War. The usual royal press took the bait. *The Sun*'s cover headline declared, "WILLS THE FREEDOM FIGHTER," but his platitudes about "defending our shared freedoms" were also a reminder that in this apolitical and unelected role, there is not much he can actually accomplish on this front. And then there is the fact that when he took on the title of the Prince of Wales, his first solo visit to his new namesake country wasn't exactly a hit. Locals there—some of whom have campaigned for the title to be abolished due its holder having no true connection to the country—were less than impressed with his inability to speak more than a few words of Welsh, despite having had years to prepare.

"He's doing his best," said a Kensington Palace source, "but he is also just a human. There is a lot to learn along the way." Indeed, as a father of an heir and two spares, and as a king in waiting, there are mounting stresses and obligations in both his official life and his private one. This requires some delicate maneuvering and a highly functioning on-off switch. The Queen managed this high-wire duality with aplomb, but with William, it's too early to tell.

I'll never forget a conversation I had with William when he was still an air ambulance pilot. He told me that after a long day's work in emergency situations that demanded everything he had in him—a rigorous mix of hard and soft skills—he often had to take some time at home "to decompress . . . watch TV or have a cry" before reentering the family world as a husband and father. It was one of the few moments over the years I've witnessed a more vulnerable side of William. Here was a person who, like many, struggles with unrelenting work-life balance and the letting go of one part of yourself to be fully present in the other. It dawned on me that this is the royal predicament in a nutshell—the juggling of inner and outer lives, ambitions and obligations, personal desire and duty. For a moment, when William, whether intentionally or not, left his formal royal persona behind, I saw a glimpse of the man behind the facade. I can't help but wonder whether the system will ever allow the public to see this side of the Prince of Wales and the future King, or whether, seven years on, that side of him still exists. If the Queen or many of those before her are any indication, the chances are slim. His recent posturing and dedication to the institutional cause suggests the carefully curated royal persona is here to stay, a crusader for a Crown.

# 9

## Gloves Off

### Prince Harry, Man on a Mission

———◆———

*For what matters in life is not whether we receive a round
of applause; what matters is whether we have the courage
to venture forth despite the uncertainty of acclaim.*

—Amor Towles, *A Gentleman in Moscow*

*I was summoned to provide backup, distraction, diversion
and, if necessary, a spare part. Kidney, perhaps.*

—Prince Harry, *Spare*

As the morning sun rises over Santa Barbara, bathing the steep Santa Ynez Mountains, and the Pacific Ocean sparkles with California's trademark glow, the sprawling Sussex compound in the wealthy enclave of Montecito is already popping. With Meghan already preparing a family breakfast in the kitchen, Prince Harry is busy getting the couple's children, Prince Archie and Princess Lilibet, ready for nursery school and toddler playgroup, respectively.

Despite the staff on hand to help during the daytime, when Harry and Meghan shift into work mode, the Sussexes keep their mornings as time "for the family only," said a source—no staff. As hands-on parents, the pair take turns doing the school drop-offs and pickups every day.

Once the kids are settled, the couple switch into their own prework morning routines. Their Tuscan-style villa (its number of bathrooms an obsession to the British press, who cite the stat in almost every article about the couple) includes a fully equipped gym they both make the most of before joining their first meetings of the day. For Harry, working out and staying healthy have become regular parts of his life in California. Sessions with his personal trainer, hikes, bike rides, acupuncture, and ice baths have all become essentials. "Spending time with Harry lifts you up," said a friend. "He's positive, happy, and motivating. He's in a great place."

It's a place a world away from the life in Britain that Harry officially left behind in January 2020. When he and Meghan announced a joint decision to step back from their royal roles, after their "half-in-half-out" working model was rejected by Queen Elizabeth II and her advisors, they had to restart from scratch. Now, the couple's calm life in California is an existence that, at many points during their working royal years, and even those first months after moving, they dared not even imagine as a possible reality.

Both openly admit that the journey to get here has been tough. Family relations were tested and ruptured (permanently, in some cases), some commercial deals were made in haste to secure sufficient money to guarantee their safety long into the future (and a home of their own), and the pressures of a watching world prodded them to go full throttle when it came to launching their own projects. "Not one step ahead could be predicted . . . they were flying by the seat of their pants at times," said a friend of the couple. "Those first two years outside of the U.K. were scary, stressful, and, while full of hope, incredibly draining. It took a long time to be able to just sit back and think, 'Phew, we're going to be okay.'"

As stressful as it was, their more recent experiences back in the royal bubble have confirmed that leaving it all behind was exactly the right thing to do for them. Even though they live completely separate lives from the royal family, key moments have seen brief returns to the chaos. Some, such as the Platinum Jubilee celebrations, were anticipated, while others—particularly the death of the Queen—unexpectedly pulled them back into the institution's whirlwind of games and manipulations, the same vortex that had hauled them toward its dark center for four years.

When the couple left their children in California with Meghan's mother, Doria Ragland, and a nanny to visit the United Kingdom and Germany for five days of engagements in September 2022, neither knew that the quick-fire trip would result in a two-week return to royal drama. Neither did I. During this visit, I joined some of their engagements and watched as Meghan gave a speech to teenagers and young adults at the One Young World summit in Manchester. In the post-pandemic world, Harry and Meghan wanted to remind people that they hadn't lost touch with the organizations and causes they were involved in before their departure. There was talk of visiting the Queen in Scotland, but her schedule, the couple was told, was already packed. Any rumors about Her Majesty possibly being in her final days had certainly not made it as far as California. With the imminent releases of their Netflix docuseries and *Spare*, family members and Palace officials were also doing their best to keep the couple at arm's length and out of the loop.

The couple intentionally kept to themselves while staying at their Windsor base, Frogmore Cottage, with no plans in place to visit family and zero room in their schedule for socializing. Plus, they were eager to get back to Archie and Lilibet as soon as their work was complete. The only private time they took was a visit to Althorp, the resting place of Princess Diana. They had never been as a couple, and Harry had long wanted to bring his wife to his late mother's grave.

Frogmore Cottage was once a home filled with promise, but after they moved overseas in 2020, their British base (which Charles wouldn't take away until the following year) didn't feel quite so cozy anymore. By the time of their last scheduled engagement—the WellChild Awards on September 8—they were more than ready to head back home, just in time to celebrate Harry's thirty-eighth birthday as a family. Still, the two of them were looking forward to the WellChild event, which celebrates the inspirational qualities of Britain's seriously ill children and the professionals who help care for them. The charity was one of Harry's first royal patronages, and he crafted a heartfelt speech for the ceremony.

As it turns out, he never got to read that speech. The night before the WellChild event, doctors for Queen Elizabeth II advised the monarch to clear her calendar and rest. Though it did not involve a hospital stay, the fact that Buckingham Palace had made an official announcement about it confirmed growing fears that her decline in health was getting worse. The news rattled the Sussexes. Just four days prior, Harry had spoken with his grandmother on the phone. She had mentioned not being well enough to attend the Highland Games, but her working schedule was still full of appointments. The monarch was, as sources said at the time, positive and upbeat.

By the next morning, the Sussexes had no idea that Buckingham Palace was already planning for the Queen's final hours and the first days of the monarchy's new era—until the duke's phone started ringing. An unknown number. He usually ignored those. "You should answer it," Meghan told him. He tapped accept just before it stopped. Harry hadn't spoken to his father much that year, but this was not the time for any father-and-son tension. Charles told him he and Camilla were about to leave Dumfries House for Balmoral, where Princess Anne was already by the Queen's side. He told Harry to make his way to Scotland immediately. William, whom Charles had just spoken to, was supposedly working on arranging travel. Harry sent a text message to his brother asking how he and Kate planned to get to Scotland and whether they could travel together. No response.

With no further information from other family members or Palace aides, the Sussexes and their team had to operate in the dark. Harry was informed that William had already secured a flight with his uncles Andrew and Edward (and Edward's wife, Sophie), but he couldn't get in touch with anyone about joining that flight. "It was upsetting to witness," said a source close to the Sussexes. "[Harry] was completely by himself on this." Buckingham Palace released a further update: "Following further evaluation this morning, the Queen's doctors are concerned for Her Majesty's health and have recommended she remain under medical supervision. The Queen remains comfortable and at Balmoral." Harry knew it was happening, and happening fast.

With the world's media now rushing to Aberdeenshire (and most flights and train tickets selling out within minutes), travel options dwindled. Another call came through from Charles, who instructed his younger son to come alone. Despite already publicly confirming that Meghan would come with him (always the plan if they were traveling from California for this very situation), he reluctantly agreed, after Charles assured him that Kate would not be there, either. Charles had cited "protocol," but the reality was that Kate chose to stay back to pick up the children from their first day at a new school. "They just didn't want Meghan there," said a former Palace aide. Meghan, a friend added, "could sense she wasn't wanted."

Harry sent another text to his brother. Nothing. Though there were available seats on William's chartered Dassault Falcon private jet, which was leaving in less than an hour, Harry was left to fend for himself. "William ignored him," said a family source. "He clearly didn't want to see his brother." Princess Eugenie reached out to Harry to see if he had any more information about their grandmother. She had heard from another family member that it was "time" but knew little more.

The Sussex team clamored to find a flight for Harry, ratcheting up the pressure on what was an already stressful situation. Meanwhile, an hour later than originally scheduled, William, Edward, Sophie, and Andrew's flight took off from an airfield just nineteen miles away from Frogmore Cottage. With no invite forthcoming from any of the family members, Harry eventually located an available option—a private charter costing £30,000 from Luton Airport, a forty-minute drive from Frogmore without traffic.

And with that, Harry started his own race to Scotland. Though rumors of the Queen's passing were rife at this point, Harry had no way of knowing whether it was true. His father doesn't carry a cell phone and his brother wasn't acknowledging his existence. When William and the others landed at 3:50 p.m. to discover the news that the Queen had passed away at 3:10 p.m., Harry still had no idea what was going on when his own plane finally took off at 5:35 p.m. And, as his phone service cut out after takeoff, he remained in the dark for the duration of his seventy-minute flight.

Back on the ground, there was a tug-of-war between the Sussexes' team and Buckingham Palace over whether to announce the news without Harry being informed. With Her Majesty's death already confirmed to the prime minister an hour before Harry left, and all other senior family members now gathered in Scotland processing the news, royal press secretaries were ready to share the news with the world. The Palace claimed Charles tried to call Harry (sources later told me there was never any proof of this), and that there was no more time left to delay. "His team literally had to beg for them to wait for his plane to land and they reluctantly agreed to hold the statement back for a little bit," confirmed a close family source. But as stormy weather over Aberdeen International forced Harry's plane to circle the airport numerous times before landing, patience at the Buckingham Palace press office wore thin—they could wait no longer and the announcement went live at 6:30 p.m. When Harry's plane finally touched tarmac twenty minutes later, he received a text from Meghan urging him to call ASAP followed by a breaking news alert via the BBC News app with the announcement of the Queen's death. Palace "sources" later briefed certain papers that Charles had personally shared the news with his younger son, but this was just a move to save face. "Harry was crushed," said a friend of the duke. "His relationship with the Queen was everything to him. She would have wanted him to know before it went out to the world. They could have waited just a little longer, it would have been nothing in the grand scheme of things, but no one respected that at all."

During the one-hour car ride to Balmoral, the silence in the security-driven BMW gave the now fifth in line to the throne time for the news to sink in. Despite the ups and downs of his royal life, Harry and the Queen were consistently close. "Granny, while this final parting brings us great sadness, I am forever grateful for all of our first meetings—from my earliest childhood memories with you, to meeting you for the first time as my commander-in-chief, to the first moment you met my darling wife and hugged your beloved great-grandchildren," he wrote in a statement. "I cherish these times shared with you, and the many other special moments in between. You are already sorely missed, not just by us, but by the world over."

When he arrived at Balmoral, Princess Anne warmly greeted him and led him to the Queen's room, where he spent a quiet moment privately paying his respects. He had hoped to see his father—who had made it to Balmoral Castle in time to see his mother alive—to express his sympathies, but he was informed that Charles, William, and Camilla had already left for Birkhall together. Again, no invite was extended to Harry. That night after eating he retired to his room, exhausted by the day's emotional roller coaster. He was glad to have had a private moment to say goodbye to his grandmother, but there was no point in sticking around. With no offer to return with William and the others in the morning (all of his texts, including a thoughtful message about the loss of their grandmother, continued to be ignored), Harry booked his own British Airways ticket on the first available departing flight.

During the days ahead, Harry and Meghan kept a low profile, praying the press wouldn't turn their attentions to them but remain rightfully focused on the loss of a beloved monarch. "There was an incredible sense of sadness," said a family source. "For them, the Queen was one of their last strong links to the family. She always made them feel welcome. Without her . . . it will never be the same."

Other senior members of the family were already meeting members of the public, and questions surfaced about whether the nation would see the Sussexes doing the same. Charles spoke to Prince William on September 10 to discuss his plans. The public, said the new King, needed to see the *entire* family putting differences to one side. "Essentially, he told William to swallow his pride and invite his brother and sister-in-law to join them when they greeted mourners and well-wishers in Windsor that day," said a Palace source. "William wasn't keen. This was *his* moment with the public, but the King put pressure on [him]."

With around forty minutes left before he planned to step out on Windsor Castle's Long Walk with Kate, William sent his first text message in months to Harry, suggesting it would be "good" if they came along, too. The couple wanted to do what was right, but time was short. Meghan, in sneakers with her hair pulled up, had only just come back from a walk. The couple's head of communications, Ashley Hansen, gave the couple a pep talk. "It doesn't matter how little time you have, just get out there and do it," she told the couple. And, with that, the Sussexes quickly got ready and made their way to the courtyard of Windsor Castle. Though they had seen William and Kate since their big exit, including at the Platinum Jubilee celebrations, this was the first time the couples had to actually talk as a foursome. The silence as they climbed into the same car (a decision made by Lee Thompson, William and Kate's press secretary) was very noticeable. Given the tension between the brothers and zero communication between Meghan and Kate, the 150-second car ride to the Long Walk felt like two hours as they muddled through light small talk. And then a feeling of discomfort and reluctancy set in as Harry and Meghan caught a glimpse of the photographers and video cameras ready to capture their arrival as a group of four. They knew there would be members of the public gathered, but this was the first time they knew of an official media presence. Kensington Palace, they later found out, had tipped off a select group of people.

Of course, once out of the car, all four were consummate professionals. Walkabouts are a staple of working royal life, and all of them have discovered their own ways to shine in this type of setting. Just like the old days of the "Fab Four," they agreed to split up and each take a different side of the Long Walk. Though appearing composed, sources said Meghan was "extremely nervous" about being in front of the crowds. By this point, the couple's rapidly declining popularity in the United Kingdom was an inarguable fact. The level of vitriol aimed at Meghan in particular, whether online or in the newspapers, was worse than ever. Armed royal protection officers were on high alert, and so was she. Some supporters gathered in the crowd didn't hide their animus toward the duchess. "Of course we would get stuck with her," moaned one woman within earshot of Meghan. Another was seen on camera grimacing after shaking the duchess's hand, while others refused to put their hand out. "When I saw the videos of Meg, I could see she was doing her best to hold it together; she looked terrified," said one of her close friends. When a fourteen-year-old fan stopped to chat with Meghan, their hug choked the duchess up. "I just wanted to show her that she's welcome here and wanted to hug her after everything that's happened," said the teen.

Kate reportedly found the outing just as difficult. Close sources told King Charles's biographer Robert Jobson that she admitted to a family member that "it was one of the hardest things she ever had to do" because of the acrimony between the two couples. Harry spent much of the walkabout speaking with well-wishers about his grandmother, recounting memories of her life. "I still think of her being in [Windsor] Castle when I look over at it," he said to one family, who had told him they were thrilled to see him back in Britain. The moments outside were a reminder that, despite the slanted media coverage, Harry still had some steady support in his home country. After wrapping up their forty-two-minute walkabout, William orchestrated a somewhat forced photo of the four together. Newspapers later cited Kensington Palace sources who revealed the decision to put on a show of unity in Windsor was William's idea, but sources in both Buckingham Palace and the Sussex camp deny this version of the tale. "Sounds like a grab for positive press," snarked a Charles aide.

Over the days that followed, communication from the Palace to the Sussexes remained minimal—mostly text messages from press aides keeping the couple's team abreast of basic information. On September 17, the Palace arranged a fifteen-minute vigil for all the Queen's grandchildren at Westminster Hall, where the Queen was lying in state. Harry was initially told he was not permitted to wear his military uniform, despite his status as a decorated war veteran. He knew his grandmother would have wanted him to, but it took a number of emails and conversations before King Charles relented and gave special dispensation for Harry to wear his Blues and Royals, Number 1 dress attire. But when the uniform arrived at Frogmore Cottage, it was incomplete. The shoulder epaulettes were missing the Queen's "ER" initials (only official aides-de-camp are allowed to wear them, and this was a title he had confiscated) and the ornamental braided cord, known as an aiguillette, had been removed by someone at Buckingham Palace. To rub salt in the wound, Prince Andrew had also been given permission to wear his military uniform for a vigil by his mother's coffin two days earlier, complete with the Queen's cipher and aiguillettes. Heated phone calls were made, but Palace officials refused to make any changes. "Some of these people are determined to make him feel like shit, determined to continue punishing him for leaving, it's bullying," a family source later told me. So incensed by the way aides and Palace officials were treating him, Harry considered wearing a regular suit to the vigil that evening, but after word had come from another aide that William would remove his aiguillette to make things a little more equal, he changed his mind. It was a rare show of support from his brother and one a source said he appreciated.

But the support ended there. For the duration of their time in Britain, the Duke and Duchess of Sussex were on the receiving end of snubs and brush-offs. At the state funeral Camilla, Kate, and Sophie noticeably went out of their way to ignore Meghan outside Westminster Abbey. "They did their best to remain focused on the importance of the trip and honoring Her Majesty, but being dragged into the royal fold again was an unpleasant experience. So little has changed, the same old power trips and dancing around various protocols. Having to deal with the insanity of the media coverage, which on many days revolved around them, made it even worse," said a source close to the couple. Indeed, newspaper articles and royal commentary ranged from cruel to completely made up. One commentator, well known for her fictitious ramblings and out-of-pocket conspiracy theories, used a Sky News broadcast about the Queen's life to falsely claim the couple would be wearing microphones and secret cameras to record their encounters with members of the royal family for future Netflix projects.

The ongoing fictionalization of the Sussexes' lives continues to be a national sport for large sections of the mainstream media. Despite him opening up his life to the public in interviews, television specials, and even a 125,000-word memoir, the caricature most of the papers draw of Prince Harry is barely recognizable to anyone who actually knows him. It's one of the many reasons why the Duke of Sussex is on a mission to reclaim his story, his life, and his image from the media and the public's fantastical accounts. And, through a series of high-profile court cases, he has slowly been able to claw some of it back.

From the libel case against the *Mail on Sunday*—which incorrectly cited "informed sources" in 2020, claiming the prince had turned his back on the Royal Marines and British Armed Forces (a legal fight for which he received substantial damages and a printed apology)—to the ongoing action against the same outlet for defamatory coverage about his security battle with the Home Office (over its refusal to allow him to personally pay for official police protection while in the United Kingdom), the duke has made it clear he's not afraid to dispute and correct the disinformation out there about his wife and him.

And it extends beyond his personal issues with the press. Emboldened by his distance from the royal institution and its fiercely protected relationships with Britain's top media barons, Harry is now free to fight a much larger issue that has quietly plagued the media landscape for decades—illegal news-gathering practices. In 2023, three legal actions for phone hacking and other unlawful intrusions directed at Harry and his inner circle continued to gather momentum in London's High Court: one directed at the *Mirror*'s publisher (MGN) for phone hacking between 1996 and 2011; another for the same allegations at the *Mail* group (Associated Newspapers) for a slightly longer time period; and a third aimed at Rupert Murdoch's News Group Newspapers (NGN), which is the parent company of *The Sun* and the now-shuttered *News of the World*. All three had preliminary hearings in spring of the same year. The MGN case was a full trial of liability for a sample of thirty-seven articles (out of a list of over one hundred) believed to have come as a result of phone hacking and other illegal methods. News Group's hearings mostly revolved around arguments over whether Harry should be allowed to get around the statute of limitations, as he didn't find out about the publisher's alleged unlawful activities until years after they had taken place (because, his lawyer argued, the newspaper hid them so well). In the end, though, the judge determined that only Harry's claims of illegal information gathering can proceed to trial, not the the phone-hacking claims.

His battles haven't gone down well with members of the royal family and their aides, who seemingly did all they could to tamp down Harry's pursuit of justice during his years as a working royal. In their view, fighting the media puts the monarchy at risk. "In short, him wanting to take on these papers posed a threat to all of them," said a former Palace aide. "No one in the family, particularly [Charles, Camilla, and William], wanted the solid media relationships they had formed to be rattled by a family member gone rogue." One of those beneficial relationships was exposed in his case against *The Sun*'s publisher, after Prince Harry's April 2023 witness statement alleged that in 2020 Prince William privately agreed to a "very large" settlement (which sources claimed was over one million pounds) with Murdoch's publisher for not formally suing them for hacking into his private voicemails hundreds of times (later described by Harry as a "favourable deal in return for him going 'quietly'").

This highlights just how different the brothers have become. Before the 2018 rebranding of William as "statesman in the making," the pair were aligned in their plans to put claims against *The Sun*'s publisher and even took first steps down that path together. But Harry alleges that at some point before 2013, Charles's household struck a "secret agreement" with senior Murdoch executives (made without William and Harry's knowledge) that promised that royal victims of phone hacking, including the brothers, would receive a settlement and an apology when all the publisher's other major phone-hacking cases had concluded. A few years later, and irrespective of any "deal" between the two sides, the Queen gave permission for two of her aides to help the brothers get their apologies (with multiple attempts being made to speak with evasive executives at the publisher), but when the monarch's private secretary

Lord Christopher Geidt was pushed out in 2017, any such efforts slowly came to a halt.

After Edward Young took over Lord Geidt's role, both he and Clive Alderton (Charles's private secretary)—a man described by insiders as Young's "partner in crime"—did their best to thwart anything that might anger the Murdoch papers. A source close to the family said, "[Charles's office] has very much ruled the roost when it comes to the relationship with the media . . . [The Queen] was doing her best to ensure that everybody was working in harmony, but Clarence House had a long-term strategy." In his witness statement, Harry described that strategy as a bid to "keep the media onside in order to smooth the way for my stepmother (and father) to be accepted by the British public as queen consort (and king respectively) when the time came, and anything that might upset the applecart in this regard (including the suggestion of resolution of our phone-hacking claims) was to be avoided at all costs." Harry added that when he finally issued his hacking claims against both the *Mirror* and *The Sun* publishers in October 2019, he was "summoned" to Buckingham Palace, where Young, Alderton, and Charles promptly demanded that he drop the legal actions because they had an "effect on all the family."

Following Harry's legal actions, the retaliatory media coverage against the Sussexes reached new levels of negativity and aggression as the industry circled the wagons. Harry remained defiant. "I'm one of the few people that is able to take this the whole way, rather than worrying about my reputation," he told a friend. "But I've got to see this through." The media coverage centered around the prince "attacking" his family (a favored phrase by the tabloids) in the buildup to King Charles's coronation. "The reality," a source close to Harry added, "was that he just wants to protect his claims. The secret Charles/Murdoch agreement was made way above his station, and he only found about it years later. That's why his action has come at this time." For his part, Charles was aware of Harry's court appearances ahead of the coronation and told his son he "understood" why he needed to see it through. Unlike William and more than one thousand other victims of unlawful press intrusion by News Group who settled out of court, largely down to the astronomical legal costs required to take a case to trial and the generous damages offered without admission of liability. Harry is not one of these—he is determined to have his days in court.

It's a bold move to make, one that is fortunately enabled by his deeply lined pockets, due to several commercial endeavors and private investments he's made since moving to California. By entering witness statements into the British legal system and joining forces with other high-profile people (Sir Elton John, David Furnish, Liz Hurley, and more are going against the *Mail* group), Harry has actually made Britain's most powerful publishers feel threatened. The efforts to expose the widespread culture of phone hacking during the 1990s and early 2000s, plus other illegal practices that are suspected to continue today, have also seen some journalists and prominent media figures join these class action cases. For full disclosure, I also testified in the phone-hacking trial against Mirror Group Newspapers, sharing my experiences as a college intern in the publisher's newsrooms, where I witnessed conversations about phone hacking by senior staff, including the *Mirror*'s editor in chief at the time, Piers Morgan. Hundreds of victims have launched civil lawsuits since 2012 and the publisher has, so far, paid out on well over six hundred claims.

Harry himself entered the witness box for the *Mirror* group trial on June 6, 2023, breaking with royal protocol as he became the first member of the family to be cross-examined in court since 1891. During his eight-hour testimony at London's High Court, the prince stated there was "hard evidence" that he was illegally targeted by MGN, who had gone to "extreme lengths to cover their tracks." Along with telling the court that many of his past relationships had failed because of press intrusion (citing an incident when he found a tracking device on the car of his then girl-friend Chelsy Davy), he stated that the way the tabloids reported on Meghan "disgusted" him and provided the motivation for his decision to take on the *Mirror*, *Sunday Mirror*, and *Sunday People* newspapers.

Andrew Green KC, the *Mirror*'s barrister, accused Harry of indulging in "total speculation" and pointed out the prince had "no evidence" his phone had been hacked by journalists working for MGN. However, invoices suggesting the *Mirror* made payments to a range of private investigators in the United Kingdom and the United States were submitted to the court and show that these PIs accessed ex-directory phone numbers, social security details, and financial records of public figures, including Harry. Appealing directly to the judge, an offended Harry responded, "My lord, my whole life the press have misled me, covered up their wrongdoing. To be sitting here in court knowing that the defense has the evidence in front of them, and Mr. Green saying I'm speculating . . . I'm not entirely sure what to say about that." By the end of his testimony, Harry appeared emotional when his barrister David Sherborne asked how he felt after the proceedings. "It's . . . a lot," he quietly replied.

In an interview in early 2023, Harry described his campaign to change the media as his "life's work." It's a statement sources say he would like to revise. "I plan on making sure this does *not* take over my life . . . I want to see it through to a conclusion," he told a friend. In fact, the prince hopes for resolutions on all cases by the end of 2025. "This is a tough commitment, but he has the balls to take them all on . . . He's never going to back down," said a source close to Harry. "He spent ten years in the military and finds it very hard to turn a blind eye to injustice. He is determined to see this through." He is not, however, naïve enough to think that even winning these cases will change how the media writes about him. "I don't see any version of pulling back or settling in the hope that they might leave us alone," he told a friend. "That's never going to happen. Unfortunately, we sell them too many newspapers and too many clicks."

An outcome he does hope for is change at a higher level. "His goal here is not to destroy the media for the sake of it, but to encourage the creation of a more ethical and reliable press," said a source close to the duke. "Destroying them for revenge won't get anyone anywhere. In fact, doing that just leaves a vacuum . . . and who's going to fill that? Probably Murdoch again." Harry hopes that his actions will simply lead to finding some solutions for improving media practices. That at some point, those in the British government, including the Department for Digital, Culture, Media & Sport, will push for a substantive overhaul. With a switch to a Labour government looking likely in 2024 (after the Conservative party—largely supported by media barons who control most of the country's papers—have been in power since 2010), that could happen. It would also be an achievement far greater than anything he could have done as a spare.

In other aspects of his work, Harry's plate is full. His input on the *Harry & Meghan* docuseries and his memoir took up the majority of 2022, but now he's finally focusing on projects that will demonstrate he is moving away from his past. Sources close to the prince confirm that "royal revelations" are now over, and rumors of additional chapters or updates being added to *Spare* are false (the book will remain unchanged when it eventually comes out in paperback). Instead, Harry will focus on production efforts, following the positive feedback received for *Heart of Invictus*, a documentary based on his long-running and successful Invictus Games sporting competition for wounded, injured, and sick veterans and servicepeople. The Sussexes' production company is working on two scripted projects for Netflix that Harry and Meghan acquired the rights to in 2023, including an adaptation of novelist Carley Fortune's *Meet Me at the Lake*. And he will continue his own charitable endeavors, particularly in the military space. "[That] is where he comes alive," said a spokesperson for the duke. "There is so much he plans to do for the community over the years ahead."

The decision to look ahead rather than backward will be music to the ears of the Palace. It will also serve the couple well. After two years of tell-alls about their royal story, the Sussex brand ended up synonymous with drama by the start of 2023. For a couple who hoped to carve out their new U.S. lives as global philanthropists, the soap opera–style narrative that followed them everywhere certainly wasn't the plan. "For setting the record straight, it was absolutely important to share those stories and experiences the way they did," lamented a source, "but such projects take a considerable amount of time to complete, and it kept them immersed in an old chapter of their lives during the new one for longer than was ideal. They're more than ready to move on."

As with any new operation, it has taken a while to find the perfect rhythm. Building a three-piece organization (Archewell Foundation, Archewell Audio, and Archewell Productions) during a pandemic was certainly not the ideal start-up environment. A mix of rushed decisions and hires also meant that earlier PR efforts were far from polished. An out-of-the-blue statement in January 2022 announcing that unnamed sources would no longer speak for the Sussexes is a prime example. The claim was that "only the official communications team at Archewell" will comment—or not—on any stories concerning the couple. An impressive feat if pulled off (especially given that the entire royal bubble thrives on anonymous briefing), but the pledge came across as bizarre to the public and the media, including myself, especially when just a week later (and beyond) unnamed "sources" continued to speak for the couple. Since then, the couple have reconfigured their approach to media strategies and hired a new head of communications, a former media executive at the Universal Film Entertainment Group, Ashley Hansen. And while the confusing guidance about sources is something their team has yet to properly address, it seems this type of cross-communication is already a thing of the past.

Still, mixed messaging such as this causes some distrust in the public—who have often been unclear whether information briefed by the couple's own aides is accurate. When Harry and Meghan experienced a distressing two-hour paparazzi chase around Manhattan in May 2023, additional details shared by their team on background (and cited in articles as "Sussex sources") were dismissed by even some of the couple's most ardent fans, who, as they often do, rushed to point out that "sources don't speak for the couple anymore." Years of British newspapers attempting to poke holes in the couple's every word and action has also strained the Sussexes' credibility, and sources said both Harry and Meghan reluctantly accept it's an area that needs serious improvement.

The rush to sign commercial deals after the royal institution cut them off from all funding and security in 2020 led them to sign some lucrative deals they might have thought twice about had they not been under so much financial pressure. When the couple signed a contract worth up to $20 million with Spotify to develop podcasts, neither of the two expected executives to turn down so many of their ideas. The streamer, said a company source, was only interested in paying out for juicy goods that could generate major headlines and bring in subscriptions. In the end, Spotify only commissioned one Archewell Audio Christmas special and twelve episodes of Meghan's *Archetypes* series—a podcast that explored widely used labels that hold women back. Only a portion of that $20 million was ever paid out and the two parties "mutually agreed" to part ways in the summer of 2023, although a damning review from one of Spotify's podcasting executives, Bill Simmons, who called the couple "grifters," suggested that it may not have been as mutual as implied. "There have definitely been a mountain of lessons learned when it comes to the business side of things," a source close to the couple admitted.

It was a shaky start for the couple's charitable foundation, too. They launched the Sussex Foundation in the summer of 2019, but a source working on the project later told me that plans for the nonprofit were ultimately shelved as Harry and Meghan didn't want to focus on providing grants, an effort that requires constant fundraising. The Archewell Foundation's launch in October 2020 came with grand ambitions to provide something different, but as the months went by they realized again that grants would become the ballast for this foundation as well. No shame in that, and the money given out has gone on to do great things, such as helping move eight thousand individuals out of Afghanistan with the Human First Coalition and providing additional resources to the tech-focused civil rights advocacy organization Color of Change. For a couple who want to create change around a myriad of issues, it makes sense that they have so many irons in the fire. But at the time of this writing, two and a half years into the foundation's life, the true purpose and mission of their charitable vehicle is still not completely clear. A lot of everything, but little in terms of major anchoring projects.

As it turns out, the grant work they avoided at first has taught them how to support small charities and build new partnerships. Now, said the head of the foundation and former Kensington Palace aide James Holt, a "significant change" in direction will become more visible over the next two years. Moving forward, programs are being developed with a key thread in all three areas of the foundation's work—mental health. It starts with the couple's efforts to build a better online world, which includes a project and partnership with the Social Media Victims Law Center and families who have suffered the most extreme impacts of social media.

Linking back to Harry's media battles, Archewell is also seeking ways to "restore trust in information." As well as looking at structural reform, a spokesperson added that they want to use their platform to "promote and highlight media organizations they think are doing the right thing." And the third area is uplifting communities. Picking up from Meghan's work supporting victims of the 2017 Grenfell Tower fire tragedy in London, who came together to prepare food for displaced residents and the wider community, the foundation is introducing the sentiment and drive behind the Hubb Community Kitchen to communities across the United States. By mid-2023, ten projects were already quietly in pilot phases (from sewing groups to cooking clubs), with a focus on women-led initiatives supporting Afghan immigrants who fled the Taliban.

Archewell's decision to work with William Morris Endeavor (WME), a powerhouse agency headquartered in Beverly Hills, has also helped the duke and duchess accelerate some of their charitable work. "It takes a long time to build a lasting legacy but *this* is their life's work," said a Sussex spokesperson.

As for Meghan, following the release of the *Harry & Meghan* docuseries in November 2022, the duchess noticeably distanced herself from the dramas and labels associated with the royal family. By February 2023, Archie's fourth birthday was cited as the primary reason she would not be attending the coronation of King Charles, but sources later told me that her strong feelings about not getting hauled back into royal dramas also played a "significant role."

During that low-profile year, she appeared in public for only a handful of key moments, such as receiving a Women of Vision Award for her advocacy for women and girls. Meghan kept her head down to focus on building her own business. Though there were rumors that she might follow in the footsteps of Gwyneth Paltrow's Goop or revive her lifestyle blog *The Tig* (both tempting options), a source said Meghan is building "something more accessible . . . something rooted in her love of details, curating, hosting, life's simple pleasures, and family." Added a friend of the duchess, "Meghan is busy working on creating something safe and timeless. And something that won't be accused of riding on the back of anything royal."

The couple's decision to enjoy a more relaxed summer in 2023 allowed them to retreat a little from the public eye for the first time since stepping back. Naturally, the quieter moments provided a perfect opportunity for the press to fill in the gaps with their own narratives. Britain's *Telegraph* wasted no time in suggesting that the couple's "frazzled, fraught and lacking romance" relationship was in trouble. Meanwhile the couple—who used to focus on all the coverage about them—remained unconcerned and, at times, blissfully unaware at home in California. "Closer than ever," said a close friend of the couple. "They're genuinely happy."

At times it seemed like the couple would never find complete happiness after leaving the royal fold. Some events of the past still hurt today, particularly those involving their children, Archie and Lilibet. Although convention dictates that the two should have automatically become prince and princess when the King acceded to the throne, it took Buckingham Palace six months to finally confirm the title changes. Charles had initially avoided the subject but eventually told Harry in early 2023 that he would "make it official" if they wanted it (they did), but uttered no further word on it until his press secretary casually informed the couple's team a month later that a change would be made. Officials finally updated the royal line of succession on the Palace's website—the children's "Master" and "Miss" stylings were replaced with "Prince Archie of Sussex" and "Princess Lilibet of Sussex" (sixth and seventh in line, respectively). The Palace blamed the delay on the site's periodic update schedule but refused to explain why they didn't just change the children's titles at the same time as publishing William and Kate's new Wales titles in September 2022. "They see the way their children are treated differently and that's hard to feel comfortable with," said a friend of the Sussexes.

As for Harry, who started the year claiming in interviews that he was hoping for reconciliation with and accountability from his family, he dramatically shifted after his father and brother actively continued to avoid conversations about their part in the difficulties that the Sussexes experienced. In February and March, the prince turned to a mutual friend back in London to try to set up a conversation with his brother, but the attempts were ignored. Harry, said a source, chose to "keep focused on the future, not the past."

As the duke left California on May 5 for King Charles's coronation—a decision he had made because "it was the right thing" to support his father on such a big day—his emotions were a world away from how he felt landing in London with knots in his stomach for the Platinum Jubilee just a year earlier. "Though he hasn't found closure with his family, he's accepted that things are unlikely to change, particularly with his brother—who refuses to even properly talk with him," said a source. As Harry later explained to a friend, "I'm ready to move on past it. Whether we get an apology or accountability, who knows? Who really cares at this point?"

# 10

# The Men (and Women) in Gray

Royal Courtiers and the Struggle for Power

———·———

*The courtier's final aim is to become his prince's instructor.*
—Baldassare Castiglione, *The Book of the Courtier*

*A prince's court*
*Is like a common fountain, whence should flow*
*Pure silver drops in general, but if 't chance*
*Some curs'd example poison't near the head,*
*Death and diseases through the whole land spread*

—John Webster, *The Duchess of Malfi*

When the showy, obsequious courtier Osric appears in Shakespeare's *Hamlet*, Prince Hamlet inquires whether his friend and confidante, Horatio, knows the young Palace aide. As Osric ingratiatingly introduces himself, Hamlet, in a wry aside, asks Horatio, "Dost know this waterfly?" Osric then shares the details of the King's wager—a duel refereed by Osric that eventually causes Hamlet's death—while the prince haughtily toys with the courtier, forcing him to agree with everything he says, despite intentionally contradicting himself. One minute Hamlet says he's hot, the next he is cold, and Osric zealously concurs both times. With a touch of a sneer, the prince scolds the aide for not wearing his hat like a proper courtier: "Put your bonnet to its right use. 'Tis for the head."

Shakespeare's gentle mocking of Osric would have easily landed with his Elizabethan audiences. During Queen Elizabeth I's reign in the sixteenth century, the stereotypical courtier dressed extravagantly to signal their wealth and position in the court. The women literally assembled their outfits, attaching puffy sleeves to bodices and draping elaborate skirts over hooped petticoats known as farthingales. With long, frizzy hair swept up from the forehead into hair helmets and elaborate buns, necklaces, and dangling earrings, female courtiers dazzled like cockatiels. But they were often outdone by the men. Adorned in cloaks, decorative doublets with ruffled collars (think: a gaudy, snug jacket topped by a frilly dog collar cone), ballooning knee-length trousers, tight hose, and, of course, a flamboyant hat, male courtiers were the peacocks of the Elizabethan court.

Colorful, noisy, and always hovering, Queen Elizabeth's advisors and hangers-on were also the insects of the House of Tudor, hence the bard's reference to a waterfly. Like Osric, they buzzed around the monarchs and their advisors, flitting here and there from situation to situation like bugs, carrying messages, refereeing duels, and doing their bosses' bidding. They were the waterflies who dropped in to deliver troubling news; the butterflies who fluttered through the palace, with whispers and scandal providing the uprush of air for their wings; the bees who pollinated the rumor mill and guarded the nest; and the flies who fed on the waste from their devious schemes.

Minus the doublets and farthingales, a courtier's work profile and behavioral traits haven't changed all that much over the centuries. To this day, modern courtiers retain similar responsibilities and perform comparable tasks to their sixteenth- and seventeenth-century predecessors. Current members of the court still diligently guide, protect, and serve their monarchs, often with great skill and even some of that old Elizabethan flair. But instigating and umpiring Palace duels also remain part of the job description, though leaks and press releases have now replaced daggers and swords. The flashy capes may be gone, but Palace advisors still operate in cloaks of secrecy and often trade in gossip and favors. You may not see a courtier donning a feathered bonnet or carrying a scrolled message in the twenty-first century, but King Charles and Prince William continue the tradition of dispatching loyal aides to announce, arrange, fix, and, at times, provoke. Now they're professionally trained and, in some cases, groomed for the job. Today's Osrics sport office attire from Savile Row and have earned their stripes in the creative but wily realms of public relations and communications.

Palace advisors and aides may now come tested and highly qualified, but one royal family member still refers to them as mere insects. In *Spare*, Prince Harry singles out three courtiers—without ever naming them—for the bug treatment, dubbing them "The Bee. The Fly. And the Wasp." Beyond Harry's zoological monikers, courtiers have been subject to an array of nicknames over the years. Queen Elizabeth I referred to her top consultants as "Spirit," "Eyes," and "Elf." One of these, Robert Dudley, Earl of Leicester, was purportedly her lover, so it's fortunate for him that she labeled him Eyes instead of Elf. Both Prince Philip, who often butted heads with members of Queen Elizabeth II's court, and Princess Margaret called them the "Men with Mustaches." A long-serving courtier for both King George VI and Elizabeth II, Sir Alan "Tommy" Lascelles, wore a rather sizable 'stache and did in fact routinely clash with both Philip and Margaret. In *The Crown*, Lascelles is portrayed as a rigid, assiduous member of the old guard—an emblem of establishment order and duty to the monarchy—and the show's Prince Philip character derisively calls him the "dreaded mustache." Princess Diana's well-known tag for the courtiers in her orbit was "the Men in Gray," because of their ubiquitous gray suits; the Duchess of York, Sarah "Fergie" Ferguson, jumped on Diana's train and referred to them as the "Gray Men," while Meghan and her friends privately called them "Palace Vipers."

But who are these men, and now women, in gray, these wasps and mustaches? And what exactly do these courtly bees and elves get up to? Full disclosure: it's a vast and intricate subject, one that is beyond the scope of one chapter, though I will hit some highlights. One could write an entire book about British courtiers and their powerful positions in the monarchy. In fact, some have, including historian Lucy Worsley's *Courtiers: The Secret History of the Georgian Court* and royal reporter Valentine Low's *Courtiers: The Hidden Power Behind the Crown*. Low's book mostly looks at major players from the House of Windsor, which came into being in 1917, including the scornful and "unhelpful" Commander Richard Colville and the modernizing Lord Altrincham, a man who daringly told Queen Elizabeth II and her family that they were out of touch, and then, later in his tenure, let some fresh air in on what he considered an over-stuffy institution buzzing with too many upper-crust drones. Worsley's book pulls the curtain back on the eighteenth-century court, revealing how it's often not just senior officials who wield enormous power in the Palace. King George I's Turkish valet, Mohammed, not only helped dress the King (and treat the monarch's, erm, hemorrhoids) but, because of his intimate access, was considered as important and influential as a government minister.

Centuries later, similar was said about Elizabeth II's personal assistant and senior dresser of three decades, Angela Kelly, whom the late monarch confided in more than any other aide or family member. Discreet and trustworthy, Kelly (nicknamed by some staff as "AK-47" because of her easily triggered temper) knew all Her Majesty's secrets. She was one of the first and few to know about (and keep) the secret of the Queen's health diagnosis and related struggles (revealed by family sources after Her Majesty's death as myeloma, a form of bone cancer). Kelly was also a shoulder to cry on, often sitting with the Queen for hours at a time after the death of her husband, Prince Philip. Charles is said to have never trusted Kelly and, after his mother's death, made one of his first acts as king to evict the sixty-five-year-old from the Windsor grace-and-favor home the Queen had gifted to her. "He wanted to keep her at arm's length and away from the goings-on in Windsor," said a source. And so Kelly was moved four hours away to a property in Yorkshire. Even that came with a condition. After publishing two books about her life working with his mother (with Her Majesty's blessing), the *Mail on Sunday* reported that Kelly was made to sign a new NDA with Charles promising that any future commercial projects don't include the words *King* or *Palace*.

Lowly or high ranking, emblematic or modern, these individuals worked in a position that goes back thousands of years. The 1528 book *Il Libro del Cortegiano* (*The Book of the Courtier*), essentially a how-to guide for aspiring courtiers, described court life as one that "revolved around the monarch or prince it served"; it is a world that has existed since the first monarchies. "Whenever there is a monarch, there is a court; and whenever there is a court there are courtiers," said Low.

The line of British monarchs stretches far back into the mists of time. Sometime during 924–939, Saint Dunstan served as an influential attendant at the court of King Æthelstan, a sovereign whom many consider the founder of the English monarchy. Dunstan was the King's favorite until other jealous courtiers hatched a sabotaging plot: they started a rumor about Dunstan to disgrace him (some things never change). After convincing Æthelstan that his chosen courtier practiced black magic and witchcraft, the King sent him packing. On his way out, his rivals attacked him, threw him in a cesspool, and left him to die. He survived and later joined a monastery. One can hardly blame him.

Two hundred years later, Sir William Marshal transformed the role. As a knight and soldier, he broke the mold of the mere court attendant, becoming King Henry II's most trusted advisor and influencer. An exceedingly powerful courtier who joined military crusades and signed on for administrative posts, he shaped medieval English politics and society in the process. A fellow knight who eulogized him said he was "the best knight who ever lived" and Sir William's legacy is a lasting one—a statue of "the Marshal" was unveiled at Pembroke Castle on the rugged southern coast of Wales in 2022.

Sir Nicholas Carew's legacy is not so grand. As a master of the horse—a top position in the royal household that remains a ceremonial title to this day—Carew was an important figure at the court of King Henry VIII, a transforming but execution-friendly monarch who reigned and terrorized in the early to mid-1500s. Letters between Carew and a fellow conspirator revealed there was a movement afoot to depose the King, and somehow these ended up in Henry's possession (it appears there were leaks then, too). Carew was tried for treason and beheaded on the infamous Tower Hill on the north bank of the River Thames in 1539.

The influential, trailblazing Duchess of Marlborough, Sarah Churchill, kept her head, but she did experience a steep fall from being Queen Anne's favored courtier in the early 1700s. Churchill was Queen Anne's right-hand woman and a quintessential gatekeeper—those who wanted to sway the Queen or sought favors from the monarch approached the duchess first. Anne rewarded Churchill for her loyalty and counsel by promoting her to Keeper of the Privy Purse. Churchill was the first of only two women to hold this powerful position. The second to hold the royal purse strings was her challenger, Baroness Abigail Masham, an ambitious protégé of the duchess whose rise to power eventually eclipsed her boss's, leading Queen Anne to outright dismiss Duchess Churchill from her court.

Although modern courtiers won't find themselves face-to-face with a hooded executioner or at the bottom of a cesspool (not literally anyway; metaphorically the list is long, with finding oneself floating in the sewer of British politics at the top of it), they, too, are often overlooked, plotted against, and caught up in political beef and family feuds. This has much to do with the nature of their work. The label of courtier is synonymous with "Palace aide," and it broadly applies to those who work in royal communications or serve as private secretaries, estate managers, equerries, event coordinators, ladies of the household, dressers, valets, and much more.

More narrowly, though, the term *courtier* is most often linked to press officials and private secretaries. When royal correspondents or talking heads reference courtiers or aides (including quoting them anonymously), chances are they are referring to those Palace staff who manage and offer advice to working royals or those in the communications offices who strategize engagements and release calibrated information. Toiling behind the scenes, they also advise, consult, and, like their ancient predecessors, finagle—surreptitiously directing and promoting their bosses (and, in theory, the Crown) whenever an opportunity presents itself.

Working so closely with the family members puts them in a tough spot. Courtiers must tread carefully to achieve a certain balance. If they are too fawning, principals (the term commonly used by courtiers when referring to their boss) and other influential Palace staff may grow weary of them and discount them, but if they are too direct, their bosses may quickly show them the door. And while they're walking this tightrope, they often have the odious task of persuading monarchs to do some things they might not want to do, like, for instance, stripping Prince Andrew of his titles or disallowing Princess Margaret to marry her beloved Captain Townsend. The hours are long, the pay is often nothing to write home about (after all, it mostly comes from the public purse), and it can be a thankless position with minimal job security. Some stick around for years, but for many it's a brief stint—a springboard to a well-paid job elsewhere.

But underestimate courtiers at your peril. As the historian and royal biographer Robert Lacey says, "[The] courtiers in the British system are the rulers of their masters and their mistresses, they're not really underlings." This is an overstatement, as the monarchs always have the final say, but courtiers are most certainly powerful players. The system promotes a hierarchy and, as a result, aides look for ways to exert their own power to consolidate it for their bosses. This sometimes requires hush-hush dirty work and brutal machinations. Being adjacent to power can be an intoxicating if sometimes corrupting position. Courtiers are the ultimate institutional insiders who—invisibly but with great influence—assist their principals with strategies around work and family complications, and they do what it takes to keep ugly stuff out of the media's relentless gaze. They help them navigate the churning waters where the rivers of their personal lives meet the wild, expansive sea of public opinion.

In this respect, courtiers have played key roles in pivotal moments throughout the monarchy's history, acutely so in more recent times. The information age tore up the ledgers and rule books and reformatted the cultural layout, even scrapping the entire design in some cases. It engendered "truthiness" and introduced multiple platforms for consistent messaging and content overload or campaigns of disinformation.

Through all this change and rearrangement, an ancient monarchy has hung on and stayed relevant—at least enough to survive anyway, both as an institution and a cultural attraction. They've done this by serving the tyrannical notion of image and practicing "brand management"—work that primarily falls under the purview of the courtiers. Essential to the royal brand is the reputation of the monarchs, so courtiers are responsible for managing and repairing the reputations of the family, both individually and collectively. When it's going well, the marching orders are promote, promote, promote! In times of duress or when under attack, it's defend, defend, defend! Or sometimes the edict is to simply stay silent. Either way, the brand must be maintained, the image upheld at all cost, and senior courtiers are on the front lines of these efforts.

Sometimes they do this ethically and responsibly, and sometimes they do not, which leads to the more important questions about senior courtiers: How do their practices and ploys impact the royal family, both as a family and as a brand? Do their ethics and values always reflect those that the monarchy is supposed to uphold? This brings us back to Harry's insects.

"The Bee" is Queen Elizabeth II's former private secretary, Sir Edward Young. A former banker and advisor to Conservative politicians, Young looks the part of both. An "oval-faced" (Harry's words) middle-aged white man with neatly parted salt-and-pepper hair, he looks like two different people depending on whether or not he is wearing his glasses. Bespectacled, he's all business administration with a touch of the professorial; without, he appears a little softer around the edges and slightly lost. But don't let the latter look fool you. Following a three-year stretch as head of communications for the Granada media conglomerate (now ITV plc), he joined the royal household in 2004 as an assistant private secretary to the Queen until Her Majesty promoted him to the head job thirteen years later. Dedicated to his role, he was fiercely protective of the late monarch, particularly during the engulfing drama of Harry and Meghan's departure. Harry's contention is that Young abused his gatekeeping power, gaslighting him when it came to passing along important messages about his lawsuits against the media, and then prohibiting access to his grandmother when Harry needed her the most, all under the guise of "protecting the sovereign."

I first wrote about Young's tactics when revealing the final hours of preparations for the Sussexes' exit from Palace life at the start of 2020. After the couple announced that they were stepping back from their royal roles (and initially blocked by Young from talking to the Queen about it with a lie that her schedule was "full"), Palace officials planned the "Sandringham Summit," a boardroom-style meeting sold as a discussion to determine the Sussexes' future in the monarchy. On the agenda at the January 13, 2020, gathering was whether Harry and Meghan would be granted the "half in, half out" working model they pitched (keep their security, perform royal work to support the Queen, and fund their own charitable projects with commercial endeavors), or would be granted a clean break ("full severance," which meant the Sussexes would lose their entire security detail, and their royal obligations and responsibilities would come to a complete halt).

Edward Young and the Queen joined Harry (with his short-lived private secretary Fiona Mcilwham), William (who brought private secretary Simon Case), and Charles (who arrived with his private secretary Sir Clive Alderton) for an hour of discussion, before leaving only the family members for the final talking points. Soon after, the institution made the call: *full severance*. Harry argues, however, that the "fix was in" from the start—his family went into the discussion with their minds already made up. For the Duke of Sussex, proof of this was that Young had brought along a copy of a drafted press release for only this one particular scenario and not for the others that were also discussed. Young told Harry the office printer was broken. "Is this some kind of joke?" he asked with a laugh. He expected an open and honest conversation with his family but received a premeditated verdict from the Firm instead.

The prevailing opinion on Young is that he was an uninspired private secretary who lacked imagination. Critics pointed to the fact that when Meghan first joined the family, Young was slow to help find patronages and active roles for the newly minted Duchess of Sussex. Sources say he "dithered" for eight months before nudging Queen Elizabeth II to appoint Meghan as the royal patron for the National Theatre, a no-brainer considering her years as an actress. This initial failure to help Meghan create a suitable lane as a working royal ushered in a pack of problems for the Sussexes, who ended up taking matters into their own hands when it came to carving out their roles (and we all know how that ended). As a result, Young is often blamed for a portion of the Sussex vs. Palace fiasco.

The countervailing opinion is that Young was a skilled liaison between the Queen, the government, and those who seek her favor, and that he was a committed, undaunted protector of the monarchy's interests. It is widely believed that Young was the driving force behind the Queen releasing her own personal statement following Harry and Meghan's Oprah interview rather than let communication aides speak on behalf of the institution. Though he was less than keen on the Kensington Palace–concocted "recollections may vary" response to the couple's race-related allegation (a sentence he felt could perhaps come back to cause problems for the Queen and provoke the Sussexes to reveal even more), his decision to employ the word *family* three times in the statement helped to subtly remind the public that this was a family affair. While there were many hands involved in the official response, it was Young and the Queen who had the final say before hitting the send button on what many believe is a PR triumph of evasion and measured incredulity, packaged and sold as concern and love—truly a coup de maître of deflection, whether you agreed with it or not.

As for pressing buttons, Charles's private secretary, Clive Alderton, aka "the Wasp," was instrumental in the plot to convince the Queen to green-light the ouster of Young's predecessor, Sir (now Lord) Christopher Geidt. An establishment figure par excellence and a former military intelligence officer, Geidt was a favorite of the Queen's. He ran a tight ship, exercising prudence when necessary and forward-looking vision when modernizing pressures demanded it. Once described by a former colleague as "suave and charming, very proper, clipped and British with a regimental tie, but also with a touch of the spook about him," Geidt was discreet, professional, and plugged into the circuit board of British politics. A bald and calmly assertive middle-aged white man (a reflexive choice for the Palace), Geidt earned the trust of those around him—including Princes William and Harry—as a decisive but aboveboard leader. His colleagues insisted he could "see around corners" and considered him the eyes and ears of the Palace. He was an effective manager of complicated people and complex situations, and many in the Firm approved of and lauded his work ethic, judgment, and penchant for making himself invisible at the right time.

Prince Charles, however, was decidedly not in this camp. The relationship between the then Prince of Wales and Geidt had deteriorated over the years, but it totally collapsed in 2017. The Queen was ninety-one at the time and Charles was pushing for more involvement in sovereign duties in preparation for his own reign. According to royal sources, Charles and his aides were eager to "accelerate" his activities and visibility by his seventieth birthday in November 2018. Insiders called it "Project 70," and the goal was to further position Charles as the king in waiting and show that a transition of power was already underway. Ever the Palace guard and a man of caution, particularly about matters concerning the Queen, Geidt—who didn't personally believe the heir had what it takes to be a worthy successor to his boss—stood firmly against the project.

Further infuriating Charles, around this same time Geidt called a staff meeting to announce Prince Philip's retirement without conferring with Charles's aides beforehand (their opinions weren't particularly valued or wanted). It was all too much for a prince itching to be King. With Alderton's help, Charles enlisted Prince Andrew (not exactly the most dependable of siblings, but the one person who always had their mother's ear) to convince the Queen to remove Geidt from his post. Andrew had his own issues with Geidt. Like so many others, Geidt had long envisioned a slimmer monarchy as the key to a secure future for the Crown, and he believed one way to get there was to cut back on funding for the problematic Duke of York and his family—in particular, monies for Princesses Eugenie and Beatrice. Though Andrew knew Charles also wanted to cut his family out when his turn on the throne arrived, he felt it would be one fewer obstacle if Geidt was no longer around. The brothers' united front against the Queen's man eventually worked, and Geidt stepped down in July 2017, allowing the Firm to pro-mote Edward Young to the head position. The effort involving both royals and their courtiers, a Buckingham Palace insider said at the time, was like "something out of monarchies in the middle ages."

The backroom maneuver irked Prince William, who thought the whole stunt reeked of unprofessionalism and personal grudges run amok. The press would later call this the result of a "Palace power struggle," the climax of increasing tensions between Buck-ingham Palace and Clarence House. Some, including Princess Anne and Prince Edward, believe that letting Geidt go was the worst mistake of the Queen's later years. Looking back, many in the family and households are certain that Geidt would have steered the monarchy through the Harry and Meghan dramas with much more control and forethought. "He just wouldn't have al-lowed it to get so out of control," a longtime Palace staffer who worked with Geidt said. "He would have listened to both sides and worked hard to ensure that everyone was happy, looked after, and, more importantly, [the Crown] would not get tainted."

Participating in a palace coup was not out of character for Alderton. Some behind palace walls have referred to him as the "hatchet man" for his expertise in delivering bad news to his princi-pals. This may be the case, but he certainly doesn't look like a man comfortable wielding a deathly axe. Tall and poised, with an older but cherubic face and floppy, sand-colored hair, Alderton looks like a preparatory schoolboy all grown up. Like Charles, Sir Clive is a sharp dresser, perhaps a stylish instinct honed while working in the Foreign Office, Britain's version of the United States Department of State. It was there that Alderton started his career in 1986 and over the years held diplomatic posts in France, Belgium, Singapore, and Poland. He joined Charles and Camilla's team at Clarence House as a deputy private secretary in 2006, but jumped ship to take on two ambassadorships, one in Morocco and the other in Mauritania. He rejoined Charles's inner circle in 2015 as the then Prince of Wales's private secretary. By all accounts, Alderton is intensely intelligent, and he also likes to charm and schmooze. A former colleague says he "thrives" on his adjacency to power but is also a social butterfly who is enjoyable to be around. In terms of his relationship with certain senior members of the press, he's "always up for a drink," one longtime royal reporter told me.

Resilient at the pub, but also in his job. Recognizing that Geidt was the primary obstacle for Charles's play for power, Alderton and Charles initiated a fight against an exceedingly strong opponent and won. This obvious power grab required thick skin, strategic thinking, and persistence, three essential qualities for a modern courtier. If Charles ever doubted Alderton's loyalty or his capabilities, his willingness to go the distance to install the more pliable Edward Young surely banished any concerns. And it solidified Alderton's position. Nine months after the Queen's death, Young retired with honors (appointed as a Lord in Waiting) and was given a £150,000 "compensation payment," but Alderton stayed on and now serves as the King's principal private secretary.

Of course, it would be wrong to assume that all courtiers at the House of Windsor are ruthless manipulators. Over the decades there have been some senior aides who have successfully managed to support the Crown, climb the company ladder, become universally liked by staff and royal family members across all households, *and* leave with their ethics and values intact. During her seventeen-year rise at Buckingham Palace, Samantha Cohen achieved just that. Starting in the communications office before reaching the role of Queen Elizabeth II's assistant private secretary for eight years, Australian journalism graduate Cohen quickly earned herself the nickname "Samantha the Panther" within palace walls (and the press) for her feisty spirit and no-nonsense attitude. She was one of the few colleagues to speak up at the appalling treatment of Lord Geidt in 2017, and the late Queen greatly valued her quick thinking and strong opinions. Prince Harry felt the same way, too. When his much-loved private secretary Ed Lane Fox (or "ELF" to those on friendly terms with him, though not as friendly as Queen Elizabeth and her Elf) left in 2018 after five years, Harry turned to Cohen to fill the role. He had known her since he was a teenager and always felt she was one of the "good eggs." The Queen thought it was a "marvelous idea," said a source, and encouraged Cohen (who at this point was ready to leave the royal fold for greener pastures) to stay on and serve as a stand-in until the Sussexes could find a permanent replacement. Many credit Cohen for the success of the couple's 2018 tour of Australia, New Zealand, Fiji, and Tonga, having helped meticulously plan a diverse itinerary that highlighted the Commonwealth, the Queen, and the couple (not an easy feat, as more recent tours by other royals have proven . . . ahem).

In 2019, Cohen was ready to continue her journey elsewhere. A royal source said that Cohen was fond of Harry and Meghan but found the pair "a bit like teenagers" at times. The Sussexes attempted to keep her on but, seeing the stormy seas ahead, the senior aide felt like it was the right time go. Cohen—who was awarded a Royal Victorian Order in 2016 for her services to the monarchy—remains a trustee of the late Queen's Commonwealth Trust, a charity that supports young leaders across the Commonwealth.

While some courtiers shine like stars in the royal orbit, others are more comfortable in the gutter. This brings us to "the Fly." Harry had this to say about Simon Case: "[He'd] spent much of his career adjacent to, and indeed drawn to shit. The offal of government, and media, the wormy entrails, he loved it." It's a damning portrait, but many behind the gates of the Palace and Parliament would argue that it is also spot-on. At the age of forty-four, Case has a résumé that already reads like that of an establishment stooge, a political player who's been in the game for much longer than he actually has. He started his career in civil service in 2006 as a policy advisor in the Ministry of Defence. After a few years of working in the Northern Ireland Office and the Cabinet Office,

Case went to work at Downing Street under then prime minister David Cameron. Here he retreats further into the shadows. In 2015, Case signed on as a director of strategy for the Government Communications Headquarters (GCHQ), an intelligence and security apparatus based in "The Doughnut," a circular fortress-like hive of offices (think a round version of the Pentagon) tucked away in Cheltenham. Seemingly always buzzing from one influential post to the next, Case then joined Cameron as his principal private secretary. He continued on in the same position for the first year of Theresa May's short stay on Downing Street, before Prince William poached him in 2018.

Case's appearance matches his résumé. Practically born in a suit, these days his combed and parted brown hair accompanies a meticulously trimmed beard and rimless glasses. Many consider the GCHQ a spy agency, and Case does resemble a spy in the pulp thriller sense—slick but normal enough. There is something about his eyes that conjures up a comparison to a weary politico who can't unsee what he's already seen. Having enjoyed a positive working relationship with William's previous private aide—the affable and skilled Miguel Head, who was in the role from 2012—I didn't feel so positive about my first in-person encounter with Case during the summer of 2018. There was just something about him I didn't trust—and most of it was in his eyes. "I look forward to hearing more about your book—I trust it will all be glowingly positive," he said with a chuckle. With cracks already in the relationship between the Sussexes and Cambridges, we both knew that would not likely be the case. A political operator dressed up as a civil servant, Case is intelligent and undaunted by difficult jobs. In a short but revealing BBC News profile, a cabinet minister described Case as a "fixer by nature," and a former university tutor claimed Case is a natural "keeper of secrets." A Tory colleague was less guarded with their words: "I like Simon, but he's a snake."

Prince William brought Case on in March 2018, just a couple

of months before the Sussexes' wedding. Harry and William's relationship was already on the skids, their "divergent paths" growing further apart but still a year away from becoming front-page news. Case, said several sources, saw an opening in this deteriorating relationship, a chance to elevate his "principal." Despite the obvious difference in the line of succession, Harry and William were publicly on equal footing at the time. Before Meghan's arrival, William, Kate, and Harry were a unified trio on their chosen causes and I always saw them smiling and laughing together at engagements. This was largely thanks to Miguel Head, who regularly encouraged the brothers (and Kate) to find ways to work together, not apart. Case was different—he saw the cracks, and his actions helped widen them. To change the narrative for William and move him away from his work-shy image to that of a resolute and industrious second in line, some drastic measures were required. His plan: reposition William, the heir, as the responsible one, the adult in the room, while casting Harry, the spare, as the wayward one, the selfish brother with a competing agenda.

Harry's wedding was an ideal event for Case to kick off his campaign to elevate William. A source told me that Harry was unwavering in his decision to have a close friend be his best man instead of William, with whom he was already becoming at odds. In *Spare*, he reveals he asked "old mate" Charlie van Straubenzee to take on the role. Recognizing that the optics—and the headlines to follow— of Harry passing over his brother for the role would certainly be detrimental to William's image and, by extension, problematic for the Firm at large, Case made sure that at the very least the media received word his boss was selected for the task. Harry's aides were instructed not to correct the inaccurate reports that followed.

In late August 2019, Case sniffed out another opportunity for PR gamesmanship. That summer the Duke and Duchess of Sussex were under fire for flying on private jets so soon after Harry announced his new sustainable tourism initiative, Travalyst. By their fourth private jet trip (in eleven days)—this time to Nice, France, on a plane that belonged to their host, Sir Elton John—sections of the press were calling out the couple's hypocrisy. The argument was that it contradicted Harry's public stance on the environment. Given that private jets consume ten times more fuel per person than commercial jets, it was not one of Harry's wisest decisions from a public image standpoint. Even his communications secretary Sara Latham had advised him to reconsider his jet travel plans for a solo Google Camp appearance in Italy the previous month. But, for this particular family trip, the media failed to account for the Sussexes' growing security concerns, particularly when traveling with a newborn. Sir Elton ended up defending his friends and tweeted that he and his husband, David Furnish, paid for the trip for safety reasons and that they always offset their carbon emissions with donations to environmental groups.

Reasonable arguments on both sides resulted in a reasonable outcome. Harry and Meghan had valid reasons for flying by jet but privately acknowledged that the criticism served as a "lessons learned" moment. As for the complaints that they were in France instead of visiting the Queen and Prince Philip in Balmoral during their summer stay (they hadn't been explicitly asked, but all family members had an open invite), their answer was simple—they felt four-month-old Archie was too young for all the hunting, shooting, and fishing that fill up the family itinerary at the Highland getaway.

But Simon Case had another idea. Seizing this moment, which he perceived as a highly embarrassing one for Harry, he took another step in his PR long game for his boss. Just days later, William, Kate, and their three children were spotted boarding a commercial budget airline flight from Norwich to Aberdeen for a trip to Balmoral. Although there were no photographers on the tarmac, a conveniently captured phone video popped up in the press showing William, Kate, and their children casually making their way off the plane at the airport. Palace-friendly papers were quick to report that their seats on the Flybe aircraft cost only £73 per adult, adding that the cheap travel proved William and Kate were entirely comfortable taking their children on a commercial flight. Champing at the bit to compare and contrast, the *Daily Mail* (who, like some other papers, was given a heads-up about the trip by a Kensington Palace aide) reminded readers about the recent row over Harry and Meghan's trips before breathlessly reporting how Prince William was "looking like your archetypal family man on holiday . . . [and] can be seen clutching a number of bags while George, six, and Charlotte, four, run excitably alongside him."

A premediated publicity setup; this was all Case's handiwork. A stroke of backhanded artifice, it was a successful stunt—at first, anyway. As *London Evening Standard* royal editor Robert Jobson said at the time, "It's a shrewd move by the Duke of Cambridge and great for the public . . . and if they can fly budget then surely Harry, Meghan and their child are able to as well." He added, "A lot of people are claiming the royals are costing too much at the moment, and William is putting his money where his mouth is by going budget." His commentary was exactly the kind Case was hoping for— a perceived stark contrast between the brothers and an elevation of William at the expense of his brother.

Of course, all is not always as it seems and, unknown to the public at the time, William and Kate's casual trip wasn't quite as environmentally friendly or spendthrift as it first appeared. After a Kensington Palace aide discussed their plans (and the fact that photographs would likely end up in the papers) with a Flybe executive, officials at the company made some moves of their own. As it turns out, there wasn't a plane emblazoned with corporate branding at William and Kate's outgoing airport—the daily flight from Norwich to Aberdeen is operated by Loganair for Eastern Airways, a franchise of Flybe. So as to not miss this golden advertising opportunity, the Flybe team decided to fly over an empty, properly branded aircraft from their headquarters in Humberside, a coastal town 123 miles north of Norwich. The plane also returned empty to Humberside after the Cambridges and other passengers disembarked in Aberdeen. All told, the two empty flights released upward of four and a half tons of carbon emissions. Kensington Palace claimed they knew nothing about Flybe's switcheroo, but the whole farce turned it into a fail for all involved regardless. Their perfect family trip was exposed for what it really was: a showy publicity stunt. Even in this early stage of his Kensington Palace post, some officials in the other households were less than impressed with Case's stratagems. A Buckingham Palace aide (who was no fan of the private secretary) laughed to me at the time: "Nice try, but in the end, they looked like even bigger hypocrites than the couple they were trying to show up." Added another communications staffer at that time, "I feel like it's a new era with [Case]. I'm not sure if it's a good or a bad one."

In retrospect, as the crevasse between the brothers deepened to the point that reconciliation still seems like a long shot, even Case's PR gambits can now be viewed as successes for Kensington Palace. The results are in: William is firmly in the role of a decisive king in waiting and Harry has been cast by the Palace and the press as a perceived lost soul. This so-called success came at an exceedingly high cost. While other circumstances—some unforeseen, but many of them devised—hammered on the wedge between William and Harry, Simon Case's moves activated a chain of events that have helped damage a brotherly relationship beyond repair. "That was a dark time," a source close to the family told me.

Similar sentiments were shared when Charles and Camilla's longtime press secretary Julian Payne left in 2021. Never afraid to get his hands dirty ("he's the resident playground gossip," a senior aide of the Queen once said to me), Payne happily shared tales about family members, including Harry and Meghan, to other staff and preferred media allies who wrote favorably about his bosses. He also gave details about Charles's relationships with Harry and his grandchildren for *Finding Freedom*, although, prior to publication, I found out that some of the information (such as how regularly Charles would visit Prince George, Princess Charlotte, and Prince Louis) was not accurate.

As for "the Fly," well, he buzzed off back to the intestinal system of British politics, joining former prime minister Boris Johnson's team as cabinet secretary, the youngest to ever hold the position. He survived Johnson's ugly resignation and his successor's short tenure, and Prime Minister Rishi Sunak kept him on as his cabinet secretary. But it wasn't a successful journey for Case. He was implicated in the "Partygate scandal" and its swarming allegations that Johnson and staff flagrantly violated Covid-19 lockdown restrictions by hosting social gatherings at 10 Downing Street and other locations during the pandemic. Loyal only to himself, it seems, Westminster watched as Case seemingly threw his former boss under the bus. Johnson revealed he was advised by Case that Covid protocol was followed for the rule-breaking get-togethers, but Case later told an investigating committee that he said no such thing.

The Firm needs to look no further than the example of Simon Case as a reminder that Svengalis ultimately seek to control and exploit, and gurus tend to fall from grace. Waterflies never hang around for long. Lest we forget the messy situation that Charles's former right-hand man Michael Fawcett found himself in. Even Niccolò Machiavelli, the Renaissance diplomat and philosopher whose name is now synonymous with calculating plots and ruthless power grabs, was eventually arrested and banished. In the end, relying on deception and trickery ultimately leads to destruction. Image control is a fool's errand. And it should be obvious to the royals by now that when it comes to family, truth always outsmarts cunning.

# 11

# Ghost at the Feast

## Princess Diana and Revisionist History

———•———

*Thy bones are marrowless, thy blood is cold . . .*
*Can such things be*
*And overcome us like a summer's cloud,*
*Without our special wonder?*

—William Shakespeare, *Macbeth*

Body. *People kept using that word. It was a punch in the*
*throat, and a bloody lie, because Mummy wasn't dead.*

—Prince Harry, *Spare*

Hounded as she was into a subterranean darkness, Princess Diana's life was cut short on August 31, 1997, by excessive speed, shattering glass, and twisted metal. After her chauffeur Henri Paul was blinded by a "major white flash" from a paparazzi photographer on an overtaking motorbike, he lost control at sixty-five miles per hour and collided with a concrete pillar in the Pont de l'Alma underpass in Paris. She was thirty-six. Her journey from a spirited young woman to a "royal body" to a corpse in a French morgue was devastatingly brief. Into a tunnel and then gone.

But her story, tragic ending and all, her time as the "people's princess," and her élan endures—and continues to inspire the public and haunt the monarchy. In some ways, it's as if she never left. This is especially true for Prince Harry, who avows in *Spare* that he grappled with the reality of her death from what was left of his splintered childhood through his turbulent teenage years into early adulthood, often tricking himself into believing she was just in hiding and would soon come back for him and his brother. Who of us wouldn't, at his age and in his circumstances, surrender to this kind of magical thinking?

Harry kept up these wishful fantasies until he was twenty-three. After a driver drove Harry through Pont de l'Alma at the exact same speed as his mother's car, he internally acknowledged that no escape plans were executed, that his mother was not, in fact, in hiding. Speeding through the tunnel, watching the spectral zone lights ratchet up the windshield, he finally accepted that his mother was gone. "Closure" is a powerful influencer, one that steered both brothers to the scene of their mother's death. After Harry recounted his trip to his brother, he and William then went through the tunnel together. It's an experience that led both to conclude that the police inquest into her death—which depicted the tunnel as a bumpy death trap and laid much of the blame at the chauffeur's feet for drinking—was a joke. We don't know how William reacted or if he found any solace, but for Harry, it did bring closure, as he claimed, "I got it in spades." However, instead of stopping the pain, it brought "Pain, Part Deux." As novelist Andrew O'Hagan points out in a *London Review of Books* essay, over the course of his four-hundred-and-sixteen-page memoir, "Harry never says that his mother is dead, only that she has 'disappeared.'"

He still feels her presence, especially in the hinge moments of his life—his wedding, the births of his children, and when he absconded to California to protect his family from the British press and the realities of his untenable situation within the Firm. During the publicity sprint after the book's publication, and in the years leading up to this moment, Harry often cited in interviews that a fear of "history repeating itself" (Meghan meeting a horrific end) was the prime motivator for leaving the royal bubble, saying goodbye to all of that. Harry believes his mother was undeniably there for him, revealing the tidal force Diana's story exerts on her younger son. In a *Good Morning America* sit-down, Harry told host Michael Strahan that he "felt the presence of [his] mum more so in the last two years than [he has] in the last thirty." He trusts she's still out there, in spirit form, leading him as he reinvents himself beyond the strictures of royal life.

Diana's indelible presence may serve as an attending spirit for Harry, but for other members of the royal family and the institution behind them, her legacy is a haunting narrative, one with which they must continually contend, and another tragic episode they are doomed to never forget. Diana's absence and the press coverage it receives is an inextricable part of the royal story. There is incessant reminiscing from the global media, which has created a niche industry of Diana nostalgia that the business at large relies on and the royal institution leans into—when convenient. The flip side of this for the monarchy is that it never goes away. Diana created a visual brand for the family, and when the outside world pictures the Firm, Diana is still present.

A web of its own making, the saga of the late Princess of Wales was not a fait accompli. The Palace effectively installed her and then manufactured the gilded cage she never stopped rattling. Queen Elizabeth II and her backers rejected Charles's choice, Camilla Parker Bowles, and helped groom the young Diana Spencer for the role. And, wow, did she ever tick their boxes: young, elegant, and, most importantly for them, slim, virginal, and aristocratic. Born into nobility—the youngest daughter of Viscount and Viscountess Althorp—Diana, along with the rest of her family, ran in the same circles as the royals for decades. Just as the Queen selected her thoroughbred racing horses, the Firm chose Diana for her pedigree and her usefulness. They trusted Diana would bring home the big prize to Windsor—an heir and a spare.

The system had a blueprint for Diana as a vessel for hereditary power, but when it came to Diana as a human being, the Palace was completely unprepared. As she matured, she proved to be all things the monarchy was not—modern, vital, mercurial, savvy, and, to the institution's eventual dismay, wildly popular. Some of this attractive but unpredictable dynamism was expected, even planned for. The Palace knew that adding Diana to the roster would boost their public profile. She would, as former *Guardian* royal correspondent Stephen Bates put it, "enliven it, rejuvenate it, refresh it and be glamorous, and [serve as] proof that the family were not stuck in the mud."

She certainly brought the glamour, but she also brought empathy, sensitivity, and a worldly outlook. To borrow a cliché, she wore her heart on her sleeve, something that is categorically *un*-royal. The "people's princess" was more approachable and sincere. Often to the frustration of Palace aides, who furiously watched the clock as they regularly ran over a precise schedule, she always made time for others during her royal walkabouts, clasping the hands of well-wishers as she attentively listened to their stories. The public responded to this new personable royal style, which left other working royals looking cold and stiff. The Palace took notice and eventually adopted her approach as a matter of company policy, and then other family members followed her example (and have been ever since). Even King Charles, a man not raised to be outwardly warm, now physically embraces members of the public when he's on walkabouts. After his mother's death, a time of undeniable personal grief, he allowed members of the public to hug him and hold his hands in theirs. (Some haven't quite managed it, though—Prince Edward still famously avoids most physical contact with the great unwashed. "He's a massive germaphobe," a royal source said.)

# Five Years of Highs and Lows

Happier times for the "Fab Four" at the February 2018 Royal Foundation Forum in London.

William and Kate followed tradition, sharing their third child, Prince Louis, with the world outside the Lindo Wing of London's St. Mary's Hospital on April 23, 2018.

Harry and Meghan were at the peak of their popularity on their wedding day at St. George's Chapel, Windsor, on May 19, 2018, though the vultures were already circling.

The Queen of the United Kingdom, Elizabeth II, shares a laugh with the Queen of Fashion, Anna Wintour, during London Fashion Week in February 2018.

Charles and Camilla host Donald and Melania Trump during a June 2019 state visit. President Trump later tweeted about meeting "the Prince of Whales."

The Queen and Prince Philip meet their great-grandson, and the first mixed-race child born to a senior royal, Archie, after his May 6, 2019, birth. "I cherish these times," Harry later wrote.

Proud parents: Prince Louis makes his Trooping the Colour debut alongside siblings Princess Charlotte and Prince George in June 2019.

Prince Andrew's catastrophic November 2019 *Newsnight* interview, where the duke deflected and fumbled answers about his friendship with Jeffrey Epstein and underage sex allegations.

A painfully obvious divide as William and Kate turn cold shoulders to Harry and Meghan at the Commonwealth Day service on March 9, 2020—the Sussexes' final engagement as working royals.

A united front: William and Kate took a break from their March 2020 royal tour of Ireland for a romantic stroll in front of the cameras.

After Harry's departure, the Palace were keen to show William and Charles—here at a medical rehabilitation center in February 2020—working in "lockstep" together.

Strict pandemic protocols were still in place for the funeral of Prince Philip, with the Queen one of only thirty attendees for this solemn occasion on April 17, 2021.

Harry and Meghan's March 2021 interview with Oprah was the first step in the couple sharing their side of the story. The Palace's response? "Recollections may vary."

William and Harry briefly put their differences to one side in July 2021 to unveil a commemorative statue of their mother, Princess Diana, in the gardens of Kensington Palace.

Charles, Camilla, William, and Kate sparkle at the premiere of *No Time to Die* at London's Royal Albert Hall in September 2021.

The Netflix docuseries *Harry & Meghan*—which debuted in December 2022—was the first project born of the Sussexes' deal with Netflix and gave a peek into their new life in California with Archie and Lilibet.

As the Queen slowed down, Prince Charles took on her monarchical duties bit by bit. Here he delivers the sovereign's speech at the opening of Parliament in May 2022.

William and Kate's misjudged and colonial-tinged May 2022 tour of the Caribbean ended with Jamaica announcing their intent to cut ties with the British monarchy.

Harry and Meghan make a low-key appearance at the June 2022 Platinum Jubilee celebrating the Queen at St. Paul's Cathedral for a service of thanksgiving.

During the Trooping the Colour parade to mark his great-grandmother's birthday in June 2022, Prince Louis lets his feelings about the very loud Royal Air Force flyover be known.

The last photo: Queen Elizabeth II awaits the new (and short-lived) Prime Minister Liz Truss at Balmoral Castle on September 6, 2022—two days before she passed.

An uncomfortable reunion for the Wales and Sussex couples, who briefly came together after the death of the Queen to greet mourners on the Long Walk at Windsor Castle on September 10, 2022.

Harry carried out a major publicity tour for his candid memoir, *Spare*, appearing on *The Late Show with Stephen Colbert* in January 2023. The book rocketed to the tops of bestseller lists worldwide.

A new normal: After Charles became King, egg-throwing hecklers (right, pictured in November 2022) and republican protestors (left, February 2023) became a familiar sight at the monarch's engagements.

The celebrations for the coronation begin—a Buckingham Palace garden party in May 2023—with Edward and Sophie now thrust forward into prominent roles once destined for Harry and Meghan.

Despite initial plans for a leaner coronation, King Charles III's May 6, 2023, crowning laid on full pomp and circumstance as the family, including Kate and Andrew, worked hard to stoke pride for a monarchy facing challenging times. The day also marked the triumph of Camilla's image rehabilitation as she finally became queen.

With Charles's vision for a slimmed-down working lineup now a reality, a leaner June 2023 Trooping the Colour balcony appearance failed to evoke the usual annual buzz. Royal events fatigue? Or the sign of waning public support? Only time will tell.

Diana's unfeigned warmth was infectious to everyone around her. But like anyone managing the distortions of fame and the exigencies of family life, she did live a somewhat double existence: she had a public identity and a private self—one that her biographer and confidante Andrew Morton once described to me as "a little immature . . . and a little stubborn"—and these selves were often at war. But on the public stage she predominantly came across as unaffected and assured, particularly as she grew more comfortable in her role. She was real, she was genuine, and she wasn't afraid to show it. Diana passionately took on the thorny issue of HIV and AIDS research, even though, at the time, Charles deemed it an inappropriate cause for royal participation. For her good works and authenticity, a global public embraced her as one of their own, similar to how they did at first with Meghan.

Days into her life as a working royal, Princess Diana's popularity was already eclipsing that of her husband. The woman who should have been the submissive wife in the heir's shadow quickly became Charles's biggest competition, and this further irritated an already inflamed marriage. Charles's long-standing affair with Camilla, Diana's depression, and the strain of the insatiable British tabloids all led to the epic royal crisis that was the couple's three-year separation and their hyper-publicized divorce in 1996.

And so, the fairy tale came to an end. Diana's popularity no longer served the royal cause, and, as a result, the system—led by Queen Elizabeth II herself—commanded the divorce. Embarrassed by the self-perpetuating circus of Charles and Diana's imbroglios and exasperated by the fact that the couple was now airing their dirty laundry in the public arena, the Queen issued her decree via separate letters to her son and his soon-to-be ex-wife. "After considering the present situation, the Queen wrote to both the Prince and Princess earlier this week and gave them her view, supported by the Duke of Edinburgh [Prince Philip], that an early divorce is desirable," a December 20, 1995, Palace statement read. And to make sure the public knew God and Country approved, the statement went on to claim, "The Archbishop of Canterbury, senior prelate of the Church of England, which British sovereigns head, and Prime Minister John Major were both consulted and agreed with the Queen's action." All of this was just official gloss for Her Majesty's decision—that she'd had enough of the couple's dramas and the damage it was inflicting on the monarchy's image.

So much of the couple's messy, human ordeal led to the Queen's "Basta!" moment, but it was Diana's November 20, 1995, BBC *Panorama* interview with Martin Bashir that pushed the late monarch into the red zone. It was a sensational prime-time special that twenty-three million people in the United Kingdom tuned in for, and the source of Diana's famous line, "There were three of us in the marriage, so it was a bit crowded." The interview's many intimate disclosures are well-trodden history, and chances are you know them well. But it should be noted that for a member of the royal family—or any public figure back in the sanctimonious 1990s—to discuss her struggles with depression, self-harm, bulimia, and extramarital affairs so openly was extraordinary. It's hard to fathom now in our social media age of oversharing and grievance gorging just how explosive and astonishing Diana's raw honesty was. This was a time when the royal family was still adhering to the dictum of "never complain, never explain."

Finally breaking free of her royal cage, Diana directly addressed her issues, many of which were verboten for discussion—not only by the royal institution, but by the culture at large. Sweeping under the rug was a national (and royal) pastime—you just did not talk about certain things. But Diana did. And she did it head-on and without any rote tap-dancing. After it aired, the interview was lauded by some but mostly disparaged in the press, and her candor seemed reckless to many, considering she had two small boys to protect. But one thing was indisputable: in fifty-four minutes, Diana had wrested her story (and life) back from the royal system that had been shaping and defining it for her. She had taken control of the narrative in front of the camera for the very first time. *Her* very own "Basta!" moment. And she was immediately punished. Just a month after the interview, the Queen issued the letters that ordered the divorce.

But Diana didn't own her narrative for long. Just a year later, as she attempted to find happiness outside of her old life, the princess sped off into the unknown with her forty-two-year-old lover and Harrods heir Dodi Fayed, their fatal crash an awful denouement that only deepened the complexity of her short but stormy life. So, it was a feeding frenzy of others making sense of it, trying to package her "life and legacy," airbrushing out the untidy reality. First came the international spectacle of grief and mourning and the mountains of flowers; then the reactive finger-pointing started. The first target: media giants and the shutterbugs who did their bidding. American royalty quickly weighed in. Tom Cruise indignantly informed the mourning public that the media was guilty. "It was harassment," he told CNN. Then it was the royal family's turn in the crosshairs, particularly after the Queen, accused of cold disinterest, remained in Scotland after Diana's death was announced to the world, also refusing to break protocol and raise the royal standard flag at half mast over Buckingham Palace to honor her passing. *The Sun* ran the headline "Where Is Our Queen? Where Is Her Flag?"

Mass catharsis often requires a sacrificial lamb. In this case, the complexity of truth was hauled up to the altar. Blaming was easy; understanding was hard. Following a preferred narrative was undemanding—and more beneficial—than taking responsibility or simply admitting that things were more complicated than they seemed, that Diana was more than just a princess, that she was more than just a victim. Her tragic death was the result of a young, modern woman entering an unforgiving, archaic system that failed to protect her, a mother caught between loving and hating the glare of the celebrity spotlight, and an ordinary human being facing extraordinary pressure. But this entanglement of facts? Who benefits from that? Where's the money in that? That narrative is too untidy.

So the Firm and the media have been cherry-picking Diana's legacy ever since. Palace officials, media outlets, movie and TV makers, and "royal experts" continually cannibalize her life and death to limn a caricature-like portrait to suit their needs—casting Diana as an impossibly perfect saint, reducing her to a reckless adulteress, or, in the case of the Palace, attempting to erase her suffering to avoid the blameful fingers being pointed.

The media is the media—we've come to expect this from an enterprise hell-bent on creating necessary narratives for their bottom lines. But it is truly bewildering to watch the royal institution speak out of both sides of its mouth when it comes to Diana. Knowing that she continues to be one of the most talked about members of the family to this day, the institution still shamelessly leverages her popularity. I recall the feeling of slight horror when a former Kensington Palace staffer told me how a senior aide encouraged the then Duke and Duchess of Cambridge to make more nods to the princess on an overseas tour, from restaging iconic photographs taken on her travels to Kate mirroring her sartorial choices during poignant moments. During the past thirteen years, Diana cosplay has become a royal staple. Both the current Princess of Wales and the Duchess of Sussex (during her working royal years) regularly replicated her iconic looks, complete with accessories once owned by the late princess. Considering they are both married to Diana's sons, the connection makes sense. But while finding a trend untouched by Diana's iconic style is almost impossible, the huge amount of effort that goes into channeling her exact look sometimes goes beyond the pale. "Those decisions were always discussed with [William or Harry], so much work and time goes into outfit choices," said a source who had worked with both royals. "Were there gentle pushes from others? At times, yes. It had been known for someone to go back and pull images of Diana at a certain place or time for ideas."

At the right moment this can be a sweet gesture, but there is also a slightly queasy feeling when you realize it's often orchestrated within the same system that contributed to her living misery, an institution that still wants some of Diana's shine to rub off on them. And then there are the money-spinners. "Diana: Her Fashion Story," a collection of clothes, photographs, and glossy expositions on her life displayed at Kensington Palace from 2017 to 2019, attracted tourists in droves. The tasteful curation of gowns and accessories was a fascinating and comprehensive chronicle of memories, but not a single one of the accompanying museum labels acknowledged the darker or more difficult sides of her story. It was Diana's life—before, during, and after her marriage to Charles—presented how the institution of the monarchy would like you to remember it: glamorous, dutiful, and very happy.

Put on by Historic Royal Palaces, visitors to the Kensington Palace exhibit could also pick up replicas of jewelry worn by the late Princess of Wales, including a £150 version of the sapphire-and-pearl choker she wore to dance with John Travolta, a £24.99 "Princess Diana faux sapphire brooch," and a £50 "Spencer tiara ring." All thirty-two items were available to purchase in a gift shop a stone's throw away from the apartment she once lived in and were marketed in time for events commemorating two decades since her passing. (A spokesperson for HRP argued at the time that, as an independent charity receiving no Crown funding, the retail sales were essential for the organization to maintain certain unoccupied royal residences across the country.)

Because the institution's health is so heavily reliant on script and image, the Palace has historically tussled with two occasions when Diana shared her real story: Andrew Morton's book *Diana: Her True Story*, first published in 1992, and, of course, that unforgettable *Panorama* interview. "These two events have been the two times the Palace lost complete control of the narrative," Morton said. Instead, they became heavy-stitched threads in the public tapestry of her life.

Morton's biography was incendiary when the independent Michael O'Mara Books first published it—staunch royalists burned copies in the streets, and the tabloids (some of whom accused the young journalist of making up reporting in the book) set up paparazzi outside his London home for weeks. But it was nothing in comparison to the firestorm that ensued after the British author updated it for a new edition just two months after Diana's death in 1997. After denying for five years that Diana contributed to the book, claiming to have spoken only with friends and family, Morton finally acknowledged that the Princess of Wales was the main source. He changed the subtitle to *Her True Story—In Her Own Words* and included an eighteen-thousand-word transcript of the tape recordings that she gave him for source material. "If she was still alive today, I would still be saying my sources were her friends and family," he said.

Predictably, bedlam followed the bombshell news. Deep in version control hell and losing their grip on the story they had desperately tried to shape, the Palace threatened to have the book banned. Diana's brother Charles, Earl of Spencer, even sought legal counsel regarding the ownership of the tapes. Morton was singled out and pilloried for "cashing in" on her death by the very same media establishment that made millions relentlessly covering her separation, her divorce, and her sad end.

In more recent years, Morton claimed the newer edition reflected Princess Diana's belief in openness, honesty, and clarity. Suffice it to say, these values are not exactly highlighted in the monarchy's playbook. To stay afloat, especially when their brand is challenged, the institution rolls out the opposite: reticence, truthiness, and distraction. It's why journalists who help pump out the Palace narratives are often rewarded with the best access. Biographer Penny Junor, for example, has spoken and written about Diana as a bad mother, volatile, narcissistic, and violent. She has also enjoyed top-tier access to Charles and Camilla for intimate, and mostly positive, biographies. These knocks to Diana's character, however, can achieve only so much. Diana's story—the closest we will ever come to her memoir—was already out there.

Along with Morton's tome, the *Panorama* interview remained a go-to source for Diana's "true story" for twenty-seven years. It was everywhere—until it wasn't. After a BBC-led and royal family–supported 2020 investigation restated that journalist Martin Bashir committed "deceitful behavior" and used unethical practices to obtain the interview, the BBC outright banned it, announcing in July 2022 that the corporation would never air it again.

For the institution and King Charles, removing *Panorama* from the public eye was a long time in the making. "They had no control over the Morton book, but this was something they hoped people would forget about," a family source opined. "This investigation was the only way to secure that. They had no interest in doing it for Diana; it was all about removing what continues to be incredibly damaging to the monarchy from the public domain."

The process started in 1996, when Earl Charles Spencer, and others in Diana's family, began to question Bashir's tactics to land the interview. An internal investigation at the time saw Bashir admit that he forged bank statements to convince Diana and her brother that Rupert Murdoch's News International and U.K. intelligence services were bankrolling a surveillance operation on her and other members of the Spencer family. In his quest to land the unprecedented interview, Bashir went as far as to tell the earl that his own head of security was in on it and had accepted payments from a shadowy offshore account in the Channel Islands. For a family on edge and a princess already convinced that operatives in the institution were spying on her, this was the spark that lit the fire. After Earl Spencer relayed to his sister that he had the smoking gun—bank statements that showed their security team was in on it—she agreed to Bashir's interview proposal, despite the fact that he was a relatively junior, little-known reporter at the time.

Bashir confessed to this deceit, but the BBC let him off with a slap on the wrist. Case closed. The story all but vanished, and Bashir went on to have a successful career at ITV, NBC, ABC, and then back in the saddle at the BBC as a religious affairs correspondent in 2016. But Diana's brother was not done fighting. Just a month prior to the twenty-fifth anniversary of what was still referred to as the "interview of a generation," the earl wrote a letter to the BBC director-general, Tim Davie, formally asking for the public service broadcaster to open an inquiry into this matter alongside a dossier of new evidence illustrating the underhanded methods adopted by Bashir to win Diana's trust. "I have to leave you in no doubt—because I want to be absolutely clear, not to threaten: this is all going to come out now," he signed off rather ominously in the November 2020 note, which was also shared with the *Mail on Sunday*.

Threat or not, the BBC took notice and hopped to it. For his part, Bashir quit before he could be fired, citing "health issues." The corporation's board appointed Lord Dyson, former justice of the Supreme Court of the United Kingdom, to reinvestigate the circumstances around the interview. Completed in May 2021, Dyson's inquiry found that Bashir was in "serious breach" of BBC guidelines and, even more damning, that the BBC "covered up in its press logs such facts as it had been able to establish about how Mr. Bashir secured the interview" and "fell short of the high standards of integrity and transparency which are its hallmark." It wasn't the misdeed but the cover-up that heaped on the trouble.

For the Palace, apologies were not enough, considering the reputational damage from the interview. This was a golden opportunity to stop it once and for all. Prince William personally contacted BBC executives to take whatever steps were necessary to ensure that the interview never again sees the light of day. With the help of Diana's older son, they finally had the chance to remove her voice from the record. Without hesitation, the BBC agreed. The one small caveat would be that in certain circumstances ("for journalistic purposes"), it may be justified to use a short clip. But "these will be few and far between and will need to be agreed at Executive Committee level and set in the full context of what we now know about the way the interview was obtained," the BBC said in a statement. The disappearance of Diana's interview has prompted Andrew Morton to find archives outside of Britain to store the tape recordings Diana made for his book. "She did only two interviews and now there is only one left, so it's important to protect her voice," he told me.

Already at odds with each other, Prince William's and Prince Harry's official responses were as far apart in tone as their locations in the world. The Duke of Sussex's written statement issued from California reminded the public that his mother was "an incredible woman who dedicated her life to service" and someone who was also "resilient, brave, and unquestionably honest." Harry went on to share his concern that the "ripple effect of a culture of exploitation and unethical practices [that] ultimately took her life" still thrives and devastates. "Our mother lost her life because of this, and nothing has changed," he wrote. "Let's remember who she was and what she stood for." To Harry, a friend of his later told me, the purpose of the duke's brief and targeted response was to acknowledge the outcome but also protect his mother's legacy and her words. "This wasn't about wanting to silence her . . . He knew that what she said in that interview was how she felt at the time. The means used to convince her to do it were ugly and unethical, but if it wasn't Bashir it would have been someone else. His mother just wanted to be heard."

In a white shirt, tie, sweater, and jacket, William personally opted to read his statement in front of a camera at Kensington Palace. He did not prevaricate as he said, "It is my view that the deceitful way the interview was obtained substantially influenced what my mother said." He also claimed that the BBC "made lurid and false claims on the royal family which played on her fears and fueled paranoia . . . [The] BBC's failures contributed significantly to her fear, paranoia, and isolation that I remember from those final years with her." With conviction and force, in an almost officious tone, he added that the interview "established a false narrative" and the program "should never be aired again."

The differences in the brothers' statements are stark. Both expressed understandable outrage over Bashir's duplicity and the BBC's moral and professional failures. But while Harry stopped to acknowledge and honor Diana's strengths, despite the whole fiasco, William reinforced the counternarrative that his mother was paranoid at the time. While there is no doubt that William's rebuke came from a place of love, sources explained he was also keen to toe the company line without any concessions to what his mother said during the interview itself. To write his statement, William turned to a number of aides within the royal household, including former private secretary Simon Case, who had left a month earlier for his new role as cabinet secretary for then prime minister Boris Johnson. He embraced the institution's version that, because Diana was duped, the interview was null and void as a result—even if what she said was completely in line with what she had previously expressed in Morton's book. By disparaging Bashir's trick and by extension the entire interview, William ended up discrediting a large part of his mother's own story. To make his points, he did not remind the public that his mother was candid and truthful, despite Bashir's dirty work, but, instead, maintained the royal version that she was emotionally fragile and thus easily manipulated, and therefore her claims are not to be trusted.

It was more proof that the institution leveraged this ordeal as a way to wipe the interview from the collective consciousness, to get rid of a source of inconvenient truths, to finally free itself of a haunting narrative that just won't go away. And to do so, they sent out the good son, the heir to the throne, to make it official.

William was convincing in his lead role, but a source close

to Harry believes William may have felt some pressure to word his statement as he did, speaking not just for himself but on behalf of the institution. Either way, it demonstrates just how far the brothers have drifted apart, even though they once promised to never allow the institution to come between them and their feelings toward their mother. Harry's statement was a missive from exile issued from the heart of his crusade to reform a press establishment that he believes caused his mother's death. And he wasn't shy about bringing it up again. Just over a year later, Harry allowed and encouraged director Liz Garbus to use a clip from his mother's *Panorama* interview in Netflix's 2022 docuseries *Harry & Meghan*. "I think we all now know that she was deceived into giving the interview but at the same time she spoke the truth of her experience," Harry says in an episode. William was said to be "infuriated."

Let us also remember that it was in this interview that Diana suggested Charles might never be ready for the throne, claiming that such a "suffocating role . . . would bring enormous limitations to him, and I don't know whether he could adapt to that." Charles is now on the throne, and the Firm no doubt appreciated the opportunity to bury this insightful candor from a woman whose legacy and popularity still eclipses their own. The hard truth in all of this: we'll never know for certain whether Diana would have agreed to the interview and shared everything she did without Bashir's trickery. But the fact remains that she had already risked it all for Morton's book. "That interview was simply an amplification of what she had already said to me," said its author. Even in Lord Dyson's damning report, the judge states that he believes Diana probably would have agreed to the interview without Bashir's unscrupulous inventions (a fact conveniently sidestepped by some newspapers). Published as part of the investigation was an authenticated handwritten note from Diana on Kensington Palace stationery that read, "I consented to the interview on *Panorama* without any undue pressure and have no regrets concerning the matter."

Bashir also wanted to get something of his own on the record. After the Dyson report, he issued a statement that claimed mocking up the bank statements was "a stupid thing to do" and an action he "deeply regret[s]." But, he added, it is "saddening that this single issue has been allowed to overshadow the princess's brave decision to tell her story, to courageously talk through the difficulties she faced, and, to help address the silence and stigma that surrounded mental health issues all those years ago." The sanctimony is perhaps a bit much from someone who faked their way into fame, but he makes a good point. The melodrama once again occluded Diana's all-too-real human story: her suffering and bravery under fire, her vanity and guile. Distraction upstaged a knotty truth. Now *this* was straight from the Palace playbook.

For the royal establishment, the timing of all this couldn't be better. As the family continues to transform their shape with King Charles and Queen Camilla at the head and Prince William waiting for his turn, it proved an opportune moment to derail the Diana narrative. And with Harry and Meghan's own storyline out there dredging up similar issues, particularly the institution's indifference when it comes to women and mental health, this is a propitious moment for the Firm to, at the very least, rewrite this one notorious chapter. By casting Diana as a paranoid dupe in this fabled interview, they can pave the way for others (particularly the onside press) to raise issues about every other Diana story out there. Well, was she of sound mind when she said that? Who was pressuring her at the time? Questions about anything Diana-related that troubles the family brand can be raised. Meanwhile, the version of Diana they are comfortable with, the one that still brings in money and boosts their image, *that* one they'll be fine with. "Harry has experienced something very similar after sharing his own experiences and truth," said a source close to the duke. "He understands exactly what his mother went through because it's happening to him, too."

It was a masterful snow job from the Palace. In one go they delegitimized a disquieting narrative, laid blame on the media, and, once again, sidestepped any responsibility for Diana's misery. In a campaign of mass distraction, Diana's story was buried under a barrage of statements and reports primarily issued by powerful men. Her voice was almost lost to a mostly male echo chamber of opinion, interviews, and "findings."

When it was the Duchess of Sussex's turn for her own *Panorama*-style moment, a prime-time interview with Oprah Winfrey in March 2021, the royal institution had learned its lesson. This time, a campaign was activated before Meghan's words were even broadcast. And certain aides had just the ammunition that was required. After members of the royal household, past and present, worked closely with a British journalist, Meghan's reputation took a hit five days before *Oprah with Meghan & Harry* aired on CBS. On the front page of the March 2 edition of *The Times of London*: "Royal aides reveal Meghan bullying claim before Oprah interview." Inside, a lengthy dossier-style reportage featured a number of allegations from sources and insiders all claiming Meghan had "bullied" and "humiliated" staff during her time at Kensington Palace. According to the newspaper's royal correspondent Valentine Low, aides chose to "hit back" at the duchess, fearing "that only a partial version" of her two years as a working member of the royal family would be shared in the prime-time special. "They wanted to give their account of the turmoil within the royal household from Meghan's arrival," Low claimed, with details of how Meghan reportedly drove two personal assistants out of their jobs and undermined the confidence of a third staff member. One of them, he reported, told a colleague, "I can't stop shaking," before a meeting with the newly minted Duchess of Sussex. Others, the article added, were "reduced to tears."

Spearheading these claims at Kensington Palace was Jason Knauf, who at the time of the story's publication was CEO of William and Kate's charitable umbrella but was previously the communications secretary for both the Sussexes and Cambridges. He first expressed concerns about Meghan's bulldozing behavior, including her treatment of his friend and Sussex assistant Melissa Toubati, with the Palace's head of human resources, Samantha Carruthers, back in October 2018. Knauf told Carruthers he was worried that "nothing will be done," then followed up by emailing Simon Case.

"I am very concerned that the Duchess was able to bully two PAs out of the household in the past year. The treatment of [name one, redacted] was totally unacceptable," he wrote in the memo, which was passed on to *The Times*. "The Duchess seems intent on always having someone in her sights. She is bullying [name two, redacted] and seeking to undermine her confidence. We have had report after report from people who have witnessed unacceptable behaviour towards [name two, redacted]."

Interestingly, despite claims that the former "tormented" staffers were keen for their stories to be heard before the Sussexes' special aired, several sources confirmed to me that two of the "victims" mentioned in *The Times'* piece had actually rescinded their stories. "When they heard Jason had raised [the issue], they did not want it to become an official HR complaint," said a former member of the Kensington Palace team. Regardless, Knauf went ahead with internal conversations, including, a second source confirmed, several meetings with Prince William. "William wanted the story out there at the time . . . but it was tricky; it would have meant potentially putting members of staff who didn't want to be identified or part of this in a vulnerable position." It should come as no surprise then that, ahead of the Oprah interview, William was happy to overlook any prohibitive terms in staff members' employment contracts before email communication between Knauf and Case was shared with *The Times*.

Essentially, this was your classic "oppo dump," no different from when a political candidate collects information on their opponent and unleashes it in the final stages of an election or campaign to weaken them. Inside *The Times'* explosive report were a number of other unrelated claims, including the fact that Meghan had worn earrings gifted from Crown Prince Mohammed bin Salman of Saudi Arabia, the same royal who U.S. intelligence agencies say approved the murder of the journalist Jamal Khashoggi. Surprisingly, the duchess chose to wear the jewels three weeks after his killing at an October 2018 dinner in Fiji hosted by the nation's president. But a Sussex source claimed that the earrings were a wedding gift from the entire Saudi royal family and presented at Buckingham Palace on March 7, 2018, where the Sussexes weren't present and that the earrings "remain property of the Crown." Another allegation in the report suggested that Meghan ditched a visit to an initiative run by U.N. women on the same Fiji trip because of reservations about the organization (a biographer, briefed by the same former Palace aide, later added that Meghan took issue because they failed to make her an ambassador). "Ridiculous!" a staff member on the tour, which I was also on, told me. "We had to end the engagement early because there were security concerns at the market [where the engagement was at], which was quickly getting overcrowded. She was pregnant and security pulled the plug."

The timing of the allegations was obvious to even the most diehard royalists. Team Sussex was given the opportunity to comment a few days before the report, and the couple was devastated. Harry felt certain that the institution was behind it. "Let's just call this what it is—a calculated smear campaign based on misleading and harmful misinformation," a spokesperson for the couple pointed out. "It's no coincidence that distorted several-year-old accusations aimed at undermining the duchess are being briefed to the British media shortly before she and the duke are due to speak openly and honestly about their experience of recent years."

Meghan's London-based lawyer, Jenny Afia, later explained, "What bullying actually means is improperly using power repeatedly and deliberately to hurt someone, physically or emotionally. The Duchess of Sussex absolutely denies ever doing that. Knowing her as I do, I can't believe she would ever do that."

From the time before the couple's wedding to their January 2020 departure, I was deep into the reporting for *Finding Freedom* and in regular contact with the majority of Palace staff working for the Sussexes (sometimes several times a day). And though I was aware of how tense and fraught the atmosphere was for all on that team, largely down to the couple's increasingly fractured relationships with the institution and members of the royal family, there was never a word uttered or overheard about "bullying" or anything that resembled such behavior. In fact, it wasn't until Meghan's final week in Britain as a working royal that I first caught wind of potential staff hostility on the horizon. "Don't write that the staff were sad to see her go," one of the couple's aides said to me a couple of months later. This was after I had watched two team members wipe away tears as they bid farewell to the duchess. "Not all of us are or want to be portrayed as such." That aide went on to help at least two journalists with stories about the couple, particularly Meghan.

Even though there were no definitive examples of the alleged bullying (to this day, neither Low nor any other reporter has shared an account or anecdote involving bullying), Buckingham Palace made the rare move of going public with their response, announcing in a statement sent to global media outlets that a full investigation would take place. "We are clearly very concerned about allegations in the *The Times* following claims made by former staff of the Duke and Duchess of Sussex," read a statement issued less than twenty-four hours after the report ran, adding that the Palace's HR team would be investigating the article's allegations, and that staff from that period of time, including those who have left, would be invited to share their experiences. "The royal household has had a dignity at work policy in place for a number of years and does not and will not tolerate bullying or harassment in the workplace."

At a time when she was about to share her royal experience with the world, Meghan's new image as a bully was the reputational hit the Palace needed. Three people connected to those involved in the fiasco tell me that it was intentional to launch it just before her big interview. "I think some were worried that they would come out looking bad and no one was prepared to let Meghan have the final word," said a former Buckingham Palace staffer. "To some, they truly believed Meghan was these things . . . but to others it was about revenge. It was their way of putting her in her place in the final hour."

And it worked. When Meghan spoke about her difficult times working in the institution, media coverage in Britain still focused on the bullying allegations, and some used them to suggest she may have been to blame for the treatment she received. Behind the scenes, the Palace made a half-hearted attempt at conducting interviews (only a handful of people were ever approached) and carried out light investigative work. "It wasn't a thorough investigation," said the ex-staffer. "There really was never any intention to go much further with it. The claims served their purpose." Indeed, as the months went by, so did the memories of the investigation.

Sir Michael Stevens, the Keeper of the Privy Purse, told reporters during a July 2022 Sovereign Grant Report briefing, "I can confirm though that it was a review of the handling of the allegations aimed at enabling the royal households to consider potential improvements to HR policies and procedures. The review has been completed and recommendations on our policies and procedures have been taken forward, but we will not be commenting further." A Buckingham Palace spokesperson adds that conclusions were kept private to protect those taking part. It was an unsatisfactory outcome for all, including the participants of the investigation and the Sussexes, who—through their lawyer—filed a twenty-five-page report in early 2022 to Buckingham Palace's HR department to refute all the bullying allegations. To this day, details of the institution's report remain unknown to the public, unseen by the Sussexes or their lawyers, and somewhere in a vault at Buckingham Palace.

Harry, said a source, "was gutted that his family would watch this kind of dirty game play out." During a conversation just hours after the September 19, 2022, funeral of Prince Philip, Harry confronted his father and brother about why nothing was done on Meghan's behalf. "You must understand, darling boy, the institution can't just tell the media what to do!" Charles told him.

In both Diana's and Meghan's cases, the institution showed it can be masters of PR sleight of hand, but it comes with tremendous fallout. Royal Family, Inc., does not exactly have a spotless reputation for how it treats the women who enter into the family business. Discrediting Diana's account and posthumously labeling her as overly suspicious and unstable won't help. Before her death, Diana was ordered to suffer in silence. Though now back in the fold, Sarah, Duchess of York, spent years being punished for speaking up after her divorce from Prince Andrew. She spent almost thirty years shunned and unforgiven for allowing someone to suck her toes five months after their separation, despite the depravities of her former husband, which have forever disgraced the entire organization and himself. As for Meghan, the full story is *still* emerging—the Oprah interview, the Netflix docuseries, and Harry's memoir all revealed a shocking amount, and there are still things the couple has not shared. Maybe they never will. When it comes to Meghan's grim experiences behind palace walls, the royal family may stand by "recollections may vary," but it is now accepted truth that, at the very least, the institution ignored Meghan when she was in pain.

It's a dismal record, and with William now openly claiming his mother was essentially too paranoid to speak the truth, it proves the institution still operates under the principle that women not born into the family are, ultimately, disposable. Kate, of course, counters this, but then she's never challenged the system with public struggles or oversize aspirations. Comfortable in her role, willing to bring the requisite smile and elegance to her duties as princess, Kate glides under the radar. For now, anyway. It doesn't hurt that she is the wife of the heir to the throne and mother to the next in line. In many ways, Kate is protected in a way that other unrelated women were not. Norman Baker, who is not shy about criticizing the Sussexes, said that he was told by the boss of the major national newspaper he was writing for at the time, one with close ties to the royal family, that he could "say what I want about Harry and Meghan, but I had to lay off William and Kate. That was the instruction from the editor."

In the Sunken Garden at Kensington Palace there now stands a commemorative statue of Diana. It tastefully adorns one end of an ornamental pond that serves as the terraced garden's centerpiece, attracting tourists far and wide. On a sultry July 1, 2021, morning, William and Harry temporarily set aside their differences to unveil the bronze Ian Rank-Broadley–designed sculpture for its first public viewing. Many hoped this reunion would signal a thaw between the brothers, that this occasion to honor their mother would somehow bridge the widening gulf between them. Instead, it proved just a polite photo op that is now inconsequential in comparison to the transfiguring events that followed in the coming years. Harry left less than fifteen minutes after the photographers got their shot, exchanging only a few pleasantries with his brother.

Now, visitors can stroll the gardens and "reflect and celebrate" the life of Princess Diana, hopefully also spending a little money in the nearby Palace gift shop (complete with Diana-related memorabilia) or the on-site Orangery where you can indulge in afternoon tea overlooking the grounds where she once walked and chatted to gardeners. As for the brothers, we are unlikely to see them visit this site together anytime soon, if ever again. Not even her legacy can fix that.

But her human suffering, her impact, her eminence as a pattern breaker, these will never leave the many of us who lived through her time in the sun. And they're also stamped on the history of the royal family, whether they like it or not. An inverted mirror image, her statue's reflection in the palace pond is a reminder of how, depending on the light, her true story briefly vanishes but always reappears.

# 12

## Skilled Survivors
### Camilla and Kate, Windsor Women

———•———

## Part I: Camilla
### The Transformation of a Mistress

*The two most powerful warriors are patience and time.*
—Leo Tolstoy, *War and Peace*

*I feel as if I have been blessed to undergo a transformation from*
*"gangster" to "redeemed sinner with gangster proclivities."*
—Cornel West , 2016, *60 Minutes* interview

Resting in the rugged but fertile valleys that stretch between Crete's majestic Mount Psiloritis and the towers of sun-bleached limestone that make up Mount Spathi, the Lyrarakis Winery is a family-owned business best known for its first-rate wines and commitment to sustainability and environmental stewardship. It was a natural spot for Camilla, then the Duchess of Cornwall, an earthy woman who shares her husband's zeal for eco-friendly ventures, to stop for a tour and taste some wine during the couple's

2018 visit to Greece. Dressed in a flowy cream and white outfit fit for a sunny day in the mythologized Greek countryside, Camilla walked the dusty vineyard paths, visited the vine museum, and tasted several of the Lyrarakis wines.

A photographer snapped the requisite photos as Camilla raised a glass to toast her hosts, claiming, "I [have] never had Greek wine before, but it is delicious. I will certainly have it again."

With that it could have been job well done for Camilla—a natural end to the engagement and time to pack up and move on to the next leg. But, with time to spare, Camilla stuck around and enjoyed the views from the winery's taproom—and got to know Robert Jobson, a royal correspondent of nearly thirty-five years. As luck had it, Jobson was the designated journalist from the royal rota covering the engagement, and he was also gathering reportage for his book on the then Prince of Wales, *Charles at Seventy*. The heir and his team gave Jobson unrivaled access during this time, so Camilla was well aware that he was in the thick of it. An old hand at working rooms, Camilla called Jobson over. "Do you want to join us doing the wine tasting, Robert?" she asked with a smile. Alongside Camilla's private secretary, the trio relaxed and chatted under the watchful gaze of her protection officer Inspector Mark Andrews as they sampled wines with a selection of cheeses. "I thought, that's a very kind move, and a smart one, too," said Jobson. "I didn't see it as her trying to be manipulative or an attempt to suck up to a journalist. It was just a relaxed atmosphere and something any normal, considerate person would do. And it was great wine; neither of us needed the spittoons!"

This is modus operandi for Queen Camilla—schmoozing and delighting come naturally. Speak to anyone who has spent more than a few minutes with her and they'll talk about how charmed they were by her sense of humor and her ability to hold a conversation. Much of that is down to her personality, but it also comes from how she was raised. Camilla was brought up old-style near the picturesque rural village of Lewes in East Sussex; her parents, Major Bruce and Rosalind Shand, were both considered charming aristocrats from a bygone era. Major Shand was a handsome World War II hero who was well-versed in wine, fox hunting, and conservative politics. Before she married the debonair major, Camilla's mother mixed in society circles as Rosalind Cubitt, daughter of the 3rd Baron of Ashcombe. Rosalind, the debutante of the year in 1939, was a radiant beauty who was comfortable holding court among that era's beau monde. In *Palace Papers*, former *Vanity Fair* editor in chief Tina Brown wonderfully describes her as "generously bosomed, vivacious, and witty." She was known to puff on small cigars, but she was strict about manners when it came to her children. Rosalind embodied old money and all the trappings of aristocratic life. Her triple great-grandfather was Thomas Cubitt, a famous nineteenth-century builder who oversaw construction of many of the mansions that still grace London's tony neighborhood of Belgravia, as well as the iconic east front of Buckingham Palace. On the other side of Rosalind's family tree, her grandmother, socialite Alice Keppel, was King Edward VII's favorite highborn mistress and illicit plaything of twelve years. It seems even the inclination to become a royal paramour was passed down the family line to Camilla.

On the edge of the undulating green and chalk hills of East Sussex's "magical" South Downs, Camilla's childhood home, the Laines, is a study in "rustic elegance." A former rectory made of brick and timber in the Georgian style, the seven-bedroom estate oozes country charm. It features rooms that are at once spacious and cozy, rambling flower and vegetable gardens, fruit trees, and a Gothic-style orangery with wrap-around windows. By all accounts, the Shand family filled this bucolic home with familial warmth and affection. Major Shand passed on his love of horses and hunting to Camilla and her two siblings, Mark and Annabel. Rosalind taught Camilla the ways of the garden. And there were of course grand dinner parties and lively drinks in the orangery, times when the Shands turned on the charm and their country home glowed with bonhomie and social dazzle. In one of her many interviews with the *Mail on Sunday*, Camilla joked that those gatherings prepared her for life as a royal. "We used to complain and say, 'Can't we stay here and watch the television over fish fingers?' and [my mother would] sit us down at the dinner table and the minute there was a silence, she used to say, 'Talk! I don't care what you talk about, talk about your budgie or your pony but keep the conversation going . . .' And so I've never been able not to talk. It's in the psyche, not to leave a silence."

When it was time for school, Camilla got a good dose of the city. From the age of ten until her late teens, Camilla attended the exclusive Queen's Gate School in London's South Kensington. There, social training came first, academics a distant second. At the time, the school focused on preparing upper-crust girls for a life of socializing and administering to a big, grand house. Instead of formal higher education, Camilla attended a Swiss finishing school next to the shimmering waters of Lake Geneva, and then went to the capital of France, where she studied French literature (naturally) at the University of London Institute in Paris. Much of this traditionally patrician education took place during the sixties, a decade that was swinging and full of flower power and protest, one that eschewed convention and patriarchy. But there was Camilla studying the blueprint for the bluebloods, dutifully learning how to mix and mingle and drop a perfectly timed French phrase, while many young women of her generation were burning their bras as part of an effort to dismantle the system that prized this sort of old-fashioned behavior. (Today, Camilla stands for women's equality but, interestingly, hates it when someone suggests she is a feminist.)

Camilla was fine with her outmoded upbringing then, and she's proud of it now, a fact that is both admirable and a little troubling, considering where we are as a society two decades into the third millennium. Looking back, Camilla says she's grateful to have been "brought up with the grounding of my parents, and taught manners. It sounds, especially in this day and age, sort of snobbish but . . . nobody went on to university unless you were a real brain-box. Instead, we went to Paris and Florence and learned about life and culture and how to behave with people, how to talk to people." Not snobbish at all. You won't hear the likes of Hillary Clinton, Michelle Obama, or even Catherine, the Princess of Wales, espousing the virtues of elite, erstwhile social training. And while her royal understudy, Kate, spent a "gap year" abroad at the British Institute in Florence, she followed that up by working as a deckhand in South-ampton for £40 a day that same summer. This is all before she went on to the University of St. Andrews to earn a degree in art history. In Camilla's defense, she was part of the last generation of upper-class women who were born into these antiquated practices—it was expected of them, and deviations from it were frowned upon. "This was very ingrained in my upbringing and if I hadn't had that, I would have found royal life much more difficult," she has said.

You could say Camilla was born to play the part the royal system demands of its actors, and she demonstrated these skills from the very start of her long and twisting love affair with Charles. From the chrysalis of her loving but privileged childhood and her debutante-styled education emerged a dazzling, self-assured social butterfly who was not only trained to flit to and fro as prescribed, but also ready to face whatever circumstantial winds blew her way. Camilla might not have stood on the barricades in the sixties, but she did enjoy the sexual freedoms ushered in by that radical genera-tion. Over the years, some who knew Camilla during this time have told various authors and journalists that the young Ms. Shand was known for being "raunchy and randy" and the sort to "throw her knickers on the table." This reputation is one of the reasons why Queen Elizabeth II and the Firm rejected Camilla as a spouse for Charles, alongside the fact she was a "commoner" (the air around her family home not rarefied enough) and an "experienced woman" (read: not a virgin).

The result of this Palace meddling: Camilla married the horse-crazy, swashbuckling Andrew Parker Bowles, a man who at one time was also coiled around Princess Anne (though not at the same time as he was with Camilla, contrary to rumors and the third season of *The Crown*); Charles begrudgingly put one foot into his union with the Palace-approved, beautiful but naive Diana; and Charles and Camilla started a decades-long affair that flagrantly smudged the monarchy's reputation and gassed up the tabloids for years. The two marriages engendered two sets of children, but the extramarital romance produced splintered families and, as can now be said with confidence, broke the hearts of those very same children.

But it was in this trail of wreckage that Camilla found her footing and started playing what can only be called a long game. Before Charles eventually married Diana in 1981, he floundered around with other women, but Camilla made sure he was always more than welcome at the Parker Bowles residences whenever he wanted to return to his true love. Brigadier Andrew knew about Charles and Camilla's fling but enjoyed the whole aristocratic gamesmanship of it all—and the royal associations, even if it meant shuffling around his private clubs as a cuckold. So, Charles and Camilla threw caution to the wind, coming dangerously close to displaying their love in public, and, at one point, making it fodder for staff gossip. The rumor that one of Charles's bodyguards found the passionate couple "doing what Lady Chatterley enjoyed best" in the garden at Camilla's grandmother's house has become an old (but probably false) fable in royal circles.

It wasn't until after Diana entered the mix that Charles and Camilla added colluding to their canoodling. Marrying the woman the Firm demanded left Charles demoralized and in constant need of bucking up, a typical state of mind for the famously mopey prince. Enter Camilla, who kept up the sensual mistress routine, but she also, like her ancestor Alice Keppel did for King Edward VII, became Charles's biggest champion and a dependable advisor. And Camilla managed to do this without scuttling her own marriage. When it came to Charles, Camilla leaned on that same self-assuredness and natural affection that made her so appealing and unique as a debutante, qualities that flowered from seeds planted during her upbringing. She confidently took on the role as the future King's closest confidante and lover.

Charles admitted to his official biographer, Jonathan Dimbleby, that what made Camilla so exceptional was that "she laughed easily and at the same silliness" as he did, while in a letter to his favorite uncle, Lord Mountbatten, he claimed he and Camilla experienced near perfection: a "blissful, peaceful, and mutually happy relationship." Camilla became essential for Charles. No matter how high the stakes, he had to have her in his world. She shared his interests in hunting and country life and made herself indispensable when Charles fled Palace duties and a struggling Diana to while away in his prized gardens and don his tweeds at his rural retreat. This was made easier by the fact that his refuge, the vast country mansion of Highgrove, is only a fifteen-minute drive from Camilla's beloved Ray Mill House, an almost Proustian re-creation of her childhood haven in Sussex that she still uses to this day. Their pastoral conniving involved others from their inner sanctum who opened up the doors to their own country manors for Charles and Camilla's trysts when Ray Mill or Highgrove wasn't an option. A housekeeper from one of these conspiratorial homes complained to a tabloid that she always knew when Camilla had been there: "After she's been staying, I find knickers all over the place." Camilla's undergarments making yet another appearance.

The pair carried on like this until the calamitous 1990s sent them both reeling. In 1992, the Queen's famous annus horribilis, Diana and Charles finally called it quits and separated. Enough was enough—Charles was checked out and, from the royal institution's point of view, Diana was causing untold damage by openly discussing their marriage woes. And it quickly got so much worse, for Camilla in particular. After the new year celebrations of 1993, Australia's *New Idea* magazine published the scandalous transcript of a bawdy phone call between Charles and Camilla. Former *Mirror* editor Richard Stott, who broke the story but didn't run the transcript, claims that an amateur radio enthusiast from Merseyside gave him the tape after he randomly—and after "a few pints of lager"—picked up the call on his radio and recognized Charles's voice. Dubbed "Camillagate," the contents of this proto–sex tape are old news; even a 2022 episode of *The Crown* rehashed it in all its gory details. It's worth noting, however, that after Charles says he wants to "live in [Camilla's] trousers or something, it would be much easier," Camilla laughingly responds with, "What are you going to turn into, a pair of knickers? Oh, you're going to come back as a pair of knickers." Those knickers seem to be a running theme in this story.

The barrage of lurid news tanked both of their reputations, forcing Camilla to batten down the hatches at Middlewick House, the Wiltshire manor she shared with Parker Bowles at the time. Charles, of course, had the Palace apparatus in his corner, and the system's instincts to protect one of its own kicked in. Wasting no time to initiate an image-rebuilding effort for Charles, the spin machine went into high gear for the heir to the throne. Camilla, on the other hand, was left to manage on her own. It was a tough outcome for someone who had just been branded the most hated woman in Britain. She faced an unabating Hydra of scorn: hate mail, threatening phone calls, people scowling in her direction in public (though that famous story about shoppers throwing bread rolls at her is just a tabloid myth), and, of course, strikes from the papers and the wider world's press. For her part, Diana nicknamed Camilla "the Rottweiler," which, as she probably intended, the media picked up and ran with. Harassed and stalked, Camilla retreated into Middlewick, often afraid to step outside.

While in hiding, Camilla began her long climb back to normal life. She taught herself how to paint (a hobby she still enjoys to this day) and buried herself in books. Proving her resilience, she privately withstood her mother's death from crippling osteoporosis and Charles's disastrous TV interview with Jonathan Dimbleby in July 1994, where he publicly confirmed that he had cheated on Diana. The nineties weren't done with her yet, though. Camilla and her brigadier finally divorced in 1995, and Parker Bowles went on to marry his own favorite mistress, Rosemary Pitman, shortly after. In February 1996, Charles and Diana's divorce was finalized. The musical chairs of extramarital sex, collusion, and public humiliation were finally brought to an ignoble end for all involved.

After the ink dried on the divorce papers, Camilla found herself utterly alone in her cavernous Wiltshire home, but, because of her ability to "just get on with it" and her commitment to Charles, the cocoon of her new life started to form. Camilla's stability and endurance during these hardships was recognized by those close to her and quietly by those in the orbit of the Palace. She never publicly aired her grievances or rushed to correct the record (at the time), no matter how vicious the rumor—she rode out the storm, prioritizing her relationship with Charles (who did the same in return, much to the frustration of young William and Harry, who a family source said "often felt like they came second to Camilla"). That grin-and-bear-it upbringing had already prepared her for a life of "never complain, never explain" as a member of the royal family. "The duchess is resilient . . . down to earth," Julian Payne, her communications secretary during the 2010s, previously said to me. "She is focused on the bigger picture." Her natural composure and confidence would see her through.

This time she had some serious help. After Charles and Diana's divorce, the Queen and the institution slowly started to accept that Camilla wasn't going anywhere—her gravitational pull on Charles was too strong, and their long affair had solidified into something that the Palace couldn't easily dismiss. Diana's tragic death in 1997 forced the couple to retreat from any plans to step out publicly, going to great lengths to avoid being be seen together. They wanted to change this unwelcome reality and, to achieve that, Charles and Camilla as a couple would need a PR miracle. So Charles promoted assistant private secretary Mark Bolland to a deputy role—tasking him to work with private secretary Stephen Lamport to incrementally rehabilitate Camilla's image. Now widely known as "Operation PB" (Parker Bowles), the duo masterminded a long-term campaign as subtle as it was powerful, at least at first. When the press finally got the official first words about Charles and his ongoing relationship with Camilla, Bolland told journalists she was a "nonnegotiable" part of his life. However, they waited eighteen months before making their first photographed public appearance—a birthday party for Camilla's sister at London's Ritz hotel. Bolland personally phoned the likes of *The Sun* and the *Daily Mail* to assure them that the January 28, 1999, bash was "T-Day" (Together Day). The Queen was unimpressed—she felt her son was "over-promoting" their relationship. But it worked. Suddenly, at least in certain media quarters, Camilla had gone from being called "the other woman" to the "woman who waited."

For Camilla's own fiftieth birthday celebration in June 2000, Clarence House scaled up their efforts with a sparkly to-do at Highgrove, where she would meet the Queen for the first time (and Bolland would go on to share all the details with the *News of the World*, edited by his close friend Rebekah Brooks, now the managing director of Rupert Murdoch's News UK). That night Camilla "dazzled," and Charles and his "woman who waited" shared the spotlight in the same house they previously snuck away to for trysts. At the time, I'm told, both William and Harry struggled to come to terms with the reality of their family's new normal. "They had few people they could share their anger with," said a mutual friend of the siblings. "Here was a woman who had destroyed their family and tormented their mother, now having the time of her life. In those early days, they were angry with her."

It would be another five years before Charles and Camilla would marry, and in the spring of 2005—in a toned-down civil ceremony at Windsor Guildhall in front of their children, including Princes William and Harry—Camilla Parker Bowles completed the first stage of her transformation. Taking Charles's hand in marriage, the vilified royal mistress became the Duchess of Cornwall, wife to the heir. Patrick "Paddy" Harverson, then Charles's communications secretary and the PR chief responsible for taking the reins of Operation PB a year prior, counted the wedding as a crowning accomplishment for the couple. The former communications director for Manchester United Football Club (he turned David Beckham from a national hate figure to hero after the football legend was blamed for England's loss against Argentina in the 1998 World Cup), Harverson was an experienced, likable, yet determined "comms guy" dedicated to his one mission: "protect and promote." He embraced that position from day one with Camilla, recognizing how her outgoing nature and calm under pressure could benefit the monarchy's reputation. He also quickly realized that Camilla was indispensable for Charles—she reanimated him in a way that no one or nothing else could. "She has been by his side, working diligently, supporting him while pursuing her own causes," said Harverson. "They love each other. She is a source of great support and comfort and love to [Charles]. They share the same sense of humor and they blend together beautifully."

Good for Charles, and good for the institution, as it turns out. The wedding meant that the Palace finally embraced Camilla and formally established a working role for her. The Queen had also come around to agreeing that the union was the best thing for the Firm. It had the potential to clean up the mess the couple had made over the years.

For William and Harry, it took a long time to get there, but they finally accepted Camilla for what she was and still is—an anchor for their father, an unflinching, steady support system for which he could not do without. But while she may technically be their stepmother, the relationship she has with both is "more professional and respectful than loving and familial," described a family friend. In the years that followed, the new Duchess of Cornwall finally became tolerated, then later accepted, by the public (and now even approved of by some). In the early days it would have been unimaginable to think that one day William and Kate would meet Charles and Camilla for laugh-filled lunches, but the two couples have grown increasingly closer over the years, especially since the Sussexes' departure. As for her relationship with Harry and Meghan, there is none. Camilla has told others she has "great sympathy" for what Meghan went through but, according to a royal source, has "no respect for the way they handled themselves."

The rehabilitation of the mistress could be called a success, a sanitizing process that turned a "Rottweiler" into a duchess. But there was still work to be done, and Camilla, Charles, and their Palace teams continually fueled the engines for different iterations of Operation PB, orchestrating most of them from the shadows. Camilla has also taken matters into her own hands, building relationships with a number of high-profile (and some notorious) media figures. Though former morning TV host Piers Morgan was responsible for some of the most aggressive tabloid coverage about Princess Diana and the royal family during his time as editor in chief of the *Mirror* and has also spent more than five years attacking the Duchess of Sussex in articles and on TV, Camilla continues to enjoy a close relationship with him. Not even accusations of *Mirror* journalists hacking the phones of Harry and other high-profile figures during Morgan's tenure has tempered the friendship. The pair have been close for more than twenty years and enjoy regular chats on the phone and the occasional boozy lunch. In addition to their shared love of East Sussex (they grew up in neighboring villages), they have a mutual disdain for all things "woke" (in its 2.0 sense). Behind closed doors, Camilla usually rolls her eyes when topics such as gender identity, unconscious racial bias, and even veganism are raised. "It's all 'lefty nonsense' to her," a former aide revealed. "Even gluten-free or dairy-free options on a restaurant menu irk her."

It seems they might have similar views on Meghan, too. When Piers called the Duchess of Sussex "Pinocchio Princess" and then a "race-baiter" on *Good Morning Britain* after she admitted that she had suicidal ideations during her time as a working royal (also asserting that there was unconscious bias within the family), it was Camilla who quietly thanked him for defending the Firm. "[Camilla] will never publicly comment on anything or speak ill of others, but she will *always* know someone who can do that for her," a former Palace aide told me. "I've had some messages communicated to me on behalf of several members of the royal family," Morgan admitted to *Extra TV* in April 2021. "I'm not going to go into who it was, but [it was] gratitude that somebody was standing up."

Even her friendship with legendary actress Dame Judi Dench came in handy when a fifth season of *The Crown* threatened to knock Camilla's reputation once again. The (mostly accurate) portrayal of her as a chain-smoking adulteress who made Diana's life hell saw her popularity tank once again, as viewers were reminded of Camilla's pre–Operation PB antics. To prevent the negativity experienced during the release of *The Crown*'s fourth season from happening again, friends in the media (including the *Mail* group of newspapers, where she enjoys a close relationship with the paper's owner, Lord Rothermere) activated a defense strategy. The "vicious" series, the tabloid barked on its front pages and website, is bullying the royal family, would have "destroyed" the Queen if she were still alive, is "verging on defamatory," and should be boycotted. Dench did her bit to help the cause and wrote an open letter in *The Times* accusing Netflix executives and show producers of blurring the lines between historical accuracy and crude sensationalism, thereby damaging the monarchy. The show should, she insisted, have a disclaimer at the start to "warn" viewers of its fictionalized scenes. It was a curious fight for the usually press-shy actress to take on, especially given her own depictions of the Queen's great-great-grandmother in the movies *Victoria & Abdul* and *Her Majesty, Mrs. Brown*, both of which received some criticism from historians about accuracy.

Though those in Camilla's world all echo the same high praise when it comes to her sense of humor and mischievous "twinkle in her eye" (both true), one can't deny that many of these friendships have also served a greater purpose when it comes to the rehabilitation of her image. That prize charm is also how she won over the majority of the royal press pack. While most senior royals tend to largely ignore the gaggle of reporters and photographers at engagements, Camilla is always the first (and often the only) to say hello and give a wink. When the photographers point their lenses, Camilla doesn't turn away or play hard to get; instead she will ask, "Where do you want me?" She will even give a nudge to Charles at times if she senses that snappers aren't getting the best shot.

It's a smart and simple move—especially in the cases of some longtime royal reporters, who harbor a need to be liked by the subjects they write about. Most in the royal rota now sing her praises when given the chance in opinion pieces and documentary appearances. With some, the relationship has gone even deeper. The *Daily Mail*'s royal editor Rebecca English is regularly the first to be spoon-fed Camilla-related scoops. A canny strategy that has paid off in droves, as the reporter has never written a critical word about the paper's star royal source since taking the job in 2004. "For Camilla, having a little pet in the [press] pack has been essential," a former Palace aide revealed. "After the wedding, it was absolutely her mission to make that happen."

In *Spare*, Prince Harry revealed his "complex feelings" toward his stepmother. "In a funny way I even wanted Camilla to be happy," he wrote. "Maybe she'd be less dangerous if she was happy." That dangerousness, he told journalist Anderson Cooper, comes from her willingness to forge interdependent relationships with the tabloid press and media figures. "With a family built on hierarchy, and with her, on the way to being Queen Consort, there [were] gonna be people or bodies left in the street." It is no secret that his own body was one of those sacrificed on Camilla and Bolland's "personal PR altar." In those earlier days, information about him and his life were currency to curry favor with Fleet Street editors. Today, a similar arrangement with sections of the British press still exists, as Harry's courtroom revelations have revealed.

Still, the Duke of Sussex also says he sees Camilla as just as much of a victim of the inner workings of a cold institution as any of his other family members. "I have a huge amount of compassion for her, you know," he said. "She had a reputation, or an image, to rehabilitate. Whatever conversations happened, whatever deals or trading was made right at the beginning, she was led to believe that that would be the best way of doing it . . . [She] has done everything that she can to improve her own reputation and her own image for her own sake." Even today there is no animosity on Harry's side. A source close to the Duke of Sussex—who has said he doesn't consider Camilla an "evil stepmother"—called their relationship "respectful . . . and kept at a safe distance." Camilla, I'm told, may not feel quite the same. "To say she wasn't hurt by what he wrote [in *Spare*] would not be the truth," said a royal source. "But she won't retaliate. "A friend and one of Camilla's "Queen's companions," the Marchioness of Lansdowne, told *The Sunday Times*, "Of course it bothers her, of course it hurts. But she doesn't let it get to her. Her philosophy is always, 'Don't make a thing of it and it will settle down—least said, soonest mended.' "

The marchioness is one of a group of six women Queen Camilla keeps close, in place of what previous female monarchs called ladies-in-waiting. Other "Queen's companions" include Baroness Carlyn Chisholm, a British peeress and member of the House of Lords; and Lady Sarah Keswick, who has known Charles and Camilla since the first days of their affair. Camilla's sister, Annabel Elliot, whom she considers her best friend, joined the Marchioness of Lansdowne to serve as "Ladies Attendants" during the May 2023 coronation. Elliot's appearance made the ceremony somewhat of a family affair for Camilla, whose three teenage grandsons, Gus Lopes, Louis Lopes, and Freddy Parker Bowles, were selected as pages of honor.

Camilla has long enjoyed close relationships with her two children. Her son, Tom Parker Bowles, a restauranteur, is tight-lipped when it comes to talking about Camilla the royal, but he's the first to sing her praises as a mother. Her roast chicken "with all the trimmings" on a Sunday, with everyone getting together at Ray Mill House, is something they strive to do regularly, no matter how busy everyone gets. "We all love our food and to be able to share that with each other is wonderful," he told me during an interview. As grandmother to his children, Freddy and Lola, she's also happy to step in to babysit (something she is "brilliant" at, he said). Despite the fact that they're now children of the King's wife, neither Tom nor her daughter, Laura, expect their lives to change. "You're not going to find us with great estates or being called the Duke of Whatever, no, that would be appalling," he has said.

In addition to fulfilling her duties as grandmother and pushing overtime to repair her reputation, Camilla has done the necessary work in her role as a senior royal, namely through philanthropic endeavors and awareness raising to help others. In an unassuming way, Camilla has put her energies into more than ninety charities, including grittier, less-glamorous issues that demand more than just ribbon-cutting. The National Osteoporosis Society, a cherished charity for Camilla after her mother died of the disorder in 1994, was renamed the Royal Osteoporosis Society in 2019. The name change was Camilla's idea, said the charity's executive Craig Jones, a business-minded decision Camilla believed would give the charity more "clout and credibility." More clout is important because, as Jones said, "osteoporosis is a difficult cause . . . it's surrounded by stereotypes and defeatism . . . people think breaking bones is an inevitable part of getting older. Camilla knows it isn't." She also passionately raises awareness about domestic abuse, which she rightly calls a "global pandemic of violence against women"; literacy, through her "Queen's Reading Room" initiative; animal welfare (both of her dogs, Beth and Bluebell, were rescued from the Battersea Dog Home); and loneliness among the elderly. Unable to lean on widespread popularity or tabloid interest in her sartorial choices (blame an ageist society and, by her own admission to an aide, a "less exciting" wardrobe for that), Camilla has carried out many of her charitable efforts without splashy, big-budget campaigns. "She was very explicit with me that she didn't want [that] and simply let her work speak for herself," said Julian Payne.

This natural style toward work and her ease in her role has scored Camilla points with the Firm, the public, and influential figures. It has also impressed her husband. In his first address as King in September 2022, Charles had this to say about his other half:

> *I count on the loving help of my darling wife, Camilla. In recognition of her own loyal public service since our marriage seventeen years ago, she becomes my Queen Consort. I know she will bring to the demands of her new role the steadfast devotion to duty on which I have come to rely so much.*

And with that the second stage of Camilla's royal journey was a success: Camilla, Queen Consort, now sharing her husband's rank and status. Before she passed away, Queen Elizabeth II promoted the idea for Camilla to take on the consort title before Charles's ascension, making her wish clear before the Platinum Jubilee celebrations in 2022. Seventeen years earlier, after the couple's wedding, Palace aides had assured the public that Camilla would only take on the title of "Princess Consort"—an effort to appease a nation that mostly disliked her. But with Camilla having managed to achieve acceptance since then, the late monarch felt it was the right time to put her stamp of approval on an upgraded title. Unbeknownst to the public, that, too, was only temporary. A month before the May 6, 2023, coronation, Buckingham Palace released invitations without the consort styling. The former mistress would now be crowned by the Archbishop of Canterbury as Queen Camilla. Transformation complete.

Ironically, and perhaps hard to believe for some, it was never Camilla's wish to sit on the throne. Those I have spoken to over the years say she has simply accepted that the role comes with the territory of being with the man she wanted to spend the rest of her life with. Nevertheless, she takes the job seriously. Despite her age, she consistently carries out more engagements than most royals, including Prince William and Kate, the Princess of Wales. She also remains a committed and effective advisor to the King. She can probably say more with a half-raised eyebrow than the rest of his well-informed staff combined (it's why she was never a fan of Charles's right-hand man Michael Fawcett—she felt he was the only other person who had his ear as much as she does). An aide close to her has told me that "she doesn't take herself too seriously. She isn't lost in a sense of self-importance, but she understands the importance of the institution." Added a royal source, "To be around her you would never think she is Queen. She's still the same as she was years ago, friendly with everyone, always up for a natter."

Payne, who worked for Charles and Camilla for five years, told Times Radio, "She has an innate understanding of the institution but also fifty years of living in the real world. She's a very good bridge between the two. You see her voice and her impact in all facets of the life of the King and as a couple."

Whether she wanted it or not—and whether the public wanted it or not (polls at the time of the finishing of this book say a lot of the nation still aren't sure)—she is now Queen Camilla. And what now appears like an inevitability actually took a lot of backstage maneuvering and horse-trading. While communications campaigns and PR gurus certainly played significant roles in Camilla's decades-long metamorphosis, it would be a mistake to underestimate her own handiwork in this massive image overhaul. But her long game is finally over, and Camilla and the Palace PR corps can finally file the strategies and plans for Operation PB. Perhaps they'll come in handy for someone else in the future. She's come a long way from the Shand family haven in Sussex, but, in many ways, this is exactly where Camilla thought she'd be when she became Charles's mistress more than forty years ago. Her troubles endured, and her final act planned for all along.

# Part II: Kate

## Suddenly Front and Center

*We've all seen the families of the skilled survivors. Their strength comes from within and was put there . . . from their earliest days.*

—Diana, Princess of Wales, 1993, keynote speech

*It is the nature of stone*
*to be satisfied.*
*It is the nature of water*
*to want to be somewhere else.*

—Mary Oliver, *The Leaf and the Cloud*

As the final throes of summer tapered into an unusually hot start to the fall of 2019, September's late afternoons brought longer shadows and slanting light to the hills and woodlands of Surrey. Only twenty-five miles southwest of London, the Royal Horticultural Society's flagship site at Wisley basked in the warm glow of England's unseasonably long summer and served as a testament to the wonders of horticulture. The grand gardens cover 240 acres, and its Glasshouse centerpiece, a greenhouse the size of ten tennis courts, was thriving with exotic plants from around the world enjoying the early-autumn sun. An arcadia for anyone with even a passing interest in the natural world, Wisley is home to a world-famous rock garden with a tumbling stream, alpine plants, and a fern grotto, as well as the meandering walkways of the Bowes-Lyon Rose Garden and its four thousand plants. That month, RHS Wisley was also the proud new home of the Back to Nature Garden, a woodland ramble and wildflower meadow for families and children with treehouses, a hollow log, swings, a willow pond, and a large sand pit. The brainchild of Kate, who was then the Duchess of Cambridge, the garden opened on September 10. Just like the usually bashful autumnal sun, Kate, too, was ready to shed her shy side for the garden's grand unveiling. She visited the garden with *Great British Bake Off* star Mary Berry to tour the grounds and take part in a host of fun activities with local schoolchildren. "I hope I do this right!" she said with a laugh as she planted a weeping blue cedar sapling in front of photographers in the garden's family play zone. The natural sprawl of the tree's drooping branches—which grow outward rather than up—added visual curiosity to the grounds and would eventually provide a den-like structure for children to play under.

In a signature Emilia Wickstead blue floral dress, Kate also gave a speech on the importance of family, friends, and community recreation in the development of young children. "The physical benefits of being outdoors and in nature are well documented," she said. "More recently, however, I have learned that these often safe and supported environments can also bring significant benefits to the cognitive, social, and emotional development of our children, too." The speech underscored Kate's mission to get children back outdoors. And, unlike public speeches in the past, where she often stumbled on her words, she wasn't nervous this time. "She practiced it a few times before giving it and was just really at ease," her communications secretary told me afterward. "I'm definitely seeing a new level of confidence in her."

Her self-assured demeanor was a world away from four months prior, when she launched her first Back to Nature concept garden at the Chelsea Flower Show in June. To promote that she filmed a surprise appearance on BBC's *Blue Peter*, Britain's longest-running children's television show. On air, viewers saw Kate wander around the rangy Paddington Recreation Ground in London's Maida Vale with host Lindsey Russell talking about her passion for the great outdoors and how she constantly encourages her children to spend time outside, "rain or shine." Smiling, relaxed, and motherly around the local schoolchildren featured in the program, Kate took the small group to "pond dip" for tadpoles, an activity she claimed was "massively up her street," as well as some old-fashioned fort-building using sticks, logs, and leaves.

But, behind the scenes, it was a different story. Though it was a low-pressure, small-stakes broadcast appearance, Kate was feeling nervous and "well out of her comfort zone" before the taping. "It was just not an area she felt confident in and, up until that point, other household staff hadn't really pushed her," a Kensington Palace source said. Naturally timid and introverted, Kate had historically eschewed giving interviews or public speaking, instead finding comfort in engagements that were often led by a host while she quietly followed, giving a speech from a script or teleprompter. She also favored outings that involved interacting with children or sporting activities, where it's more about her actions than her words.

Where other senior royals are out and about several times a week, meeting people across the length and breadth of the country, Kate has long maintained a smaller work schedule that helped her check off the required royal boxes while saving time for her roles as a mother and a wife. Prince William was called work-shy for his initial hesitation to fully sign on for royal duty; Kate, too, gained some disparaging media nicknames of her own. Not long after their marriage, some critics deemed her "lazy" because she avoided regular royal duties. Over the years, several factors made it easier to circumvent too many public-facing events, including William's fierce protectiveness and her vital role of producing an heir (and spares) first and foremost. The Palace gatekeepers have always been more vigilant when it comes to Kate, never pushing her too hard, as the road to Queendom is a marathon, not a sprint. "I think for a long time people were afraid to make her do something that would make her uncomfortable," a senior aide told me. But with the sun setting on the Queen's reign, the heir and spare tasks achieved, it was time to slowly push Kate out onto center court.

Her lead press secretary Christian Jones—who had six years

of experience working with two government departments before starting at Kensington Palace in early 2019—was the one who suggested the *Blue Peter* appearance to the duchess. While it was designed as a slow pitch for Kate to hit a crowd-pleasing home run, there were difficulties getting her up to the plate. Kate, Jones later told me, wasn't thrilled with the idea of doing an interview and initially wanted to turn it down. But after some encouragement from both himself and William, she reluctantly agreed. On the day of the mid-June shoot, Kate was "a bag of nerves."

Jones joined her for the weekday outing and reminded Kate that the interview would be short and the majority of the filming would be with children. But it was William's words that eventually filled her with enough courage to stay calm. As she arrived, a text message from her husband popped up. "William was texting her regularly to see how she was doing and make sure she wasn't nervous," said a source. The taping itself went smoothly, Kate later admitting to Jones that she "worried for nothing." William called afterward to make sure everything was all right. Everything, she assured him, was great. "She was always nervous about speaking on camera," an aide said afterward, "but it feels like today was a bit of a breakthrough." Given that Kate was in a public-facing role for eight years up to this point, the journey to this breakthrough took longer than anyone expected. Still, progress is progress.

The Back to Nature projects formed part of the buildup to Kate's early-years development advocacy, dubbed "her life's work" by Kensington Palace officials. What started back in 2012 as a curious interest in how experiences in childhood often shape a person's life, for good and bad, gradually expanded into the focus of her royal efforts. Through the Royal Foundation Centre for Early Childhood, which she launched in 2021, Kate is now working with professionals "to transform society for generations to come." Along with it have been splashy nationwide campaigns, numerous research reports, and red-letter events to drum up interest and awareness. It's all for a worthy cause, but the restrictive nature of Kate's role means that she's unable to get involved on the political front and push for the urgent solutions the early-years sector desperately needs—namely, government funding.

Instead, say royal aides, Kate hopes her focus on amplifying "key findings" and issues will influence policymakers, including politicians and those in government. Within the sector itself, feedback has been a mix of appreciation for her efforts and a feeling that much of the initial work done (surveys and reports that offer statistics and information already discovered by other organizations, as well as endless convening of "roundtable discussions") seemed a shade performative. Case in point: there were no early-years experts on the team that drafted a key report from her foundation in 2022. Dr. Mine Conkbayir, a leading voice in the early-years sector and founder of several related scientific programs and educational courses, said, "We are well accustomed to MPs and royalty visiting early-years settings. But nothing is done. The time has long passed for 'awareness.' We need action—long-term investment and funding in the early years." Indeed, in 1999 the Labour party launched an early-years program in Britain offering grants and centers for health care, education, and mental health support for children and parents. Due to funding cuts, however, over 1,400 of the 3,600 centers that the Sure Start program has operated in are now closed. Campaigners say this could have been avoided if prominent figures such as Kate helped advocate for their importance. Nevertheless, it's clear that Kate genuinely cares about the issue, and Kensington Palace often reassures journalists that she remains committed to the cause for "the rest of her life."

Like so much royal philanthropy, Kate's early-years work is part of a broader institutional campaign to flaunt and elevate her importance to the monarchy and to the nation. Every royal is expected to have their flagship cause, and this is hers. Flaunting is, of course, the easy part. Without fail, those in the media—now as a matter of reflex—will always reference Kate's elegance, charm, and grace. There is also always a focus on what Kate is wearing—her clothes, her jewelry, her shoes, her hairstyle—to such an extent that often what she says and does is usually an afterthought. Compared to other royals, mainstream coverage of Kate in the British papers is overwhelmingly positive, often bordering on infantilizing the princess, with articles marveling at her ability to perform the simplest of tasks (think enthusiastic reporting about kicking a soccer ball or flipping a pancake, or how amazing it is that she can assume the perfect "princess pose" in photographs). Admittedly, Kate has rarely put a foot down wrong in public. But in the instances where criticism would be fair, such as carrying out fewer engagements than other senior royals, or the fact that she has had *five* different private secretaries in six years (one, I'm told, simply found the role "uninspiring and frustrating"), you'd be unlikely to read about it in any British newspaper.

For many of those in the press, Kate is the monarchy's last "shiny thing" for many years to come, even more so given William's slow fade into his staid institutional role and the departure of Harry and Meghan. Put a new, glamorous photo of Kate on the front page of a paper and a sales boost is guaranteed. Charles, Camilla, and William? Unless it's family drama, not so much. In the first months after her wedding to Prince Harry, the Duchess of Sussex was also a shimmering ornament in the royal family tree. And with her outgoing nature and leadership potential, qualities for which Kate isn't known, early coverage of Meghan's royal engagements were far less about fashion choices and more about her work or her role in the Firm. Until they weren't.

Though new to the Windsor fold, Meghan assuredly took to her role as a working royal. With her acting experience and upbeat demeanor, Meghan was supremely comfortable in her public-facing role, even when she initially knew very little about it. Her confidence alarmed some at Buckingham Palace, who found it intimidating or obnoxious at times. Before it all went wrong, the Firm's American outsider and underdog was becoming the star of the show. Whether it was guest-editing an entire September issue of *British Vogue* while heavily pregnant, releasing a bestselling book for charity, or collaborating with British fashion brands to launch a capsule collection to raise money for her patronage of the women's employment coaching charity Smart Works, Meghan got things done fast. It was Princess Diana all over again.

William, Kate, and their team took notice and altered course. Harry and Meghan had introduced the world to a new, more modern-looking royal, and it suddenly made the Cambridges—who for years had been the monarchy's hot young couple—appear a little dull in comparison. Though all similar in age, it's undeniable that during their glory days the Sussexes connected with a younger generation of Brits in a way William and Kate never had. And so, over time, Kate's private secretaries and communications aides encouraged her to change her approach to engagements—less "listening and learning" and more *doing*. Even her working wardrobe of formal coat dresses and structured pieces started to slowly transform into the more relaxed, business-casual attire chosen by the California duchess. Fashion choices change over time for anyone, but even a few aides at Buckingham Palace separately commented that Kate's sartorial evolutions seemed far from coincidental. As an aide working with the Cambridges and Sussexes said to me in 2019, "Meghan's arrival was a bit like a rocket up the . . ." He paused mid-sentence, but I knew where he was going.

Much has been written (and mostly speculated) about the relationship between Meghan and Kate. In past articles and *Finding Freedom*, I wrote about how—contrary to reports—the lukewarm distance between the two women was initially down to the ever-growing cracks in William and Harry's relationship. They may have had very little in common, but they probably could have made things work in those early days if there was peace between the warring Windsor siblings. Still, for Meghan, who found much of her time as a working royal a lonely and isolated experience, there was a hope that Kate would be someone she could at least turn to for an encouraging word during her lowest points, including her emotional difficulties during her pregnancy. They were once both outsiders, middle-class women brought into the House of Windsor for unimaginably different lives. Kate, however, was uninterested in forming this kind of bond with Meghan. "She can be cold if she doesn't like someone," said a source who had worked with Kate in the past. Does that mean she didn't like her from the start? The source paused. "She wasn't a fan, no," they replied. Added another, "She spent more time talking *about* Meghan than talking *to* her." This is a side of Kate that rarely gets written about. Advocating for mental health causes—the mental health of mothers, for that matter—but ignoring her own sister-in-law's cries for help seemed out of character for someone the public knew as sweet and easy to get along with. And when the *Telegraph* accused the Duchess of Sussex of making Kate cry (front-page news that resulted in days of critical Meghan coverage), Kate watched in silence as the Palace refused to set the record straight, even though it was the other way around. She later apologized to Meghan (with flowers), but the damage from the public rift was already done.

On more recent occasions, Kate has jokingly shivered when Meghan's name has come up around her, and there has been almost zero direct communication, bar a few short pleasantries, between the pair since late 2019. For the princess, there's no going back, even in her relationship with Harry. "She was close to Harry, and she will always look back fondly on those moments . . . and the relationship he had with their children . . . but to her there is no way she could ever trust them after all their interviews," said a source who knows the family. There's also the fact that the Sussexes' departure put more pressure on the other half of the "Fab Four" to scale up and fill the working void left behind.

After Harry and Meghan broke ranks and fled to North America at the start of 2020, sources at the time said Kate was put in the hot seat. But perhaps the extra push was also a silver lining. That period saw the introduction of Kate 2.0—a slightly more relaxed, more relatable duchess with a voice that could be (needed to be) heard. First up was an appearance on the *Happy Mum, Happy Baby* podcast with mommy blogger Giovanna Fletcher. During their candid conversation, Kate opened up about her own childhood and shared some of her struggles as a mother. The interview was the first time the public heard Kate speak at length, and it was universally lauded in the media as "groundbreaking," which is *maybe* a little hyperbolic. But even as a somewhat jaded royal reporter it was fascinating to witness her showing a different side of herself when Kensington Palace invited a group of us to come and listen to the recording before it went live. There was the future Queen discussing her severe morning sickness, "mum guilt," and giving a peek into her world, all the while reminding listeners that the girl next door had made it to the top without losing her everywoman qualities.

I remember having a similar conversation with Kate at a Kensington Palace media reception after the birth of Princess Charlotte in 2015, one in which she spoke about the challenges of parenting. "I look at my friends and think they have it all figured it out . . . while I'm just making it up as I go along," she said with a laugh. I always thought this more frank, real side of the sometimes Stepford-like royal wife was something that others should see more of. Attending her engagements and traveling on the couple's tours for the better part of a decade, I was around for brief glimpses of Kate away from the cameras. At India's Kaziranga National Park in 2016, I was the only reporter with William and her on a mini-safari to spot the elusive one-horned rhinos for which the stunning region is famous. As we rode through the wild terrain in two open-topped Jeeps, our guides instructed us to remain silent if a rhino crossed our path and to let the accompanying park ranger make the necessary animal calls to scare it if it got *too* close. As luck would have it, we encountered two on our journey, one of which decided to stop right in the middle of the muddy road we were traveling on. Clearly not in a rush, the beautiful female rhinoceros slowly stomped around in front of us . . . and then stopped to poop. As we sat there in dead silence giving the rhino absolutely no privacy whatsoever, I looked over at Kate, who was in a fit of muted giggles. For someone usually so poised and inscrutible, it felt like the mask momentarily fell away, and it was a refreshing sight. Her silent laughter triggered the rest of us and we all ended up pretty much holding our breath, trying not to let out immature chuckles after each massive plop.

It was a genuinely candid moment. And so, the podcast and its chance for the public to experience a tiny bit of that same openness was an inspired PR push. If the Palace needed Kate to generate some positive news in the wake of Harry and Meghan's departure, it was a solid start. In the summer of 2020, during the height of the pandemic, Kate spearheaded a successful photography project with the National Portrait Gallery. Hold Still was a community project in which Kate, an avid photographer and art history graduate, invited members of the public to send in photographs they snapped during the national lockdowns. Documenting the effects of the virus outbreak and the subsequent quarantines, the digital exhibition gathered and organized photographs under the themes of "Helpers and Heroes," "Your New Normal," and "Acts of Kindness." It was a compassionate project, and Kate scored accolades and solid media coverage for another solo venture. A year later, she wrote an introduction and helped curate content for the book *Hold Still*, which made its way to the *Sunday Times* bestseller list. It was reminiscent of Meghan's 2018 *Together* cookbook in aid of the Grenfell survivors of London's Hubb Community Kitchen—and it worked. In September 2021, the same Kate who was exceedingly nervous for a brief appearance on a children's television program confidently took to the tennis courts to play doubles with teen ace Emma Raducanu. An avid tennis player and patron of the All England Lawn Tennis and Croquet Club (AELTC), Kate showed off her forehand and appeared unfazed by the cameras and the many in attendance who were there to welcome Raducanu back to the United Kingdom after she took the trophy at the U.S. Open just a few weeks before.

After the autumn leaves fell and the 2021 holiday season kicked into high gear, Kate readied herself to host the televised *Together at Christmas* carol service at Westminster Abbey. Christmas has always been a high-return, low-risk holiday for the royal family, and Kate seized it for a moment. Billed as a "tribute to the incredible work of individuals and organizations across Britain who have supported their communities through the Covid-19 pandemic," the holiday occasion primarily provided the family a much-needed reason to convene in public. Still staggering from an unnerving few months that started with the April 2021 death of Prince Philip, the Queen's October hospitalization, and the ever-unfolding Sussex story, the senior members of the Firm were determined to put on a united front. And, with Kate at the helm—even playing the piano—it was a success.

With the exception of Princess Anne (who had schedule conflicts), the extended royal family appeared with much fanfare—which also helped gloss over the fact that the Queen was too fragile to attend. When it came time to doing it all again in 2022, the family was in even more dire need of a celebratory set piece. Earlier that year, Prince Andrew was humiliatingly defrocked and settled out of court with his family's money. The monarch's death further destabilized the family and the Firm, while Harry's candid memoir was lurking around the corner. There was an immense and powerful feeling that the other shoe was about to drop. The family gathered for a *Together at Christmas* redux featuring a stirring tribute to the recently deceased Queen Elizabeth II. And, by coincidence, the carol service took place on the same night as the premiere of Harry and Meghan's Netflix docuseries. A perfect distraction, they hoped. From a PR point of view, the evening wasn't quite the draw it was the previous year, but Kate appeared even more confident. And the family, despite their troubles, were adequately cheerful. The absence of Covid masks this time around might have helped, too.

For someone more than comfortable in the background, Kate has come a very long way. She did this with the help of the Palace machine, sure, but also on her own and with some guidance from Bucklebury Manor, the Middleton family home. Kate's stable childhood and strong parental guidance, especially from her mother, inculcated in her strains of resilience and acceptance unique to those who are *not* born into incomprehensible wealth and privilege. Kate's comparatively modest beginnings started in a simple semidetached house just outside of Reading. Her parents, Michael and Carole Middleton, who met while working at British Airways, bought the house shortly after their marriage. During Kate's early years, Carole set up shop in the shed behind the house, forming a mail-order party supply business. Her company, Party Pieces, was a multimillion-dollar operation for many years before it was sold at a loss to an entrepreneur in 2023. Back then Carole added self-made millionaire to a résumé that also included loving mother of three, and Michael continued at British Airways until he later joined Party Pieces to help his wife manage the growing company. After selling their first home, the Middleton family moved to a larger property in Bucklebury village and then to the nearby sprawling manor house on the nearby Pease Hill.

The Middleton ancestors who married into money left an inheritance large enough for Michael and Carole to send Kate and her siblings, Pippa and James, to some of the country's top private schools. As two caring parents who worked hard, made their mint, and climbed the social ladder (no small feat in a country *still* obsessed with class), the Middletons—mostly Carole—saw that the pretty and grounded Kate was ready to carry the family name further to the top. So, they began orchestrating her life, ensuring she was at the right places at the right time and spoke the right way. Kensington Palace has never denied that Kate had several rounds of elocution lessons as she became more serious with William. Friends have noted over the years that her accent now sounds "posher" and "even more plummy" than her husband's. The Middleton strategy involved more than just aristocratic affectation—Carole calculatingly placed Kate right at the center of young Prince William's world. It was first reported in royal biographer Katie Nicholl's *Kate: The Future Queen* that when Carole learned that Prince William was slated to attend the University of St. Andrews, she encouraged her daughter to turn down a spot at her dream school, the University of Edinburgh, take a gap year to study abroad in Florence, and enroll at St. Andrews the following year.

Carole set things up, and Kate took it the rest of the way. It wasn't long before William and Kate's friendliness turned into a loving relationship, one that included natural ups and downs—periods when they were on and times when they were off. During the flush and passion of their early romance, the pair spent lots of time with Kate's family in Bucklebury. William took to the cozy Middleton enclave in a village where time seemed to stand still. The echoing bells of the sixteenth-century parish, the clink of glasses and last call in the traditional Bladebone Inn, and the low lights and trailing chimney smoke from thatched-roof houses all proved irresistible for a young man used to gated entries, long corridors, and private secretaries.

He also fell for the Middleton family. Although less frequent these days, William has always looked forward to Sunday roasts at their house and helping load the dishwasher at the end of it. They live in comfort, but it's down-to-earth, snug, and congenial compared to the decorous, hushed rooms at the cavernous royal residences he grew up in. The wellies-by-the-back-door and home-cooked meals of it was an environment that both he and Kate have continually tried to re-create for their own children.

Bucklebury Manor was the house at the end of the lane. And it was this home with its familial affection and quiet ambition that shaped and equipped Kate for her life as a future Queen. As Tina Brown noted, "Bucklebury provided the backbone for Kate's aspirational resolve." And Kate was forced to call up this resolve long before the two were married. Their courtship lasted eight years, long enough to give birth to the cruel tabloid nickname "Waity Katie." Knowing he would soon be immersed in his monarchical duties, William struggled to commit for the long haul, even pushing the two to completely break up in spring 2007. Kate retreated to Bucklebury for Carole's motherly advice, while William took refuge at Bovington Army Camp in Dorset.

Kate didn't pull back for long. She soon resurfaced and demonstrated some of that Middleton determination and took a few bold steps of her own. While William was off in Dorset—ostensibly for armored reconnaissance training, but photographic evidence suggests he spent much of his time sowing his wild oats—Kate rallied her sister, Pippa, and some close friends for London's nightlife scene. The paparazzi swarmed, and Kate was regularly photographed on raucous nights out. Long before my royal reporter days, I saw her inside the members-only Boujis club in South Kensington a few times, where she and her friends would knock back complimentary trays of shots and jump up on the seats and tables to dance to whatever hip-hop or house music the DJ was spinning. There was an option to leave the building secretly, but Kate left through the main doors, where the photographers waited.

During that spring, the media ran with the "single and ready to mingle" storyline long enough for William to take notice and come racing back from Bovington. Game, set, match. Less than three years later, I combined reporting efforts with Nicholl to break the news on the front cover of *Us Weekly* that the "Royal Wedding

Is On!" A week later, Clarence House confirmed the engagement. William and Kate married in the spring of 2011. An estimated two billion people around the world watched in awe as Kate Middleton stepped out of the church as Catherine, Duchess of Cambridge, the grand and dulcet chimes of Westminster Abbey eclipsing the bells of Bucklebury's little parish church.

In many ways this is where Kate's personal story comes to an end: she traded in Carole's training for the Palace playbook, and the young woman disappeared behind a Palace-constructed mold. Before her engagement to William, Kate was left to fend, manage, and ward off the stalking tabloid press who seemed to buzz around her wherever she went and create whatever narratives they pleased. There may have been no social media negativity or online trolls to deal with, but Fleet Street's interest was obsessive: Kate was regularly tailed by paparazzi, her voicemails were repeatedly hacked (155 times alone by one reporter at *News the World*), the likes of the *Daily Mail* poked fun at her un-royal family and former air hostess mom, and body-shaming commentary was written about her weight loss. The misogynistic and snobbish way many of the tabloids wrote about Kate was reprehensible. After her marriage, however, she had full Palace protection and spinmeisters on the payroll to assist her with media harassment and reputational management.

Aides at the time told me they were keen to avoid "the past" (i.e., the institution's mistakes with Princess Diana) from happening again. Because of the Middletons' strategic guidance and Kate's instincts for reticence and discretion, the public knew scarcely anything about her inner life even when she was simply Kate Middleton from Berkshire. As the Duchess of Cambridge, wife of the heir to the throne and future Queen, her genuine identity receded even further. Transfigured by her new role and completely dedicated to indiscriminately supporting William, Kate—with institutional assistance—successfully sublimated her authentic self, becoming an enigma to the public and perhaps even to herself. Unimpeachable, relatable Kate was also now an inscrutable queen in training—an institutional dream come true.

Kate quickly assumed her royal positions: a vessel for a dynastic family and a token of glamour and youth. She gave birth to an heir in the requisite time frame—Prince George was born in 2013. Following years of tradition, she introduced her firstborn (and the subsequent births of Charlotte and Louis) to the world on the steps of the Lindo Wing at St. Mary's Hospital in London. My experience of waiting for weeks outside the hospital with the dozens of other journalists and photographers for the mother of an heir to give birth is still as surreal as it sounds. Lying on the floor just ten steps away from them (to stay out of shot) as hundreds of cameras clicked was just bizarre. After the body image–obsessed tabloids tracked every pound of her postpartum weight loss, she was back on the royal A-team for the daily drudgery: ribbon-cutting, ceremonial piffle, and well-timed photo ops. And she looked great doing it. Always elegant and serene, she wore her role well. The late Hilary Mantel got into some hot water for saying so, but during Kate's early royal career, it almost seemed that appearing this way was Kate's sole purpose for the Firm, especially after she birthed an heir. "I saw Kate becoming a jointed doll on which certain rags are hung," Mantel wrote, adding that the duchess appeared like a "shop-window mannequin, with no personality of her own, entirely defined by what she wore." A harsh observation to be sure, but also a truth most find hard to swallow. Like Diana, Kate became a sparkling showpiece for the Firm, a symbol of refined beauty and those white, English Rose genetics the British newspapers love so much. Freya in an Emilia Wickstead coat dress.

And now, like Diana, she, too, is the Princess of Wales. It's a title that carries a huge and extremely important legacy, but sources close to the royal (who, for those wondering, "is just as happy being called Kate as she is Catherine") say she is surprisingly "unfazed" by her new designation. Respectful of the past but graciously "keen to carve out her own" path in the new role.

Unlike strong-minded Diana, who, saddled with a cruel and taxing marriage, proved to be a woman unwilling to fully submit to the royal cause, so far Kate has been a much more teachable, pliable future Queen. She's coachable, which is something Queen Elizabeth II admired in Kate from the start. "There has rarely been a moment where Kate has said 'This is *my* way' or pushed an opinion on others," said a royal source. "She is happy to follow the advice and leadership of those around her, people she trusts to take charge and [who] know what's best." To mitigate the fact that, in terms of actual work, she has technically been a part-time working royal, the Kensington Palace communications team always stress in press releases and other communiqués that Kate is "keen to learn." So, yet another nickname was born. "Katie Keen" was a popular refrain on social media for several years.

A Kensington Palace source called her approach to philanthropic work a "shift" in how royal duties have been executed over the years. Where in the past royal patronages were collected in the hundreds (Queen Elizabeth II had more than six hundred when she passed), the Waleses have both streamlined their lists. Princess Anne is currently patron or president for more than three hundred organizations and rarely goes a few days without carrying out an engagement at one of them, while Kate has taken on only about twenty (a spokesperson for the couple said the smaller slate gives more time to make an impact on each one, rather than infrequent visits, though statistically there isn't much proof of this). All are said to reflect her own interests (such as the Royal Photographic Society), but it's resulted in a much leaner schedule of engagements for the publicly funded Princess of Wales. In 2022, she attended just ninety engagements; Anne, on the other hand, topped out at 214. In 2023, before the coronation, both William and Kate took off an entire month from work for the children's Easter break from school, leaving Charles and Camilla to hold the fort and the attention of the public. It followed almost two weeks off in January, a week in February, and seven weeks over the summer for other school-related vacations. "That one's a nonnegotiable," said a royal source. "It's essential for her and William to have the school holidays with the children." Another source told me that Kate doesn't plan to increase her workload for another ten to fifteen years, once the children reach adulthood. It's a privilege most parents can only dream of. The late Queen, too, would take off blocks of time throughout the year to recharge, but she was also known to carry out *at least* three hundred engagements annually. Sources said Kate remains "laser focused" on her duty to the family first, and then the Crown.

Unlike so many others in the royal family, Kate has no history of bringing scandal or shame to the Firm, and it's likely that the Palace machine will ensure it stays that way. When she was photographed topless while vacationing in France with William in 2012, she met the horrendous moment by staying mum and out of the fray—the definition of grace under fire. I joined Kate for an engagement in Kuala Lumpur, Malaysia, on the day France's *Closer* magazine released the photos in print and online. William's private secretary Miguel Head had just shared the news with the couple over breakfast when I arrived at the As-Syakirin Mosque ahead of the Duke and Duchess of Cambridge for a tour of the Islamic place of worship. For someone who had just experienced such a traumatic and gross invasion of privacy, Kate seemed unshaken. William was tense, his fists clenched and, from a source who had been with him earlier in the day, "filled with rage." But Kate smiled and got on with the work. Rather than "freak out," I was told, she relied on the royal institution and her vehemently protective husband to handle the situation, which they eventually did by winning a lawsuit against the French outlet and scrubbing the photos from many parts of the internet. A senior aide likened Kate's faith in the institution to do-ing a trust fall: "She has absolute confidence that they know what's best."

When rumors repeatedly circulated and trended online about her marriage, Kate never publicly addressed or acknowledged the is-sue, letting William, the Palace, and the passage of time do the work for her. In our current age of oversharing, when most people snatch up the opportunity and platform to set the record straight, Kate—who reportedly never looks at social media or reads newspapers—seems content as a voiceless symbol of courtly resolve, a totem of stoicism in a time of emotional overdrive. This side of her most resembles Queen Elizabeth II, a woman after whom Kate has long modeled her approach to royal life—the late sovereign's allegiance to the Crown and her commitment to the stability and continu-ity of the monarchy. Perhaps more than anything else, Kate has learned what is paramount for survival in the system: vanishing into your role, giving away nothing, and allowing yourself to embody what the public sees in you. And with those elocution lessons, the Princess of Wales even sounds a bit like her former boss—polished, regal, and appropriately distant.

Kate may have achieved a Queen-like detachment, but it's still a guess as to whether she can maintain this now that natural occur-rences and unanticipated conditions have pushed her further into the spotlight. Even to this day, the public knows so little about her, and we haven't yet seen her display the gravitas and commanding power that the late Queen mustered so effortlessly. Some journal-ists who have been approached by publishers to author biographies about the Princess of Wales have turned down the chance. "I'd barely be able to do a chapter, let alone an entire book," one joked to me. As the Princess of Wales, Kate has now entered a more pressur-ized, demanding phase of her royal life, which has put much of the fate of the monarchy's popularity on her shoulders. William will one day be King, but the closer he gets, the more rigid he becomes. His future is a stately, silent one. Kate's is more of a question mark, but we know it will involve more public participation and civic engagement. She can still easily draw a crowd and land a front page like no other (working) royal, and the Firm heavily leans on that. With Charles and Camilla already aging out of the long overseas tours, William and Kate will be expected to carry some of that load—even if they have already told senior courtiers that they would prefer to keep any travels focused on their own flagship projects rather than those at the request of the Foreign & Commonwealth Office. Still, there are commitments with being married to the next in line to the throne that are unavoidable, including new military honors. In December 2022, King Charles named his daughter-in-law the new honorary colonel of the Irish Guards—a position previously held by Prince William that requires more than appearing with the guard's regiment for St. Patrick's Day. The following March, she dressed up in camo and visited the 1st Battalion Irish Guards at a very snowy Salisbury Plain Training Area to participate in training exercises. And in August 2023, she became the commodore-in-chief of the Royal Navy's Fleet Air Arm (one of Prince Andrew's former roles), colonel-in-chief of the 1st Queen's Dragoon Guards, and Royal Honorary Air Commodore of Royal Air Force Coningsby.

But at home, titles are left at the door, and she relishes just being "mama" or, in Princess Charlotte's case, "mummy." Since moving to the smaller Adelaide Cottage on the Windsor estate, the family enjoy "plenty of outdoor time," said a source, who noted that both William and Kate enjoy riding bikes with their three children. "It's cute . . . like ducks in a row," they joked. Without the live-in help they had at Kensington Palace's Apartment 1A (staff now just come and go), Kate has "really gotten into cooking." Above all, and this is where she differs from Elizabeth II, the children will *always* come before duty, several sources commented.

Raising an heir has also presented its own unique challenges. After Prince George's tenth birthday in 2023, media coverage and opinion pieces about his future role increased. It was also reported that the second in line to the throne will be allowed to skip the obligatory stint with the Armed Forces "if he wishes." Controversial, according to some in royal circles, given that he will one day become the head of the British Armed Forces when taking the throne. But William and Kate, a source told me, "want to allow George to make as many of his own decisions as he can in life."

Mother but also the future Queen—it's quite a balancing act. And it puts Kate in an almost impossible position: when the time comes, she will have to leave the mum role at the palace gates, shuck her natural diffidence, balance her regal rectitude with some everywoman charm, and, for the never-ending presence of the press, dazzle whenever needed. It will require every ounce of the Middleton resilience that got her this far. For a woman who is so tightly controlled and carefully assembled, this is a lot of shape-shifting and pressure to perform. Under such continual duress, facades tend to crumble. The institution will do anything to prevent this from happening. The Palace knows the fallout when it does.

After that successful 2019 appearance on *Blue Peter*—an undeniable confidence booster considering her pre-taping nerves almost got the better of her—with a big smile Kate confidently asked her head of communications, "Okay, what can I do next?" Perhaps we'll see more of this self-assurance and enthusiasm from the Princess of Wales as she grows even more accustomed to the spotlight. Maybe that Back to Nature garden day was a turning point for Kate—planting the weeping blue cedar a means to encourage her own growth. Here's the thing about that species: it's naturally slow-growing and requires adequate space for its sculptural branches and cascading needles. But if there is too much pruning, or the space around it is too restricted, the tree ends up taking on an odd shape and loses the character that made it so special in the first place.

# 13

# A Dangerous Game

Royals and the Media

———·———

*The press is our chief ideological weapon.*
—Nikita Khrushchev (former premier of
the Soviet Union), 1957, speech

*If we amplify everything, we hear nothing.*
—Jon Stewart, 2010, speech at "Rally to Restore Sanity"

Sitting in a dimly lit corner of a South London pub on a brisk autumnal evening, Prince William was about as incognito as a future King could get. Swapping his usual uniform of a crisp Oxford shirt and chinos for a more casual jeans and baseball cap combo, the then Duke of Cambridge would have looked like any other patron if it weren't for his protection officers sitting nearby. Not that anyone would have noticed—the buzz around the October 11, 2019, England vs. Czech Republic football game on the venue's TV screens had the most pub-goers cheering on the Three Lions in their UEFA Euro qualifier match (which they were about to lose, 2–1). William was one of them, but he also had other business to attend to.

While the senior royal is no stranger to a pint or two at the pub with friends, this visit was different. He was there to meet *Sunday Times* editor in chief and News Corp executive Martin Ivens. William first established a professional relationship with Ivens when he took on the newspaper's top job in 2013, and there was a mutual respect between the two—and an appreciation of football. But they weren't here to talk match stats. On the top of William's mind was Prince Harry, who had just seven days earlier announced phone-hacking lawsuits against News Corp's *Sun* newspaper and MGN, the former owners of the *Mirror*. Around the same time, Meghan announced she was suing the publisher of the *Mail on Sunday* after they published a handwritten letter she sent to her estranged father. The announcement of their lawsuits stunned the rest of the royal family, who found out the news with the rest of the world while Harry and Meghan were touring southern Africa.

When news outlets reported on the lawsuits, William immediately turned to his aides to vent. "It was a step too far in his opinion," said a former Kensington Palace staffer. "You just don't take on the press like that . . . It's a recipe for disaster." Added another, "William felt this would jeopardize his own relationships [with the press]." Around this time, William was already in the process of meeting a number of big-name newspaper editors to personally strengthen his connections, so someone (especially his brother) putting them at risk was not an option. After a contact had tipped him off, William was aware that Harry had also discussed their "tensions" and "different paths" with journalist Tom Bradby for a forthcoming prime-time ITV documentary about the Sussexes' royal tour. Both William and his private secretary Simon Case felt that Harry's candid confessions were going to be "a problem."

So, by the time William sat down with Ivens at the pub, it didn't take long for him to open up about Harry. "I've put my arm around my brother all our lives and I can't do that anymore; we're separate entities," he confessed. "I'm sad about that. All we can do, and all I can do, is try and support them and hope that the time comes when we're all singing from the same page. I want everyone to play on the team."

As the relationship between the Sussexes, the institution, and the royal family continued to disintegrate, William's frustrations with Harry intensified. When Harry and Meghan announced on January 8, 2020, that they would completely step back from their royal roles, William took action to deal with the oncoming Sussex storm. "He had conversations with a few in his team about getting ahead of what he felt would soon be Harry blaming them all for not doing enough [to support himself and Meghan]," said a Kensington Palace aide who has since left the royal household. Palace officials advised William to bite his tongue until he could join the Queen and Charles for a proper sit-down with Harry, a meeting already scheduled for a week later in Sandringham. But his patience was, as usual, running thin, so he discreetly took matters into his own hands.

Just a day before the now-famous Sandringham Summit, William's disapproval over his brother's decision to step back was loud and clear on the front page of *The Sunday Times*: "I've put my arm around my brother all our lives. I can't do it anymore." The article quoted William speaking to an anonymous "friend" (guess who) and positioned the heir as a caring older brother who had done everything to help his hapless sibling. When it first came out at midnight, Kensington Palace didn't like its tone. Calls were made. By early morning, the second editions of the paper made their way around the country with an updated front page: "William to Harry: We need to be team players." Perfect.

For years, the axiom "never complain, never explain" has been synonymous with the royal family. Dating back to the 1800s, legend has it that it was British prime minister Benjamin Disraeli who first uttered the phrase, but it was soon adopted by high-ranking Brits across the military, royalty, and even future prime ministers, including

Winston Churchill. During the Victorian age and beyond, the maxim reflected an established position for the royal family and those in the institution. Today, however, it's nothing more than an empty promise. Queen Elizabeth II may have genuinely kept calm and carried on, but the go-to move for most other senior family members now is to reveal their thoughts, plans, and grievances via anonymous source quotes through their staff and well-timed leaks to preferred newspapers.

This sacrosanct relationship between two of Britain's oldest institutions, the monarchy and the press, is now a symbiotic one where each leans on the other for its survival. Without the acres of coverage and the visibility the British newspapers provide, the royal family would be a shadow of itself. This drift into irrelevance has already happened to many European monarchies. And without the access, photos, and scoops from the family's constant drama that drives their revenue, the flagging industry of tabloids and broadsheet newspapers would be even closer to death's door.

While printed media is fast becoming a thing of the past, newspapers and their brands still sit at the core of the nation's media realm as many publications have found new leases on life online. Influential, expedient, subsidized by deep pockets, and fueled by an information-obsessed public, the likes of the *Daily Mail*, *The Sun*, *The Telegraph*, and *The Times* have the ability to influence political votes, public opinion, and the national mood. They've wielded this power for centuries, sometimes for good, but often not. The arrival of publications such as the *London Gazette* in 1665 saw pages filled with eye-catching headlines, exaggerated tales, and titillating rumors, creating a sense of communal belonging among a widely dispersed British public. They were outraged and intrigued by the same things, motivated by the same opinions. And as a result, says openDemocracy journalist Adam Ramsay, "demands for democracy—that these publics have a say—advanced."

This synchronicity of opinion and demand for a more democratic system created a new form of nationalism among the population, one that sprung from the bottom instead of being decreed from the top. The establishment was forced to acknowledge and respond. King Charles I disregarded public and parliamentary opinion during the birth of this new nationalist era which resulted in his beheading. The late political scientist and historian Benedict Anderson pointed out that the country's ruling class, including its media-owning elite, quickly realized the advantages of maintaining pomp and ceremony, "[it] kept the plebs reverential and society hierarchical, and propped it up."

The cofounder of the *National Review* and editor of the *Economist* in the 1860s, Walter Bagehot, maintained that the British monarchy's raison d'être was to "impress the many" while Westminster and Whitehall press on with "governing the many." The Crown is the "dignified" part of the constitution—the monarchy is there to "excite and preserve the reverence of the population." Strategically, this located the hereditary principle—a dynasty of white privilege and the rusty class system that goes with it—right at the heart of British identity. The emergence of radio and TV amplified this notion. Lord Reith, the first managing director of the BBC, said in 1929 that the national broadcasting corporation would guarantee that the ringing bells of Big Ben, "the clock which beats the time over the Houses of Parliament, in the center of Empire," would echo "in the loneliest cottages in the land."

In 1924, Reith convinced King George V to address his subjects over the radio via the BBC with great success. Twenty years later, for Queen Elizabeth II's coronation, the royal family fully embraced modern media, allowing TV cameras inside Westminster Abbey to broadcast the ceremony for the first time. This historic occasion doubled the number of television owners in Britain and established royal pageantry as a form of entertainment. Because the sovereign's roles include the head of British Armed Forces and the head of the Church of England, the monarchy was already conjoined with the institutions of the military and religion. But after

Her Majesty's coronation, the institution of the media—one that now was connected to the people by way of a TV or radio in virtually every British home—also became an essential component of the royal pantomime.

The media kept the appeal of the royal family alive throughout Queen Elizabeth II's reign and beyond. And the monarchy has needed it. The huge decline in religion (only 6 percent of the adult British population currently identify as a practicing Christian) and a vast reduction in the country's military power have left the media as the only viable institution left to effectively prop up the monarchical system. As a result, the institution has heavily leaned on the media for connection and prominence. Some new media efforts worked (Charles and Camilla's assorted appearances on popular British TV shows such as *The Repair Shop*, *Gardeners' World*, and *Antiques Roadshow* have been solid PR boosts, particularly among older Brits) and some were misfires. In 1969, Prince Philip encouraged Buckingham Palace to commission the BBC documentary *Royal Family*, which was essentially a one-episode reality show that followed the royals for just over three months. It revealed never-before-seen intimate moments such as family mealtimes and Balmoral barbecues. Publicly it was a well-received program, but it also briefly destabilized the family. The "behind the palace walls" approach allowed *too* much access to the monarchy, and the portrait of a somewhat "normal" family cut through the carefully maintained veil of secrecy and fantasy that is so vital to the monarchy's existence. If the people who were supposedly given divine sanction to rule are just like us, then what was the point of it all? The Palace's successful campaign to remove the 110-minute special from all archives has left behind only bootleg cuts to occasionally surface on the internet.

This "now you see, now you don't" relationship is what made the second half of Queen Elizabeth II's reign so interesting. While she gave plenty of scripted speeches in front of the cameras, and even shared stories about the Crown Jewels in a 2018 BBC documentary, the Queen famously never gave a full-length interview. The public rarely knew her opinion on matters beyond horse racing and corgis; as for her personal life, much of it remains a mystery even after her death. Kate, the Princess of Wales, has mostly followed the same model, while the majority of the family have clearly deviated from it. The disastrous results that come from more forthcoming moments reveal just how important having a protective media strategy is for the monarchy—their secrecy is their weapon.

Of course, apace with this give-and-take relationship with the traditional media come their tortured alliances with Britain's newspapers and manic tabloids. For many of those outside the United Kingdom, the country's tabloid culture is hard to fathom. In the United States and most of Europe, tabloid periodicals are rarely taken seriously—they are trivial publications (in the past referred to as "yellow journalism") usually relegated to grocery store checkout lines and doctor's waiting rooms. But for those living in Britain, they are part of the national fabric and the country's collective conversations. Even for those who purposefully avoid such material, there is little escape from tabloid journalism. When the more elevated outlets like BBC News, Sky News, and BBC Radio 4 analyze the day's newspaper front pages across numerous shows, tabloid headlines are discussed as seriously as the stories from the *Financial Times* or the *Guardian*. Whether people want it or not, the narratives from the likes of *The Sun* and the *Daily Mail* easily become part of one's subconscious—whether it is through other media or their presence at the front of every corner shop, supermarket, and gas station in the country. And in any case, for a society obsessed with surfaces and superficialities, addicted to gossip and celebrity, and demanding of beauty and gore in equal measure, the tabloids give people what they want (even if they will rarely admit it). As Martin Amis said, "They wouldn't be there if there wasn't something in the British character that wanted it to be so." Too much junk food, however, can make you sick.

Where British newspapers were once clearly separated into a trio of categories: broadsheets (*The Times*, the *Telegraph*, the *Independent*), the mid-markets (*Daily Mail*, *Express*), and the tabloids (*The Sun*, the *Mirror*, the *Daily Star*), the lines are now blurred. While *The Times of London* may posture and advance a more elevated style (and it does contain some of the country's finest hard news coverage), when it comes to royal news, the contents are often no more or less salacious and gossip-ridden than the stories found down a rung in the *Mail*. And while one was once guaranteed a break from the screeches and tawdry gossip of the *Mirror* or *The Sun* by opening the pages of the *Telegraph*, that supposedly high-minded paper is now home to some of the most coarse, tabloid-style royal articles out there, including gossipy fiction such as Prince Harry spending nights alone in a Montecito hotel to get away from his wife. For the royals, this means nowhere is safe—every publication is capable of sinking to this kind of questionable, even vicious, coverage.

———·———

While they are constantly evolving, the relationships between the press and the institution can be separated into three silos: the royal rota; sources, leaks, and briefings; and the darker world of interference, obstruction, and control.

For years, the royal rota has been the official way for media to access taxpayer-funded royal engagements and activities. Similar to the White House press corps, members from this assemblage of journalists from various print outlets take turns reporting back to the group the relevant information and scuttlebutt from engagements where open coverage isn't possible—usually intimate gatherings in venues with limited space, or when the general humdrumness of it all doesn't require more than a reporter or two. For each engagement there is usually one print reporter, a representative from the Press Association, one TV camera (broadcasters have their own pool system, too), and a couple of photographers—everyone else, including those who aren't part of the official rota, waits outside in a "fixed point" pen to capture the royal departures and arrivals.

The rota's existence ensures that nothing is missed as members of the royal family carry out their work, but it's not a system without flaws. Established British national newspapers are the only ones allowed in from the print world, and journalists of all stripes from the Commonwealth—including Australia, New Zealand, and Canada—are banned from joining. Some exceptions have been made for the London-only *Evening Standard* newspaper and the glossy royal-friendly *Hello!* magazine. Even though online outlets are now the dominant news source for people across the world, journalists from the U.K. divisions of all-digital news organizations, such as *HuffPost* (which William and Kate have even contributed opinion articles for) and *Newsweek*, are also blocked from the rota.

With newspaper sales on a fast decline and newsrooms shrinking, it's no wonder that, unlike the White House press pool (which is open to any permanent U.S.-based editorial staff working across any platform), access to the rota (and its reporting notes) is fiercely managed and maintained by its members, which at the time of the writing of this book is just ten print journalists. Though there is much more to royal coverage than just engagement reporting, the additional rota-only briefings and front-row access to major occasions, such as funerals and weddings (though Harry controversially banned them from his nuptials), means rota members have become indispensable assets to their newspaper bosses. Front-page stories on the royals still guarantee a boost in newsstand sales of up to 15 percent.

Though it was the Palace who green-lit the group's formation more than forty years ago, the implementation was left to a British trade body, the News Media Association (NMA), who assigned a "captain" to manage the pool. For the past thirteen years that captain has been the royal editor of the *Daily Mail*, Rebecca English, who is solely in charge of managing the rotation of members covering each royal engagement and ensuring reporting is filed among the group. "We call them the cartel—it's a strange system that has a complete monopoly on coverage [of royal engagements]. And no one wants to change the system," a Buckingham Palace communications aide once told me. Even among the rota there has been frustration over English's seemingly permanent role. "They essentially put the *Mail* in charge of it all," a royal reporter at a popular newspaper told me. "She often rigs things to make sure she gets all the good engagements, gatekeeps certain information [from the Palace], and will do anything to make sure the rota doesn't grow." There's also the glaring fact that the captain of the rota has been accused, with evidence in a court of law, of illegally paying a private investigator to spy on Prince Harry and track one of his former girlfriends. She has refused to comment on the matter.

Prior to Meghan's arrival, a couple of us in the royal press pack enjoyed rota access in a more honorary fashion. As members of the U.S. media, we didn't meet the official criteria, but because we offered continual royal coverage for American publications that cater to a different audience (i.e., not considered industry competition), the rota reluctantly allowed us full access to the pooled reporting notes and rota positions on engagements. From 2011 to 2017, all was fine. But as I grew closer to the Sussexes' team (a situation that led a few reporters to privately complain to the Palace about my "unfair" access) my rota privileges were restricted. "I'd love to help but . . . you're more of a TV role now," English said with a sigh, referring to my ABC News gig and conveniently ignoring my role as royal editor for *Harper's Bazaar*. The other honorary member, who also worked for a U.S. outlet with close connections to the Duchess of Sussex's inner circle, also had their rota access reduced.

The Sussexes were the big story, so, under English's fabricated rule, anyone, *especially* an honorary member, with strong access to the couple's world should not be allowed additional benefits as well as rota perks. "Newsroom budgets were shrinking fast, job security was becoming a concern to many, and the focus of some in the rota became less about what was fair and more about protecting one's job and the ability to pay school fees or a mortgage," one long-time royal correspondent admitted to me. The Palace, on the other hand, quietly made sure that foreign correspondents excluded from the rota had everything we needed (I was "snuck" out of barricaded media positions and inside engagements by certain press secretaries on many occasions) but, as one aide said to me with a sigh, "We really don't want to interfere with the rota." They were, as several expressed to me over the years, scared. After all, if unhappy rota members had the power to shift the tone of their coverage with the wave of a pen, the Palace was most definitely going to do whatever they could to keep it that way.

Restricted access for Commonwealth outlets, digital news organizations, or U.S. publications (the latter being relevant to a newly installed American duchess in the House of Windsor) didn't make much sense to many of us. With the support of two senior Palace aides, I wrote a letter to relevant senior individuals at Buckingham Palace about why it was important to open an additional position in the rota—one that could at least be shared by the aforementioned groups. Harry, I was told, was also keen to back the effort. But it quickly hit a dead end. Rather than decide themselves, Palace aides called in English and *The Times*' royal correspondent Valentine Low, the rota's overseas tour captain (who was admittedly far less bothered about petty politics and mostly attempted to be fair in this less-involved role), for a meeting. English told them that letting "others" in would be unacceptable. "To be honest the rota is just a headache none of us want to deal with. It's easier to just leave it as it is," a senior courtier said with a shrug over coffee with me. Yet another case of institutional fear and blinkered acceptance of the status quo when it comes to the media.

Harry and Meghan, who were having their own conversations about the same issue, were then told that if they wanted to break away from the rota system and give other journalists access to their work, they would have to foot the bill for their own engagements. The list for their reasons to leave was getting longer by the month. Harry vented in *Spare*, "I'd had it with the royal rota, both the individuals and the system, which was more outdated than the horse and cart . . . It discouraged fair competition, engendered cronyism, encouraged a small mob of hacks to feel entitled."

To Harry, the rota wasn't just a symbol of the prevailing but noxious link between the media and monarchy, but proof of the backroom deals made between the two institutions, the underhanded agreements that are often personally destructive. He famously called this pact the "invisible contract"—a tacit agreement in which orchestrated public exposure is offered with a certain level of scrutiny accepted, in return for privacy behind palace gates. Amol Rajan, who produced the BBC documentary series *The Princes and the Press* (which, for transparency, I participated in), describes it like this: "Journalists are always doing unspoken deals with people. I worked in newspapers for the best part of a decade; I cut a few deals myself. The Windsor deal is: The royals get to live in a palace, they get some tax-payer funding. In return—so long as they grant access and a steady supply of stories and pictures—they get favorable coverage. But that deal only works if both parties stick to their side of the bargain."

Prince Harry's black-and-white description of this invisible contract in *Spare* and more recent interviews reveals a world in which almost every press officer and courtier has a hotline to the press—a wide-open connection to dish dirt on other family members in order to protect their own bosses and bank future favors. Of course, it's not quite as simple as that. Many old hands in the royal press pack will (and do) categorically say that no such invisible contract exists whatsoever and that this is all part of Harry's axe-grinding campaign to take down his family and the media along with it. In my own experience, the real truth lies deep in the murky middle. The *Express*'s longtime royal correspondent, Richard Palmer, has said in interviews he doesn't recognize Harry's description in the slightest, while veteran royal editor Robert Jobson said in 2021, during the period of leaks around Harry and Meghan's troubles, "They can deny it all they like until they're blue in the face, but there's been an awful lot of leaking, particularly from Kensington Palace."

While royal "churnalism"—the regurgitation of press releases, rewriting details from royal rota reports, and parroting briefing notes sent out by Palace aides—takes up the majority of the slate for some journalists on the beat, bigger outlets also need their own stories. Exclusives, leaks from sources, and on-and-off-the-record briefs make up the second type of relationship between the Palace and press. While big scoops do sometimes come directly from Palace aides (especially those hunting for favors or armed with an agenda), many are still down to good old-fashioned reporting efforts. Having access to the world the royals occupy provides journalists, myself included, with the perfect opportunity to build relationships with an assortment of those who live and work up close and personal with the royal family. Sometimes it's their communications secretaries or private secretaries, and other times it's those who are not based at the palace or work independently, such as assistants, stylists, hairdressers, and protection officers. It's no different to the way in which one covers politics, sports, or entertainment news—you cultivate sources wherever you can find them. Some of these sources are on a mission from HQ and others simply dish up the goods because they love to vent, gossip, or feel heard. And, of course, there are those who do it for the money—British papers historically pay handsomely for insider information (even when it's illegal, in some cases).

Off-the-record briefings and sources speaking anonymously are by no means a bad thing in and of themselves, and journalists depend on these things for reporting. Publicists and representatives for the likes of celebrities, sports stars, politicians, businesses, and governments all rely on an open channel to discuss stories or issues that are best talked about on background or off the record. In the Palace's case, it is often a convenient way to share useful or sensitive information ahead of an engagement or a royal mile-marker, or to address a story they want to quash, derail, or explain without the fuss of putting out a statement. While the Palace often chooses to "no comment" most things, staff in the communications offices will sometimes instead give quotable "guidance" as a source to provide further information or context. It's partly why we have a WhatsApp group with the communication aides to fire off questions and comment requests at all hours of the day.

What makes the House of Windsor unique in this dance with the media is the competing households within it, all with their own agendas, and all doing their best to please their royal bosses. Up until the Queen's death there were three houses, each with a team assigned to work with the media: Kensington Palace for William and Kate, Clarence House for Charles and Camilla, and Buckingham Palace for the monarch. There were also smaller teams under the BP umbrella who worked with other family members like Edward and Sophie, Princess Anne, and (pre-departure) Harry and Meghan. Though all part of the same institution, the rivalry between these teams is real in many ways and often derails a unified message. Each house is often angling for the same space in newspapers, hand-waving for attention with regards to their work, grabbing the ideal dates and locations for their tours and engagements, or scrambling for first dibs on charitable causes. And this rivalry often causes rifts, problems, and confusion downstream after a particular household offers breaking news or choreographs a PR operation. It was an "absolute headache" when Charles, William, and Harry all wanted to do similar high-profile environmental work, an aide once told me. "None of them were into the idea of collaborating; they all wanted their own big moments away from the other ... It was all about competition, and the households were purposefully holding information back so others couldn't try to get ahead," they explained.

Naturally, as paid members of the team, household staff for each of the three offices look out for the royals they represent. This is where "briefings" get complicated, because while the aides are all working to prop up the Crown, they owe nothing to the family members they don't report to. In the stormy days of Charles and Diana's fractious marriage, both had friends in the press that they directed their aides (and friends) to saddle up to. In recent years, the Sussexes have repeatedly claimed that staff from other households betrayed them by briefing negative stories to journalists about them, and that Charles specifically authorized aides to give out details and fabrications to his preferred media outlets. Harry called it a "dirty game" in his Netflix docuseries.

When it comes to this game, it involves more than just standard communication efforts for their bosses. Palace courtiers, as previously discussed, also have a long history of leaking information about other royals—for a multitude of reasons. With different households, it is common for an aide to look out for the royal they represent by using information about another member of the family (from a different household, and preferably less senior) as currency to win over the more ruthless media outlets or to kill a potentially damaging story about the "principal" they serve. Just think back to the 2018 tabloid stories about Meghan's 5:00 a.m. emails and the supposed drama around her wedding tiara. These reports, and many others, included anonymous quotes from Palace sources and aides working for *other* members of the royal family. And this was hardly a secret. Over the years, many Palace staff have described what can only be called a toxic culture of leaking and negative briefings within the institution, especially poisonous when it comes to Harry and Meghan. Some of the staff I have spoken to in the past and for this book said the couple was an easy target because they believed other family members were jealous of their unrivaled popularity at the time, while two others shrugged and said that was "just how it goes." And a handful of aides told me they thought that much of the venom was a result of the fact that some family members and staff just flat-out disliked Meghan for both rational and irrational reasons.

Journalist Anna Pasternak, who received legal threats from the Palace and attacks from British newspapers for a *Tatler* profile on Kate, which included mild criticism, in its July/August 2020 issue, said briefings often come to those journalists playing the right game. "[To receive them] you have to consistently write pieces that flatter the relevant members of the royal family, that you have to be seen to be more negative about others [in the family]," she explained.

These conspiratorial briefings happen much less often with broadcast journalists because they so rarely have the ability to lean on anonymous source quotes for reporting (although background information can easily shape the tone of a news script), but it's exceedingly common with traditional print outlets and their online companion sites. Journalists who say otherwise either haven't managed to build those kinds of relationships with the Palace or are lying to avoid putting their access at risk. But this doesn't mean television doesn't get dragged into the drama. And when it does, it can get heated, fast. Case in point: when I reported details of an insidious briefing war between Kensington Palace and Prince Harry, the Palace hit back hard. For a 2021 investigative show on Britain's ITV network, I said that it was no coincidence that stories of Prince William's "fears" for his brother's "fragile" state of mind appeared in newspapers less than a day after the Duke of Sussex publicly opened up about the growing distance between him and his brother. Based on information I had confirmed from several sources and Palace aides, I added that the Sussex camp were well aware that a senior member of the then Duke of Cambridge's staff cynically used supposed concerns about Harry's mental health as an opportunity to spin positive press for William. Furious that I had exposed this, Kensington Palace—personally instructed by William, one of his aides let slip—rapidly intervened and applied the requisite pressure to stop the truth from spreading. Such claims would not paint their boss in a positive light, especially given his active role as a mental health advocate.

The producers of the show were sternly encouraged by Prince William's lawyers to remove my comments from the documentary. Aides at Kensington Palace warned the network that my accurate revelations were "potentially" defamatory. The tug-of-war rose to ITV's executive level until the broadcaster made an eleventh-hour agreement to mute the audio of my voice when it aired. I was told by a source that ITV was concerned about losing access to the royal family for other big-ticket TV items (such as Kate's Christmas concert specials).

Dead air on network television is extremely rare, so when my voice cut out for five seconds the night *Harry & William: What Went Wrong* aired, it made for an incredibly awkward silence noticed by viewers and pundits alike. Kensington Palace continued their damage control by telling certain royal correspondents that I had "no evidence" to support my claim. Eager-to-please reporters repeated this accusation, despite knowing the truth. "It provided a vivid example that Kensington Palace is certainly more prepared to wade in to influence media coverage when it chooses to," said the documentary's award-winning journalist-turned-director Richard Sanders. "On the day of transmission, the Palace demanded that we remove [the] quote. People more important than myself acquiesced, although it seemed to me perfectly, legally defensible." Defensible, indeed. And somehow, in all this back-and-forth and he said–she said nonsense, the real story was lost to the noise.

Continuing William's campaign to emerge from the brothers' public squabble looking like the caring older sibling, the heir's Kensington Palace team did everything they could to carefully control that narrative. They were determined to paint him as the more mature and responsible one who had done all he could to salvage the relationship. But they can't bury the articles that included the strategic briefings I initially exposed, which clearly quote Kensington Palace sources. "WILLS: MY FEARS FOR FRAGILE HARRY" was *The Sun*'s October 21, 2019, front page. Inside the paper, a senior royal source revealed that William was worried about Harry's "fragile" state of mind after *Harry and Meghan: An African Journey* aired that week. Another source in the story added, "Harry is not in great shape . . . I'd say he's not well." And a Kensington Palace source was also quoted by BBC News on the same day, revealing that the Duke of Cambridge was "worried" about his brother. Harry and Meghan, they added, were in a "fragile" place. Similar language appeared in a number of other outlets, including the front page of the *Daily Mail*: "WILLIAM'S FEARS FOR TROUBLED HARRY."

My proof of Kensington Palace's schemes at work wasn't just in the newspaper coverage. I also had close working relationships with Buckingham Palace aides and people on Harry and Meghan's team. Back in 2019, one of the Sussexes' main communications aides felt strongly that William's staff, led by press secretary Christian Jones, crossed a line with the mental health stories. One of the couple's team called me the moment the "William's concerns for Harry" front pages dropped. "It's pretty disgusting that they would pull out the mental health card for this . . . None of them care for his health," the aide said. As Harry later shared, "They were happy to lie to protect my brother. They were never willing to tell the truth to protect us."

This wasn't Christian Jones's first rodeo, and he was just one of many at Kensington Palace who engaged in these tactics. William's private secretary Simon Case and communications secretary–turned–senior-advisor Jason Knauf also shared details with preferred reporters to quell rumors about the broken relationship between the Cambridges and the Sussexes. When William and Kate went to see Harry and Meghan after the birth of Archie, Jones made calls to a *Mirror* reporter and me to share an exclusive—the couple had just *minutes* ago stopped by for a special visit. "It's a great story that shows that the relationship isn't as bad as everyone makes out," he said. "It was really sweet." What he failed to mention, as I later found out from Sussex sources, was that the couple's lukewarm drive-by lasted less than twenty minutes.

There are also times when certain false information is purposefully given out just to give the institution a proper whitewash. For *Finding Freedom*—which initially started life in 2018 when Harry and Meghan were excited about their years ahead as royals—two Kensington Palace aides working for the Sussexes at the time told my coauthor Carolyn Durand and me that Meghan had received SAS-style security training ahead of her marriage to Harry. Perfectly believable, given the fact that Kate and other senior royals went through the exact same taxing instruction course. But the Sussexes were surprised to read this when the book came out in August 2020. "Meghan *wishes* that was true," her new U.S. representative admitted to me after publication. Harry called the story "nonsense," adding, "On the contrary, the Palace floated the idea of not giving her any security at all because I was now sixth in line to the throne."

Looking back on that period, a current senior Kensington Palace staffer called the "briefing wars" that took place during the Sussexes' fallout a "dark time." They claim the Prince and Princess of Wales are now keen to move on and operate differently. After I exposed the details behind the "fears for Harry" stories leaked by Kensington Palace, William had me excluded from access to engagements and even press releases for almost ten months. A former aide in the prince's circle revealed that it was the last straw. "There was a frustration that control of the narrative was slipping away when *Finding Freedom* came out, then Oprah . . . [William and Kate] were exhausted and angered by it all." But in the summer of 2022, I was told by a senior aide that the household wanted to "wipe the slate clean." The arrival of Lee Thompson, NBC's former vice president of global communications and strategic partnerships, as William and Kate's new head of press has certainly resulted in new, more transparent strategies. There's a sense that under his watch at least, the past might not repeat itself. "That's not how I operate," Thompson told me shortly after taking on his new role. He vowed to staff at the start of his role that he doesn't have favorites and doesn't have plans to get involved in any games. A supposed new era.

But the lasting damage of many years of deceit and cynical tactics still lingers. The impact on family relations seems as raw as ever when you consider Harry's tormented odyssey. There were times, the Duke of Sussex says, that even brother William had been a victim of manipulation and trickery in an effort to boost his father's and Camilla's images. Charles's former press secretary Sandy Henney revealed that William was "furious" when, at sixteen, *The Sun* published details of his first proper meeting with Camilla. The author of the story later revealed that the source was, once again, Mark Bolland, Charles's deputy private secretary and public relations advisor. Henney described the briefings as "transactional," adding, "When I joined his office in '93 [Charles] was going through some pretty virulent criticism—'Bad father, unloving husband.' I think he was pretty hurt."

Bolland worked hard to change Charles's image, leaking all sorts of details in the process and helping journalists shine an extremely positive light on his boss, even if it meant bringing others down along the way. "[Mark] had a meeting with me at the publisher's office, at the very beginning of [my biography *Charles: Victim or Villain*]," revealed journalist Penny Junor. Details provided to the author included the claim that Charles's marriage to Princess Diana was a lost cause because she had multiple personality disorder. This was a low point in Charles's desperate attempts to reconstruct his image, and the public took notice. The Palace disassociated itself from the book, but Junor still claims Bolland was behind much of the reporting in the tome, a huge share of which glorified Camilla as the woman who "saved" a forlorn prince.

Bolland was also accused of approving a *News of the World* scoop claiming a sixteen-year-old Harry was "taking drugs," in exchange for spinning the story into one that praised Charles as a caring, involved father who took time out of his busy royal schedule to take his pot-smoking son to a "heroin rehab clinic." To complete the fabrication, misleading photographs from an unrelated royal engagement Harry and his father carried out at an entirely different rehabilitation facility were used to illustrate the article. While Harry has admitted to spending many nights at Highgrove getting high and drunkenly falling into trouble at a local pub in Wiltshire, the story failed to mention that this rebellious time in his life was partly the result of Charles leaving him alone at his country mansion for a majority of the summer in 2002. "This was a child that needed guidance, that needed a parent, and [Charles] was too busy and involved with other things to notice," said a family friend. In *Spare*, Harry writes that the front-page tabloid story, which went on for an additional six pages, left him feeling "sickened" and "horrified." Bolland later admitted that the sequence of events in the now-defunct newspaper was "distorted" to make Charles look good.

When rumors about Prince William and gossip about Kate's "fallout" with Rose Hanbury flooded social media feeds and American tabloid magazines in 2019, Kensington Palace press secretary Christian Jones took a leaf out of Bolland's book and pulled out all the stops to get *The Sun*—the first outlet to allude to the gossip— to stop poking around in the detritus of the rumor and back off. Crises such as these require more than just strategic briefing, which drops us right into the third media relationship: tactics that teeter on the edge of ethical boundaries, and in some cases run right past them.

While there was no proof that there was any truth to the Rose gossip, the tale's trip along the grapevine was damaging enough. "Christian was desperate to stop [the rumor] and made it his mission to do so," a former courtier told me. Jones even tried to include me in his attempts. While the tabloid continued to dig around on the story, even sending a reporter to canvass Hanbury's home in Norfolk, Jones—who had already admitted to me that the paper's persistence was stressing him out—suggested that I connect with the journalist behind the initial reports—*The Sun*'s "showbiz" editor Dan Wootton. Christian clearly wanted to give Wootton something in exchange for standing down on the rumors. If he promised Wootton scoops from elsewhere, maybe *The Sun* would do him a solid. As for my supposed gain from this, Jones claimed, it would be a "great move" to help promote *Finding Freedom* before it was launched in August. "He would be helpful," Jones wrote in a late-night text. "I reckon a story [from your book] to Dan that goes in *The Sun*, and then he goes on [morning TV show] *Lorraine* [to talk about it]."

At this point I was already aware and dubious of the triad relationship between Jones, Callum Stephens (his partner and PR executive), and Wootton. I had zero interest in collaborating with the tabloid and Wootton, let alone with a notorious hack best known for bullying and hounding celebrities, including the late *Love Island UK* host Caroline Flack (who Prince Harry was romantically linked to in 2009), as well as a long list of worrying allegations, including blackmail, coercion and other repulsive acts. (In July 2023, Wootton responded to the publication of some of the allegations, calling it a "witch hunt" by "dark forces," and admitted that, while he has "made errors of judgement in the past [the] criminal allegations . . . are simply untrue.") But Jones continued to push the idea—at least three other times.

It was soon clear my book was not the only carrot Jones would dangle in front of his pal at *The Sun*. In late June the paper suddenly pulled reporters off the hunt and then dropped digs into the story entirely. "Christian helped make it end," one high-level courtier told me. Curiously, Wootton and the paper—which does not have a reputation for giving up on potential scoops—shifted their focus to a series of revealing stories about the Sussexes.

For Prince Harry and some other Palace staff, including one who was confiding in me at the time, the timing of this shift was dubious. And those suspicions reached fever pitch when, a year later, a report was published by a grassroots news outlet run by a team of media lawyers and former Fleet Street journalists that focuses on the activities of Britain's newspapers. Strict U.K. laws prevent me from repeating the details contained within it.

At this point, the Sussexes and two of their aides were on high alert. It didn't go unnoticed that just months prior to the report, Wootton let slip to Talk Radio listeners that most of the negative stories about the Sussexes are "coming from within the royal family."

For this book, several separate sources—including two *Sun* staffers—confirmed that Jones helped provide details to *The Sun* about the Sussexes' move to Canada and their decision to step back from royal life. "Leaks got really obvious toward the end," a senior ranking courtier confided to me. When Harry and Meghan's head of communications Sara Latham sat down with Jones and Prince Charles's press secretary Julian Payne in January 2020 to prepare a joint statement from Buckingham Palace confirming the couple's official departure, details about it leaked to the newspaper while they were still working on the draft. "They hadn't even spoken to anyone at that point and Dan [Wootton] was already calling her to ask for comment about details in the statement . . . It felt like Christian had literally been texting him under the table."

The steady stream of information to *The Sun* appeared to have had an upshot. The paper that once dubbed William "Workshy Wills" and called him the "cringey" heir went on to write mostly enthusiastic, positive pieces about the Prince of Wales. Since 2020,

*The Sun*'s coverage has called Prince William a "hero," labeled him a "man of the people," and—after years of negative commentary—declared that the future of the monarchy now rests in his "safe hands." A "proud" Kate even joined forces with the tabloid in the summer of 2023 to launch a drive for baby bank donations. Quite the reversal.

As for Prince Harry, he attempted to sound the alarm on Jones's movements with Wootton early on but, to his frustration, found himself up against resistance from all fronts in the institution. At the infamous Sandringham Summit in January 2020, the duke brought up the matter to his brother for the first time, a conversation to which William was surprisingly receptive. A source said he was willing to hear Harry out. "Yeah, we've also got our suspicions," William responded. They both agreed to do "something" about it—but three months went by, and nothing was done. Instead, William promoted Jones from press secretary to personal private secretary, a station much closer to the future king.

But the Duke of Sussex wasn't relying on his brother's cooperation anymore because, by this point, he had all the evidence he needed: relevant documents, intel from Scotland Yard, and information from other journalists (including sources at the paper itself) who had passed details along to his team. Armed with a dossier, Harry went to the very top of the institution with a formal complaint and a suggestion that they take appropriate action against *The Sun*. The response Harry received, however, was far from what he expected. There, on Buckingham Palace–headed paper, was a reply from the Lord Chamberlain at the time, Earl William Peel, who had a particularly close relationship with Charles. The letter, a source said, included "some of the most strong" language seen on official household stationery, aimed at Harry, not Jones. "It was a threat," said a source close to the situation, who added that the Queen wasn't consulted before the Palace issued it. "[The Lord

Chamberlain] said either drop the charges or face severe consequences in twenty-four hours." A message from a lawyer for Jones, arranged by the Palace, soon followed. The decree: stand down from legal action against Prince William's aide.

An exasperated Harry pointed out to Palace aides that he was not suing the aide or anyone on this matter—he simply had a desire for the situation, a public official with deep connections to private information about a senior royal being shared with a national newspaper, to be properly dealt with. For the duke, enough was enough. *The Sun* had a long and controversial history of inappropriate relationships with public officials, and the Palace, at one point, was also keen to put an end to these practices. "The Palace basically accused Harry of wanting to sue his brother's [private secretary] and causing great distress to Christian," the source continued. When they asked him to provide more evidence, Harry refused. "At this point he already had plenty and, given how defensive they were being of Christian, it was clearly going to be used to help *him* and not Harry."

Within weeks, it was clear to all involved that the Lord Chamberlain's threat of "severe consequences" was no bluff. Harry received two further letters in July 2020, one from Charles's private secretary Clive Alderton and the other from the Queen's, Edward Young, both stating the same thing: he was to be officially and immediately cut off from *all* financial support, including official security, which Charles had been privately covering with his Duchy of Cornwall income.

"I have *never* seen the Palace circle the wagons like they did with Christian," a source later reflected. "In my experience, anyone who puts a risk to the survival of the monarchy is out." It seems, however, that the actions of Christian Jones, who continued to work for Prince William until April 2021, were seen as a help, not a hindrance. As it turns out, William knew about Jones's friendship with

Dan Wootton since day one. Multiple sources confirm that during an early 2018 interview with Simon Case for his job at the Kensington Palace press office, Jones, in the interest of transparency, shared that he has a "working relationship" with Wootton.

Joining *The Sun* in the collusion club with the royal family is the *Daily Mail*. Often the go-to when it comes to setting the record straight or controlling certain narratives, the consistently favorable coverage of the royal family in the country's most read daily newspaper has greatly benefited the monarchy in the last fifteen years.

Queen Camilla's mutually advantageous friendship with *Mail* editor Geordie Greig now orbits the *Independent*, a once left-leaning paper where Greig landed in January 2023 as editor in chief. Since the Eton College alum's arrival, the *Independent* has gone from a paper that went out of its way to avoid covering the royal family to routinely publishing insidery reports that have at times quoted a mysterious "senior royal family source." And her ongoing relationship with the *Mail*'s publisher, Lord Rothermere, arguably the most powerful man in the British media, has helped matters, too. "Camilla has been canny," said former BBC royal correspondent Peter Hunt. "She's kept the media close and the *Daily Mail* even closer."

So it's no surprise that when the Duchess of Sussex announced in October 2019 that she was suing Associated Newspapers and the *Mail on Sunday* on the grounds of copyright infringement and invasion of privacy after they published a private letter she wrote to her estranged father, Thomas Markle, both Clarence House and Kensington Palace aides became "very worried" about how it might affect their ties with the *Mail*. "Even aides on [the Sussex] team were saying it would be best to stand down," admitted a source, who added that once Harry and Meghan made the legal action public, Charles, Camilla, and William were "furious." "So much work had gone into getting the *Mail* in their corner . . . The paper had pretty much become an extension of the Palace communications team, and to lose that would have had detrimental impact on the monarchy as a whole. It sounds extreme, but the *Mail*'s positive coverage and its huge audience do a huge part in helping prop up the popularity of the royal family."

A number of sources confirmed that in an effort to make it clear to Lord Rothermere and his executives that the Palace was against the duchess's legal move, Palace officials furtively told the *Mail*'s lawyers that they would "get the help they need [from the institution]" to defend themselves in the trial. Evidence of this support arrived in December 2020 when the publisher's lawyers filed a witness statement from the *Mail on Sunday*'s editor in chief Ted Verity. In the statement, he shared information received from a "senior member of the royal household" referred to only as "Source U." Verity wrote, "They were fully aware of the matters in dispute in these proceedings and how important they were to me and the company I work for." This Source U, an anonymous high-ranking courtier, informed Verity that William and Kate's head of communications at the time, Jason Knauf, worked on drafts of Meghan's letter to her father. In their eyes, this *legally* ensured that Meghan was not the sole copyright owner.

With this one source statement, the *Daily Mail*—with Palace assistance—tried to submarine one of Meghan's copyright claims and paved the way for Knauf to step forward with evidence. The kicker: Source U also claimed that *I* was given a copy of the letter for a "big reveal" in *Finding Freedom*. A ludicrous claim that I hardly feel the need to correct, but, as the pages of the book itself confirmed, this is untrue.

Still, none of this mattered by February 2021. After more than a year of hearings, the judge decreed that because the case was so clear-cut, there was no need for a full trial. The court awarded Meghan a victory over the newspaper group for both invasion of privacy and copyright infringement. For the publisher and a number of individuals at the Palace, it was a crushing blow, as both parties hoped the trial would result in a victory for the paper and a timely opportunity to traduce Meghan's character yet again.

The legal drama was far from over, though. Claiming they had new evidence and that it was essential for their witnesses to be heard (including Knauf and Thomas Markle, who bizarrely sided with the same paper that famously screwed him over days before Harry and Meghan's wedding), the *Mail*'s lawyers appealed the ruling. With Prince William's blessing to circumvent an employment NDA concerning emails and text messages, Jason Knauf provided a statement of his own to prove he was a legitimate coauthor of the letter (having helped Meghan go over every draft), and that the two of them had meticulously worded it in the event that the press got hold of it. In other words, could it have really been that private then?

The emails that Knauf provided to the *Mail*'s lawyers and the court also showed that he and Meghan repeatedly discussed *Finding Freedom* after my coauthor and I asked him for input on some topics in our biography. During a fall 2018 lunch at Nobu (a spot we had taken Knauf on a number of occasions), Durand and I gave him an overview of what was needed for the book. He was keen to help us in his role as Harry, Meghan, William, and Kate's joint communications secretary, so I followed this up with the first wish list of topics and queries (mostly regarding Meghan's family and upbringing) with which we thought he could help—all standard practice for most journalists writing a book on the royal family.

Knauf's emails showed that Meghan had provided him with answers to some of the questions on this list, and the press raced to turn this into some sort of *gotcha* moment—supposed "proof" that she had invaded her own privacy by helping us with the book (which is exactly the point Associated was hoping to make). And also "proof" that I had lied about the couple not cooperating. It was incredibly frustrating, as I was clear in hundreds of media interviews—and even two witness statements for this very case—that the couple did *not* cooperate with us on the book.

It was all completely ridiculous. Not a week goes by when a royal press secretary doesn't have to ask a member of the family whether something is true or not, or discuss a response to a story. The same goes for when a journalist calls Buckingham Palace for a "right of reply" on a big scoop they are about to break. If it's of interest (or alarm), this usually spurs the Palace official to contact the relevant royal to discuss the matter (often unbeknownst to the reporter making the request). It's standard operating procedure, and it certainly doesn't mean the royal is in cahoots with that exact journalist. Of course, this is all information that Knauf omitted from his statement (and the British tabloid press would choose to ignore). Too much of the truth would have spoiled the narrative he was attempting to spin.

The Palace has always worked closely with the press, but this combined effort in the High Court was like nothing seen before. Meghan's U.K. lawyer, Jenny Afia, points out that Knauf didn't have to step forward if he didn't want to—there was no official request for his evidence. "The witness statements had no legal significance on the case ... [They were] filed because the impact on Meghan's reputation was potentially damaging," she said. Indeed, for the *Mail*, the Palace, and Knauf this was just a mission in optics. And for William, it was his opportunity to watch the institution strike back after Harry and Meghan went so public with private details about the Firm.

Still, regardless of the sideshow circus, it was clear from the beginning that the *Mail* broke copyright laws and unlawfully trampled on Meghan's privacy by publishing her letter to her father. Their appeal was destined to flop from the get-go. Almost a year after the original decision, the judge awarded Meghan her second victory in December 2021 alongside a court-mandated front-page apology from the paper. The mea culpa in the *Mail on Sunday* stopped short of saying sorry, but it did acknowledge her legal victory.

Knauf continued to work in his role as chief executive of William and Kate's foundation for a few more months before stepping down to join the board of the foundation for William's Earthshot Prize. As a loyal aide, he stuck by William through it all, from helping brief the press long after his communications role ended, leading the bullying allegations against Meghan, and joining forces with the *Mail* in court. Unsurprisingly, a year later, King Charles included him on his list of those to receive the honorable title of lieutenant of the Royal Victorian Order (RVO) for his "personal service to the monarchy." Notably, this high honor is chosen by the royal family and not the government, and it was his pal the Prince of Wales who performed the investiture on May 10, 2023, at Windsor Castle. Knauf—a man who went above and beyond to protect the royal family's relationship with a British tabloid—emerged from this fiasco as a titled hero, the personification of duty above all. His dangerous dalliance with the media in the courtroom is all part of a job description you won't find on his LinkedIn profile and a soon-to-be forgotten footnote in a celebrated career.

No one really paid attention to the *Mail*'s public apology because their coverage at the time focused on the fact that Meghan received only £1 from the newspaper for her privacy invasion. The *Mail* conveniently failed to report that Meghan also received close to seven figures for her copyright win. So, in the end the paper came out unscathed. Emboldened by their tighter-than-ever relationship with the institution, King Charles took the relationship to another level by hiring longtime *Daily Mail* editor Tobyn Andreae as his communications secretary in July 2022—the invisible contract becoming increasingly visible. Though he had no PR or communications experience, the former Eton College student's twenty-one years at the country's most aggressive tabloid was most appealing to the monarch and his Queen. With her established ties to the paper, it was Camilla who put him forward for the role after Geordie Greig sang his praises on a number of occasions. Andreae is not the first person from the news media industry to lead the monarch's press team, but Charles's other hires, such as the capable former *Newsnight* editor Simon Enright, came from the proven BBC, not the arena of downmarket tabloids. If this was intended as a modernizing effort on the King's part, it comes with more than a few questions as to why.

Buckingham Palace's head of press is now a man whose stint at the *Mail* included being an editor overseeing pieces that called out Kate's "alarming" weight loss, articles pushing the cruel "Waity Katie" nickname that followed her for years, and features mocking the princess's "trashy" eyebrows and "disastrous" gray hairs. And Andreae's two years as a deputy editor at the *Mail on Sunday* included the ugly week in which the paper viciously exposed Thomas Markle's staged paparazzi photos, the ones that initiated a chain of events that brought the Sussexes' royal wedding to its knees, destroying Meghan's relationship with her father in the process. But as the royals and those who collaborate with them have repeatedly demonstrated, it's all about keeping one's enemies—and friends in the right places—very close. It's easier to forgive previous attacks when those responsible for such cruelty are now on your side and at your disposal when enemies and obstacles get in the way.

———•———

Kensington Palace and Buckingham Palace have refused to comment on their media relationships or briefing history. Palace sources did, however, tell the *Daily Mail* in 2022 that it was "absolutely wrong" to suggest that people working at the Palace had secretly briefed damaging or confidential information about the Sussexes during their time as working royals. Sources making these claims to the same newspaper that published most of the offending articles is objectively absurd. Despite a mountain of evidence to the contrary, many royal reporters still claim no such invisible contract exists. But as the respected BBC journalist Andrew Marr said, "Either well-known journalists are making a lot of stuff up, just sitting at their laptops at the kitchen table inventing the detail of feuds and private confrontations, or a particularly confidence-rotting form of anonymous briefing has been taking place." Jennie Bond, the BBC's royal correspondent from 1989 to 2003, added, "Charles has always kept the tabloids on side, rather to my own annoyance and bemusement when I was working at the BBC . . . I was excluded from parties and events. I remember one big party at Buckingham Palace, I wasn't invited as a [senior] royal correspondent but Piers Morgan was, as the editor of the *Daily Mirror*, David Yelland was, as the editor of *The Sun*. And I used to say to [the Palace], 'Why do you give stories to the tabloids first? Why don't you come to me, and I'll broadcast it and they can follow me?' But that was never the way the Palace worked; they liked to keep particularly the tabloids on side."

But as the golden years of Fleet Street fade further into the past and the number of those who actually buy physical newspapers continues on a downward trajectory, Palace officials are making strides toward fostering stronger relationships with broadcast media. Both the Prince and Princess of Wales continue to nurture a beneficial relationship with ITV (yes, the very same broadcaster who protected William from my briefing claims), with Kate's annual Christmas concert likely to enter its third run and the prince collaborating with the network for a fly-on-the-wall documentary about his work with a homeless charity. "You cannot say a critical word about [William and Kate], no matter what the story is. They are protecting that relationship fiercely," a respected journalist at ITV told me.

And King Charles has now shifted some of his media efforts to strengthening bonds with the BBC, an expedient reversal from his previous position. Shortly after taking the throne, the King held at least two clandestine meetings with BBC executives. These discussions were part of the monarch's efforts to ensure that the network properly covers his work as King in spite of all the drama surrounding the institution. The message: His Majesty will not be overshadowed any longer. And it proved a successful run of schmoozing. In the buildup to the May 2023 coronation, the BBC ran Palace-requested items across their platforms about his charitable efforts. "It's become apparent to a number of journalists and producers that the Palace now has the BBC firmly under its control," a senior figure at the network shared on the condition of anonymity. "To many, the BBC has become an extension of the press office of the palace."

Joined at the hip, two troubled institutions now require each other for relevance in a culture that, to a large degree, is moving on without them. As a result, the relationship between the monarchy and the British media has changed. Where once the royal family needed the print press as a partner for advancing their agenda, it is now in such dire straits that the Palace has mutated into a feeder machine—there's no clear mission, just a gasping effort to provide them enough grist to keep the relationship limping forward. With the option to tell their own stories on social platforms and through other progressive outlets, perhaps it's time the Palace realizes it no longer needs to play the dirty game—that it also has the option of pulling the plug before a callous and reckless tabloid culture pulls the Firm down all the way to the bottom.

# *14*

# The Decay of Years
## The Fading Glory of the Crown

———•———

*Something as curious as the monarchy won't survive
unless you take account of people's attitudes. After
all, if people don't want it, they won't have it.*
—Charles, the Prince of Wales, 1994, ITV interview

*As yourselves your empires fall, and every kingdom hath a grave.*
—William Habington, *To Castara*

### May 3, 1951

A thin fog hunkered over the streets of London on an otherwise
agreeable spring morning. Thousands gathered to cheer King
George VI, Queen Elizabeth (later known as the Queen Mother),
and Princess Margaret as they made their way from the gates of
Buckingham Palace to St. Paul's Cathedral to officially open the
Festival of Britain. The decked-out and tasseled Household Cal-
vary Mounted Regiment escorted the open-top carriage, stopping
the horse-drawn escort only once along the way at the ceremonial
entrance to the City of London. Here, at the Temple Bar Memorial, the Lord Mayor presented the King with the pearled sword,

a bit of royal kabuki established in the Elizabethan era that is still performed every time the royal family makes a pilgrimage to the cathedral. From here the monarch's escort continued the short distance to St. Paul's, Sir Christopher Wren's magnificently domed, Neoclassical-Baroque masterpiece. After a short dedication service, other members of the royal family, including a twenty-five-year-old Princess Elizabeth (who nine months later became Queen Elizabeth II), husband Prince Philip, and George VI's mother, Queen Mary, joined Their Majesties and Margaret on the cathedral's front steps for the King's speech.

The 1951 Festival of Britain was a nationwide exhibition that emerged from the two great storm surges that altered the texture of British life: the fallout from World War II and the winding down of the British Empire. Although the fall of the empire was mostly gradual and undramatic, two particular events signaled its crumbling into the ocean of history—India's independence in 1947 and the London Declaration of 1949. The latter established the Commonwealth of Nations, which at the time was really just Britain's last-ditch effort to maintain ties and mutual interests with its former colonial strongholds and outposts. After the victory parades and end of World War II celebrations faded into memory, and Britons faced the grim economic realities of a once great nation in decline—work and food shortages being chief among them—the Festival was designed to showcase the United Kingdom's past, present, and future contributions to Western civilization and to boost the country's morale.

At the time, Britain looked and felt like a defeated nation. Lights in war-ravaged cities flickered off and on at night, food rationing lines formed in grimy streets, and heavy-headed souls trudged home after the factory whistles blew—now a haunting sound reminding the working men and women that many of their coworkers-turned-comrades never made it home from the front lines. These telltale signs of slow economic recovery and collective grief produced a dour national mood, one that tested the "Keep Calm and Carry On" resolve that carried the country through the war's crouching hours, wailing sirens, and bombs.

Dreamed up by Herbert Morrison, a senior cabinet member of the Labour party and a forward-thinking politician, the Festival of Britain highlighted the country's achievements in the arts, sciences, and industry as a means to celebrate the nation's victories beyond the arenas of war—a reminder of Britain's role in advancing civilization even while it was still recuperating from a full-on assault against it. The exhibitions were scattered across England and Scotland, but the Festival's epicenter was on the South Bank of the River Thames in the nation's capital. It featured pavilions, displays, retrospectives, and the Festival's focal point: the futurist-looking Skylon, a "floating" three-hundred-foot-high cigar-shaped steel tower meant to symbolize the United Kingdom's aspirational strides out of the rubble toward a better world. In a promotional reel, a jaunty yet instructional male voice distinctive of 1950s commercials and TV shows told viewers that the Festival was "devised halfway through this century as a milestone between past and future to enrich and enliven the present," and stressed that Britain was now a "diverse place of serious fun and lighthearted solemnity reclaimed from the bomb rack and the decay of years."

The Festival also marked the centenary of Prince Albert and Queen Victoria's Great Exhibition. Held in the massive cast-iron-and-glass wonder of Crystal Palace, the 1851 Victorian-era exhibition celebrated modern industrial technology and culture from around the world. Prince Albert, who was known as an advocate for reform and social change (including campaigning against the slave trade and child labor), said that the motivations for the exhibition were "for Great Britain [to make] clear to the world its role as an industrial leader," and to "increase the means of industrial education and extend the influence of science and art upon productive industry." Absent from this grandstanding was any mention of how it also coupled the image of Queen Victoria and her consort as patrons of the arts and sciences with showcases highlighting the power and wealth of the British Empire. It was a clever public relations coup outdone only by the fact that the Festival also solidified the monarchy's relationship with the middle class, the main audience for the exhibition. The industrial and technological achievements on display were important to this segment of Britain's population, and so the Great Exhibition was another moment to bolster and advance national pride and unity—two survival elements for a lineal monarchy at odds with middle class aspirations.

Twenty years later, with the impatient urging of Prime Minister William Ewart Gladstone, this same Victorian, PR-minded institution took it a step further—Palace officials reclaimed the old carriages and royal accoutrements that were collecting cobwebs in carriage houses and attics, and gave them a good polish to create the apparatus of pomp and pageantry that the royal family are known for today. The Victorian Firm was dealing with a public image crisis of their own—a small but intelligent republican movement was afoot and out to change some hearts and minds. After the Prince of Wales (later Edward II) "miraculously" recovered from typhoid in 1872, the monarchy leveraged the moment to make itself magical again. The Queen wanted a small, quiet thanksgiving service to mark her son's recovery, but Gladstone convinced her to accept what the late political essayist Tom Nairn called "the new limelight" by turning the service into a national public holiday. Seventy-two years later, the same would happen again when Prime Minister Rishi Sunak announced that King Charles III's coronation would be a full-fat display of pomp and celebration, rather than the cost-of-living, crisis-minded proceedings that sources said the monarch had originally hoped for.

After Gladstone's encouragement, they pulled out all the stops, creating a flashy display of regal power and tradition that also, by the way, featured a balcony moment similar to the ones we're accustomed to now. Victoria and her son, the miraculous survivor, stepped out onto the Buckingham Palace balcony to wave to the public and bask in their cheering. In one auspicious and ostentatious display of ceremony, the royal family endeared themselves to the crowd, coiled their identity around the national one, and drowned out the emerging republican chorus.

Standing on the front steps of St. Paul's decades later, King George VI would have been aware of all this as he waved to an adoring public before his Festival of Britain speech. By this point the royal apparatus the Victorians put in motion was a well-oiled machine, and the institution quickly engaged it for this hinge-moment in the nation's history. Overcoming his stammer in the speech, the King wasted no time in likening the Festival of Britain to its Victorian predecessor: "One hundred years ago, Queen Victoria opened the Great Exhibition in Hyde Park . . . All of us can paint the contrast between the calm and security of the Victorian Age and the hard experience of our own. Yet this is no time for despondency. For I see this Festival as a symbol of Britain's abiding courage and vitality."

After declaring the Festival open, Their Majesties and Princess Margaret descended the cathedral stairs to applause and pealing bells before boarding their coach back to the Palace. Off in the distance a forty-one-gun salute fired from the Tower of London and Hyde Park capped off the theatrics with a dash of militaristic zeal. Just as Queen Victoria and Prince Albert had done in 1851, the postwar royal family of 1951 deftly entwined their brand with the occasion—using the moment to stage some tried-and-true royal pantomime.

The Festival of Britain was a success, and millions attended it during its five-month run. But shortly after it closed, Winston Churchill and a newly elected Conservative government completely dismantled it, erasing it from sight. They believed that the Festival was nothing more than a display of utopian delusions and propaganda for the Labour party's vision of a Socialist Britain, and somehow the previous government had convinced the monarchy this was a good idea. Particularly that Skylon, which the era's grumbling, traditional conservatives no doubt universally condemned as a futuristic eyesore.

An almost forgotten tidepool of history, the Festival's legacy rests in how it successfully promoted a new and positive vision for a modern Britain while the country was still recovering from war. It put a benign face on modernity and change. And also, a royal one. Strangely enough, an antique horse-drawn landau en route to St. Paul's Cathedral is now an indelible image from a festival that celebrated the possibilities of the future. The royal family and the institution once again made looking back an essential component of the national mechanism for looking forward.

Just a few years later, the institution used this royal cunning to officially repackage the dead empire as a new, vital Commonwealth of Nations, and enlisted the newly crowned Queen Elizabeth II for the task. In her 1953 Christmas Day broadcast, she strategically connected her nascent reign with the Elizabethan Age and the accomplishments of her "Tudor forbear," to assert that "from the Empire of which they built the frame, there has arisen a worldwide fellowship of nations of a type never seen before." Using grandiose abstractions, she sold the idea of the Commonwealth as "an entirely new conception—built on the highest qualities of the spirit of man: friendship, loyalty, and the desire for freedom and peace."

The institutional spin continued as Her Majesty repeated that "the Commonwealth is moving steadily towards greater harmony between its many creeds, colours and races despite the imperfections by which, like every human institution, it is beset." She added her signature touches of commitment to duty, declaring: "To that new conception of an equal partnership of nations and races I shall give myself heart and soul every day of my life."

This is quite a bill of goods. The remnants of empire—damaged and forever-stained with colonial boot scuffs—reissued as equal partners in the pursuit of brotherly love and common good. The rapacious takeovers glossed over as institutional imperfections. And the state power and ancestral privilege of the Crown repurposed as a living bond between a sovereign and Commonwealth citizens who are no longer subjects. Rather than a token of colonial power, the Crown was repositioned as a symbol of stability and continuance, even as it shape-shifted to assume its diminished position in the new Commonwealth of Nations. All this in one broadcast by a young monarch prepared to tell the world that while empires are swept away, the Crown remains.

Part of the Queen's new mission as head of state was to re-decorate decolonization and postwar decline in shades of unified purpose and modernity—to normalize the essential theatrics required to conjure up Britain as a leader of this new "worldwide fellowship" while softening the blow of the nation's waning power. Times may be changing, but the British royal family can still convene and lead. This was the messaging, and it was crafty, but it was also disingenuous. The monarchy and the British government knew all along that many of these former colonies and territories would eventually "graduate" and mature into independence and a life beyond the mother country's shadow. This illusion of a leading nation was necessary to secure a place for the United Kingdom at the table of global power, even if it meant projecting itself as a soft unifier interested in the "spirit of man" while other superpowers like the United States and the former Soviet Union ferociously employed hard power to build military might and gain control of world economies.

In many ways, the British monarchy with Queen Elizabeth II at its helm continually accomplished this unifying the Commonwealth task for decades, incrementally changing the Crown's image, through soft power and image maintenance just enough to remain visible and relevant (the Queen's famous quote "I have to be seen to be believed" is applicable here). Elizabeth II and the institution charged up the Victorian royal machine when necessary—employing royal choreography and elevating, even manufacturing, tradition with all its national costume to validate the monarchy for the modern world. That whole looking-back-to-look-forward trick, what Tom Nairn called "cultivated anachronism." Fanfare and royal enchantment go a long way in selling the idea that Britain still heavily influences and leads the Commonwealth. The presentation of a pearled sword *must* mean something. Why else would they still do it?

But what exactly is this global fellowship? Members have changed over the years, but the current Commonwealth of Nations, known as the British Commonwealth until 1949, is a voluntary association of fifty-six independent member countries, many of which are former British colonies or territories like Trinidad and Tobago, Ghana, and Sri Lanka. This is different from the Commonwealth Realms, which refers to the fourteen sovereign states that have the British monarch as their official head of state, including Canada, New Zealand, Jamaica, and Australia. The Commonwealth of Nations includes the Commonwealth Realms, but a majority of the countries in the Commonwealth of Nations do not have the British monarch as their head of state. It's a lot to keep straight.

Hardly a multination partnership of shared interests, cultural understanding, and mutual respect, the Commonwealth of Nations is more a loose confederation of countries with current or former ties to Britain. Some are stronger than others and, for years, the strength of the ties between the mother country and the realms has given the entire Commonwealth an illusory glow of health and vague connection. But, toward the end of the Queen's reign and particularly after her death, even the appearance of strength started to vanish. In the case of Barbados, the country's graduation day came just over nine months before the Queen's death. After 396 years, the sun finally set on the royal family's reign over the Caribbean island in November 2021, with a handover ceremony attended by Charles, who watched in silence as the royal standard flag representing the

Queen was lowered to cheers in Heroes Square in Bridgetown. Out of respect for Queen Elizabeth II, Jamaica put their republican ambitions on hold while she was alive, but, ahead of Charles's coronation, it was announced that a referendum would be held in 2024 and would possibly see the country become a republic, complete with an elected president, before the year is out.

More worryingly for the monarchy, the growing republican movement in Australia—a Commonwealth realm known for its long commitment to the Crown—found new energy after the Queen's passing. Just five hours after her death, the Australian Green Party leader Adam Bandt weighed in on Twitter: "Our thoughts and prayers are with the family and all who loved her. Now Australia must move forward. We need Treaty with First Nation peoples, and we need to become a republic." Many found the tweet insensitively timed and disrespectful. Even the Australian prime minister, Anthony Albanese, obliquely admonished Bandt for his timing. But Albanese, too, is a devoted republican, and in May 2022 he appointed an assistant minister to his administration whose primary role is to hasten the process for the country to hold a referendum to become a republic. And in the summer of 2023, it was announced that the country would no longer host the Commonwealth Games, a major sporting event always supported by the royal family, because they do not represent "value for money" anymore.

Bandt might have been an outlier in his seeming disrespect for Queen Elizabeth II, but when it comes to King Charles, it seems he is just another voice in a growing choir. In a February 2023 decision that indicates the referendum may come sooner rather than later, Australia's central reserve bank—with consultation from the nation's current center-left Labour government—decided to remove the face of the British sovereign from their five-dollar bill. Aussie fivers were the only remaining banknote featuring an image of the Queen (which will still remain in circulation), but new ones issued will not display the new monarch. The new banknote will feature an indigenous design, something that honors "the culture and history of the first Australians." Charles has been relegated to coins only. Treasurer Jim Chalmers said, "The $5 note will say more about our history and our heritage and our country, and I see that as a good thing." One can hardly argue with that. And it's both a sign of the times and more evidence that King Charles just doesn't command the same level of admiration as his mother. There's a "why wait now" feeling to all these republican impulses—the Queen is gone, so what's the holdup?

Republicans closer to the Crown's home turf are also asking this same question. The Scottish independence movement may have hit a roadblock when Scottish National Party (SNP) leader Nicola Sturgeon resigned amid controversy in March 2023, but their historic push for independence is not going away. Fifteen years ago, the Scottish National Party was considered a mostly unimportant rabble of semi-radicals, but, as of early 2023, the party now holds forty-eight of the country's fifty-nine parliamentary seats in Westminster. Around 45 percent of Scottish voters do not want England to govern their country, and a vast majority of younger Scots are in favor of breaking away from English rule. New SNP leader Humza Yousaf says it's not a case of if, but when an independent Scotland should decide on their future with the royal family. "It's not an immediate priority, I accept that," he said. "But let's absolutely within the first five years [of independence] consider whether or not we should move away from having a monarchy into an elected head of state." It's a future the late Queen once publicly opposed, taking a rare step into the political arena. Ahead of Scotland's 2014 independence referendum (which saw 55 percent of the country vote in favor of remaining part of the United Kingdom), she expressed hope that voters will "think very carefully about the future." It was later revealed that a panicked Prime Minister David Cameron had asked the monarch to make the public intervention.

A driving force behind the current Scottish independence

movement is a desire to return to the European Union. If the Scots do vote for independence, Scotland will immediately apply to rejoin the EU. This says quite a lot about the fallout from Brexit, which came into effect in January 2020. Triggered by anti-establishment populism and anti-immigration sentiment, and sold as a return to the traditional, bygone days of ye olde British glory, Brexit further isolated Britain, hastening its decline in the global arena and at home. The numbers bear this out. Just a quick example: if the United Kingdom's gross domestic product (GDP) continues on its current path of an average decline of 0.5 percent annually as it has from 2010 to 2021, the British economy will fall behind many of its European neighbors, including Poland by 2030 and Romania and Hungary by 2040. There is a fear, particularly from those in the left-leaning parties, that a failing economy will lead to a mass exodus of young people, what Labour leader Sir Keir Starmer calls a "brain drain—not just to London and Edinburgh, but to Lyon, Munich, and Warsaw—that's not the future our country deserves." It must be said that the unanticipated disruption of the Covid pandemic and the global economic destabilization that accompanied it also greatly impacted Britain's economy like it did elsewhere around the world. One wonders, however, whether a continued British partnership with other countries in the European Union might have minimized the spiritual and economic aftereffects of the twenty-first century's first global plague.

This is what King Charles and the royal institution are facing: a shrinking Commonwealth, a retreating world presence, and a weakening economy at home. And because the royal family has so deftly—and expediently in recent years—merged itself with national identity and the "Land of Hope and Glory" instincts, when the nation's status wanes, so, too, does theirs. Queen Elizabeth II, with her physical and emotional endurance and exalted commitment to the Crown, provided a decorative and protective veil from this troubling codependency between national stability and monarchical relevance, but in the early days of the Carolean era, the veil has fallen away.

Keeping the ship afloat during these anxious times is mission number one for King Charles. He long ago reconciled himself to the fact that maintaining a smaller monarchy and streamlining the institution behind it are essential to its survival. His steps to "slim down" the family business, a dream he harbored long before becoming King, are now supposedly in full motion. Under Charles's plans, a leaner lineup of seven royals (himself, Camilla, William, Kate, Anne, Edward, and Sophie) will represent the Crown on a working level. When every other institution and major governmental body is under pressure to cut costs, it's a smart move. Whether it's fully realized is another thing altogether. So far there have been few signs from Buckingham Palace that the royal family will cost the British taxpayer less money anytime soon, and a look at the Court Circular (the official record of past royal engagements) shows that the lesser-known Duke and Duchess of Kent, Duke and Duchess of Gloucester, and Princess Alexandra have all been carrying out dozens of official engagements since Charles took charge.

Charles's efforts also include cutting back on the number of family members benefiting from reduced-rate rents at royal residences. With the Sussexes having officially handed back the keys to Frogmore Cottage in June 2023 and Prince Andrew under pressure to downsize, the King is also working with aides to open the likes of Buckingham Palace, Windsor Castle, and Balmoral to the public for longer periods around the year to generate more income. If executed, it's an operational change that could shave millions off the amount the family pulls from the public purse to fund the Firm. Instead of using Buckingham Palace—which is being renovated with Sovereign Grant funding of £396 million over ten years—as an official royal residence, Charles has chosen to stick with the nearby Clarence House as his London base. "There's a strong chance we will see BP turn into an all-year-round tourist attraction," said a senior aide.

During the first two years of his reign, we're unlikely to see further drastic changes, but sources close to King Charles say there will be more in the future. At least on paper, the new King appears to have accepted that, as the monarchy's importance at home and abroad continues to diminish, survival will largely be down to appearing as a more cost-effective, domestic-focused operation. Polls often reveal that a majority of the British public do not consider themselves royalists, nor do they enthusiastically support the monarchy, but most leave it at that—viewing the family as a harmless institution that makes Britain unique and one that doesn't present any glaringly definitive reasons to get rid of it. Royal Family, Inc., relies on this apathy and sources say King Charles, CEO, knows some belt-tightening is the key to remaining mostly unchallenged. What he wasn't counting on, though, was the increasing number of republicans at home who want to abolish the monarchy altogether—sooner rather than later.

Up until now, the British republican movement has mostly remained on the fringe with those calling for the end of the monarchy viewed as radicals or busybody academics with too much time on their hands. But this is starting to change. Since 2018, the royal family's popularity has been on the slide. At the same time, the numbers of those beginning to see the rationale for doing away with the royal system are rising. This group consists of both hardcore anti-monarchists and those who just don't see the point anymore, particularly after the Queen's death. Since then, protestors (albeit far outnumbered by royal well-wishers) have started to become a regular sight at royal engagements. Signs and banners reading "NOT MY KING" are now a familiar sight on walkabouts. Recent polls show overall abolition support from an average of one in four Britons (up from just less than 20 percent a few years ago), while the number of people who say the monarchy is "very important" for the country fell to 29 percent, from 38 percent in 2022. Individually, King Charles III has an average approval rating of 54 percent, well below that of his late mother, 76 percent, and William, at 64 percent. In 2023, outright support for the monarchy fell to 55 percent (down from 75 percent in 2012, the Queen's Diamond Jubilee Year and the peak of Cambridge mania). Generationally, the differences are huge—79 percent of over-sixty-fives in Britain back the Crown, while just 36 percent of eighteen-to-twenty-four-year-olds want it to continue. That point will no doubt be of concern to the royal institution, who are already aware that when older swathes of royalists die out, they will be replaced with more critical voices.

Since Charles's ascension, the British republican advocacy group, Republic, has stepped up its efforts to disestablish the royal institution—and the movement is growing. Hardly a "firebrand," its CEO, Graham Smith, takes a constitutional, nuts-and-bolts perspective to where Britain would go without a royal head of state. The author of *Abolish the Monarchy: Why We Should and How We Will* describes it as all "relatively straightforward" because "no one is suggesting [that Britain moves] to a U.S.- or French-style constitution. It's about moving to a parliamentary democracy." He describes a future where both houses of Parliament are filled with elected representatives, with a prime minister serving in the lower house. This system would also include a non-political head of state, who is elected by the people, but ultimately has very limited powers. Countries all across Europe already have this structure, including Germany, Ireland, Iceland, Finland, and many of the Baltic states. Anna Whitelock, a British historian and professor of the history of monarchy at City, University of London, predicts a similar fate. "By 2030 there will be definite louder clamors for the eradication of the monarchy," she has said. "The monarchy—its purpose, what it's about, will be questioned and challenged in a way that it hasn't been before."

Just five years ago, the thought of the Windsors becoming equal citizens without privileged status seemed unreal to most, but now that future doesn't seem as far-fetched. Harry and Meghan have already fled to real life, and, by the looks of it, they're not hurting for either money or status. More importantly, for Britain as a country, Smith thinks establishing a republic would be a moment of profound pride for the nation: "We would actually feel very proud of ourselves for doing it and for embracing democracy and ridding ourselves of these institutions. I hope we [will also] be a beacon to other countries."

As reasonable and seemingly straightforward as this is, the possible birth of a British republic is a long way off. A lot of this has to do with the perceived popularity of the royal family, even in their current fragmented state. Republicans argue that the members of the population who passively support the monarchy believe the family are popular, profitable, and harmless. Anti-monarchists claim this is a common fallacy that is easy to disprove. With regards to their popularity, the feeling is that most of the people who like the monarchy do so because they believe others do as well, often a direct result of deceptive polling and reporting. As an example, if there is an opinion poll that states 75 percent of the population want to "keep the monarchy," the result is often misreported in the media as 75 percent "love the monarchy," which obviously makes it sound more popular than it really is. Keeping something doesn't always mean you love it. That's why attics and garages are full of stuff we want to hold on to but don't value enough to use or display.

When it comes to the profitability belief, the anti-monarchy stance is that there's no real evidence of this. It's certainly true that they are tourist attractions, but there is no precise value attached to the monarchical revenue stream—no matter how many figures are flung around every year. Staunch royalists will say the royal family are the country's biggest attraction, but a closer look at statistics available from Britain's Association of Leading Visitor Attractions reveals that it's the country's heritage sites such as St. Paul's Cathedral and the Tower of London that consistently feature at the top of London's most-visited attractions. And while Windsor Great Park might be a popular destination, royal residences such as Kensington Palace, Buckingham Palace, and Windsor Castle have yet to feature in their annual top ten lists. To put it comparatively, Britain's average tourism revenue pre-Covid was £127 billion and royal tourism accounted for approximately £500 million of it—0.3 percent of that number.

There is a habituated opinion, however, that while the British monarchy is a peculiar, even frustrating institution, at the end of the day, it is a mostly innocuous one. In the 2014 BBC program *Martin Amis's England*, Amis, who was not known for fuzzy feelings toward the "philistine" royal family, echoed this point of view: "It's connected with our love of [1970s British TV drama set in a posh London townhouse] *Upstairs, Downstairs*—those country house dramas. It's nostalgia for that class society. It's all connected, it can't not be connected. But it's relatively harmless." For years, this notion that the family may be innocuous aristocratic buffoons has provided the monarchy with an invulnerability that protected some of their darker secrets. But this just isn't the case anymore; the monarchy is more vulnerable now than it's ever been. The popular Queen Elizabeth II's reign is long gone, Prince Andrew dragged the Crown's reputation through puddles of disgrace, the King's business dealings threw a shadow over his early days on the throne, and Harry and Meghan bore a hole through the Palace wall.

More recently, deeper insights into the royal family's private wealth and finances have revealed a world of secrecy that obscures their fiscal matters from the public. Ahead of Charles's coronation, the *Guardian* launched an investigative report to cut through the "entrenched secrecy" that the paper argues was a "hallmark of [Elizabeth II's reign]" and one that deprives the British people "of the most basic information about the monarchy." It resulted in reporting that estimated King Charles's personal fortune at £1.8 billion (the Palace later called this figure "a highly creative mix of speculation, assumption and inaccuracy"). The King's assets include jewelry passed on from his mother (diamonds, pearls, emeralds, rubies—you name it, he's got it) worth an estimated £533 million; inherited properties, including Balmoral and Sandringham; a fleet of cherished Rolls-Royces and Bentleys; and, of course, Her Majesty's horses—several stables' full that are said to be worth upward of £27 million.

Digging even deeper, investigations also showed that the late Queen and King Charles both took cash payments worth around £1.2 billion from "two hereditary estates that pay no tax," in addition to the millions they receive in public funding for their official duties. And the Duchies of Cornwall and Lancaster are the primary cash cows. In 2022, they collected £21 million from each, while a fierce debate continues as to whether these duchies actually belong to the British state. On top of this, the monarch also receives £86.3 million a year from the Sovereign Grant (made up of taxpayer contributions and a percentage of Crown Estate profit) for official royal duties, official travel, staff salaries, and the upkeep of properties. Regardless of the state of the country's economy, this number does not go down, thanks to a so-called "golden ratchet" clause inserted by former *Conservative* prime minister David Cameron during his term. In fact, from 2025, the Sovereign Grant can expect a projected rise of £38.5 million (45 percent) thanks to an increase in Crown Estate profit after Charles secured a £1-billion-a-year windfarm deal on part of its land. While the King made it clear he wants extra profit from the estate to "be directed for the wider good," a percentage of that will also go back into the pockets of the royal family instead of the public purse. "This is at a time when nurses are receiving [a] 5 percent [pay rise] and other key public workers are still fighting for a fair wage," said Nick Wall of internal pressure group Labour for a Republic. "This reward is morally unjustifiable, while also both anti-democratic and plain wrong. The people of this country should have their say on royal funding through debate between their elected representatives." It's worth noting that the royal family also cost the country approximately £345 million in security funding, which is not covered by the Sovereign Grant.

All of this heavily underlines the republican argument that, at the end of the day, monarchies look out for themselves and are propelled by their own agendas, interests, and bank accounts. This enormous fortune speaks volumes about the monarchy's motivations for sticking around way beyond its sell-by date and why they use the idea of "serving the Crown" as a protective shield. If all of this is about duty to the state and commitment to a better Britain, then it doesn't look so much like an ungodly amount of inherited wealth as it does well-earned compensation for services rendered. As long as they are cutting ribbons, sharing cute portraits of their children, and doing enough work, they trust the public will agree to keep them on as a "harmless" anachronism and a uniquely British spectacle. Just like their forebears, they will continue to roll out the carriages, unsheathe ceremonial swords, and parade the crown in a worn-thin campaign to keep their palaces and stay in the game.

After King George III went mad and was forced to abdicate in 1820, his son, George IV, nicknamed "Prinny," assumed the throne. George IV's heavy drinking and self-indulgence sorely tested the patience of the public and eventually caught up with him. He reigned as King for a brief and troubled ten years before his death. When his brother, William IV, ascended, he faced a disgruntled public and an institution in disarray. Known as "Sailor Billy" because of his storied career in the Royal Navy, he was the oldest person at that point to assume the throne, and a bit of a hopeless case. Legend has it that after a reform mob threw garbage and food at his royal carriage, the sailor king said, "I feel the Crown tottering on my head." King Charles III usurped Sailor Billy as the oldest sovereign to take the throne, and one imagines that after the eggs thrown his way, not to mention the tepid response to his ascension, he, too, may one day feel the Crown teetering on his head.

# 15

# Endgame

―――・―――

*We ransomed our dignity to the clouds . . . We're actors . . .*
*We pledged our identities, secure in the conventions of our trade that*
*someone would be watching. And then, gradually, no one was.*
—Tom Stoppard, *Rosencrantz and Guildenstern Are Dead*

*If you want a happy ending, that depends, of course,*
*on where you stop your story.*
—Orson Welles, *The Big Brass Ring*

As I quietly made my way toward the center of a virtually empty Westminster Abbey, it was hard to believe that the unassuming wooden throne in front of me was a central figure in one of the country's most ancient rituals. Patched up and timeworn, the faded wood and spotted gold Coronation Chair has been at the heart of Britain's coronations for more than seven centuries. It's the place where the Archbishop of Canterbury anoints the new monarch, where King Charles receives the royal regalia and, finally, feels the full symbolic weight of the Crown upon his brow.

With less than twenty-four hours left on the coronation count-down, the Abbey was a hive of hushed activity. Outdoor voices were left firmly at the door as workers quietly made necessary ad-justments to the center stage, lint rollers at the ready to keep the somewhat garish-looking yellow carpet lint-free. Its color wasn't tradition, but a choice made early on in the planning process so the area would "pop" on television (and, in a lucky coincidence, show some solidarity toward Ukraine—a running theme in the 2023 ac-tivities of the royal family).

Even after twelve years of covering the royal story, it was dif-ficult not to feel the gravity of what was about to take place. The 335-pound Stone of Destiny, which was brought down from Ed-inburgh Castle four days earlier and was now sitting beneath the Coronation Chair, had enough history behind it for an entire book of its own. The Anglican Church and the royal family have used this humble slab of sandstone as part of the inauguration ceremony for almost a thousand years. Covering these details for rolling ABC News coverage felt like reporting from a liminal space, somewhere between venerable old traditions and an episode of *Game of Thrones*. But one thing was for sure—the royal family had set the most dra-matic stage possible.

Westminster Abbey has been the backdrop for coronations since 1066. The church has also hosted more than sixteen royal weddings and even more funerals, including the global events of Princess Di-ana's and Queen Elizabeth II's memorials. For me, Westminster is also where I clocked in for my first major event as a royal reporter—covering the elaborate nuptials of William and Kate on April 29, 2011. Back then it was an entirely new world to me, and I marveled at the thirty-three cameras that were discreetly set up to broad-cast as many angles of the fairy-tale ceremony as possible. More than a decade later, production teams strategically placed exactly 150 cameras—now smaller and more technologically advanced—to capture Charles's big day in a level of detail unimaginable back in the early 2000s. The job at hand: broadcast every movement, every bead of sweat, and every glistening eye in full 4K resolution.

The contrast between then and now is a stark and clarifying one. When William and Kate tied the knot, we were all still caught up in the royal fantasy—the enchanting wedding provided the magic the family and institution desperately needed at the time. After a dry spell, the couple's union made the royal family exciting again and threw a spotlight on the possibilities of the next generation. The cameras were there to catch this aspect, too, but the fairy-tale filter was still on and the royal machinery provided the requisite timeless grandeur. But after several years of family disintegration, disturbing revelations, and disquieting investigations, the soft focus is gone and so is a lot of the myth, both entombed with Queen Elizabeth II. Just like those 4K cameras at Charles's coronation, we can now see the world at large more clearly, at times forced to take in unvarnished realities at a disorienting pace. And, despite institutional resistance, the monarchy is now just another part of this unmasked world.

The May 6, 2023, crowning of King Charles III was the first chance for the majority of the nation, and those around the globe, to witness the spectacle of a British coronation. Though the crowds in the rainy streets of London hoping to catch a glimpse of the Golden State Carriage or that iconic balcony wave were fewer than we saw for the Queen's Platinum Jubilee just a year earlier, it still briefly brought the nation's capital to a standstill.

With millions tuned in around the world, it was the perfect opportunity for the Firm to recaptivate and restore some of that lost mystique. Commentary notes that Buckingham Palace sent to those of us preparing for hours of television coverage placed emphasis on the fact that the ceremony was one thousand years old. But a closer look at the past reveals a different history. In fact, the type of ceremony the institution prepared for Charles dates back only to 1902, when King Edward VII was crowned. Sure, there are still medieval elements, but the majority is a more recent creation as technology allowed the world to start witnessing such events. Even the regalia on display aren't originals—those were destroyed by Oliver Cromwell in 1649 during the country's brief flirtation with republicanism. As journalist and polemicist Fintan O'Toole pointed out, "The odd thing about these British royal ceremonials is that they have become more important as the power and majesty they are supposed to project has diminished."

For Charles, this wouldn't be the first time a little creative license was needed to stir the emotions and imaginations of those watching. His investiture as a twenty-year-old Prince of Wales in 1969 was in fact largely created by his filmmaker uncle, Lord Snowdon, who shaped the ceremony to look arcane and mysterious, despite the fact that they used modern props to drape the occasion. While it looked like Charles's ornate crown was topped by a gold orb, it was actually just an electroplated plastic Ping-Pong ball. Snowdon later called the event "bogus as hell."

They say a coronation is a mirror for a monarch's reign, and Charles certainly tried to put a twenty-first-century stamp on the service. He chopped the ceremony down to two hours from three, and his procession route was just a quarter of his mother's coronation's sojourn in 1953. And though guests included monarchs from Spain, Bhutan, the Netherlands, and more, there was also representation from the general public on the 2,300-person guest list—many of those were honorable people who had bettered their communities through charitable work or volunteering. Less aristocracy, more meritocracy. There were a few celebrity sightings, too, courtesy of Lionel Richie and Katy Perry, both ambassadors for charities founded by Charles. It was still by and large an Anglican ceremony, but Charles also cosigned a new pledge authored by the Archbishop of Canterbury, promising that the Church of England "will seek to foster an environment where people of all faiths and beliefs may live freely." This was an important distinction for a man who has an impressive collection of books on all faiths, from Judaism to Buddhism, and once called Islam "one of the greatest treasuries of accumulated wisdom and spiritual knowledge available to humanity."

Of course, tradition leaves little room for true modernization. As he did for Harry and Meghan's 2018 wedding ceremony, Charles requested a Black gospel choir to perform at his coronation. The talented Ascension Choir was handpicked for the job, though it was impossible not to notice that the choir didn't sing gospel music. Their presence, said journalist Nels Abbey, could have been something truly new and refreshing—a change to what is considered the norm in worship in the Church of England. "It would be diversity doing what diversity is meant to do," he said. "What we had instead was a group of excellent Black singers swaying to a [Anglican] hymn."

And there were also changes that were not so well received. Not long before the big day, Lambeth Palace—the official London residence of the Archbishop of Canterbury—announced that, for the first time in coronation history, the public was invited to make an "homage" to the King and "pay true allegiance to your majesty, and to your heirs and successors" during the coronation. But this news was met with widespread criticism in the public and the media—a request to pledge allegiance felt like a ridiculous call for servility, a command reverberating from feudal times or heard on state-mandated television in North Korea. Sources told me that Charles absolutely hated the unnecessary, tone-deaf addition. After the backlash (which saw 84 percent of people polled in Britain say they would refuse to do such a thing), Buckingham Palace officials instructed the archbishop's office to tone it down. On the day itself, the archbishop instead "invited" those in the congregation who wished to "offer their support" to recite an oath swearing allegiance to the monarch and the Crown. To most, however, it still seemed extremely old-fashioned—and undemocratic.

This blip on the radar proved a harbinger for some rough waters ahead. The coronation was a moment Charles had spent his adult life thinking about and planning for, particularly during his mother's later years. But, despite ample preparation time, his arrival did not go particularly smoothly. Pulling up to Westminster Abbey for their grand entrance, the King and Queen were forced to wait in their carriage for six minutes before other family members arrived. "We can never be on time," Charles angrily muttered to Camilla. "There is *always* something . . . This is boring." A Buckingham Palace source initially blamed the delay on the Wales family for departing Kensington Palace late, but a spokesperson for the Prince of Wales was quick to chime in with the detail that Charles's carriage had actually traveled from Buckingham Palace to Westminster too quickly, resulting in the premature arrival. The two households' narratives at odds, once again.

As he slowly walked through the church's Great West Door and under its ten statues of twentieth-century martyrs, Charles looked like a man with the weight of the world on his shoulders—and it wasn't because of the nearly five-pound St. Edward's Crown on his head. His grandfather King George VI's heavy velvet Robe of State from 1937 appeared to pull his shoulders down even farther into a stoop that aged him beyond his seventy-four years. Some sources said it was nerves, others called it dread, but, as he and Queen Camilla sat down on matching throne chairs, he bit the insides of his pale, powdered cheeks, looking more like he was enduring the ceremony rather than basking in it. Though much could go wrong elsewhere, he didn't need to worry about his speaking parts. The few sentences—such as "All this I promise to do" and "I am willing"—that Charles had to recite over the next 120 minutes were (much to the amusement of viewers) printed out in large font on cue cards that were held up directly in his line of vision for easy reading.

Camilla, on the other hand, looked confident, though at times appeared as if she couldn't quite believe she had finally completed her thirty-seven-year journey from unpopular mistress to a crowned Queen. Her smirk as Queen Mary's upcycled crown (now bejeweled with 178 carats of Cullinan diamonds) was placed on her head became one of the most meme'd images of the day on social media. Unlike Charles, who was anointed with holy oil behind a screen as a private moment between himself and God, Camilla was anointed in full public view—her new, elevated status was reinforced in front of the world.

Of course, eyes were also on the other family members. In stark contrast to a robed Prince William, who, as the next in line, kneeled before his father and pledged his loyalty "as your liege man of life and limb" (from a cue card, naturally) with a hand on Charles's right shoulder and a kiss on his left cheek, Charles's other son sat among guests four rows back. With Meghan at home in California, Prince Harry's solo attendance was a striking reminder of the missed opportunity the monarch had to bring his entire family together before the public witnessed this royal milestone. It wasn't for lack of effort on Harry's side, who made it clear to his father after the January release of his memoir that he hoped to have a proper conversation about events of the past, a chance for both sides to take accountability where necessary. Instead, Charles was stubbornly hard to pin down. The Sussexes spent the first few months of the year unclear about whether they were even invited to the coronation. His responses to Harry's inquiries about his attendance were vague at best. "I . . . haven't decided," he told his son during an early February phone call that Harry initiated, and he didn't officially make up his mind until late March. As for Harry, while he had an extensive list of reasons for skipping the proceedings altogether, shortly before making the trip, he told a source that supporting his father as the fifth in line to the throne "still outweighed the other things."

Unsurprisingly, Harry, who left for California immediately after the service, received far more cold shoulders than Prince Andrew, who self-assuredly walked to his seat in the Abbey. Though Palace aides explicitly told the Duke of Sussex that he wasn't allowed to wear a military uniform (a request that neither he nor his team had actually made), Charles gave a firm nod to Andrew to wear his lavish Order of the Garter ceremonial robes. There were some concerns among courtiers about how this would look, with "some suggestions that maybe [Andrew] should be encouraged to wear civilian attire," said a source. All fell on deaf ears. Just like the Queen he replaced, Charles's soft spot for his brother remains exposed.

Back at center stage, Archbishop Welby put on the show of his life, dramatically holding the St. Edward's Crown high before lowering it onto Charles's head. "God save the King," he solemnly declared, before stepping back to carefully check that it fit the new monarch's head. The Abbey's pealing bells and booms of gun salutes echoed around London. "God save the King," the 2,300-strong congregation called back.

Charles, standing taller than when he entered, regained his confidence—even if just for a moment—as he walked the aisle with Camilla, their purple velvet Robes of Estate trailing behind them. As he stepped past his siblings, a smile briefly cracked from the corner of his mouth before he stopped to acknowledge the assembled faith leaders he had personally invited. It was a warm moment and an affecting modern touch—Charles's pan-religious leanings on full display as he shook their hands. Smiles, however, were left indoors, and as he stepped outside a stiff resignation returned. The hard part was over, but a look of fear fell over him—a concerned grimace clouded any faint suggestion of joy. The coronation ceremony was complete, but for King Charles III the tough part of the job is only beginning. For William, too.

The father and son are facing a long line of hurdles. Britain is in a tailspin, and the turmoil's end is nowhere in sight. In the past, the family and the institution have seized crises as opportunities to showcase their importance, to highlight monarchical "stability" and "continuity." It's different now. There isn't a war (so far anyway) that the establishment can use to galvanize support—only a nation in severe economic and reputational decline, and one fighting for a new identity. The Commonwealth Realms are not what they once were, with some countries already making quick and resolute moves toward independence. Over the next two years, Charles, Camilla, William, and Kate plan to increase formal visits to Commonwealth countries to protect and strengthen ties. It's a last-ditch attempt at bolstering relationships with what's left of Queen Elizabeth II's "brotherhood of nations" (that Charles failed to visit during his first year as King). But, as many of them continue to look at a future without the British monarchy, it's probably too little, too late.

Closer to home, the King and the Prince of Wales must contend with rabid criticism of the institution and the royal system; a younger generation who feel apathetic toward the royals and who are pushing for a more open and tolerant culture; and a growing republican movement that, while still on the fringe, will continue to find footing in the wreckage left behind by the family's rippling scandals and the institution's missteps. This all pales in comparison to the mammoth task of keeping the family and system relevant enough to stay afloat. Aspirations will fall as survival mode kicks in, and King Charles could do worse than simply embracing his position as a warden of the monarchy until Prince William takes his shot at reanimating the pageant, even if it's just for another generation.

After the dust settled from the coronation celebrations and Westminster Abbey returned to its quiet dignity, Prince William forged ahead with his new agenda—one step closer to what historians will call the "Gulielean Era." The heir is already openly discussing the changes he will make to define his own reign. His decision to forgo a Welsh investiture when he became the Prince of Wales is just a preview. "Tradition will not be the deciding factor in anything he does," said a source. Instead, his mission is to define what the monarchy means and looks like in the modern world. A senior staffer from his household told *The Times of London*, just days after Charles's big day: "[William's] Coronation will look and feel quite different."

As the official royal family Instagram account trotted out highlights from the coronation celebrations, William and Kate's social media had a slightly different take on the proceedings. In a glossy, five-minute video directed by an advertising filmmaker (whose clients include Uber Eats and Red Bull), the focus firmly rested on the Wales family. Although it was Charles's coronation weekend, the King and Queen were visible in the film for only fourteen seconds. It was a decision noticed by some senior Buckingham Palace aides and the monarch himself. A source close to William simply called the decision smart public relations. "The prince is aware of the huge amount of popularity and good favor that he and the princess receive . . . For them to take advantage of that only benefits the entire institution." Whatever the reason, it's yet another sign of the growing lack of cohesion between the King and the heir, the father and the son. Long gone is that "lockstep" narrative the Palace once pushed—Kensington Palace now regularly shares that William will do things his own way when his time comes. "There has been a sense," described a former senior courtier, "that William is slowly trying to separate himself from his father. His popularity is high, and he doesn't want his father's lack of it to affect that."

A month after the coronation, the soldiers were out marching once again—this time for Trooping the Colour, King Charles's official birthday parade. What was once a must-see calendar entry for royalists felt quieter this time around. Perhaps it was widespread fatigue from royal events over the past year, but, even at the start of the summer tourist season, the crowds gathered outside Buckingham Palace were thin. While one would usually fear getting caught in the middle of the throng of people who stand outside Buckingham Palace to watch for the big balcony moment and the roaring RAF flyover, this time you could have easily walked through Canada Gate to Bird Cage Walk on the other side of the Mall without so much as a knock to your shoulder.

The balcony moment itself, once a who's who of the royal family and the iconic setting for those vibrant group portraits, appeared quieter and less exciting without its star player and cast of colorful supporting characters. The lineup of the Wales family, the Edinburghs, Princess Anne and husband Sir Tim Lawrence, and the new King and Queen may have been the slimmed-down vision Charles had long desired, but the result felt a little lackluster.

To change, adapt, and modernize has been a repeated challenge for the royal institution throughout history. While Charles can't alter the fact that the sun is setting on the British monarchy as we know it, he can set the tone for how they will approach—and even embrace—the coming nightfall. There is honor and duty in this, too. The monarch would be wise to remember something he said almost twenty years ago. When asked about his role in the Firm, he answered, "I find myself born into this particular position. I'm determined to make the most of it. And to do whatever I can to help. And I hope I leave things behind a little bit better than I found them."

Balanced stewardship from King Charles may keep it all together for the remainder of his reign, but to secure a meaningful future for the Firm, King William and the next generation will need to usher in *real* change. Without it, they risk losing it all. In Samuel Beckett's masterpiece play *Endgame*, the servant, Clov, says to his elderly and frail master, Hamm, "I use the words you taught me. If they don't mean anything anymore, teach me others. Or let me be silent." The question of how to endure in a hostile world is also their existential predicament. At first, Hamm stubbornly believes "there is no reason for [their situation] to change," but it is Clov who cautions him, succinctly and unemotionally stating, "It may end." A poignant reminder that so much is beyond our control, even our final move on the chessboard or the last words of our soliloquies. The monarchy is now running out of meaningful words, especially if it ignores a public trying to teach it new ones. Should it continue to do so, then perhaps it's time for silence and to let their country speak for them instead—even if it means standing back and watching the curtain slowly close. In the story of Beckett's stubborn old diehard Hamm, he eventually admits he's out of moves: "Old endgame lost of old, play and lose and have done with losing."

# Acknowledgments

———•———

Albert Lee, whom I'm so fortunate to call my literary agent, told me before I signed the deal for *Finding Freedom* that it "takes a village" to get a title to market—and it has been an absolute dream to work with this one on *Endgame*.

Thank you once again to the amazing people and friends at HarperCollins and Dey Street, especially Liate Stehlik. Carrie Thornton, your editorial expertise, critical but loving eye, belief in my work, and willingness to take risks with me has made creating this book another unforgettable experience, and I thank you wholeheartedly! I also owe a debt of gratitude to Allison Carney and Heidi Richter for another stellar marketing and publicity campaign; Renata De Oliveira, Drew Henry, Rachel Meyers (We made it! Thank you for all your tireless efforts), Ploy Siripant (another iconic cover!), and Ben Steinberg.

To the HarperCollins UK and HQ Stories teams: Lisa Milton, I'm *so* glad we got to work together again. Huge thanks to Halema Begum, Claire Brett, George Green, Arthur Heard, Kate Oakley, Marleigh Price, Joanna Rose, and Lauren Trabucchi.

Albert, my old friend, thank you for continuing to steer this ship with the wisdom and skill that makes you the best in the game. It's an honor to be part of the UTA family. I'm also very grateful to Laurie-Maude Chenard, Harry Sherer, and Sam Solomons. Melissa Chinchillo, Meredith Miller, Zoe Nelson, and Ethan Schlatter, thank you for all your efforts in bringing this book to new foreign markets (even with the insane translation times!).

Brett Valley, what can I say? You guided me when I couldn't find my words, helped me see straight when the number of topics I wanted to explore made my head spin, and taught me how to become a better writer. I've learned so much from you, and I look forward to the next! Thank you.

Reena Ratan, once again you helped me bring another beautiful book to life with iconic photographs. The *Back Hill Reporter* could never!

To all the sources, contacts, experts, insiders, and peers who contributed to my reporting efforts—be it on or off the record—thank you for trusting me with your words and your stories. Some of us may not always see eye to eye, but I have the greatest amount of respect for every one of you.

Thank you to my colleagues across the lands who have been so supportive and patient while I worked on *Endgame*. To the incredible teams at ABC News, *Good Morning America*, and ABC News Live—I'm so lucky I get to experience so many of these milestone moments with you all. Simone Swink and Zoe Magee, here's to another unbeatable year of royal coverage! Big love to the über-talented and unstoppable gang at *Harper's Bazaar*, including Bianca Betancourt, Quinci LeGardye, Chelsy Sanchez, and Rosa Sanchez.

Writing a book like this at lightning speed is not easy. It's an isolating and testing experience, so I want to give special thanks to the kind souls who have helped keep me strong on all fronts while I worked. Gary Murphy, you've been an absolute legend; you kept me upbeat on crazy days and have taught me so much. Hilary, you equipped me with tools I will carry for the rest of my life. And my amazing friends who kept me topped up with memes, laughs, and distractions—love you guys!

As ever, the best comes last. To my beautiful family for supporting me always, I love you so much. Hayley and Ramin, I'm so proud of you both for your achievements together. This book is great and all, but becoming an uncle to your beautiful baby girl was easily the highlight of my 2023.

# Notes

———•———

The events described in the pages of *Endgame* draw on more than eleven years of reporting, conversations, interviews, and experiences from my time covering the royal beat, as well as firsthand accounts from hundreds of engagements, major events, overseas tours, and interactions with members of the royal family. Some names have been removed for legal reasons.

For this book alone I interviewed more than sixty sources—a leaner pool than *Finding Freedom*, which started out even smaller in the initial months of writing to ensure the project was not leaked before it was announced in June 2023. As is the often frustrating nature of royal news, a lot of interviews were given on the promise of anonymity (a move done for a number of reasons, including to acknowledge sensitivity of roles, to protect careers or relationships, and to ensure safety). The upside to this is that it has allowed sources the freedom to speak candidly and critically without fear.

A number of people also spoke "on background," which means you won't see their quotes in the book, but the information they provided has informed areas of reporting and certain scenes. Some also spoke strictly off the record.

A few additional notes before we get started with the references. Unless otherwise stated in the following pages or made clear in the book, quotes featured in *Endgame* with no attribution are from my own interviews or conversations. All information from legal actions and court cases cited in the book has been referenced from original documents and not news coverage. Where the book already cites the exact reference material or a source of information (e.g., TV show name, network, *and* date), I have not repeated it in the reference notes. There are also a few fun facts peppered throughout that didn't quite fit in the manuscript but may help give a little more background detail. Thank you for reading!

# *Prologue*

—•—

Prince Harry spoke of his family's "unconscious bias" during an interview with journalist Tom Bradby on *ITV's Harry: The Interview*, January 8, 2023.

1

—•—

Boris Johnson's "bright and focused" quote is from a BBC News interview, September 12, 2022. Queen Elizabeth II's "episodic mobility issues" were first cited by Buckingham Palace in a May 10, 2022, statement confirming she would miss the State Opening of Parliament. "It's my job" was provided by an "informed source" in a report by Matt Wilkinson, "Unseen picture of the Queen during last days at Balmoral where she insisted on doing her 'job' till the end," *The Sun*, September 16, 2022. "We have heard nothing but bagpipes . . ." was in a letter written by Queen Victoria featured in Delia Miller, *Queen Victoria's Life in the Scottish Highlands*, 1985. Scott Methven's quotes were sourced from the self-penned "Recollections of a Queen's piper," *The Spectator*, September 17, 2022; a BBC News interview on September 10, 2021; and a CBC News interview on September 14, 2022. The "drunken octopus" quote is from Prince Harry, *Spare*, 2023. Reverend Dr. Iain Greenshields and Ailsa Anderson were interviewed during ABC News' *Celebrating Queen Elizabeth* (which I was also part of) on September 19, 2022. "It has been an honor and a privilege to accompany her on her final journeys . . ." is from a statement written by Anne, the Princess Royal, on September 13, 2022.

I also found the following titles useful while researching this specific chapter: Robert Hardman, *Queen of Our Times*, 2022; Brian Hoey, *All the Queen's Men: Inside the Royal Household*, 1992; Brian Hoey, *At Home with the Queen: Life Though the Keyhole of the Royal Household*, 2003; Tom Quinn, *Backstairs Billy: The Life of William Tallon, the Queen Mother's Most Devoted Servant*, 2016.

2     The origin of the term "the Firm" is believed to be from King George VI, the late Queen's father, who used it to describe the royal family (predominantly senior royals) and the business of monarchy (including the staff working within it): "We're not a family. We're a firm," he reportedly declared. The first printed mention of Charles one day wanting a "slimmed-down monarchy" was in an interview given by Charles's former deputy private secretary Mark Bolland with Ian Katz, "Prince is very, very weak, says his former top aide," *Guardian*, October 25, 2003. Camilla's not hiring her own ladies-in-waiting being called a "modern" decision is from a Buckingham Palace media briefing given on November 29, 2022. Joe Mazzulla's comment on William and Kate's visit was given to journalists at a November 30, 2022, press conference at TD Garden Arena in Boston. BBC viewership of the Earthshot Prize ceremony from article by Abbie Bray, "BBC viewers 'switch off' The Earthshot Prize minutes into show," *Express*, December 6, 2022. The royal family approval rating falling to 47 percent after the release of *Spare* is from an Ipsos poll of 1,084 adults aged 18–75 in Great Britain between March 10 and March 13, 2023. Assorted quotes from Prince William's birthday profile by Rebecca English, "'There are things you don't do and Harry has 100% crossed the line': Prince William 'alternates between grief and anger' over his brother but—as he turns 40—their relationship remains at 'rock bottom,'" *Daily Mail*, June 17, 2022. Princess Diana's first documented use of the nickname "men in gray" was in one of her tape recordings for biographer Andrew Morton, which became part of the manuscript for *Diana: Her True Story*, 1992. The term "Fab Four" first went viral on Twitter after the then Duke and Duchess of Cambridge and the future Duke and Duchess of Sussex walked to

church at Sandringham together on Christmas Day, 2017—the *Daily Mail* then ran the headline "Side by side for the first time, it's the new Fab Four!" the following day. "Oprah *who*?" and other quotes from Prince Edward and Sophie, Countess of Wessex, from an interview by Camilla Tominey, "'We are still a family no matter what': The Earl and Countess of Wessex on grieving for 'Grandpa,'" *The Telegraph*, June 4, 2021. "She was never born to be Queen . . ." quote from Robert Hardman on a Facebook livestream interview for Viking Cruises on June 2, 2022. "Grief is the price of love" is from a statement written by Queen Elizabeth II after the September 11, 2001, terror attacks. "We will meet again" was from the Queen's Covid broadcast to the United Kingdom and Commonwealth on April 5, 2020. "If you're sorry, tell *me* you're sorry," said by Ngozi Fulani on ITV's *Good Morning Britain*, March 8, 2023.

3    "A bit of grouchiness" from a September 14, 2022, tweet by *The Times*' history correspondent Jack Blackburn. The term "Pengate" was used by the *Telegraph*, *Daily Express*, *The Sun*, and other outlets between September and October 2022. Prime Minister Rishi Sunak leaving Liz Truss's "request in place" was from an official comment made by a 10 Downing Street spokesperson on October 28, 2022. King Charles being "keenly aware" and wanting "good value" come from an article by Hayley Dixon and Gurpreet Narwan, "Coronation for the cost of living crisis as King expresses wish for 'good value,'" *The Telegraph*, September 13, 2022. "The King and Queen Consort and their advisers are keenly following the debate . . ." from an article by Rebecca English, "King Charles's first 100 days— and what 2023 will bring," *Daily Mail*, December 30, 2022. "Obviously, there will be a great deal of attention on the United Kingdom at that time . . ." is from a 10 Downing Street spokesman on December 19, 2022. "Declaration of war" is from an article by Rebecca English, "Releasing trailer for Harry and Meghan's Netflix show during William and Kate's US tour is little less than 'a declaration of war' say insiders," *Daily Mail*, December 2, 2022. "Deliberately torpedoed" is from an article by Valentine Low, Tom Ball, and Jack Blackburn, "Sussexes ac-

cused of sabotaging Prince and Princess of Wales' US visit," *The Times*, December 2, 2022. "Harry, Do You Really Hate Your Family So Much?" front-page story by Richard Palmer, *Daily Express*, December 2, 2022. Additional details on Ryan Reynolds and Rob McElhenney's Wrexham Football Club takeover via profile piece by Andrew Barker, "A Win for Wrexham: How Ryan Reynolds and Rob McElhenney Helped Bring a City Back to Life," *Variety*, June 19, 2023. "Institutional gaslighting" quoted from Prince Harry in *Harry & Meghan* (episode 4), Netflix, 2022. "I reminded him to keep his rifle pointed at the target" quote is from an article by Roya Nikkhah, "What the Palace made of Harry and Meghan's 'truth,'" *The Sunday Times*, December 11, 2022. The burgundy coats "dig" was from a front-page story by Amanda Platell, "Was the great royal burgundy parade a cheeky swipe at Meghan?," *Daily Mail*, December 21, 2022. "Instead of building bridges, the head of state is torching them . . ." is a quote from a Twitter/X post by Peter Hunt on March 1, 2023. Norman Baker spoke of Andrew "dressing up as a royal" in a story by Matt Wilkinson, "BACK FOR BASH: Disgraced Prince Andrew 'to dress-up as royal for a day' as he's invited to party alongside King Charles," *The Sun*, March 20, 2023. Jens Zimmermann's quotes were filed to newswires by the Associated Press on March 31, 2023. The headline "For Hamburg, Devastated by Allied Bombing, King Charles's Visit Is So Much More Than a Photo-op" is from an opinion piece by Helene von Bismarck, *Guardian*, March 30, 2023. "Your father always does what he wants to do" is quoted from Prince Harry, *Spare*, 2023.

Though this chapter does not quote or use its material, I found Robert Jobson, *Our King: Charles III: The Man and the Monarch Revealed*, 2023, useful in my research.

4     "The only two people who talked more about strategy and planning than [the aide] were Hitler and Stalin," from Alastair Campbell, *Winners: And How They Succeed*, 2015. Ailsa Anderson quotes from *Celebrating Queen Elizabeth*, ABC News, September 19, 2022. The term "Englishness" was first used by Tom Nairn in a series of essays on the British state published

in the *New Left Review* and later collected in the book *The Break-Up of Britain*, 1977. "British-Englishness" was inspired by Nairn's term as well, and there have also been uses of the phrase in at least three PhD theses by various authors, including Siyu Cao, "Performing Post-Britishness: A Quest for Independence in the Contemporary Literature of England," University of Warwick, Department of English and Comparative Literary Studies, April 2020. "Glamour of backwardness," "contrived timelessness," "great nation-family," and "a willful failure to quit a darkening stage" are from Tom Nairn, *The Enchanted Glass: Britain and Its Monarchy*, 2011. The Treaty of Waitangi (Te Tiriti o Waitangi) was an agreement between the British Crown and more than five hundred Māori chiefs in 1840; however, although it was intended to create unity, different understandings of the treaty—and breaches of it—have caused conflict. "New Zealand has long been renowned for its dairy produce . . ." quote from the Queen in report by Associated Press, "All in All, Queen May Want to Forget About New Zealand," February 27, 1986. Positive opinion of the royal family dropping within four months of the Queen's death is from a YouGov survey of 1,710 adults in Britain between September 13 and September 14, 2022. Story about Kylie Minogue turning down coronation performance first reported by Katie Hind, "EXCLUSIVE: Kylie Minogue REFUSES offer to star at King Charles' Coronation concert because of growing Republican sentiment in Australia," *Daily Mail*, March 4, 2023, and since confirmed by my own additional reporting. Zillenials are a microgeneration of people born on the cusp of the Millennial and Gen Z demographic cohorts, usually between 1993 and 1998. Statistics of YouTube channel "The Prince and Princess of Wales" accurate as of July 31, 2023.

The following books provided helpful background and research: Kevin Sharpe, *Selling the Tudor Monarchy: Authority and Image in Sixteenth-Century England*, 2017; Kevin Sharpe, *Image Wars: Promoting Kings and Commonwealths in England, 1603–1660*, 2018.

5 An investiture is the day when someone who has been awarded an honor receives their insignia in person from a member of the royal family (and there are around thirty

held every year). The term "annus horribilis," meaning "horrible year" in Latin, was brought to prominence by the Queen in a speech at Guildhall, London, on November 24, 1992, for her Ruby Jubilee on the throne and the end of a year marked by scandal and disaster for the royal family. "Queen's speech without the Queen" was used in coverage by news outlets including the *London Evening Standard*, BBC News, *Daily Mail*, and *The Sydney Morning Herald* on May 10 and May 11, 2022. The "bags of cash" scandal was first reported by Gabriel Pogrund, Charles Keidan, and Katherine Faulkner, "Prince Charles accepted €1m cash in suitcase from sheikh," *The Sunday Times*, June 25, 2022. Charles "will not accept bags of cash again" statement given by a Clarence House "source" to the Press Association, Reuters, and journalists—including myself—on June 29, 2022. Details on Charles accepting donation from the Bin Laden family by Gabriel Pogrund, "Prince Charles accepted £1m from family of Osama bin Laden," *The Sunday Times*, July 30, 2022. The "sins of the father" quote is from a source at the Prince of Wales's Charitable Fund to BBC News on July 31, 2022. The Mahfouz cash-for-honors scandal was first reported by Gabriel Pogrund and Dipesh Gadher, "Prince Charles aides fixed CBE for Saudi tycoon who gave £1.5m," *The Sunday Times*, September 5, 2021. Pogrund's follow-up articles are not quoted but provided additional information. Subsequent cash-of-honors details, including Michael Fawcett's resignation, were reported by Kate Mansey and Jonathan Bucks, "Charles Aide Told Saudi Donor: We'll Help You Get Knighthood," *Mail on Sunday*, September 5, 2021. "Fawcett has been there for so many years . . ." quote from Dickie Arbiter in book by Stephen Bates, *Royalty Inc: Britain's Best-Known Brand*, 2015. The existence of the "Fawcett the Fence" nickname first came to light in an article by Jamie Wilson, "Aide who 'sold gifts' adds to royal woes," *Guardian*, November 11, 2002. "We have all agreed to end this arrangement" statement from Clarence House given to Press Association and journalists, including myself, on November 11, 2021. "Ersatz Georgian and mock Scottish vernacular creations . . ." quote by Alan Dunlop from article by Laura Webster, "Prince Charles's Knockroon 'eco-village' has just 30 homes," *The National*, February 3, 2019. "He needs to rethink what he spends his money on" quote by Gabriel Pogrund from interview on *Red Box Politics Podcast* (episode title: "Prince Charles and Money"), July 4, 2022. Charles "was more than disappointed at the policy" is from an article by Matt Dathan and Valentine Low, "Prince Charles: Flying migrants to Rwanda is 'appalling,'" *The Times*, June 10, 2022. "But Americans can do anything!" is allegedly a comment made by Prince Charles, reported in a book by Sally Bedell Smith, *Charles: The Misunderstood Prince*, 2017. "Royal body . . . carriers of a blood line" comes from an essay by Hilary Mantel, "Royal Bodies," *London Review of Books*, February 21, 2013. The nickname "queen of people's hearts" first entered the lexicon after Princess Diana was asked if she thought she would ever become Queen (alongside Charles) during her *Panorama* interview (episode title: "An Interview with HRH The Princess of Wales"), BBC1, November 20, 1995. "Prince of Wails" was first used in an article by William D. Montalbano, "Prince's Marital Woes Become Britain's Problem," *Los Angeles Times*, December 30, 1995, and in dozens of articles in the years that followed. The nickname "Pampered Prince" was first used in an article (which also cites the "crested silver dispenser") by Stuart Millar and Jamie Wilson, "Pampered prince puts sun king in shade," *Guardian*, November 15, 2002.

Alongside material from these referenced sources, I also found the following two books useful for additional insight: Catherine Mayer, *Charles: The Heart of a King*, 2022; Tom Bower, *Rebel Prince: The Power, Passion and Defiance of Prince Charles*, 2018.

6    The 152 veterans of the Royal Navy, Royal Marines, and British Army who signed the letter to Queen Elizabeth II were convened by the Republic group; it was sent directly to the monarch on January 13, 2022. "Without Prince Philip the royal house of cards is falling" is from Tom Bower, *The Times*, December 12, 2021. "I cannot imagine anyone in their right mind leaving you for Camilla" is from a letter sent by Prince Philip to Princess Diana in the summer of 1992 and reprinted in a book by Paul Burrell, *A Royal Duty*, 2003. "If I walk, will you walk with me?" was first reported in a book by Gyles Brandreth, *Breaking the Code: Westminster*

*Diaries*, 2014. "I don't think any child should be asked to do that, under any circumstances," from Prince Harry interview in a profile by Angela Levin, "Prince Harry on Chaos After Diana's Death and Why the World Needs 'the Magic' of the Royal Family," *Newsweek*, June 21, 2017. "[Andrew] is a kind, good man . . ." quote from Sarah, Duchess of York, interview on *Good Morning Britain*, ITV, June 14, 2022. "He was in an invidious situation of his own making . . ." quote from producer Sam McAlister interview by Andrew Kersley, "Ex-*Newsnight* producer Sam McAlister on booking Prince Andrew and BBC's 'fatal' class problem," *Press Gazette*, July 22, 2022. "Like a platter of fruit" quote is from Virginia Giuffre in an interview with *Panorama*, BBC, December 2, 2019. The articles featuring sources close to Prince Andrew denying the authenticity of the photo with Virginia Giuffre were by Bill Gardner, "Prince Andrew's supporters say his 'chubby' fingers prove photo of him with Epstein victim is fake," *The Telegraph*, August 29, 2019, and Robert Jobson, "Prince Andrew hits back over 'witch hunt': Duke of York insists claims by Epstein's 'sex slave' are 'categorically untrue,'" *London Evening Standard*, August 28, 2019. "Any suggestion of impropriety with underage minors is categorically untrue" is from a Buckingham Palace spokeswoman on January 2, 2015. "It is emphatically denied that the Duke of York had any form of sexual contact or relationship with Virginia [Giuffre]" is a statement from Buckingham Palace in response to Virginia Giuffre's *Panorama* interview on December 2, 2019. "He denies that it ever happened . . ." quote from Virginia Giuffre interview with NBC News on September 20, 2019. "Tits and bums man" and "schoolboy humor" quotes from reporting in article by Valentine Low, "'Andrew the great' exasperated duchess with unsavoury friend," *The Times*, January 6, 2015. The tabloid nickname "Randy Andy" was born after a 1986 *Daily Mail* article, titled "Randy Andy and His Web of Arm Candy" chronicled his long list of alleged romances. "He would just be putting himself back into the same dangerous position again, facing the same deposition . . ." quote from David Boies interview on *Piers Morgan Uncensored*, Talk TV, February 21, 2023.

During my reading and research for this chapter, I also found the following titles of use: Nigel Cawthorne, *Prince Andrew: Epstein, Maxwell and the Palace*, 2022; Robert Jobson, *Prince Philip's Century, 1921–2021: The Extraordinary Life of the Duke of Edinburgh*, 2021; Sam McAlister, *Scoops: Behind the Scenes of the BBC's Most Shocking Interviews*, 2022; Sarah Ferguson, *Finding Sarah: A Duchess's Journey to Find Herself*, 2011.

7   Black women in the United Kingdom being four times more likely to die during childbirth is a statistic from a report published by MBRRACE-UK (Mothers and Babies: Reducing Risk through Audits and Confidential Enquiries across the United Kingdom), released on November 10, 2021. Young Black men in London being nineteen times more likely to be stopped and searched is from a November 2020 research study by University College London's institute for global city policing. The death rate of non-white people in Britain who died from Covid being 50 percent more than their white counterparts comes from a May 2020 analysis by the Institute for Fiscal Studies. Minority ethnic job applicants sending 60 percent more applications to get a positive response from an employer is a statistic released in January 2019 by the Centre for Social Investigation at Nuffield College, University of Oxford. The case of "retain and explain" for statues linked to slavery in the City of London was a result of a decision made by the district's Court of Common Council. Prince Charles's speech on the "appalling atrocity of slavery" was delivered in Bridgetown, Barbados, on November 30, 2021. Barbados was dubbed "Little England" after the English settled on the island in 1627, wiping away all traces of its original inhabitants (the Arawaks), and it retained the nickname due to its strong British attitude and traditions (such as afternoon tea and cricket matches). "Shouldn't be here at all" quote from David Denny in article by Victoria Murphy, "Prince Charles Calls Slavery an 'Appalling Atrocity' Which 'Forever Stains Our History' in Landmark Speech," *Town & Country*, November 29, 2021. Prince Philip's "slitty-eyed" remark was made to a group of students of Mandarin at Xian University on October 16, 1986. Prince Philip told then president of Nigeria Olusegun Obasanjo (wearing na-

tional dress), "You look like you're ready for bed," during a visit to Nigeria on December 3, 2003. Prince Philip's "Do you still throw spears at each other?" remark was made on a visit to the Tjapukai Aboriginal Cultural Park in Australia on March 2, 2002. "The Africans just don't know how to govern themselves . . ." was a quote from the Queen Mother (shared by one of her ladies-in-waiting) in an article by Tanya Gold, "The queen of unkindness," *Guardian*, September 15, 2009. Charles calling a South Asian friend "Sooty" is from an article by Tim Walker, "Member of Princes' polo club 'affectionately' known as Sooty," *The Telegraph*, January 12, 2009. Princess Michael of Kent was quoted telling Black restaurant goers, "You need to go back to the colonies!" in an article by Jeane MacIntosh, "TELLS BLACK NYERS: 'GO TO COLONIES,'" *New York Post*, May 26, 2004. "I even pretended years ago to be an African, a half caste" is from an interview with Princess Michael of Kent on *My Favourite Hymns*, ITV1, July 25, 2004. Prince Andrew's alleged use of the n-word is from a comment piece by Rohan Silva, "Andrew's use of language left me reeling—and I still regret not challenging his choice of words," *London Evening Standard*, November 18, 2019. Prince Harry's uses of the slurs "rag-head" and "Paki" were from a leaked video recording covered in the *News of the World*, January 11, 2009. The document revealing courtiers banned "coloured immigrants or foreigners" from serving in clerical roles in the royal household was first revealed in a report by David Pegg and Rob Evans, "Buckingham Palace banned ethnic minorities from office roles, papers reveal," *Guardian*, June 2, 2021. "Paraded naked through the streets . . ." is from an opinion piece written by Jeremy Clarkson, "One day, Harold the glove puppet will tell the truth about A Woman Talking B*****ks," *The Sun*, December 16, 2022. "You may not necessarily comment on this issue . . ." quote by Antigua prime minister Gaston Browne to Prince Edward was broadcast on ABSTV Antigua, April 27, 2022. "She was ahead of the curve" is a quote from historian and professor of imperial and military history at King's College London Ashley Jackson in the article "The Queen and the Commonwealth: a force for international change?," *The Queen at 90*, BBC History, March 2020. "I declare before you all that my whole life, whether it be long or short . . ." is from the Queen's twenty-first-birthday speech on April 21, 1947. That an image "would particularly appeal to a History of Art graduate such as Kate" is a quote by *Mail on Sunday* art critic Philip Hensher in an article by Sarah Oliver and Katie Nicholl, "Incredible glimpse through the palace keyhole and fiercely guarded private life of William and Kate," *Mail on Sunday*, April 24, 2016. "If the Koh-i-Noor is a symbol of East India Company . . ." quote from Danielle Kinsey in article by Brahmjot Kaur, "Camilla swaps the Kohinoor diamond for another controversial stone on her coronation crown," NBC News, February 17, 2023. "With a world stage and powerful voice that was inherited by her very position . . ." quote from article by John V. Petrocelli, "Trouble in the Castle: Unnecessary to Consult Sussex," *Psychology Today*, December 10, 2022. Prince Harry's statement condemning "racial undertones" and "wave of abuse" was released by Kensington Palace with the title "A Statement by the Communications Secretary to Prince Harry" on November 8, 2016. "I do think the Duke of Sussex and his office will bear some responsibility if a journalist is harmed . . ." comment by Richard Palmer on Twitter/X, December 18, 2018. "If you'd seen the stuff that was written and you were receiving it . . ." quotes from Neil Basu to Channel 4 News, November 29, 2022. The "Meghan made Kate cry" story first ran in an article by Camilla Tominey, "Kate and Meghan: Is the royal sisterhood really at breaking point?," *The Telegraph*, November 26, 2018. The "What Meghan wants, Meghan gets!" tiara story was first reported by Dan Wootton, "MAJ RAPPED MEG: The Queen warned Prince Harry over Meghan Markle's 'difficult' behaviour after row over bride's tiara for royal wedding," *The Sun*, November 9, 2018. The story claiming Meghan, the Duchess of Sussex, "bollocked" Kate, the Duchess of Cambridge's staff was reported by Dan Wootton, "ROYAL STRIFE: Meghan Markle and Kate Middleton locked in bitter fallout as Hollywood starlet takes on royal court," *The Sun*, November 30, 2018. The claim that Meghan refused to wear M&S tights first appeared in a column by Sophia Money-Coutts, *The Sunday Telegraph*, November 18, 2018. The nickname "Duchess Difficult" was first used in a headline by Roya Nikkhah, "Meghan loses second close aide, Samantha Cohen, as rumours swirl of

'Duchess Difficult,'" *The Sunday Times*, December 9, 2018. The nickname "Me-Gain" was reported in an article by David Jenkins, "Two years on from the Royal Wedding, the cult of 'Meghanomania' endures," *Tatler*, May 18, 2020. The descriptor "narcissistic sociopath" being used by ex-staffers was reported by Valentine Low, *Courtiers: The Hidden Power Behind the Crown*, 2018. "Degree wife" first appeared in an article by Sophia Money-Coutts, "Cambridge v. Sussex: is there a rift between Prince William and Kate and Prince Harry and Meghan?," *The Sunday Times*, June 16, 2019. "Calling someone the b-word, labeling them as difficult . . ." quote is from Meghan on the podcast *Archetypes* (episode: "To 'B' or not to 'B'?"), Spotify, November 2022. "Melissa is a hugely talented person . . ." source quotes from article by Richard Eden, "Palace shock as Meghan Markle's closest aide quits her job just six months after royal wedding," *Daily Mail*, November 10, 2018. The Meghan "friend" the Buckingham Palace aide said had also made comments about Melissa Toubati was actress Janina Gavankar, who was interviewed on *This Morning*, March 10, 2021, where she said, "I also know why someone had to leave, and it was for gross misconduct. The truth will come out, there's plenty of emails and texts about that." "I just didn't want to be alive anymore . . ." quotes from Meghan from *Oprah with Meghan and Harry*, CBS, March 7, 2021. "As far as the family was concerned . . ." quotes from Prince Harry from *Harry & Meghan*, Netflix, 2022. Only 8 percent of Britain's journalism workforce being non-white is a statistic from an Office for National Statistics Labour Force Survey reported by Charlotte Tobitt, "Survey finds growing UK journalism workforce of nearly 100,000 still lacks ethnic diversity," *Press Gazette*, May 13, 2021 (updated September 30, 2022). The first use of "British-Iranian" in an article about me was by Ian Gallagher, "The celebrity writers chosen by Meghan to tell her 'real' story," *Mail on Sunday*, April 25, 2020. "What was able to just be manufactured and churned out, it's almost unsurvivable . . ." quote from Meghan to *Teenager Therapy* podcast, October 10, 2020. The statement denying Kate's "baby Botox" was issued by a Kensington Palace spokesperson on July 24, 2019. "For us, for this union and the specifics around her race . . ." quote from Prince Harry from *Oprah with Meghan and Harry*,

CBS, March 7, 2021. The letter written by Holly Lynch was sent to the Duchess of Sussex on October 29, 2019. The nationwide poll about sympathy for the Sussexes or the royal family after the Oprah Winfrey interview aired was conducted by YouGov (who surveyed 2,111 adults living in the United Kingdom) on March 8, 2021. Kate's "History will judge this statement" was reported by Valentine Low in the paperback release of *Courtiers: The Hidden Power Behind the Crown*, 2023. "We are very much not a racist family" was William's comment to Sky News reporter Inzamam Rashid on March 11, 2021, who asked the question, "Have you spoken to your brother since the interview?" (the prince's reply, "No, I haven't spoken to him yet, but I will do"), followed by, "And can you just let me know, is the royal family a racist family, sir?" The Buckingham Palace employment diversity percentages were released in the Sovereign Grant Report for the financial year 2022–23, and additional information was gathered by my own reporting. "Everything they said was going to happen hasn't happened . . ." quotes by Prince Harry from *Harry: The Interview*, ITV, January 8, 2023.

This chapter would be incomplete without the additional insights, stories, and research provided in the following sources: Akala, *Natives: Race and Class in the Ruins of Empire*, 2019; Naomi and Natalie Evans, *The Mixed-Race Experience: Reflections and Revelations on Multicultural Identity*, 2022; Catherine Hall et al., *Legacies of British Slave-ownership: Colonial Slavery and the Formation of Victorian Britain*, 2016; Afua Hirsch, *Brit(ish): On Race, Identity and Belonging*, 2018; Kenneth Morgan, *Slavery and the British Empire: From Africa to America*, 2007; Safiya Umoja Noble, *Algorithms of Oppression: How Search Engines Reinforce Racism*, 2019; David Olusoga, *Black and British: A Short, Essential History*, 2020. A huge hat tip also goes to the R. S. Locke article "House of Windsor II: Prince Harry and the Flight of Icarus," Medium, March 1, 2001; a journal article by Emily C. Bartel, "Too Many Blackamoors: Deportation, Discrimination, and Elizabeth I," *Studies in English Literature, 1500–1900* 46, no. 2, Tudor and Stuart Drama (Spring 2006); the YouTube channel "LonerBox" for its documentaries "Racism in the UK," October 14, 2020, and "The

British Monarchy," September 30, 2022; and the documentary "How Black Britons experienced racism in the shadow of COVID-19," Al Jazeera, March 14, 2022.

8 Prince William said he was "sickened by the racist abuse aimed at England" in a tweet from the Kensington Palace Twitter/X account on July 12, 2021. William's speech about ensuring diversity in future BAFTA nominations was delivered at the start of the 73rd British Academy Film and Television Arts Awards ceremony on February 3, 2020. "The public look to him to keep royal work looking modern . . ." and (later on in the chapter) "middle-class job" and "ordinary people" are from sources quoted in a profile by Roya Nikkhah, "Up close and personal with Prince William: an intimate portrait of the future king," *The Sunday Times*, March 20, 2021. Cholmondeley is pronounced "Chum-lee." The first report about Kate, then the Duchess of Cambridge, and Rose Hanbury's alleged "fall out" was by Dan Wootton, "ROYAL RIVAL: Kate Middleton has fall-out with glamorous best friend and tells Prince William to 'phase her out,'" *The Sun*, March 22, 2019—it was removed from the newspaper's website in 2021. The nickname "Turnip Toffs" was first used in an article by Catherine Ostler, "The Turnip Toffs! Meet Kate and Will's new neighbours, the party-loving Norfolk set with bigger homes than the royals. And, dahling, everyone knows each other (sometimes EXTREMELY well)," *Daily Mail*, September 12, 2014. "The real victim of aristocratic dinner party gossip" from an article by Richard Kay, "Is Kate's 'rural rivalry' just a vicious rumour to damage her?," *Daily Mail*, March 24, 2019. The legal warning to U.K. newspapers about rumors was reported by Lachlan Cartwright and Tom Sykes, "Prince William's Lawyer Tries to Suppress Rumors . . . ," *Daily Beast*, April 9, 2019. The claim that Harry and Meghan's marriage was in trouble was reported by Aaron Johnson, "Harry and Meghan TRIAL SEPARATION: 'Nasty Fights, Humiliation and Failure' Lead Prince to Pursue 'Peace'—Inside the Drama," Radar Online, July 18, 2023. "He wanted me to hit him back, but I chose not to . . ." by Prince Harry from *Harry: The Interview*,

ITV, January 8, 2023. "Far from seeming cold and unfeeling . . ." in an article by Camilla Tominey, "There's never been a better time for the Princess of Wales's new private secretary to shake things up," *The Telegraph* ("Royal Appointment" digital newsletter), February 8, 2023. "We are uniquely bonded because of what we went through . . ." is a quote from Prince William during a seven-minute video released online by Kensington Palace on April 21, 2017, to launch Heads Together. "Look, we're brothers, we'll always be brothers . . ." quote by Prince Harry on *Harry and Meghan: An African Journey*, ITV, October 20, 2019. The report that William had "bullied" Harry out of the family is by Valentine Low, "Princes 'fell out because William wasn't friendly towards Meghan,'" *The Times*, January 13, 2020. The "source close to the royal family" who said Harry has been "kidnapped by a cult of psychotherapy" was quoted in an article by Alastair Jamieson, "Royals despair as Prince Harry 'kidnapped by cult of psychotherapy,'" *Independent*, January 10, 2023. "The worldwide privacy" tour episode of *South Park* (season 26, episode 2) was first aired on February, 15, 2023, on Comedy Central in the United States. William was first called "work-shy" in an article by Emily Andrews, "Meddling Wills is throne idle," *The Sun*, February 18, 2016. The photographs of William at a Swiss nightclub appeared in an article by Emily Andrews and Nick Parker, "LETTING HIS HEIR DOWN: Prince William shows off his dad dancing skills as he throws his hands in the air to hip hop classic on lads' holiday," *The Sun*, March 14, 2017. "My mother did put herself right out there . . ." quotes by Prince William from interview by Alastair Campbell, "William: A Prince in His Prime," *British GQ*, May 29, 2017. "Following on from my time in the military . . ." is from Prince William's statement released by Kensington Palace, "An update from Kensington Palace about the plans for The Duke and Duchess of Cambridge in 2017," January 20, 2017. "I'll never know as much as he does, but I'll try my best . . ." quotes by Prince William in an article by Hannah Furness, "Prince William on making his mark on father's Duchy of Cornwall legacy," *The Telegraph*, October 11, 2019. "Homelessness can be prevented when we collaborate . . ." quote by Prince William from Kensington Palace press release, "The Prince of Wales and The Royal Foundation launch UK-wide programme to end homelessness," June 26, 2023. William spoke of his "unique bond" with Harry in a Heads Together video released by Kensington Palace on April 21, 2017. Miguel Head is quoted in an article by Roya Nikkhah, "Up close and personal with Prince William: an intimate portrait of the future king," *The Sunday Times*, March 20, 2021. William's "lifelong mission" was first reported by Russell Myers, "Prince William's pledge after Israel and Palestine visit: 'Middle East peace will be my lifelong mission,'" *The Mirror*, July 1, 2018. "WILLS THE FREEDOM FIGHTER" was the front page of *The Sun*, March 23, 2023.

Additional reading and research was useful in the books Robert Jobson, *William at 40: The Making of a Modern Monarch*, 2022; Penny Junor, *Prince William: Born to Be King, an Intimate Portrait*, 2012; Anna Pasternak, *The American Duchess: The Real Wallis Simpson*, 2020. The research on the "Turnip Toffs" by author Meredith Constant (published to TikTok and YouTube, March 2023) was also very helpful.

9     "Granny, while this final parting brings us great sadness . . ." from tribute statement written by Prince Harry and released on September 12, 2022. "I just wanted to show her that she's welcome . . ." quote from unnamed fourteen-year-old girl to Scott McLean, CNN, September 10, 2022. "It was one of the hardest things she ever had to do" from a source quoted in Robert Jobson, *Our King: Charles III: The Man and the Monarch Revealed*, 2023. The interview in which Harry said changing the media was his "life's work" was with Tom Bradby, *Harry: The Interview*, ITV, January 8, 2023. Bill Simmons called Harry and Meghan "the fucking grifters" on *The Bill Simmons Podcast*, Spotify, June 16, 2023. The Sussexes' marriage was described as "frazzled" and "fraught" in an article by Camilla Tominey, "The Sussexes are frazzled, fraught and lacking romance—like any couple with young kids," *The Telegraph*, May 19, 2023. Though not directly quoted, references to Prince Harry's *Spare*, 2023, are also made during this chapter.

10 Queen Elizabeth I called Robert Dudley, Earl of Leicester, her "Eyes," William Cecil her "Spirit," and Robert Cecil her "pigmy" or "elf," per letters she had written during her life and quoted in a number of books on her life, including Alison Weir, *Elizabeth, The Queen*, 2011. Prince Philip's and Princess Margaret's references to courtiers as "the Men with Mustaches" has been documented in numerous biographies, including books by Gyles Brandreth, *Philip: The Final Portrait*, 2021, and Tim Heald, *Princess Margaret: A Life Unravelled*, 2007. Sarah, the Duchess of York, referred to "Gray Men" in her autobiography, *My Story*, 1996. Angela Kelly's NDA was first reported by Kate Mansey, "Angela Kelly 'is made to sign gagging order,'" *Mail on Sunday*, May 21, 2023. "Whenever there is a monarch, there is court . . ." quote from Valentine Low, *Courtiers: The Hidden Power Behind the Crown*, 2022. "Courtiers in the British system are the rulers of their masters . . ." quote from Robert Hardman in an article by Latika Bourke, "The 'men in grey': The true powers behind the palace," *Sydney Morning Herald*, March 13, 2021. The "half in, half out" working model was shared by Prince Harry and Meghan, the Duchess of Sussex, on the website SussexRoyal.com, as well as within the royal institution, on January 8, 2020. "Something out of monarchies in the middle ages" is attributed to "Buckingham Palace insiders" in an article by Chris Ship, "Why has the Queen's most loyal aide suddenly left his role?," ITV News, September 17, 2017. "Palace power struggle" was first used to describe Sir Christopher Geidt's departure in an article by Valentine Low and Alexi Mostrous, "Queen's aide Sir Christopher Geidt ousted in palace power struggle," *The Times*, September 16, 2017. Sir Clive Alderton's "hatchet man" nickname was first reported in an article by Kate Mansey, "King Charles III will keep the Queen's Private Secretary—known as a 'hatchet man' for his ability to deliver bad news—in his post," *Mail on Sunday*, September 17, 2022. Samantha Cohen's "Samantha the Panther" nickname was first reported by Martin Robinson, "Meghan gets the Queen's special advisor," *Daily Mail*, May 24, 2018. "[He'd] spent much of his career adjacent to, and indeed drawn to shit . . ." quotes from Prince Harry, *Spare*, 2023. The

article that refers to Simon Case as "a fixer by nature" and "keeper of secrets" is by Ben Wright and Joshua Nevett, "Simon Case: 'Keeper of secrets' under scrutiny," BBC News, February 3, 2023. "I like Simon, but he's a snake" quote is from article by Emilio Casalicchio, "From spy chief to Prince Harry's bête noire—the many lives of UK Cabinet Secretary Simon Case," *Politico*, January 10, 2023. The term *divergent paths* was used often used by Kensington Palace aides in 2019 to describe Harry and William's "natural progression" into establishing different roles at different royal households. Elton John defended Harry and Meghan's use of his private jet in a series of posts on Twitter/X, August 19, 2019, where he said, "To maintain a high level of much-needed protection, we provided them with a private jet flight." Prince William "looking like your archetypal family man on holiday . . ." is from an article by Rebecca English, "Who needs a private jet? Kate and Wills' £73 budget flight," *Daily Mail*, August 23, 2019.

The following books also provided invaluable research and background: Baldassare Castiglione, *Il Libro del Cortegiano* (*The Book of the Courtier*), 1528; Ophelia Field, *Sarah Churchill Duchess of Marlborough: The Queen's Favourite*, 2003; Paul Hill, *The Age of Athelstan: Britain's Forgotten History*, 2004; Niccolò Machiavelli, *The Prince*, 1532; Marc Morris, *The Anglo-Saxons: A History of Beginnings*, 2022; Kathryn Warner, *Edward II: The Unconventional King*, 2014; Alison Weir, *Henry VIII: The King and His Court*, 2001; Lucy Worsley, *Courtiers: The Secret History of the Georgian Court*, 2010.

11 The term "people's princess" was used by the then British prime minister Tony Blair to describe Diana, Princess of Wales, on the day of her death, August 31, 1997. "Harry never says that his mother is dead . . ." quote from article by Andrew O'Hagan, "Off His Royal Tits," *London Review of Books* 45, no. 3, February 2, 2023. Harry has publicly shared his fears of "history repeating itself" on at least three occasions, including his docuseries created with Oprah Winfrey, *The Me You Can't See*, Apple TV+, 2021. "Felt the presence of [his] mum . . ." quotes by Prince Harry to Michael Strahan, *Good Morning America*, ABC, January 9, 2023. Diana

was going to "enliven it . . ." quote from former *Guardian* royal correspondent and author of *Royalty Inc.*, Stephen Bates, in an article by Suyin Haynes, "*The Crown* Doesn't Fully Explain Why Princess Diana Was So Popular. Here's How She Became a Global Celebrity," *Time*, November 16, 2020. Tom Cruise spoke about media "harassment" over the phone to CNN on August 31, 1997. "Where Is Our Queen? Where Is Her Flag?" was the front page of *The Sun*, September 4, 1997. The sentence on Diana's influence on fashion trends was inspired by an article by Emma Mackenzie, "Why are people so obsessed with buying Diana's things?," Yahoo! News, August 9, 2023. The "Diana: Her Fashion Story" exhibition traced the evolution of the royal's style and was organized by Historic Royal Palaces and ran at Kensington Palace from February 24, 2017, to February 17, 2019. Biographer Penny Junor wrote about Diana as a bad mother, volatile, narcissistic, and violent in her books *Charles: Victim or Villain*, 1999, and *Prince Harry: Brother, Soldier, Son*, 2014. Additional details on the Martin Bashir/*Panorama* investigation from the "Report of The Dyson Investigation by The Right Honourable Lord Dyson," published on May 14, 2021. Earl Spencer's letter to BBC's director-general Tim Davie was published in the *Daily Mail*, "SPENCER'S ULTIMATUM TO BBC'S NEW BOSS," November 3, 2020. Martin Bashir stepped down from his BBC role in April 2021, and it was announced in a statement by Jonathan Munro, the deputy director of BBC News, on May 14, 2021. Both Prince Harry's and Prince William's statements on the outcome of Lord Dyson's investigation were released under embargo by their respective offices at exactly 10:00 p.m. U.K. time, May 20, 2021. "What bullying actually means . . ." quote from Jenny Afia is from *The Princes and The Press* (episode 2), BBC Two, December 8, 2021. "You must understand, darling boy . . ." quote by Charles is from Prince Harry, *Spare*, 2023. "Say what I want about Harry and Meghan . . ." quote by Norman Baker is from interview on GB News, December 13, 2022.

Other books that provided helpful research for this specific chapter: Noel Botham, *The Murder of Princess Diana: The Truth Be-*

*hind the Assassination of the People's Princess*, 2017; Tina Brown, *The Diana Chronicles*, 2017; Patrick Jephson, *Shadow of a Princess: An Intimate Account by Her Private Secretary*, 2000; James Patterson and Chris Mooney, *Diana, William, & Harry: A life cut short. A love that endures*, 2023; Ken Wharfe with Robert Jobson, *Diana: Closely Guarded Secret*, 2016; Ken Wharfe and Ros Coward, *Diana: Remembering the Princess*, 2022.

*Part I*

**12**

Quotes from Camilla's *Mail* interview (including "just get on with it" later in the chapter) were given to Geordie Greig, "EXCLUSIVE: Camilla up close! Duchess of Cornwall opens up as never before, saying: 'If you can't laugh at yourself, you may as well give up,'" *Mail on Sunday*, May 28, 2017. "Raunchy and randy" and "throw her knickers on the table" come from an article by Caroline Murphy, "Squidging about," *London Review of Books* 26, no. 2, January 22, 2004. "Doing what Lady Chatterley loved best" is a quote from a butler in the book by Gyles Brandreth, *Charles & Camilla: Portrait of a Love Affair*, 2005. "She laughed easily at the same silliness" quote is from a book by Jonathan Dimbleby, *The Prince of Wales: An Intimate Portrait*, 1998. Details of Charles's letters to Lord Mountbatten published in a book by Penny Junor, *The Duchess: Camilla Parker Bowles and the Love Affair that Rocked the Crown*, 2018. "I find knickers all over the place" quote is from a housekeeper at Glyn Celyn House, where the couple regularly stayed as far back as 1992, in an article by James Whitaker and Jane Kerr, *The Mirror*, August 26, 1996. The story about the ham radio enthusiast is from the memoir of Richard Stott, *Dogs and Lampposts*, 2002. Diana's "Rottweiler" nickname for Camilla was first reported by Andrew Morton, *Diana: Her True Story*, 1992. Patrick "Paddy" Harverson's quote is from an interview on *Good Morning America*, ABC, September 12, 2022. Piers Morgan called Meghan "Pinocchio Princess" in a March 8, 2021, Twitter/X post before calling her a "race-baiter" on *Good Morning Britain*, ITV, March 10, 2021, where he then stormed off the set when challenged by a co-presenter about his stance (and then "left" his job that same day after Meghan personally complained to the network's CEO, Carolyn Mc-Call, who defended the duchess). "New series of Netflix's *The Crown* is 'vicious' and 'would have destroyed' the Queen, one of the late monarch's closest friends says," story by Brittany Chain, Katie Hind, and Kate Mansey, *Mail on Sunday*, October 23, 2022. Judi Dench added pressure on Netflix to tell viewers its show is fiction by writing a letter that was published in *The Times*, October 19, 2022. Harry's "bodies left in the street" quote was from an interview with Anderson Cooper, *60 Minutes*, CBS, January 8, 2023. "I have a huge amount of compassion for her . . ." quote from Harry to Michael Strahan, *Good Morning America*, ABC, January 9, 2023. "Of course it bothers her . . ." quote from the Marchioness of Lansdowne in an article by Roya Nikkhah, "Queen Camilla: the 'lady boss,' by her inner circle," *The Sunday Times*, April 15, 2023. "We all love our food . . ." quote from Tom Parker Bowles to me on the podcast *The HeirPod*, ABC Audio, December 13, 2019. "You're not going to find us with great estates . . ." quote from Tom Parker Bowles on the podcast *The News Agents*, Global, April 20, 2023. "She was very explicit with me . . ." quote from Julian Payne to Times Radio, May 4, 2023. "I count on the loving help of my darling wife . . ." was from King Charles's address to "the Nation and the Commonwealth," which was broadcast on September 9, 2022.

Additional reading for this chapter: HRH The Prince of Wales and Bunny Guinness, *Highgrove: A Garden Celebrated*, 2014; Caroline Graham, *Camilla: Her True Story*, 2001; Tom Quinn, *Mrs. Keppel: Mistress to the King*, 2016.

*Part II*

**12**

"The physical benefits of being outdoors . . . are well documented . . ." from a speech delivered by Kate, then the Duchess of Cambridge, at the Back to Nature festival at RHS Garden Wisley on September 10, 2019. Kate's appearance on *Blue Peter* aired on BBC1, June 13, 2019. The Royal Foundation Centre for Early Childhood was launched on June 18, 2021. Details of Sure Start closures come from article by

Anoosh Chakelian, "Replacing lost Sure Start centres is a tacit admission of austerity's failure," *New Statesman*, February 10, 2023. Kate joined the podcast *Happy Mum, Happy Baby*, Acast, for an episode released on February 15, 2020. The book *Hold Still: A Portrait of Our Nation in 2020*, featuring an introduction by the Duchess of Cambridge, was released on May 7, 2021. "Bucklebury provided the backbone for Kate's aspirational resolve" is from Tina Brown, *The Palace Papers: Inside the House of Windsor—the Truth and the Turmoil*, 2022. The nickname "Waity Katie" was invented by the *Daily Mail* (because she was "happy to hang on until William proposes") and first used in the article "'Waity Katie' has a wobble as Prince William commits seven years to the RAF," November 8, 2008. "Royal Wedding Is On! The Secret Proposal" was the front cover of *Us Weekly* a week before the engagement was announced on November 16, 2010. "I saw Kate becoming a jointed doll on which certain rags are hung . . ." and other quotes are from Hilary Mantel, "Royal Bodies," *London Review of Books* 35, no. 4, February 21, 2013. The report that Prince George can skip a stint in the Armed Forces "if he wishes" originates from an article by Kate Mansey, "Prince George will not be expected to join the Armed Forces before becoming King breaking centuries of tradition," *Mail on Sunday*, July 15, 2023.

**13** "Demands for democracy—that these publics have a say— advanced" and other invaluable insight from an article by Adam Ramsay, "The monarchy and media are trapped in a mutually dependent relationship," *openDemocracy*, January 9, 2023. More invaluable insight in an article by Adam Ramsay, "Dismantling Britain Is One Thing. Dismantling Britishness Is Another," *Novara Media*, October 6, 2021. "Impress the many," "governing the many," and "excite and preserve the reverence of the population" from Walter Bagehot, *The English Constitution* (Second Edition), 1873. "The clock which beats the time over the Houses of Parliament . . ." quote is referenced in Todd Avery, *Radio Modernism: Literature, Ethics, and the BBC, 1922–1938*, 2006. The statistic that 6 percent of the British population identify as Christian (while

42 percent say they are nonpracticing Christians) is from a survey by Talking Jesus reported exclusively in an article by Anugrah Kumar, "'Talking Jesus' report finds only 6% of UK adults identify as practicing Christians," *The Christian Post*, May 2, 2022. "They wouldn't be there if there wasn't something in the British character . . ." quote from *Martin Amis's England*, BBC Four, March 23, 2014. "They can deny it all they like until they're blue in the face . . ." quote from Robert Jobson on *Sunrise*, Channel 7, November 24, 2021. The term "churnalism" is used for a type of journalism in which press releases and stories from newswires (or press pools) are used to create articles in newspapers and other news media—it was coined by BBC journalist Waseem Zakir in the early 2000s. The documentary *Harry & William: What Went Wrong* aired on ITV1, July 4, 2021. The documentary *Harry and Meghan: An African Journey* aired on ITV1, October 23, 2019. William and Kate's visit to Harry and Meghan was reported by me, "Prince William & Duchess Kate Have Visited Meghan at Frogmore Cottage," *Harper's Bazaar*, April 25, 2019. Sandy Henney's quote is from Zeynep Tufekci, "Prince Harry Is Right, and It's Not Just a Matter of Royal Gossip," *New York Times*, January 25, 2023. Penny Junor's quote about Mark Bolland is from *Reinventing the Royals* (episode 1 of 2), BBC Two, March 24, 2015. Dan Wootton's comment about negative information "coming from within the royal family" was made on Talk Radio, August 2, 2019. Kate, the Princess of Wales, backed *The Sun*'s "Baby, Bank On Us" appeal on June 4, 2023, telling the paper, "I'm very proud to support this campaign." "Camilla has been canny . . ." is from an article by Peter Hunt, "How Camilla came in from the cold," *Spectator*, February 5, 2022. The apology to Meghan in the *Mail on Sunday* was printed on December 26, 2021, and on the *Mail Online* on December 25, 2021. Additional Tobyn Andreae history from an article by Ellie Hall, "King Charles Hired a Former Top Editor at the Tabloids That Published Critical Kate Middleton Columns and the Story That Was an Impetus for the Breakdown of Meghan Markle's Relationship with Her Father," *BuzzFeed News*, September 30, 2022. "Either

well-known journalists are making a lot of stuff up . . ." quote is from an article by Andrew Marr, "Prince Harry's war on the Windsors," *New Statesman*, January 11, 2023.

I fell down many a rabbit hole researching for this chapter, but the following titles are some of the many additional sources of research that were helpful (even if material or quotes from them don't appear in the book): Dickie Arbiter, *On Duty with the Queen: My Time as a Buckingham Palace Press Secretary*, 2014; Nick Davies, *Flat Earth News: An Award-Winning Reporter Exposes Falsehood, Distortion and Propaganda in the Global Media*, 2008; Jackie Harrison and Luke McKernan, *Breaking the News: 500 Years of News in Britain*, 2022; Chris Horrie, *Tabloid Nation: From the Birth of the* Daily Mirror *to the Death of the Tabloid Newspaper*, 2003; Adrian Phillips, *The First Royal Media War: Edward VIII, the Abdication and the Press*, 2023.

**14** The origin of "Keep Calm and Carry On" was a slogan created by Britain's Ministry of Information in 1939 as a message of "sober restraint" to be used in the event of war. "For Great Britain [to make] clear to the world its role as an industrial leader" is quoted from a book by Mark Kishlansky, Patrick Geary, and Patricia O'Brien, *Civilization in the West*, 2008. "Increase the means of industrial education . . ." quote from an 1850 royal commission for the Great Exhibition, which Prince Albert was president of, and now available in the House of Lords Library. Edward VII's "miraculous" recovery from typhoid is covered in a book by Jane Ridley, *Bertie: A Life of Edward VII*, 2012. "The new limelight" and (later in the chapter) "cultivated anachronism" are from a book by Tom Nairn, *The Enchanted Glass: Britain and Its Monarchy*, 2011. "One hundred years ago, Queen Victoria opened the Great Exhibition . . ." speech by King George VI, delivered for the opening of the Festival of Britain, May 3, 1951 (sourced from British Pathé archives). "Worldwide fellowship" from Queen Elizabeth II's Christmas broadcast delivered on December 25, 1953. The Queen's famous "I have to be seen to be believed" quote is in a biography by Sally Bedell Smith, *Elizabeth the Queen: The Life of a Modern Monarch*, 2012. Commonwealth Games being "not value for money" were the words of politician David Andrews, Australia's premier of Victoria, during a July 18, 2023, news conference announcing that the country will be pulling out of hosting duties. The quotes from Australia's treasurer Jim Chalmers were given during a news conference in Melbourne on February 1, 2023. Humza Yousaf's quotes about Scotland becoming a republic are from an interview by Laura Webster, "Humza Yousaf: Indy Scotland should look at breaking with royals," *The National*, March 13, 2023. The Queen made the comment about the people of Scotland needing to "think very carefully about the future" during a walkabout outside Crathie Kirk church in Balmoral on September 14, 2014. The data used to highlight Britain's economic trajectory (that it will soon be overtaken by Poland et al.) came from calculations shared by Labour party leader Sir Keir Starmer on February 27, 2023, based on World Bank data and the assumption that the United Kingdom's gross domestic product (GDP) per capita continues to grow as it has between 2010 and 2021. Keir Starmer's comment about "brain drain" is from a speech given at the office of U.K. Finance in London on February 27, 2023. The phrase "Land of Hope and Glory" is from a British patriotic song (set to the theme of Edward Elgar's "Pomp and Circumstance March No. 1"). Its references to Britain's colonial history, with lines like "By freedom gained, by truth maintained, thine Empire shall be strong" have made it controversial. The government-funded £396 million, ten-year refurbishment of Buckingham Palace (agreed to by then Conservative leader and prime minister Theresa May, chancellor of the exchequer Philip Hammond, and Buckingham Palace's Keeper of the Privy Purse Sir Alan Reid) was announced in November 2016 and began in April 2017. Buckingham Palace is usually referred to as "BP" by staff and royal family members (same for Kensington Palace, which is called "KP"). Poll data for abolition support comes from British market research and data analytics firm YouGov (total sample size was 1,754 adults, and fieldwork was undertaken between April 30 and May 2, 2022); the percentage of Britons thinking the monarchy is "very important" comes from the National Centre for Social Research (based on 6,638 interviews carried out in 2023 and building on forty years of data collected for their annual "British Social Attitudes" survey); King Charles's approval rating based on polling by Ipsos in April 2023 (data is from three representative quota samples from adults between eighteen and seventy-five years old: 1,079 interviewed online between March 31–April 1; 2,000 interviewed online between April 12–13; and 1,008 interviewed over the phone between April 5–11); young and older support for the monarchy was polled in April 2023 by YouGov for BBC's *Panorama* (4,592 U.K. adults questioned). Anna Whitelock quoted by Press Association on April 14, 2016. Royal tourism site statistics from the Association of Leading Visitor Attractions (AVLA) and based on visits made in 2022 to known attractions. The *Guardian*'s "Cost of the crown" series was launched with a report by David Pegg and Paul Lewis, "How the British royal family hides its wealth from public scrutiny," April 5, 2023. Charles's estimated fortune and assets come from a report by the "Cost of the crown" team, "Revealed: King Charles's private fortune estimated at £1.8bn," *Guardian*, April 20, 2023. "Be directed for the wider good" quote from Britain's finance minister Jeremy Hunt, January 20, 2023. Nick Wall's quote comes from a Labour for a Republic letter to opposition Labour leader Keir Starmer sent in July 2023.

The following books were useful for historical research and additional insight: Becky E. Conekin, *The Autobiography of a Nation: The 1951 Festival of Britain*, 2003; Phillip Hall, *Royal Fortune: Tax, Money & the Monarchy*, 1992; Philip Murphy, *Monarchy and the End of Empire: The House of Windsor, the British Government, and the Postwar Commonwealth*, 2013; Tom Nairn, *The Break-Up of Britain: Crisis and Neo-Nationalism*, 2021; Lynn Picknett, Clive Prince, and Stephen Prior, *War of the Windsors: A Century of Unconstitutional Monarchy*, 2002; Tim Shipman, *Fall Out: A Year of Political Mayhem*, 2018; Graham Smith,

*Abolish the Monarchy: Why We Should and How We Will*, 2023; E. A. Smith, *George IV*, 2000; Peter Fearon, *Buckingham Babylon: The Rise and Fall of the House of Windsor*, 1993.

*15* "The odd thing about these British royal ceremonials . . ." and regalia observation from article by Fintan O'Toole, "Golden Coats, Sacred Spoons," *The New York Review of Books*, May 7, 2023. The story of the electroplated Ping-Pong ball was first reported by Stellene Volandes, "Prince Charles's Prince of Wales Coronet Has an Actual Ping Pong Ball Hidden Inside It," *Town & Country*, April 23, 2019. The Earl of Snowdon's comments on Charles's "bogus as hell" Welsh investiture were made on *Timewatch*, BBC Two, July 3, 2009. "It would be diversity doing what diversity is meant to do . . ." quote from op-ed by Nels Abbey, "Brilliant Floella Benjamin and a not-very-gospel coronation choir. Is this as 'diverse' as Britain gets?," *Guardian*, May 7, 2023. The 84 percent of British people saying they would not pledge allegiance to King Charles III came from a snap online poll for *Good Morning Britain*, ITV1, April 30, 2023. "[William's] Coronation will look and feel quite different" quote from a "source close to William" in article by Roya Nikkhah, "Prince William is already thinking about his coronation—it won't be like his dad's," *The Sunday Times*, May 13, 2023. "I find myself born into this particular position . . ." quotes from Charles (then the Prince of Wales) from interview with *60 Minutes*, CBS, October 27, 2005.

I found Ian Lloyd, *The Throne: 1,000 Years of British Coronations*, 2023, useful for additional information on coronations and coronation ceremonies.

———◦———

And finally, there are so many other resources not mentioned in the individual chapter references that provided invaluable information and additional reading while writing this book, including Norman Baker, . . . *And What Do You Do? What the Royal Family Want You to Know*, 2020;

Tina Brown, *The Palace Papers: Inside the House of Windsor—the Truth and the Turmoil*, 2022; Robert Jobson, *Charles at Seventy: Thoughts, Hopes and Dreams*, 2018; Alexander Larman, *The Crown in Crisis: Countdown to the Abdication*, 2021; Andrew Marr, *The Diamond Queen: Elizabeth II and Her People*, 2021; and, of course, Prince Harry, *Spare*, 2023.